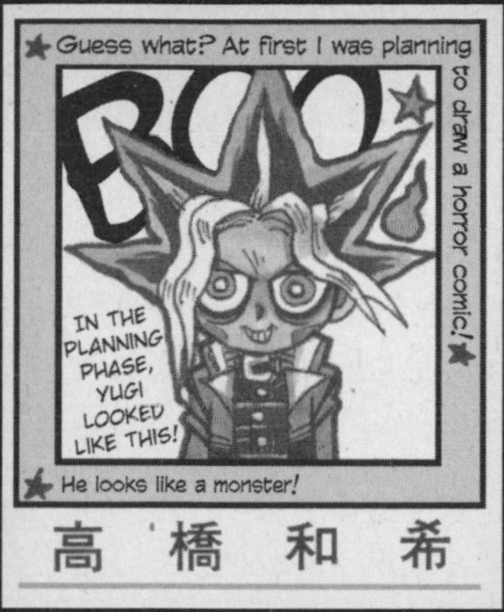
Guess what? At first I was planning to draw a horror comic!
BOO
IN THE PLANNING PHASE, YUGI LOOKED LIKE THIS!
He looks like a monster!
高 橋 和 希

IT'S A BIT LATE, BUT I'D LIKE TO TELL YOU ABOUT MY EXPERIENCES AS A MANGA ARTIST. WHEN I WAS 19, I GOT LUCKY, AND ONE OF MY STORIES WON A CONTEST IN A CERTAIN SHONEN MANGA MAGAZINE. THAT WAS MY DEBUT.

BUT AFTER THAT, IT WAS TERRIBLE! I KEPT WRITING AND WRITING, BUT ALL I MADE WAS A MOUNTAIN OF REJECTED STORIES. I WENT THROUGH SEVERAL PUBLISHERS. TEN YEARS PASSED.

THEN, I STARTED ***YU-GI-OH!*** IN *WEEKLY SHONEN JUMP*, AND I'VE BEEN DRAWING IT FOR SEVEN YEARS. YOU SEE? IF YOU DON'T GIVE UP, YOU'LL GET THERE SOMEHOW!

—KAZUKI TAKAHASHI, 2004

Artist/author Kazuki Takahashi first tried to break into the manga business in 1982, but success eluded him until **Yu-Gi-Oh!** debuted in the Japanese **Weekly Shonen Jump** magazine in 1996. **Yu-Gi-Oh!**'s themes of friendship and fighting, together with Takahashi's weird and wonderful art, soon became enormously successful, spawning a real-world card game, video games, and two anime series. A lifelong gamer, Takahashi enjoys Shogi (Japanese chess), Mahjong, card games, and tabletop RPGs, among other games.

YU-GI-OH!: MILLENNIUM WORLD VOL. 5
The SHONEN JUMP Manga Edition

This manga contains material that was originally published in English in
SHONEN JUMP #44-48.

STORY AND ART BY
KAZUKI TAKAHASHI

Translation & English Adaptation/Anita Sengupta
Touch-up Art & Lettering/Kelle Han
Design/Sean Lee
Editor/Jason Thompson

Managing Editor/Frances E. Wall
Editorial Director/Elizabeth Kawasaki
VP & Editor in Chief/Yumi Hoashi
Sr. Director of Acquisitions/Rika Inouye
Sr. VP of Marketing/Liza Coppola
Exec. VP of Sales & Marketing/John Easum
Publisher/Hyoe Narita

In the original Japanese edition, YU-GI-OH!, YU-GI-OH!: DUELIST and YU-GI-OH!:
MILLENNIUM WORLD are known collectively as YU-GI-OH!. The English YU-GI-OH!:
MILLENNIUM WORLD was originally volumes 32-38 of the Japanese YU-GI-OH!.

Printed in the U.S.A.

Published by VIZ Media, LLC
P.O. Box 77010
San Francisco, CA 94107

SHONEN JUMP Manga Edition
10 9 8 7 6 5 4 3 2 1
First printing, January 2007

PARENTAL ADVISORY
YU-GI-OH!: MILLENNIUM WORLD is rated T for
Teen and is recommended for ages 13 and up.
It contains fantasy violence.

www.viz.com

THE WORLD'S
MOST POPULAR MANGA

SHONEN JUMP

www.shonenjump.com

SHONEN JUMP MANGA

Yu-Gi-Oh! Millennium World

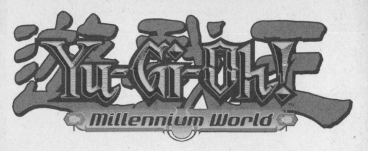

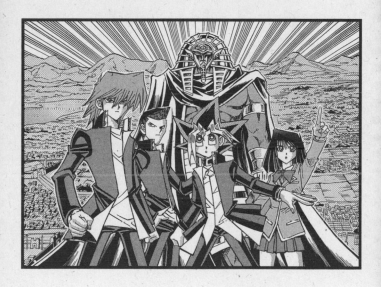

Vol. 5

TOMB OF SHADOWS

STORY AND ART BY

KAZUKI TAKAHASHI

THE MAIN CHARACTERS

KATSUYA JONOUCHI

BOBASA   ANZU MAZAKI   HIROTO HONDA

YUGI MUTOU

THE STORY SO FAR...

When he solved the Millennium Puzzle, 10th-grader Yugi developed an alter ego: Yu-Gi-Oh, the King of Games, the soul of a pharaoh from ancient Egypt! Discovering that the collectible card game "Duel Monsters" was of Egyptian origin, Yu-Gi-Oh collected the three Egyptian God Cards—Slifer the Sky Dragon, the God of the Obelisk, and the Sun Dragon Ra—and used them to travel into the "world of memories" of his own life 3,000 years ago. There, he found that he was the pharaoh, served by six priests who used the Millennium Items which had been created to save Egypt from invaders.

But unbeknownst even to the pharaoh, the Millennium Items were stained with blood. Created by the high priest Akhenaden, the Millennium Items were powered by human souls—the souls of the village of Kul Elna, which had been ritually slaughtered by troops under Akhenaden's command! Bakura, the sole survivor of Kul Elna, grew up into a revenge-obsessed madman. His goal: to gather the seven Millennium Items and summon the dark god Zorc Necrophades, so he can rule the world!

Bakura attacked the pharaoh and his priests, stealing the Millennium Ring and the Millennium Puzzle. But instead of stealing Akhenaden's Millennium Eye, he infused part of his own spirit into it, bringing Akhenaden's latent evil back to life. Filled with jealousy, Akhenaden began to plot against the pharaoh, and his dark side took on a life of its own.

Meanwhile, with the help of the Egyptian mystic Bobasa, Yugi and his friends followed Yu-Gi-Oh into the "world of memories." Their goal: to help the pharaoh by finding his forgotten name. But can they save Yu-Gi-Oh from Bakura in a deadly final fight in the Village of Kul Elna itself...?

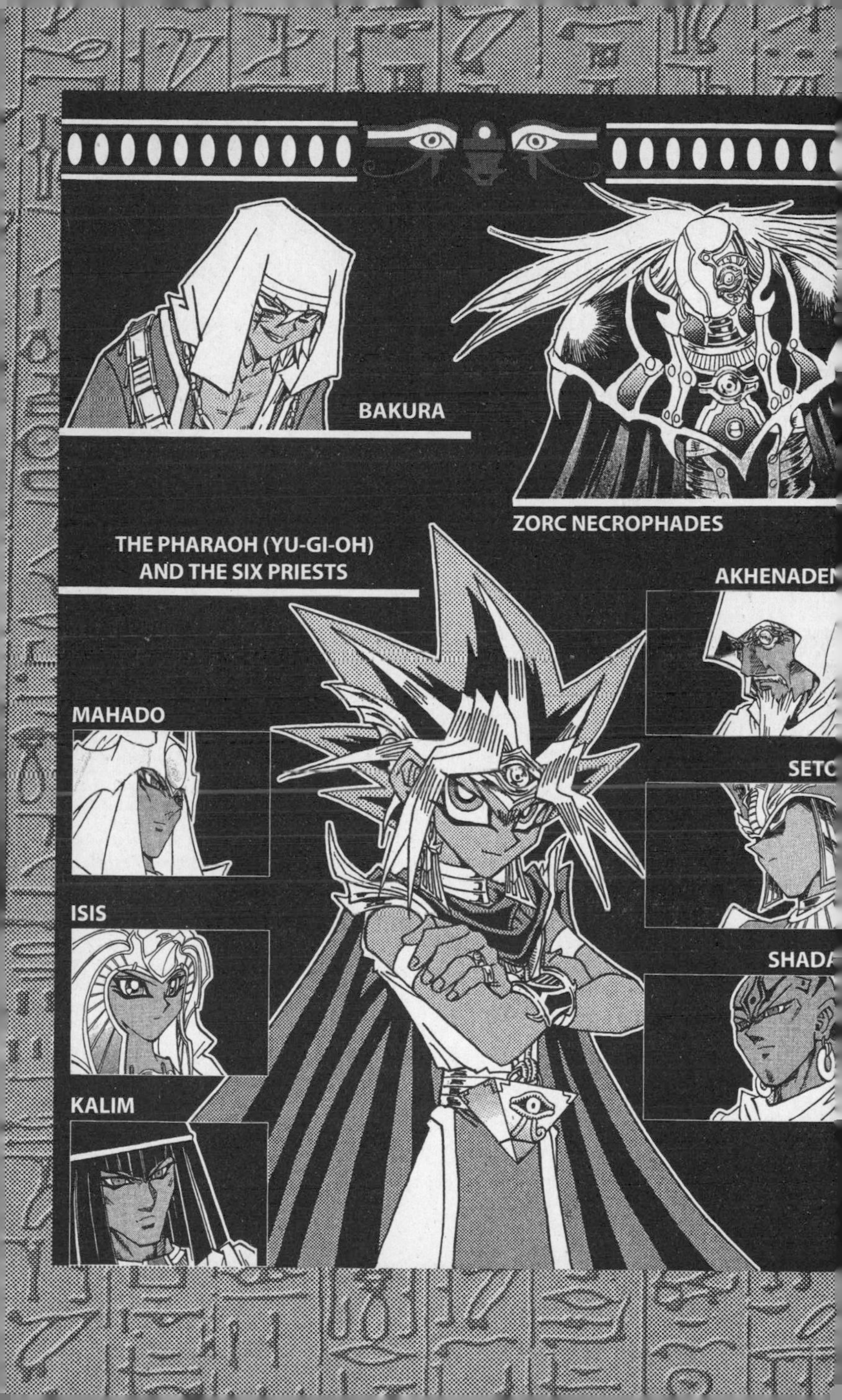
BAKURA
ZORC NECROPHADES
THE PHARAOH (YU-GI-OH)
AND THE SIX PRIESTS
AKHENADEN
MAHADO
SETO
ISIS
SHADA
KALIM

Yu-Gi-Oh! Millennium World

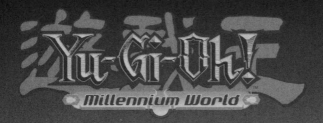

Vol. 5

CONTENTS

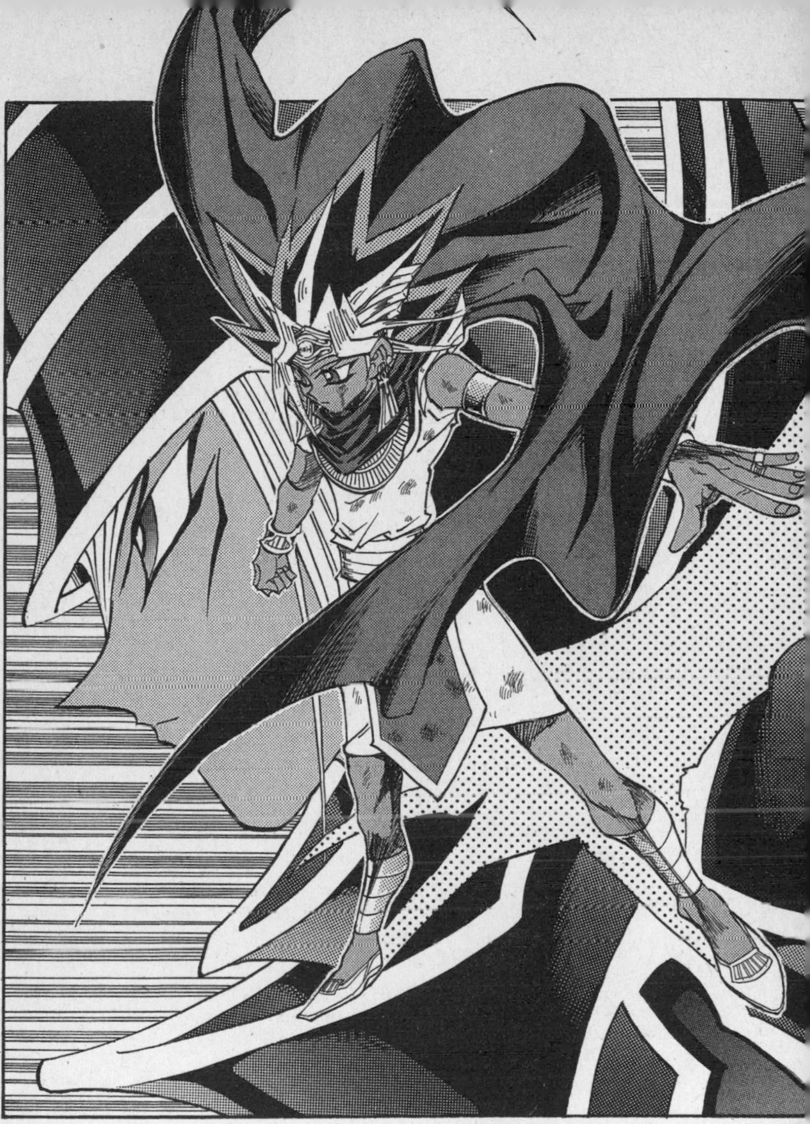

Duel 37: Shadow Camouflage!!

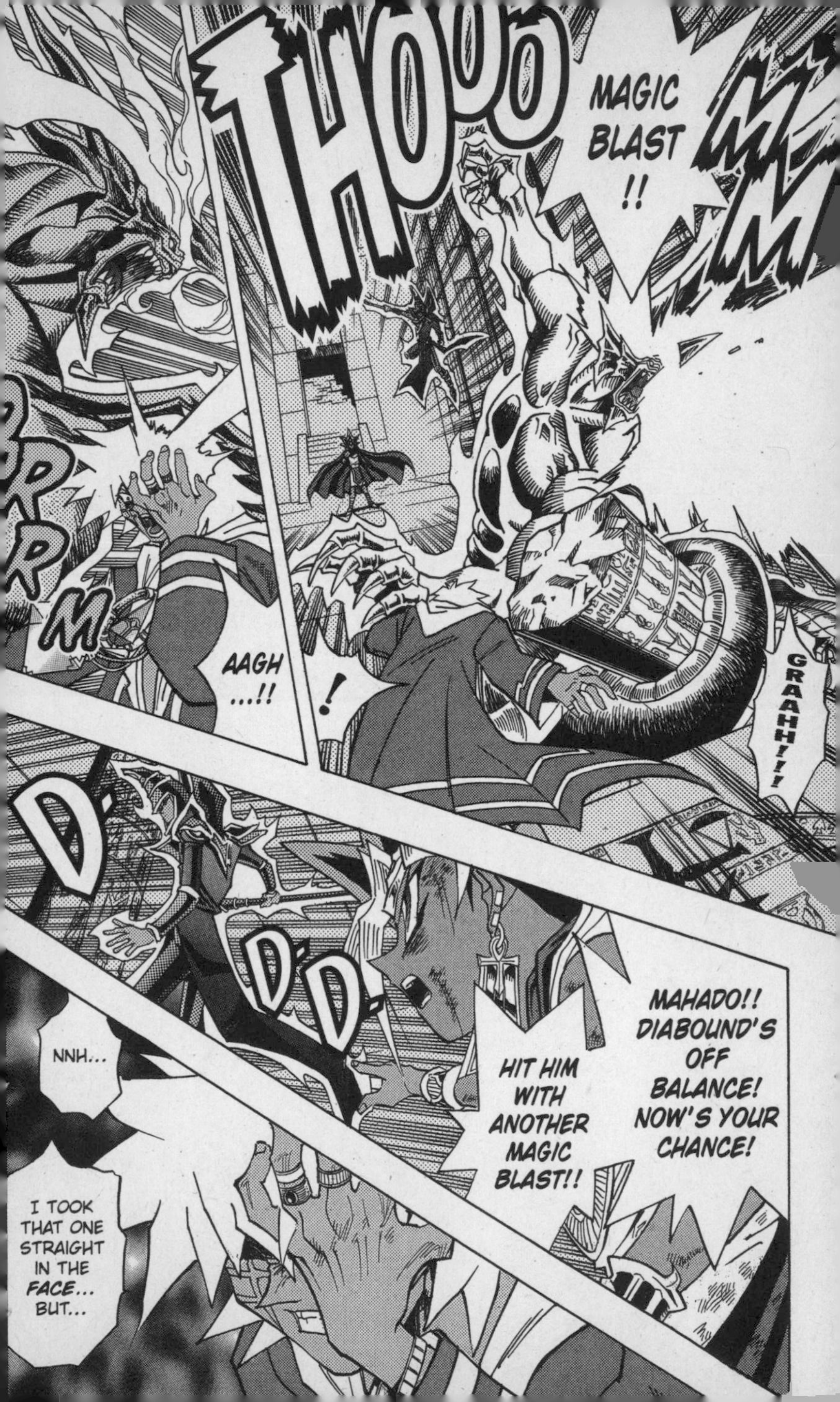
THOOOMMM
MAGIC BLAST !!
GRAAHH!!!
!
RRRM
AAGH ...!!
DDD
MAHADO!! DIABOUND'S OFF BALANCE! NOW'S YOUR CHANCE!
HIT HIM WITH ANOTHER MAGIC BLAST!!
NNH...
I TOOK THAT ONE STRAIGHT IN THE *FACE*... BUT...

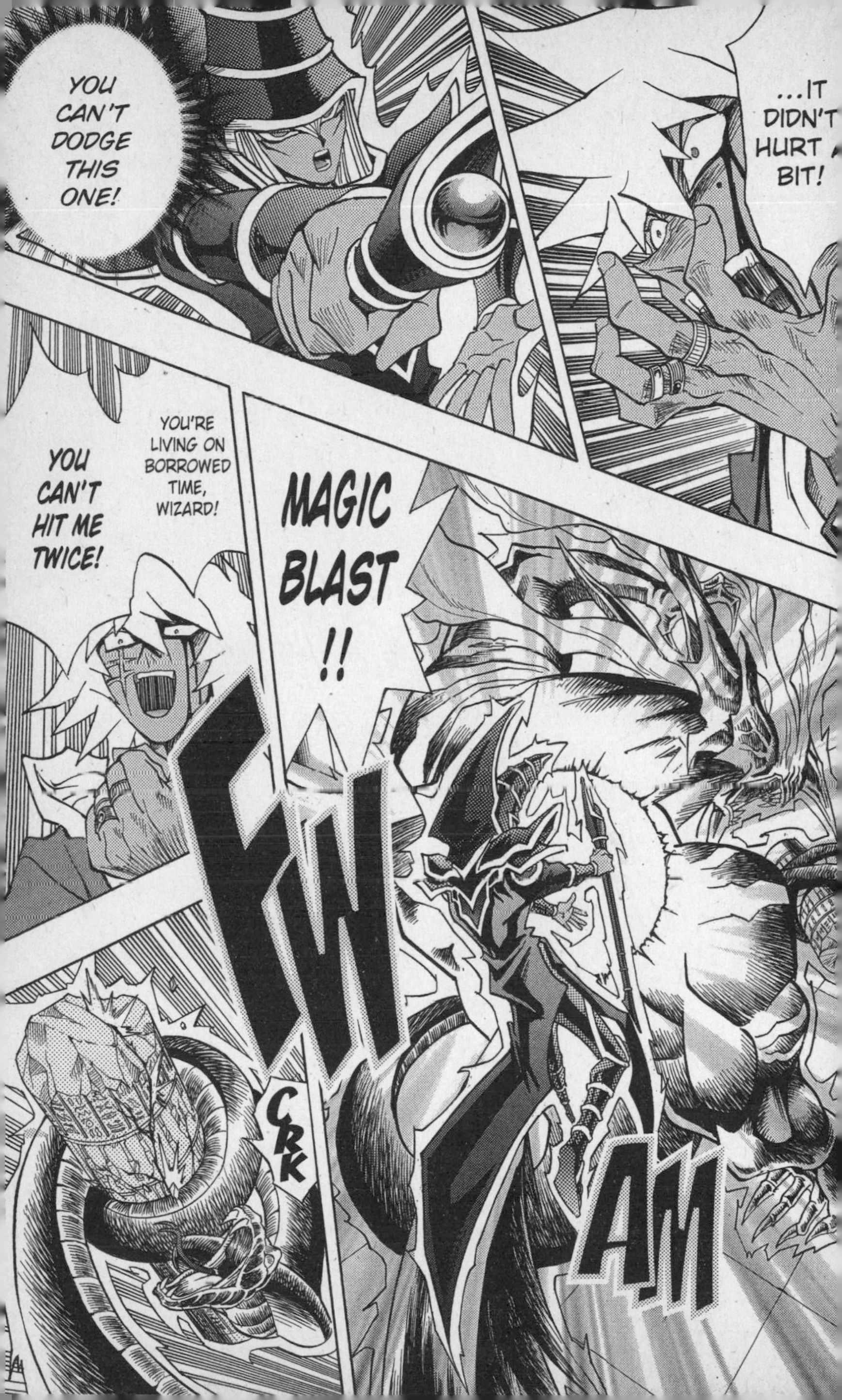
...IT DIDN'T HURT A BIT!
YOU CAN'T DODGE THIS ONE!
MAGIC BLAST!!
YOU'RE LIVING ON BORROWED TIME, WIZARD!
YOU CAN'T HIT ME TWICE!
CRK

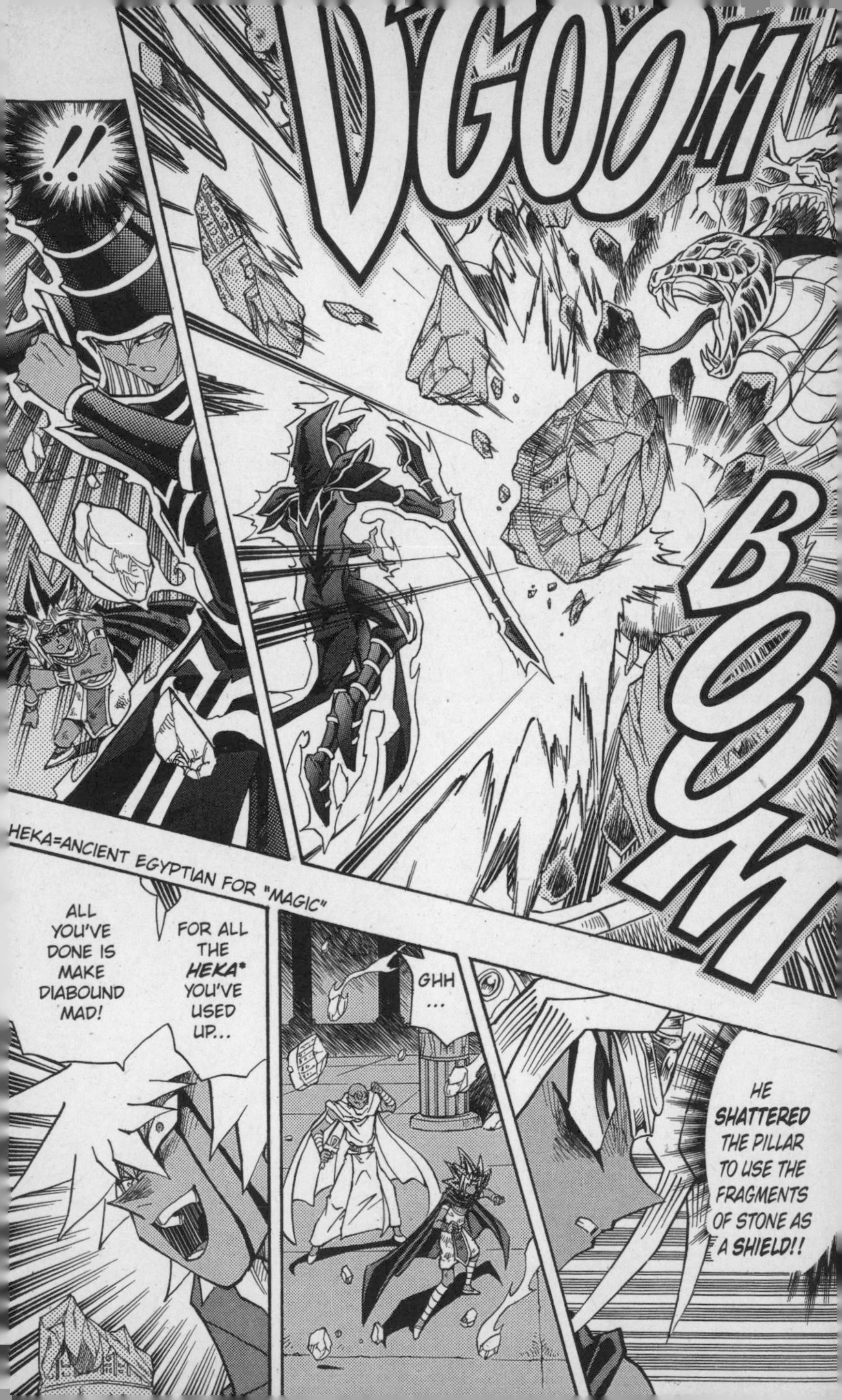
VGOOM
BOOM
!!
HE SHATTERED THE PILLAR TO USE THE FRAGMENTS OF STONE AS A SHIELD!!
GHH ...
FOR ALL THE HEKA* YOU'VE USED UP...
ALL YOU'VE DONE IS MAKE DIABOUND MAD!

HEKA=ANCIENT EGYPTIAN FOR "MAGIC"

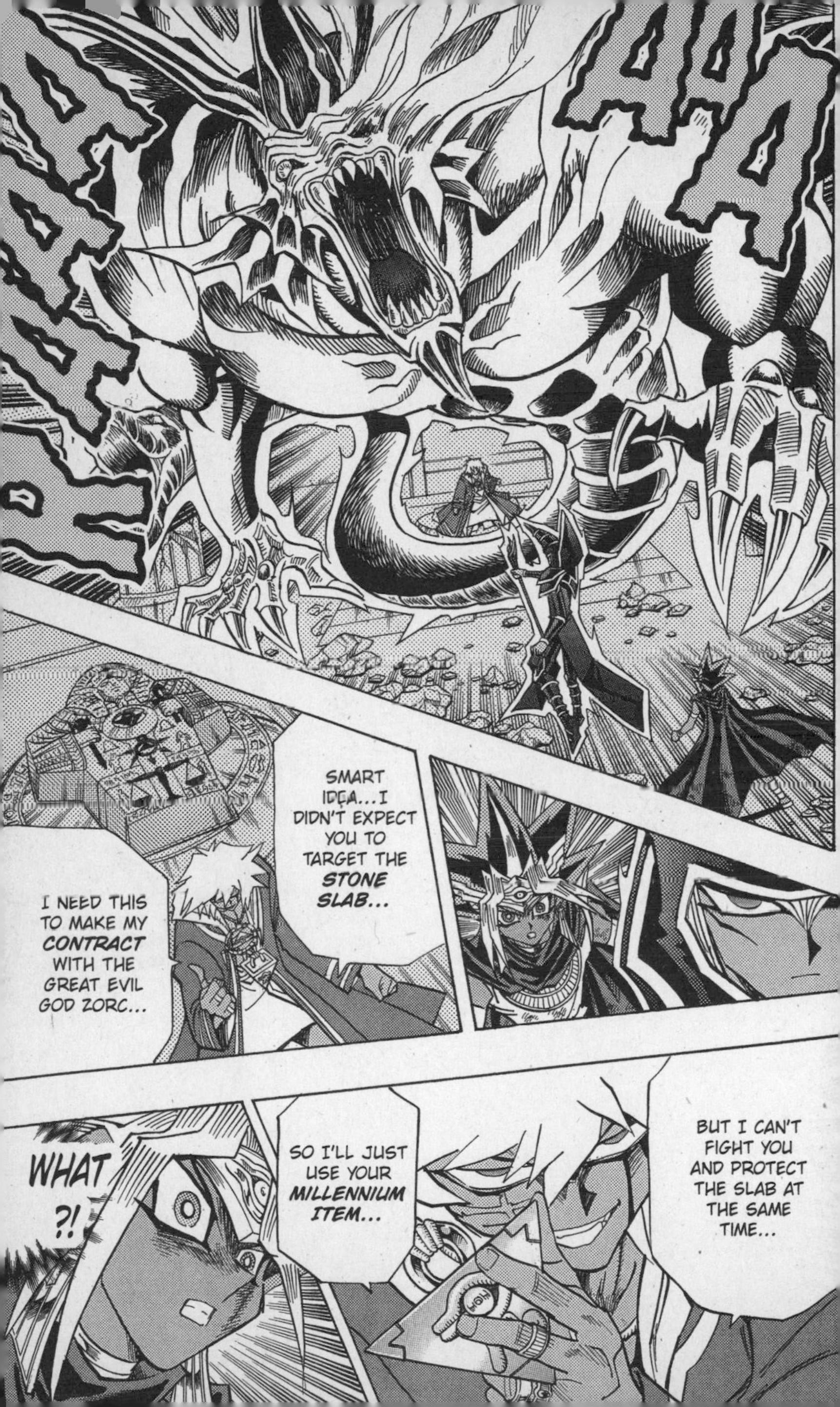
SMART IDEA... I DIDN'T EXPECT YOU TO TARGET THE *STONE SLAB*...
I NEED THIS TO MAKE MY *CONTRACT* WITH THE GREAT EVIL GOD ZORC...
BUT I CAN'T FIGHT YOU AND PROTECT THE SLAB AT THE SAME TIME...
SO I'LL JUST USE YOUR *MILLENNIUM ITEM*...
WHAT ?!

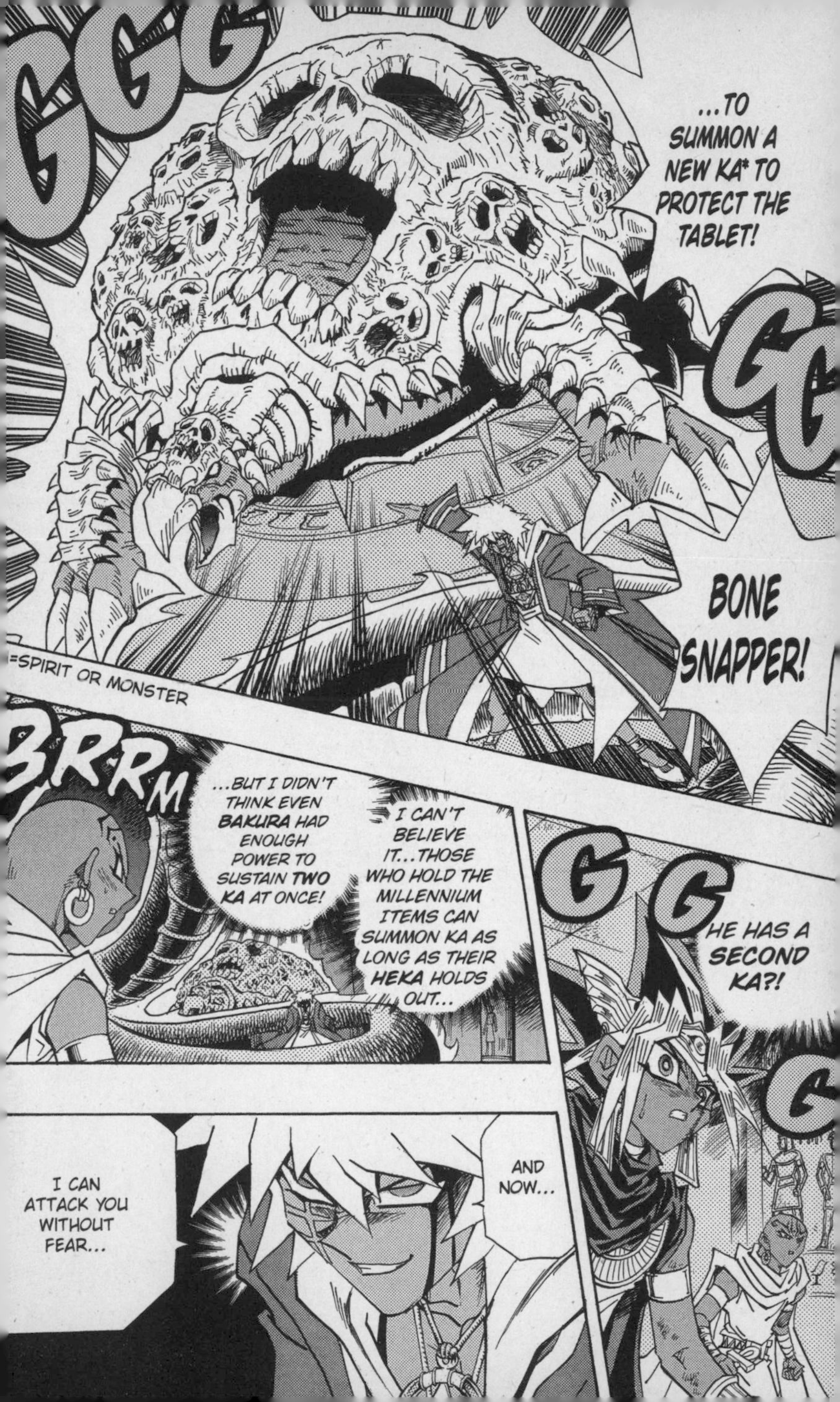
...TO SUMMON A NEW KA* TO PROTECT THE TABLET!
GGG
GG
BONE SNAPPER!
=SPIRIT OR MONSTER
G G
HE HAS A SECOND KA?!
G
BRRRM
I CAN'T BELIEVE IT...THOSE WHO HOLD THE MILLENNIUM ITEMS CAN SUMMON KA AS LONG AS THEIR HEKA HOLDS OUT...
...BUT I DIDN'T THINK EVEN BAKURA HAD ENOUGH POWER TO SUSTAIN TWO KA AT ONCE!
AND NOW...
I CAN ATTACK YOU WITHOUT FEAR...

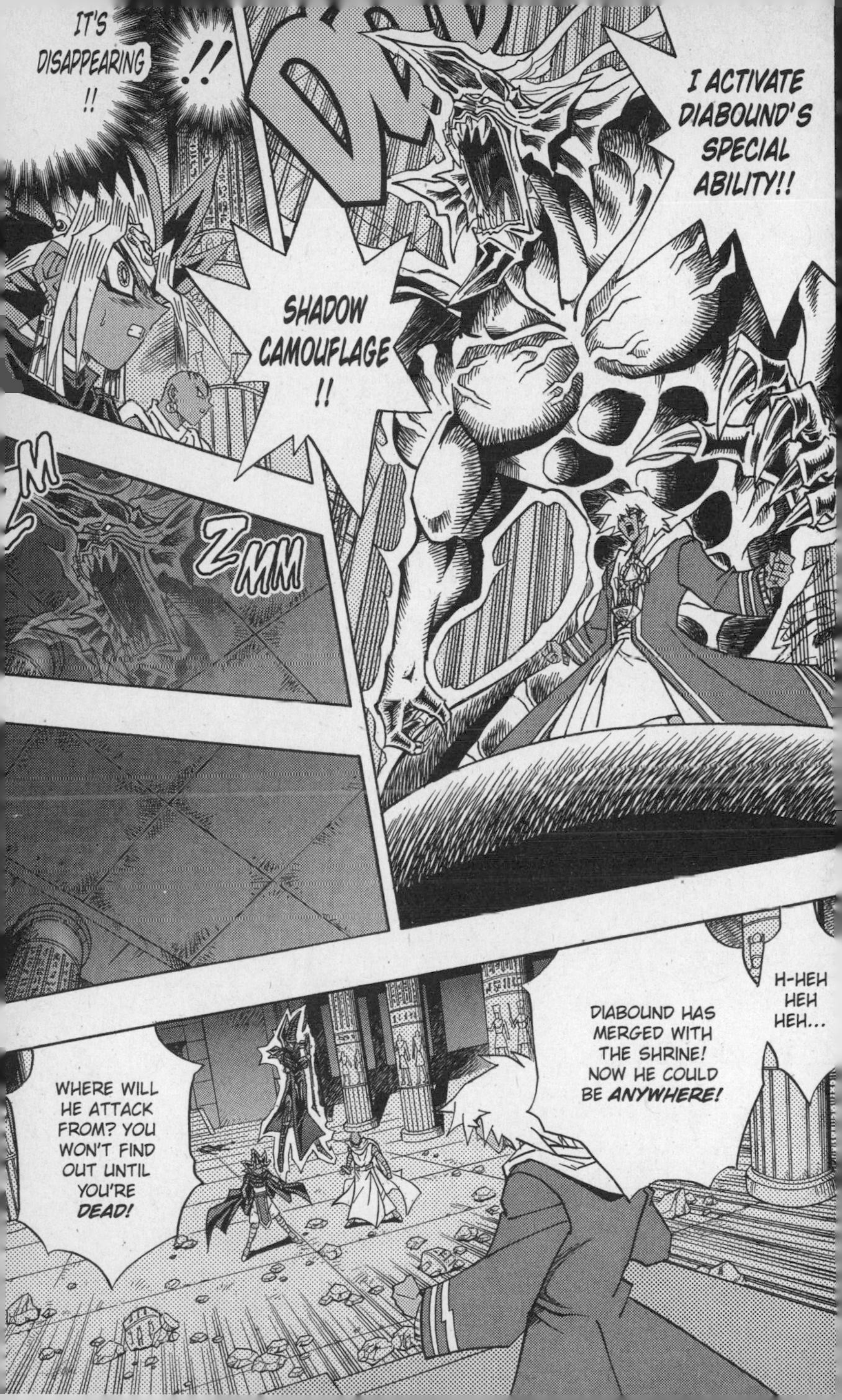
I ACTIVATE DIABOUND'S SPECIAL ABILITY!!
SHADOW CAMOUFLAGE!!
IT'S DISAPPEARING!!
!!
ZMM
H-HEH HEH HEH...
DIABOUND HAS MERGED WITH THE SHRINE! NOW HE COULD BE ANYWHERE!
WHERE WILL HE ATTACK FROM? YOU WON'T FIND OUT UNTIL YOU'RE DEAD!

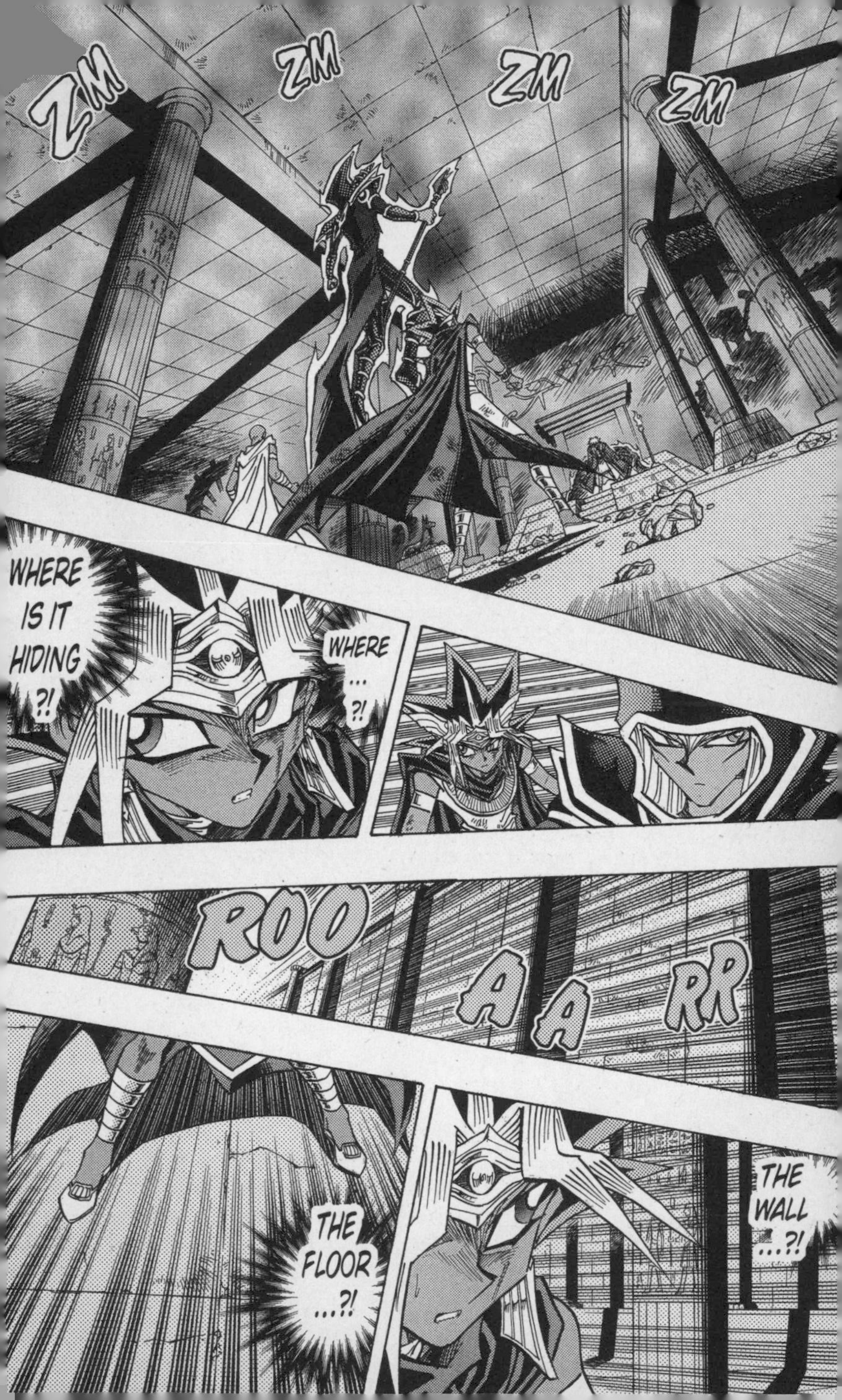
ZM
ZM
ZM
ZM
WHERE ... ?!
WHERE IS IT HIDING ?!
ROOAARR
THE WALL ...?!
THE FLOOR ...?!

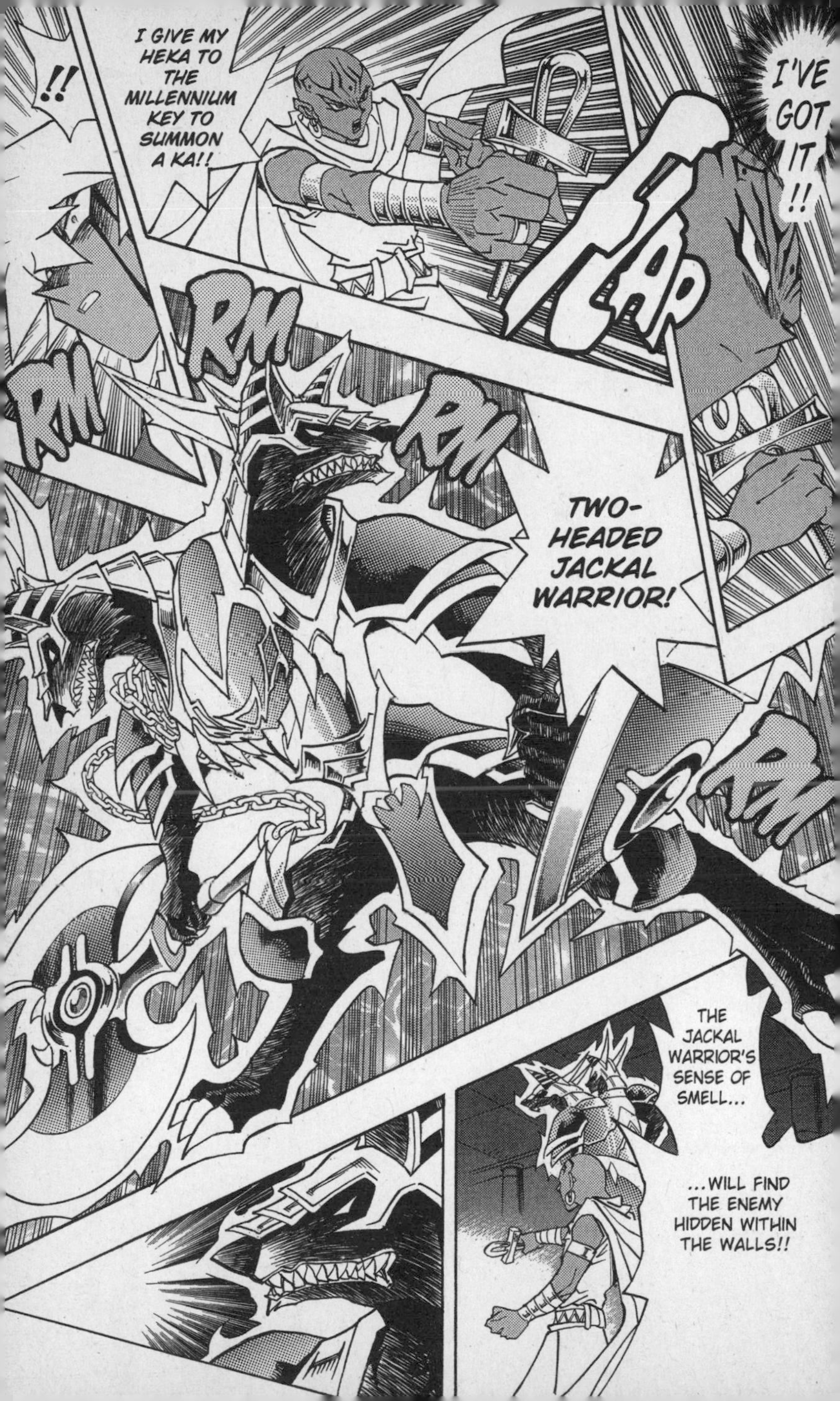

I'VE GOT IT!!
CLAP
I GIVE MY HEKA TO THE MILLENNIUM KEY TO SUMMON A KA!!
!!
RM
RM
RM
RM
TWO-HEADED JACKAL WARRIOR!
THE JACKAL WARRIOR'S SENSE OF SMELL...
...WILL FIND THE ENEMY HIDDEN WITHIN THE WALLS!!

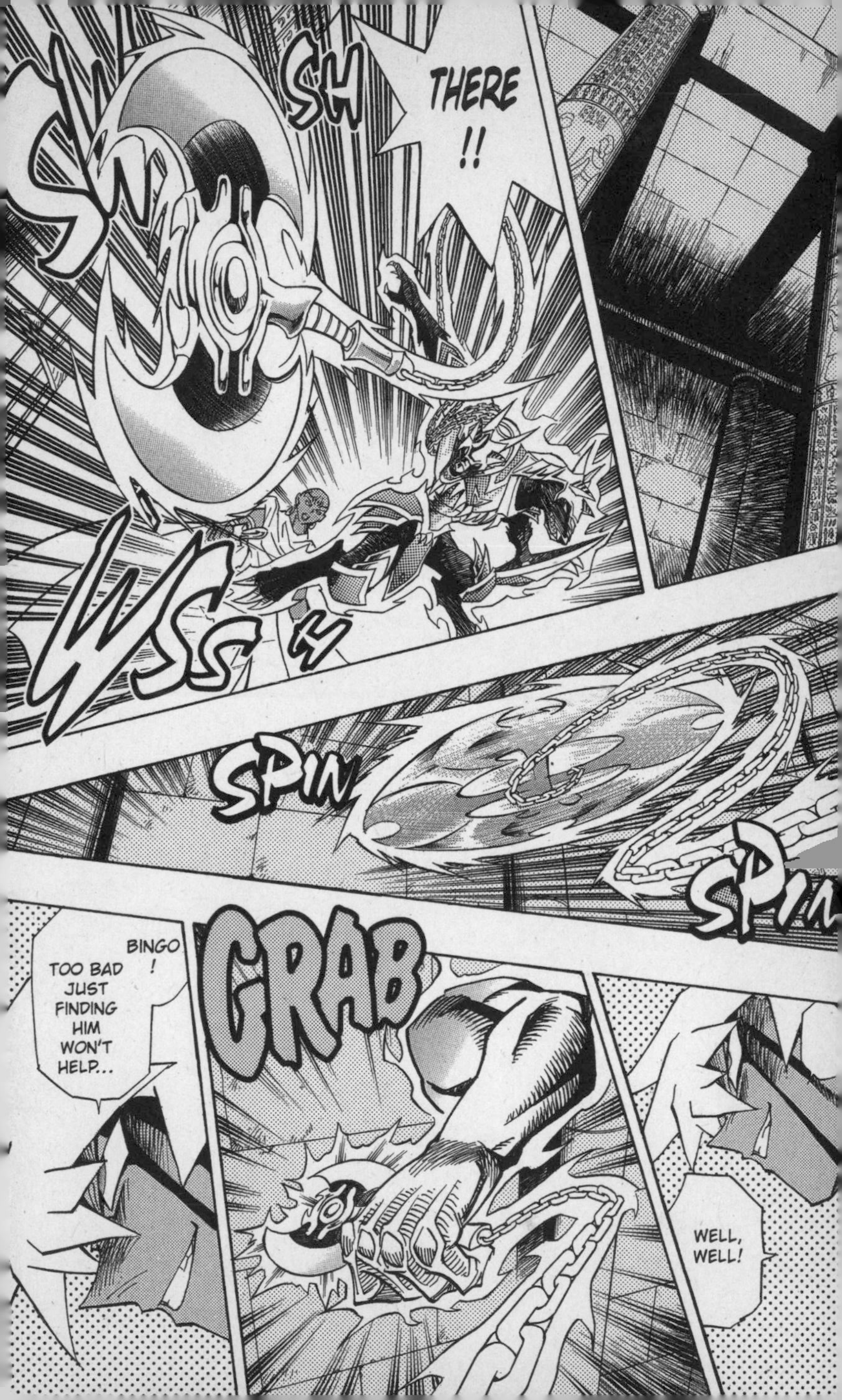

SH
THERE !!
WSSH
SPIN
SPIN
WELL, WELL!
GRAB
BINGO!
TOO BAD JUST FINDING HIM WON'T HELP...

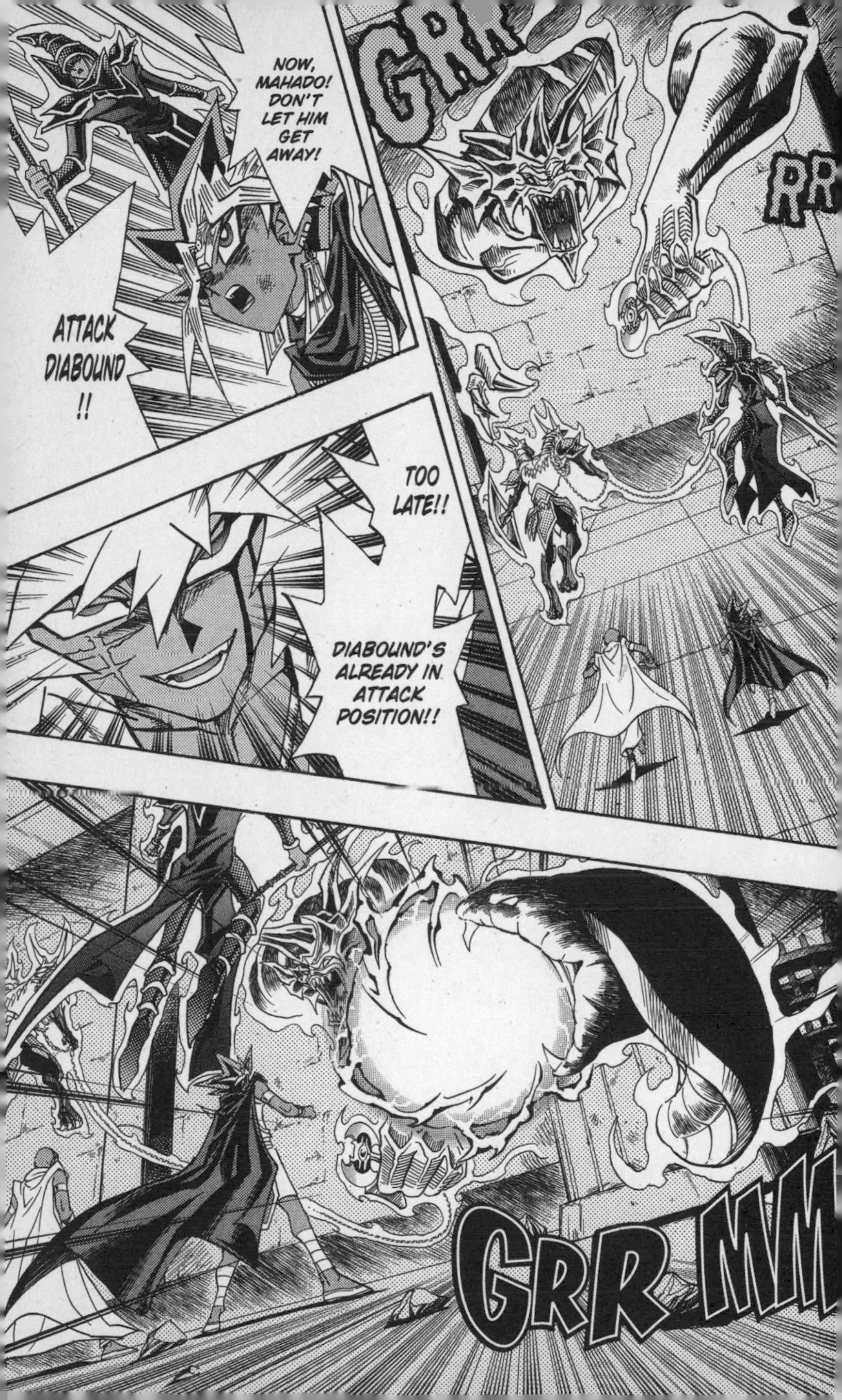
GRR
RR
NOW, MAHADO! DON'T LET HIM GET AWAY!
ATTACK DIABOUND !!
TOO LATE!!
DIABOUND'S ALREADY IN ATTACK POSITION!!
GRR MM

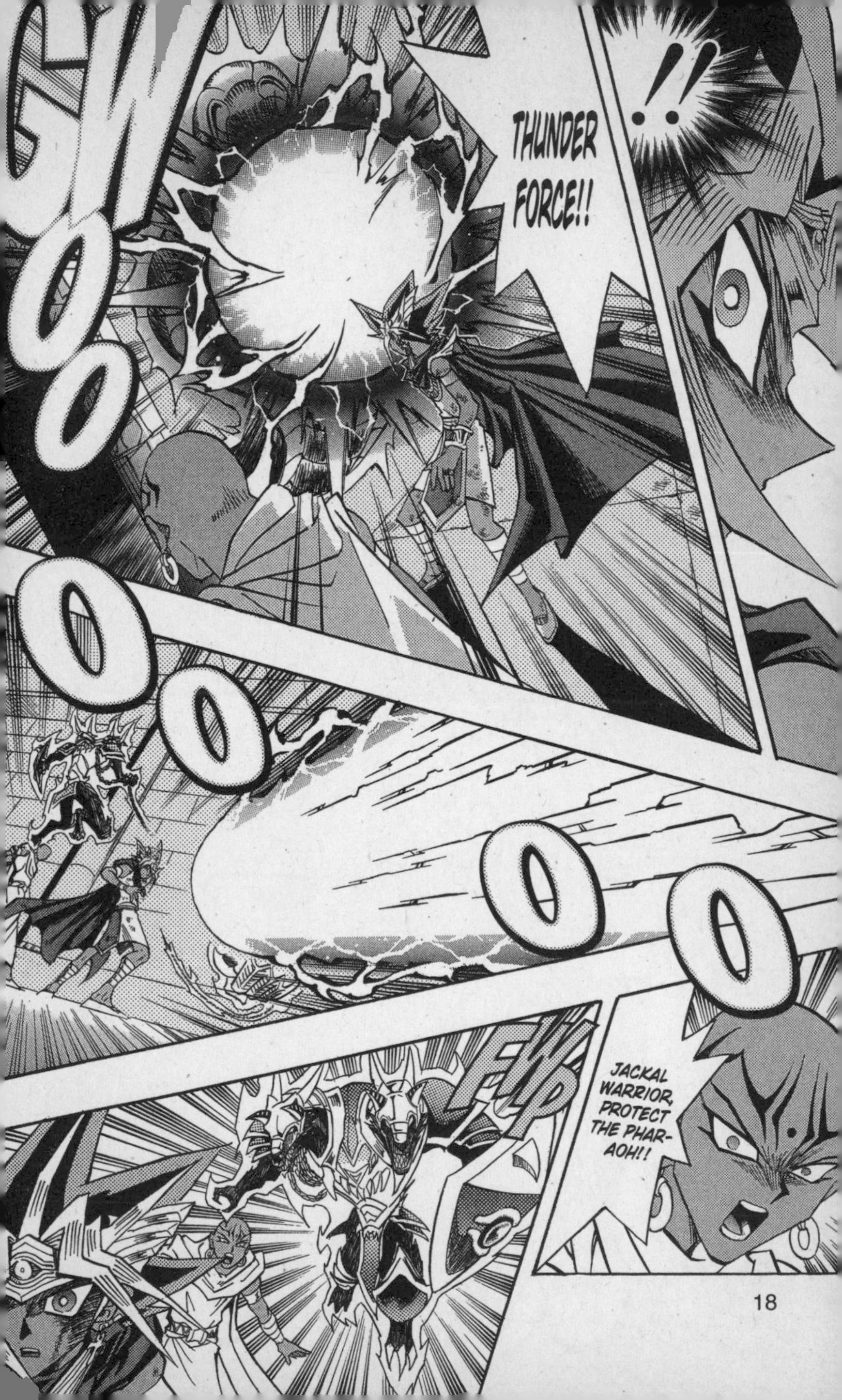

!!
GWOOOOOO
THUNDER FORCE!!
JACKAL WARRIOR, PROTECT THE PHAR-AOH!!

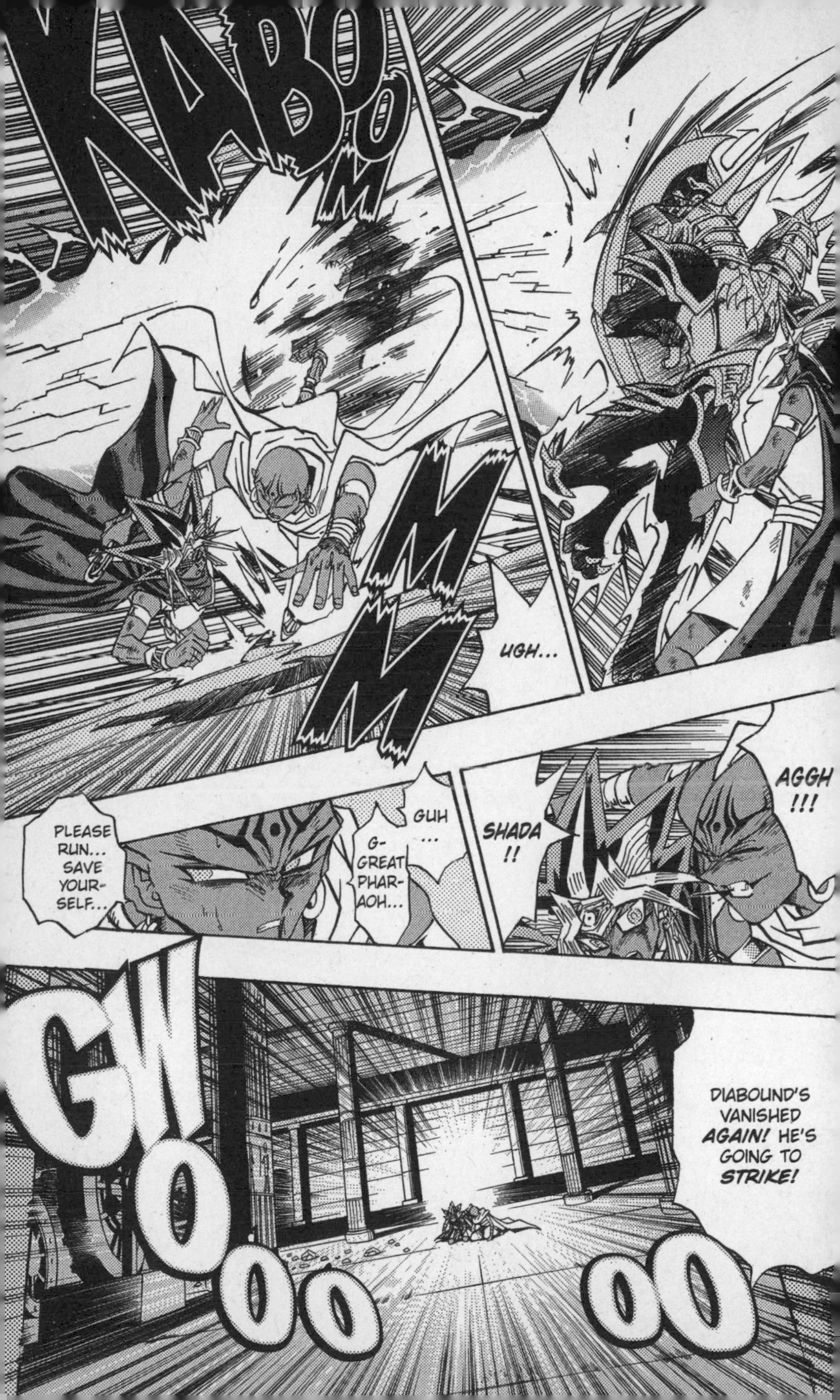
UGH...
KABOOOM
MMM
AGGH!!!
SHADA!!
GUH...
G-GREAT PHARAOH...
PLEASE RUN... SAVE YOURSELF...
DIABOUND'S VANISHED *AGAIN!* HE'S GOING TO *STRIKE!*
GWOOOOO
OO

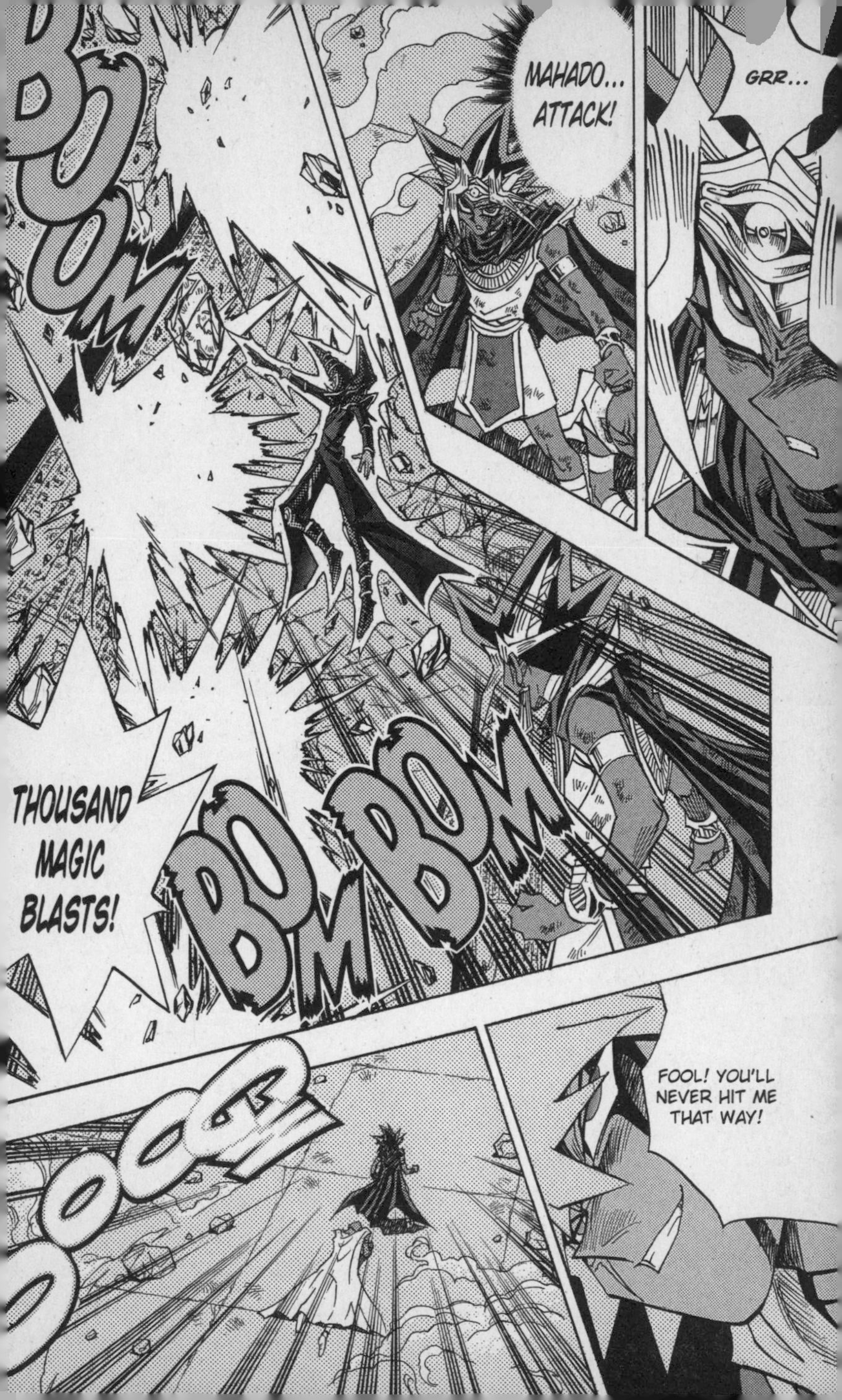
GRR...
MAHADO... ATTACK!
BOOM
THOUSAND MAGIC BLASTS!
BOM BOM
FOOL! YOU'LL NEVER HIT ME THAT WAY!

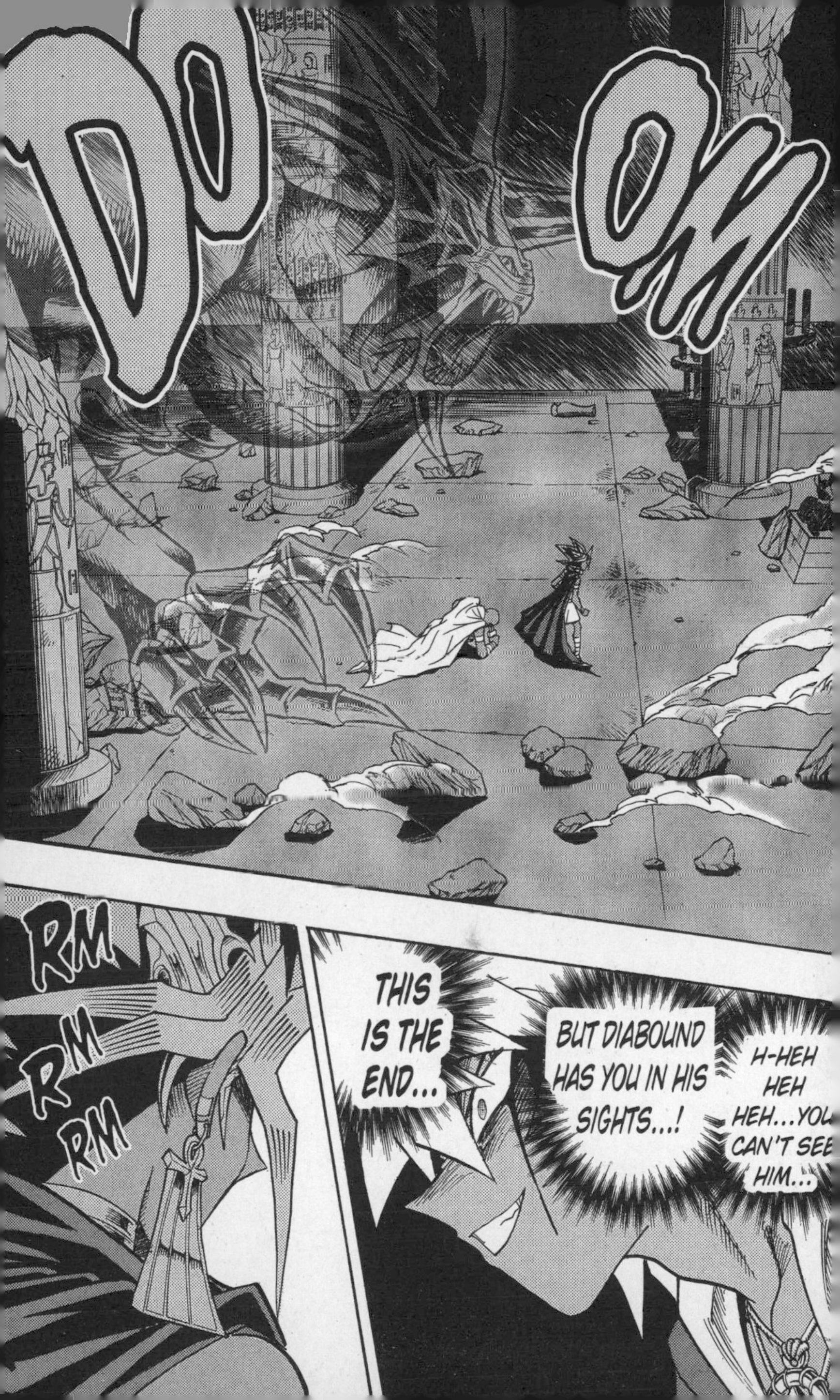
DOOM
H-HEH HEH HEH...YOU CAN'T SEE HIM...
BUT DIABOUND HAS YOU IN HIS SIGHTS...!
THIS IS THE END...
RM RM R RM

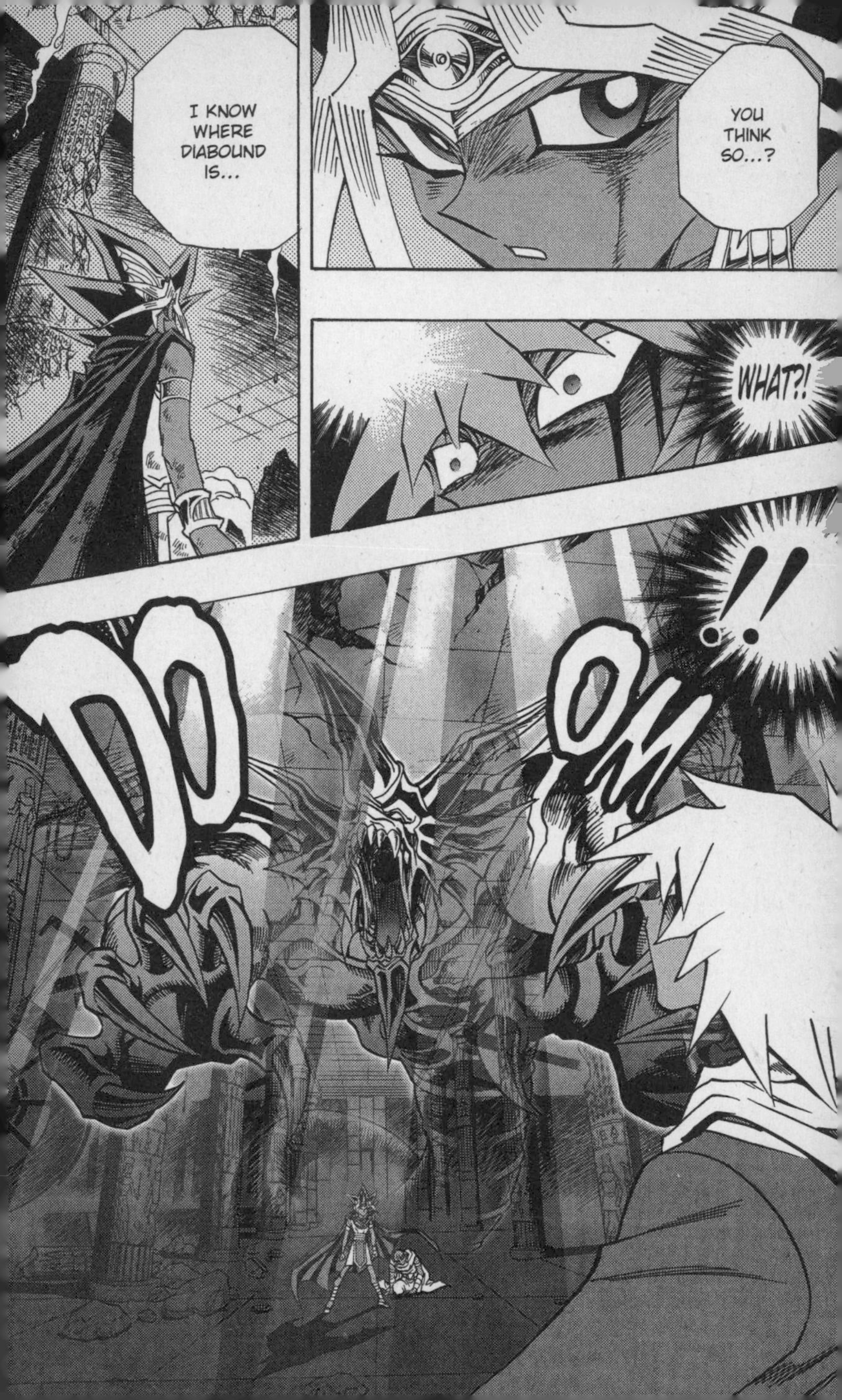
YOU THINK SO...?
WHAT?!
I KNOW WHERE DIABOUND IS...
!!
DOOM

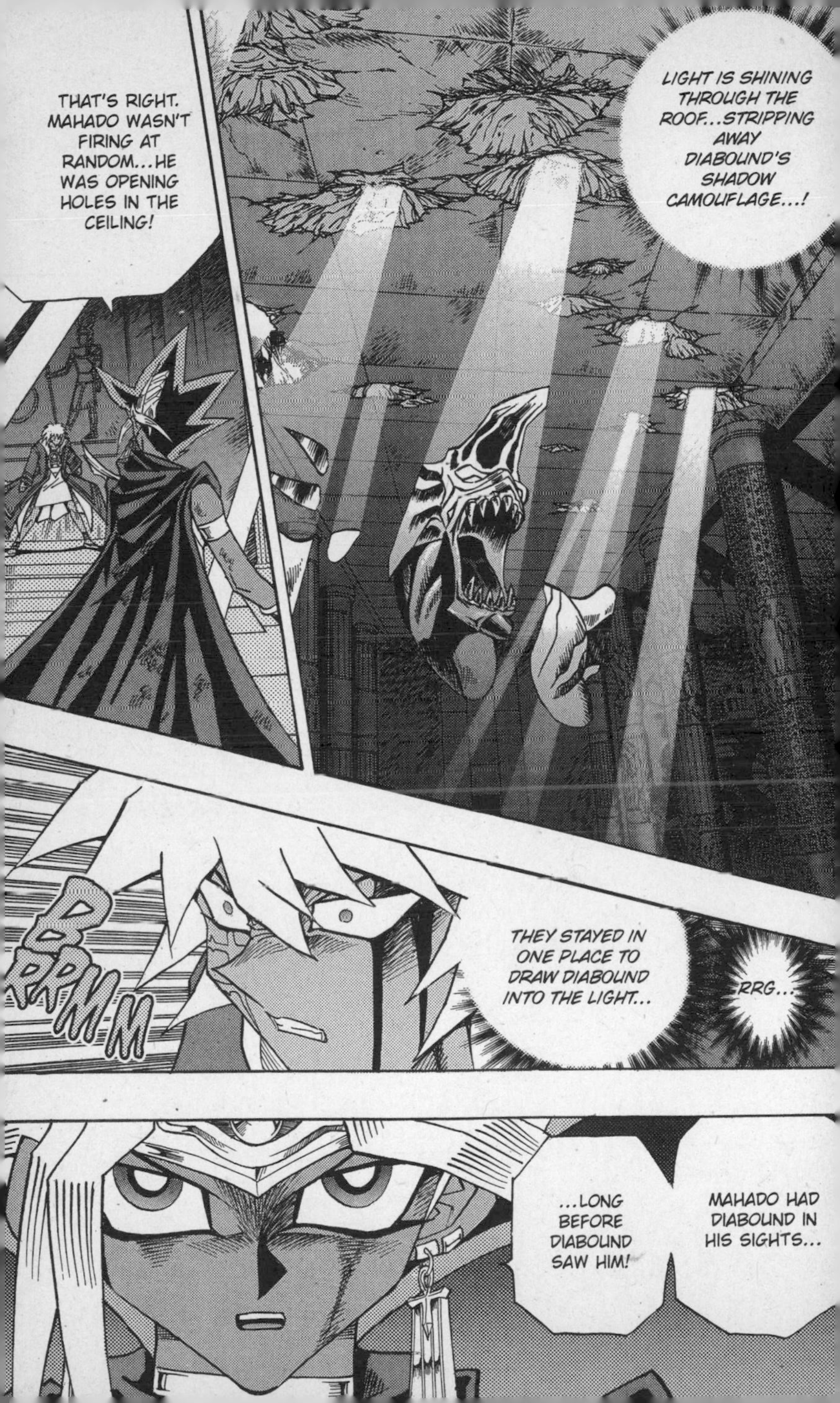
LIGHT IS SHINING THROUGH THE ROOF...STRIPPING AWAY DIABOUND'S SHADOW CAMOUFLAGE...!
THAT'S RIGHT. MAHADO WASN'T FIRING AT RANDOM...HE WAS OPENING HOLES IN THE CEILING!
RRG...
THEY STAYED IN ONE PLACE TO DRAW DIABOUND INTO THE LIGHT...
BRRRMMM
MAHADO HAD DIABOUND IN HIS SIGHTS...
...LONG BEFORE DIABOUND SAW HIM!

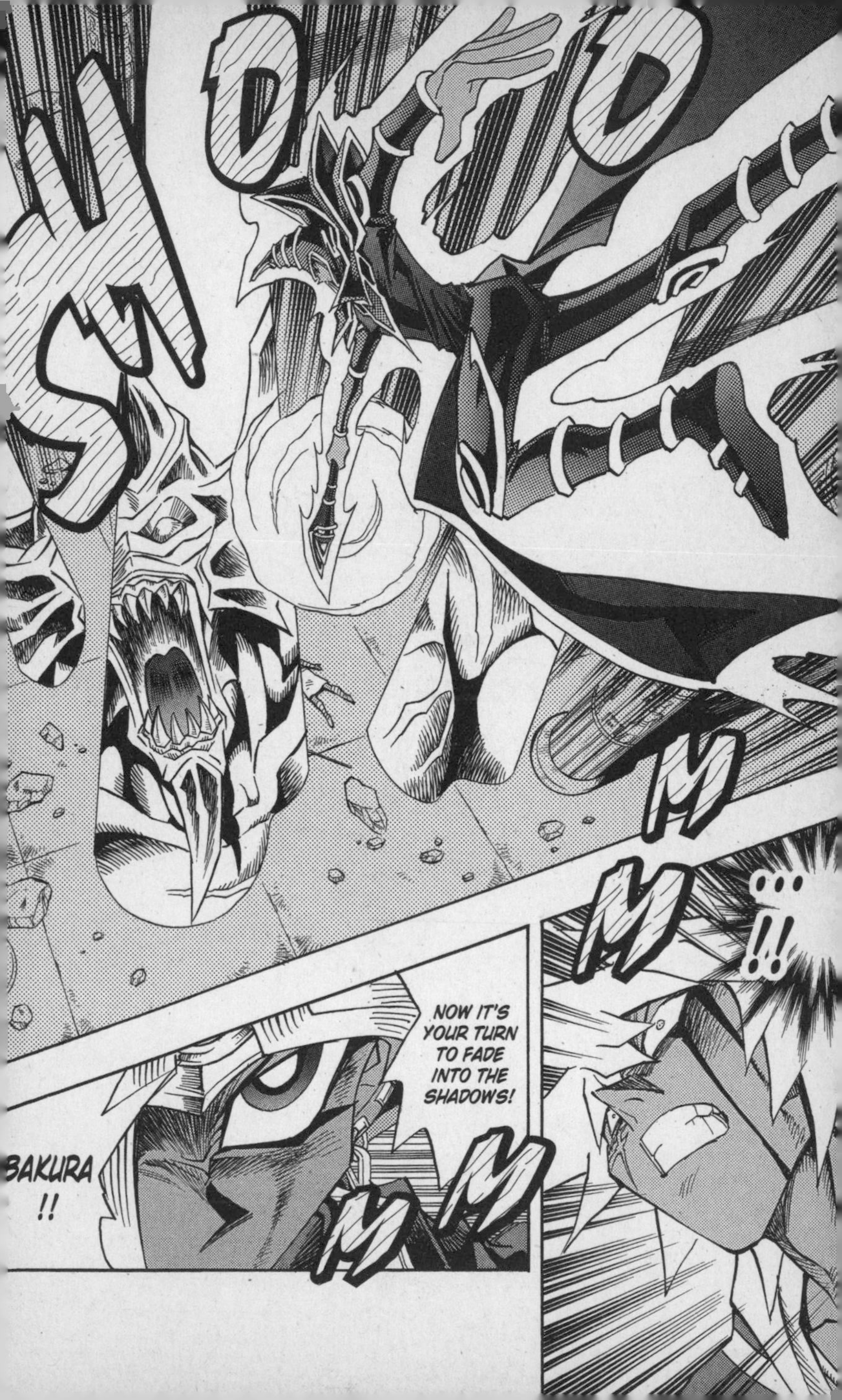
MMM
...!!
NOW IT'S YOUR TURN TO FADE INTO THE SHADOWS!
BAKURA !!
MM

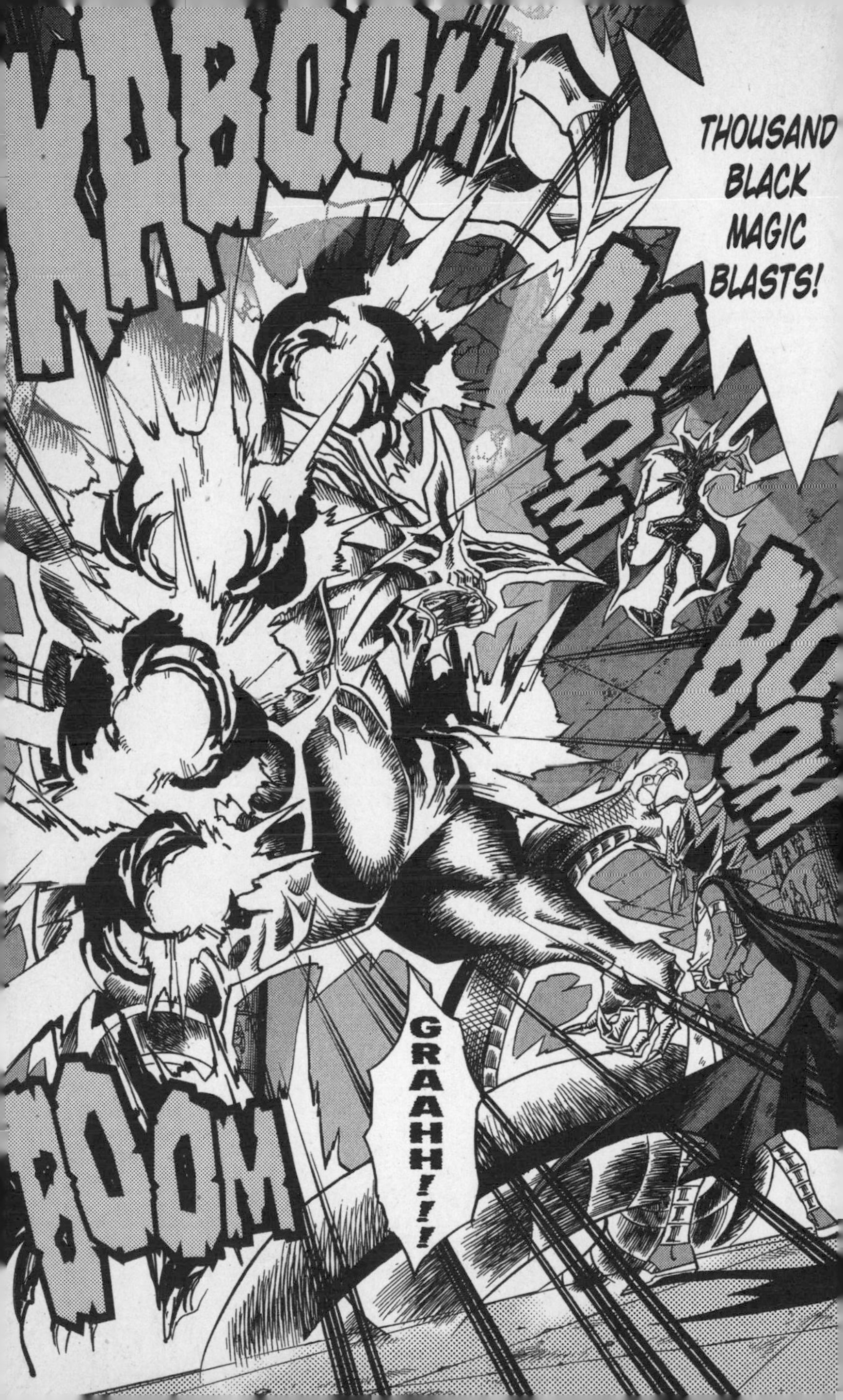
THOUSAND BLACK MAGIC BLASTS!
KABOOM
GRAAHH!!!!
BOOM

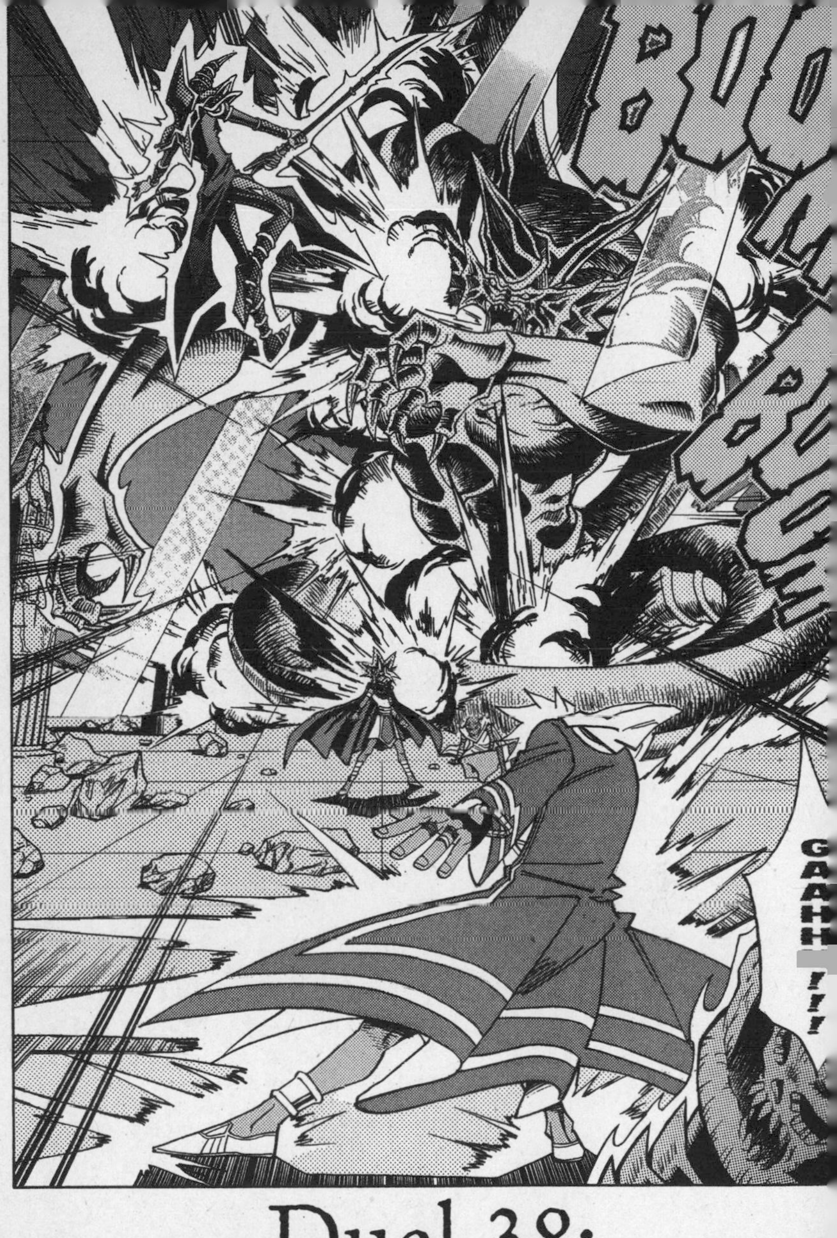
GAAHH!!!

Duel 38: Aura Shield!!

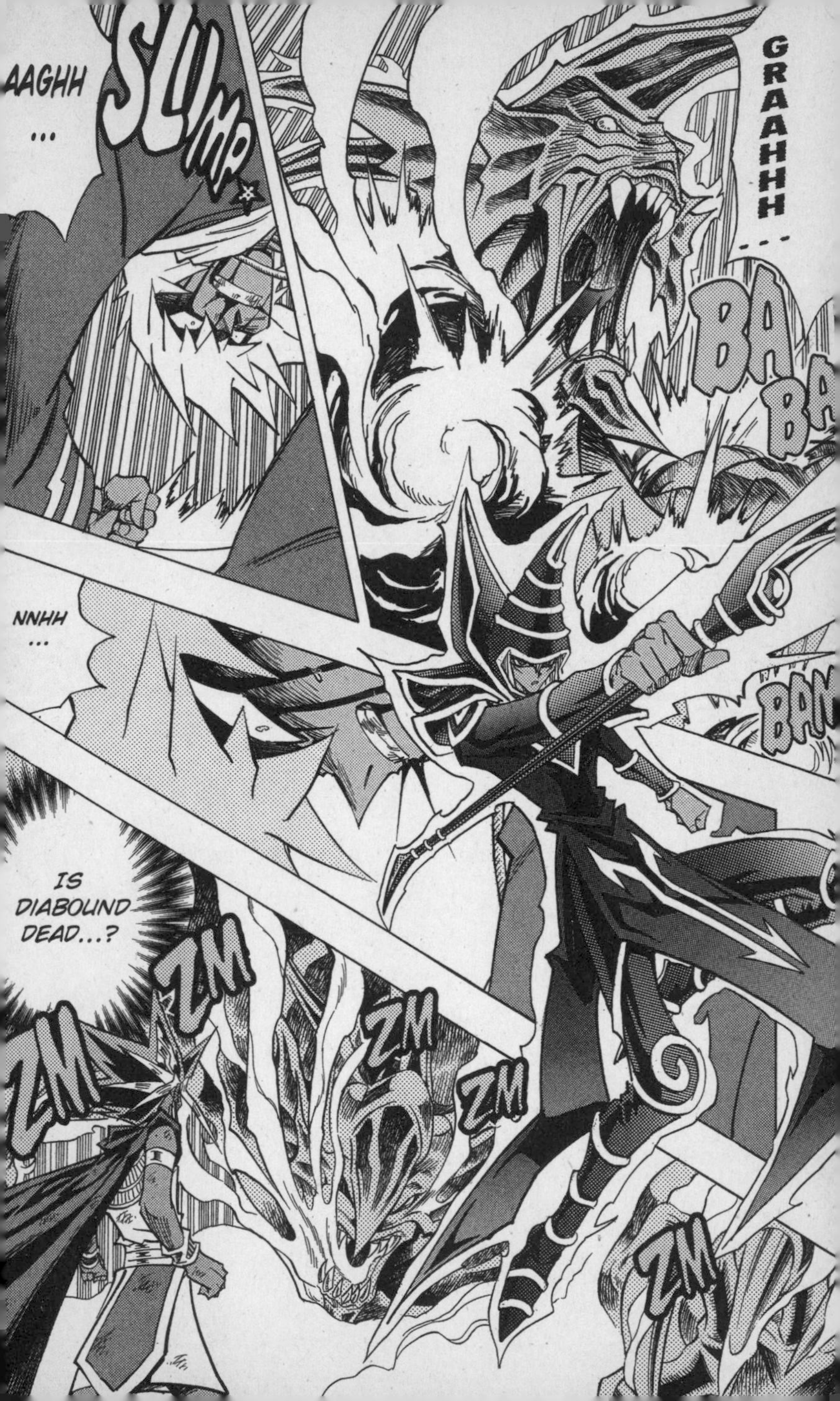
GRAAAHHH...
BA
BA
SLUMP
AAGHH...
BAN
NNHH...
IS DIABOUND DEAD...?
ZM
ZM
ZM
ZM
ZM
ZM

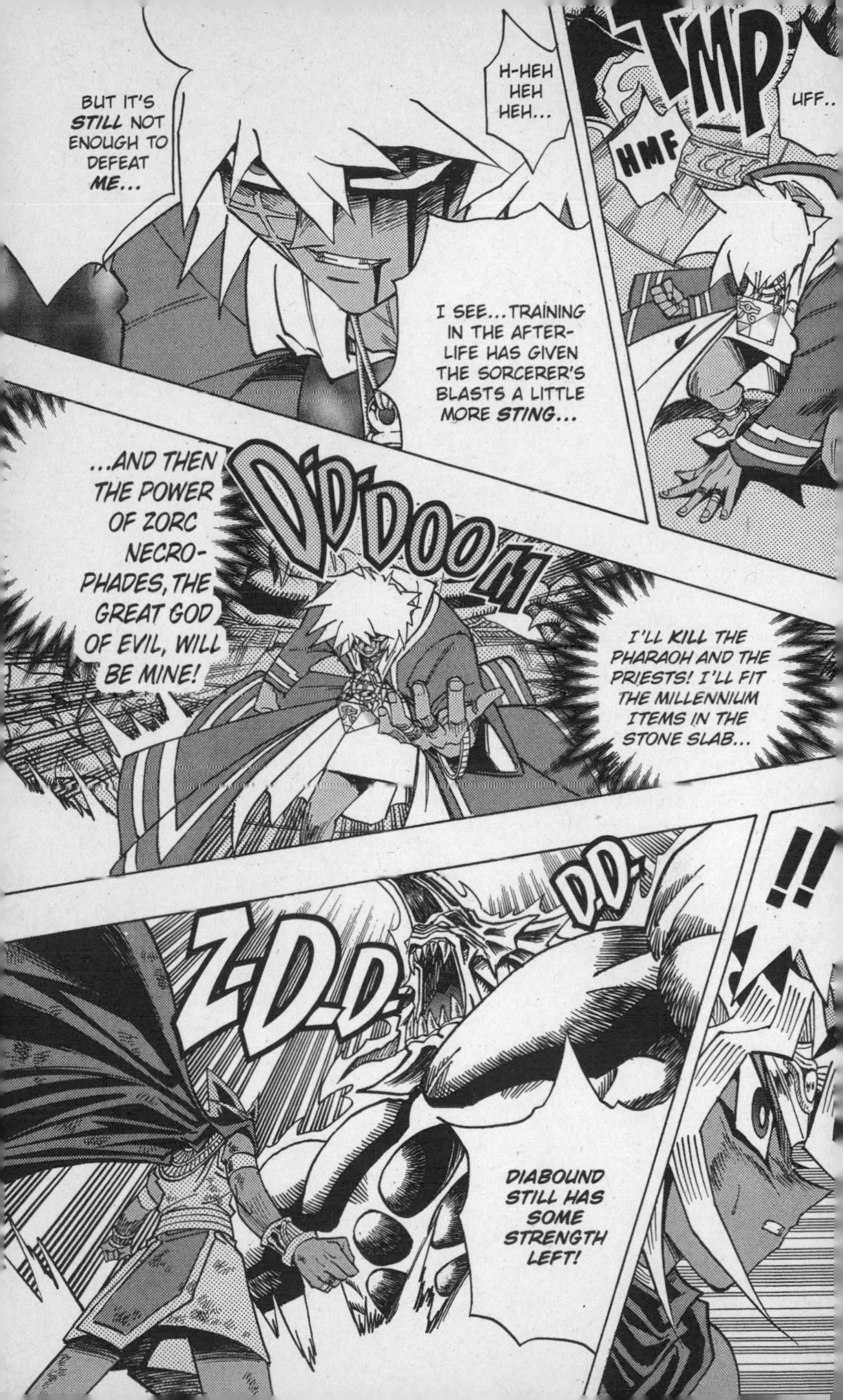
MP
HMF
UFF...
H-HEH HEH HEH...
I SEE...TRAINING IN THE AFTER-LIFE HAS GIVEN THE SORCERER'S BLASTS A LITTLE MORE STING...
BUT IT'S STILL NOT ENOUGH TO DEFEAT ME...
I'LL KILL THE PHARAOH AND THE PRIESTS! I'LL FIT THE MILLENNIUM ITEMS IN THE STONE SLAB...
...AND THEN THE POWER OF ZORC NECRO-PHADES, THE GREAT GOD OF EVIL, WILL BE MINE!
D-D-DOOM
!!
D.D-
Z-D-D-
DIABOUND STILL HAS SOME STRENGTH LEFT!

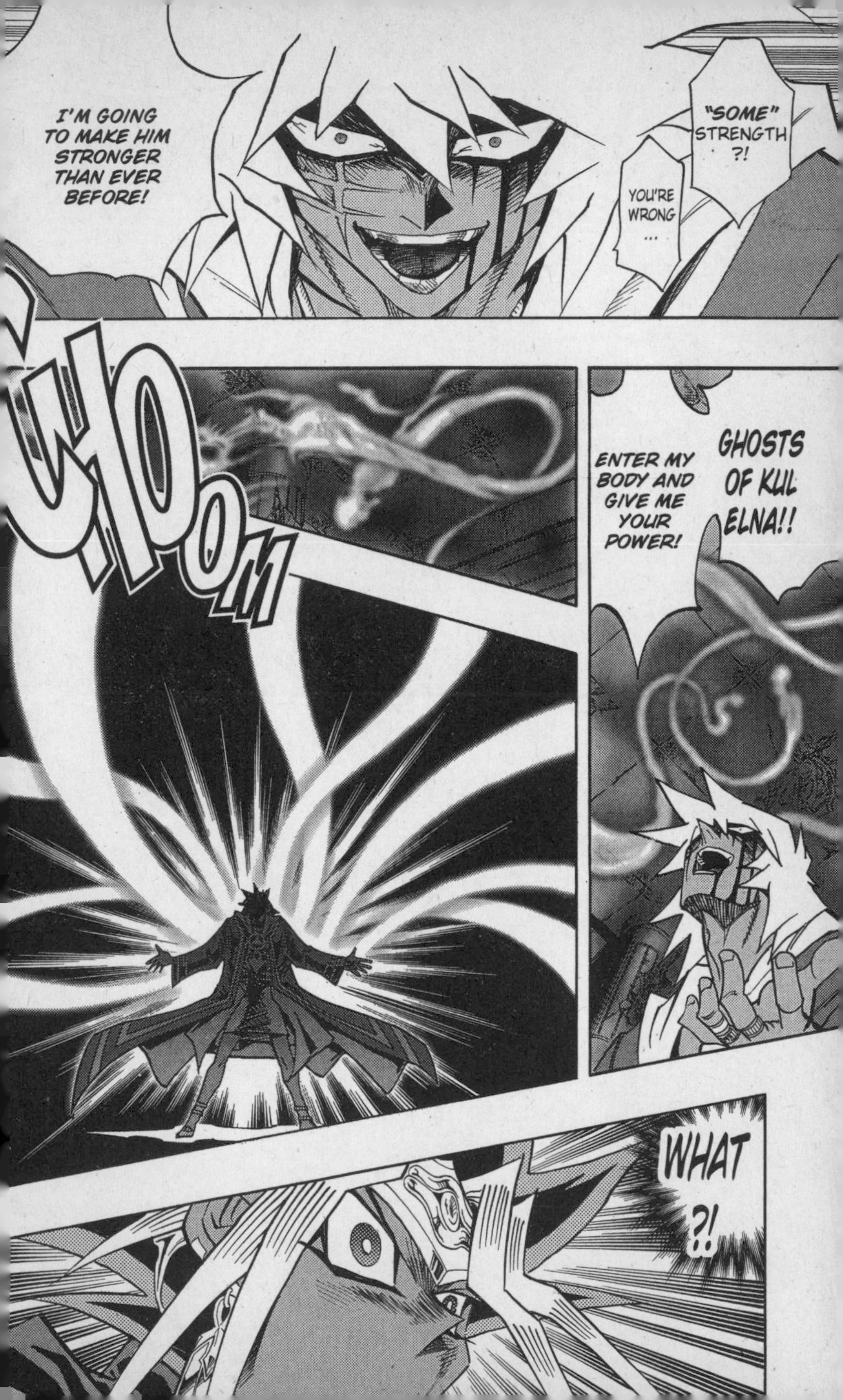
"SOME" STRENGTH ?!
YOU'RE WRONG ...
I'M GOING TO MAKE HIM STRONGER THAN EVER BEFORE!
GHOSTS OF KUL ELNA!!
ENTER MY BODY AND GIVE ME YOUR POWER!
WHAT ?!

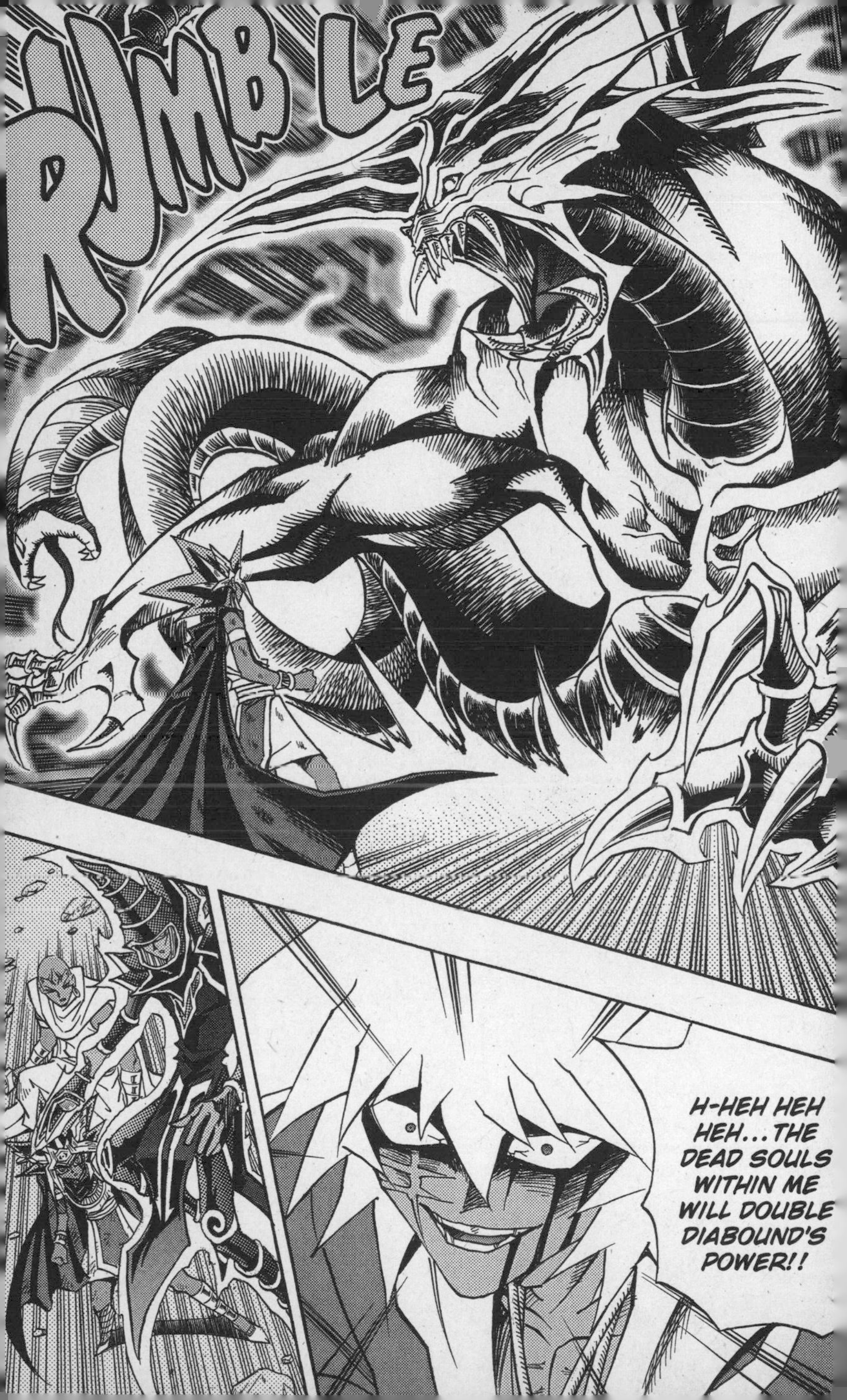
RUMBLE
H-HEH HEH HEH...THE DEAD SOULS WITHIN ME WILL DOUBLE DIABOUND'S POWER!!

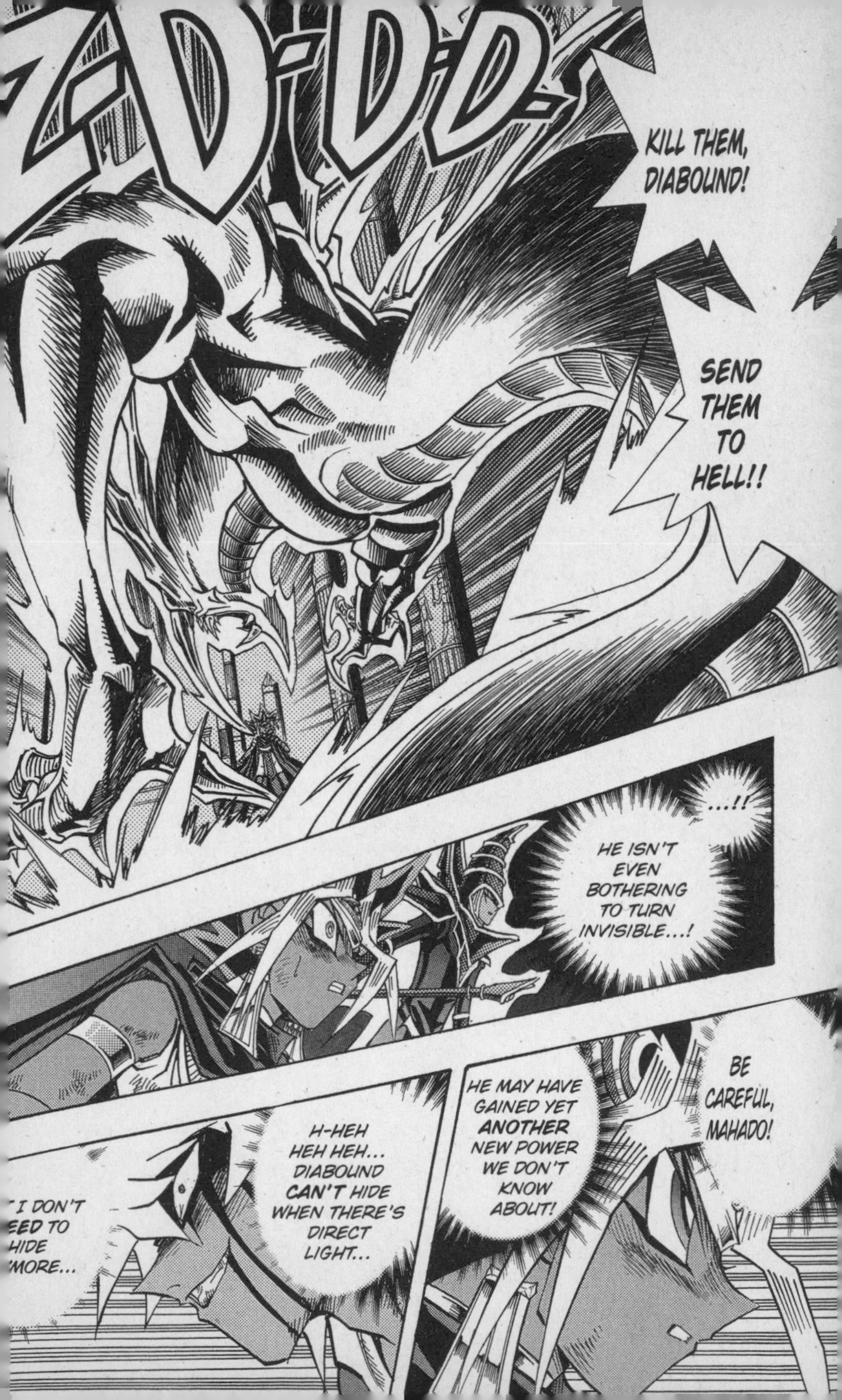
ZD-D-D
KILL THEM, DIABOUND!
SEND THEM TO HELL!!
...!!
HE ISN'T EVEN BOTHERING TO TURN INVISIBLE...!
BE CAREFUL, MAHADO!
HE MAY HAVE GAINED YET ANOTHER NEW POWER WE DON'T KNOW ABOUT!
H-HEH HEH HEH... DIABOUND CAN'T HIDE WHEN THERE'S DIRECT LIGHT...
T I DON'T EED TO HIDE YMORE...

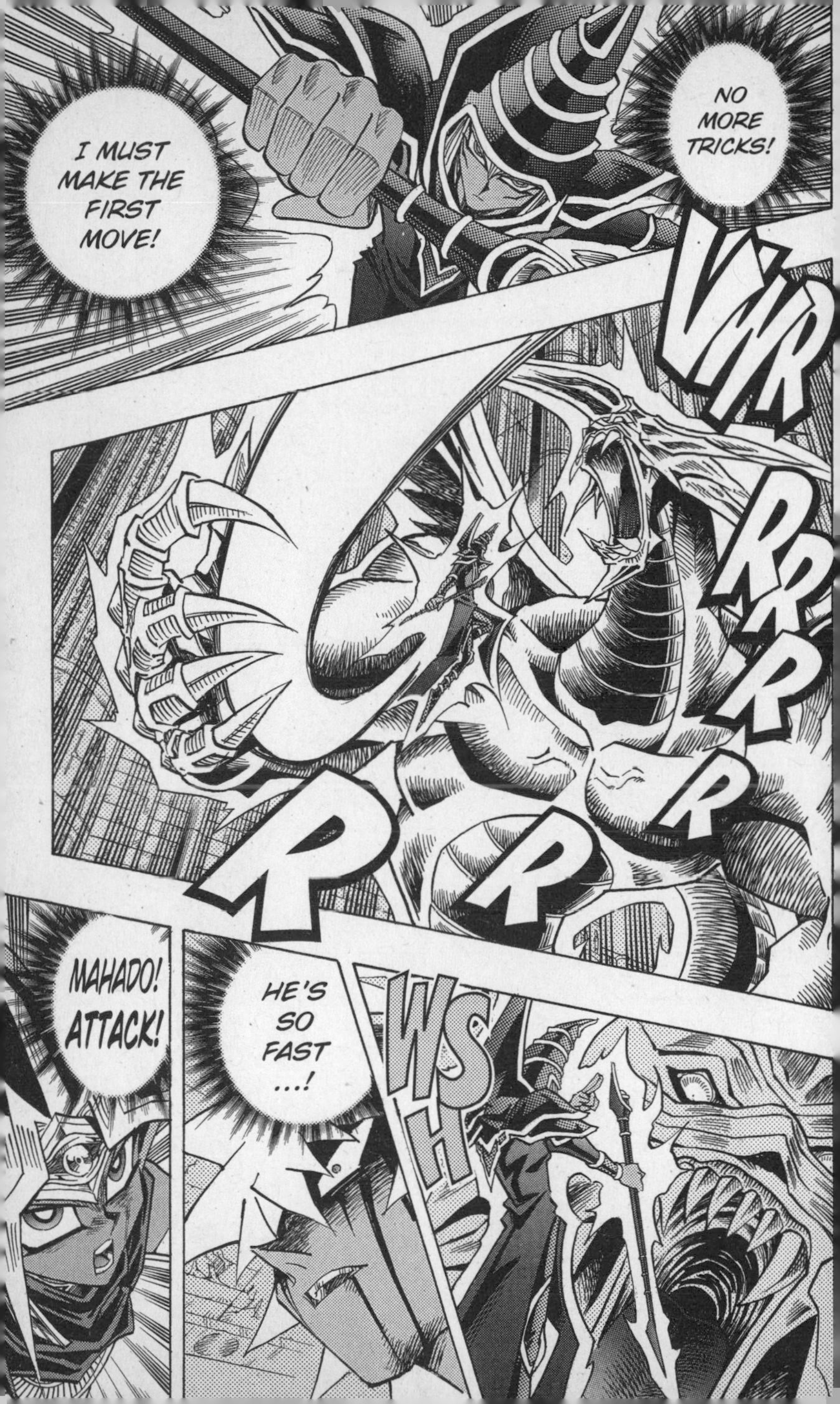
NO MORE TRICKS!
I MUST MAKE THE FIRST MOVE!
VVR
RRRRRR
HE'S SO FAST ...!
MAHADO! ATTACK!
WSH

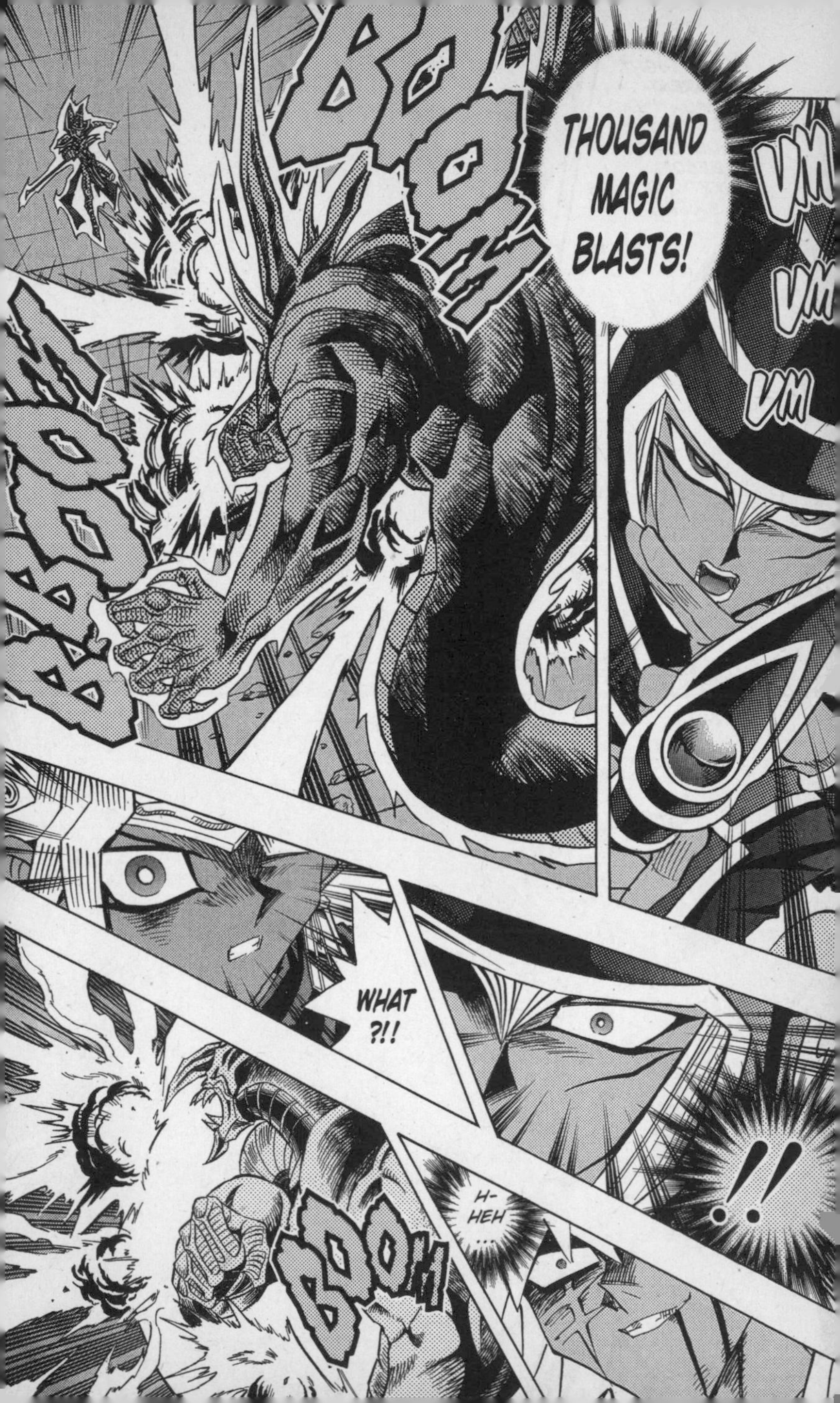

THOUSAND MAGIC BLASTS!
VM
VM
VM
BOOM
!!
WHAT ?!!
H-HEH ...
BOOM

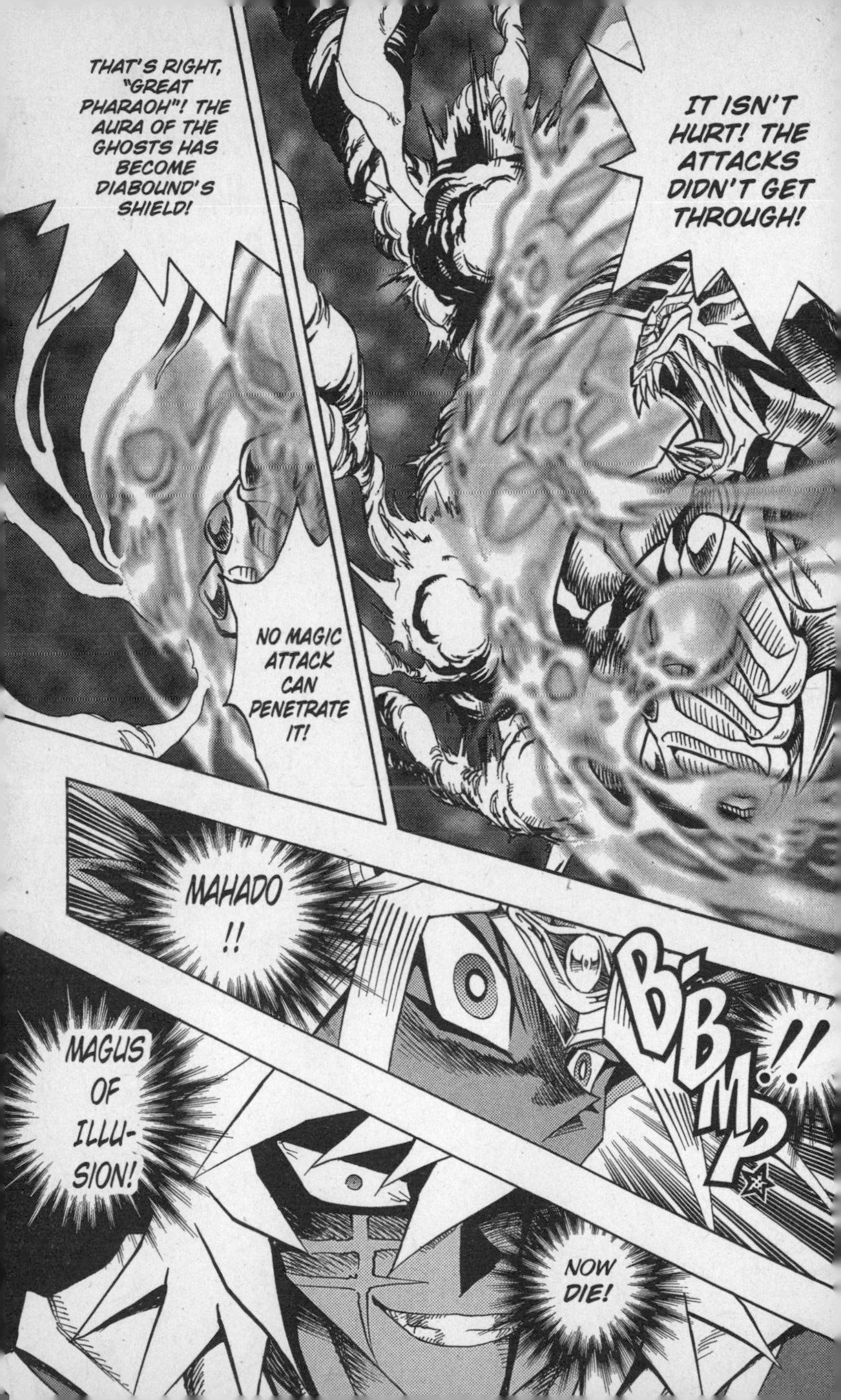
IT ISN'T HURT! THE ATTACKS DIDN'T GET THROUGH!
THAT'S RIGHT, "GREAT PHARAOH"! THE AURA OF THE GHOSTS HAS BECOME DIABOUND'S SHIELD!
NO MAGIC ATTACK CAN PENETRATE IT!
MAHADO !!
BBMP!!
MAGUS OF ILLU-SION!
NOW DIE!

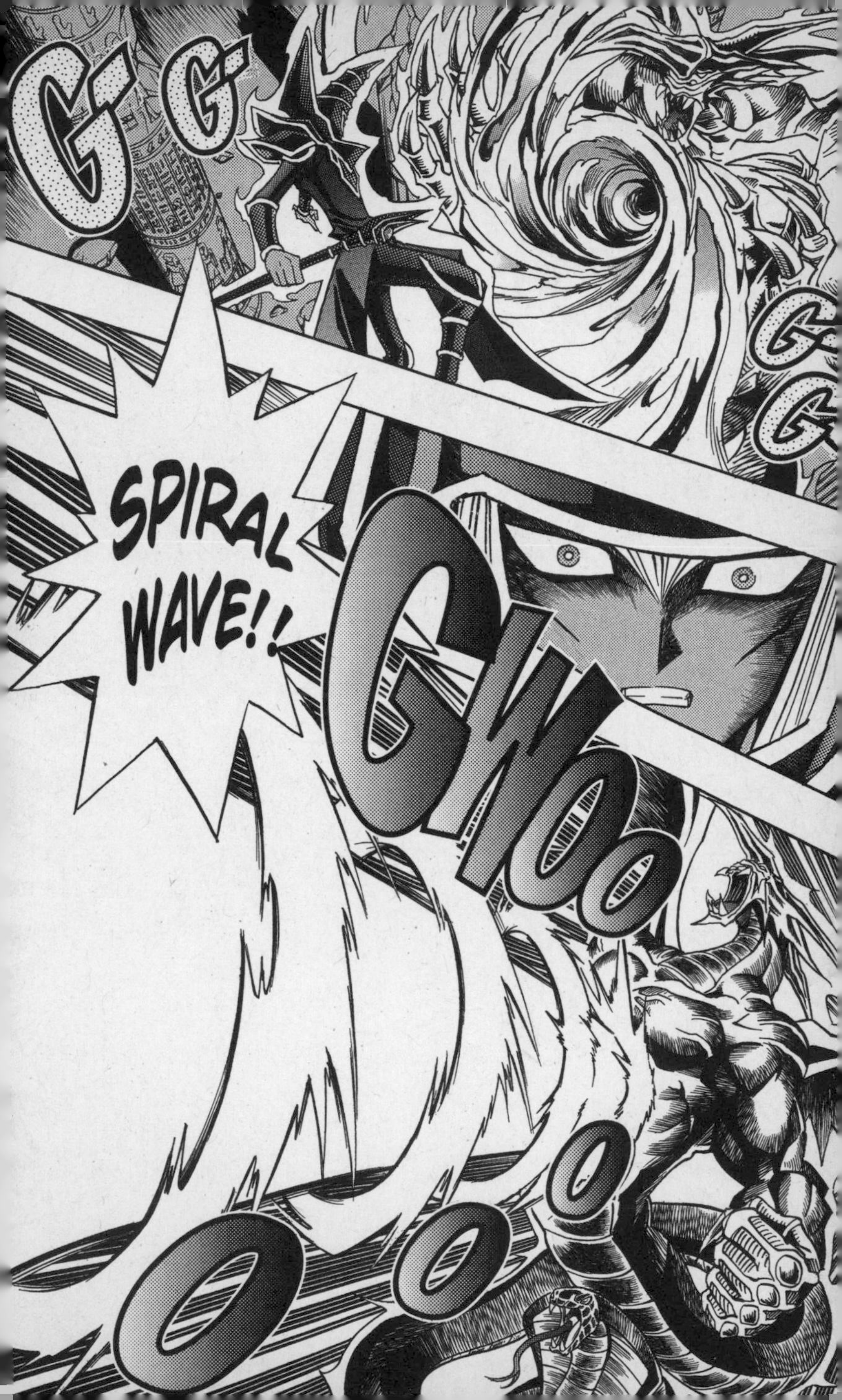

GG
GG
SPIRAL WAVE!!
GWOOOOOO

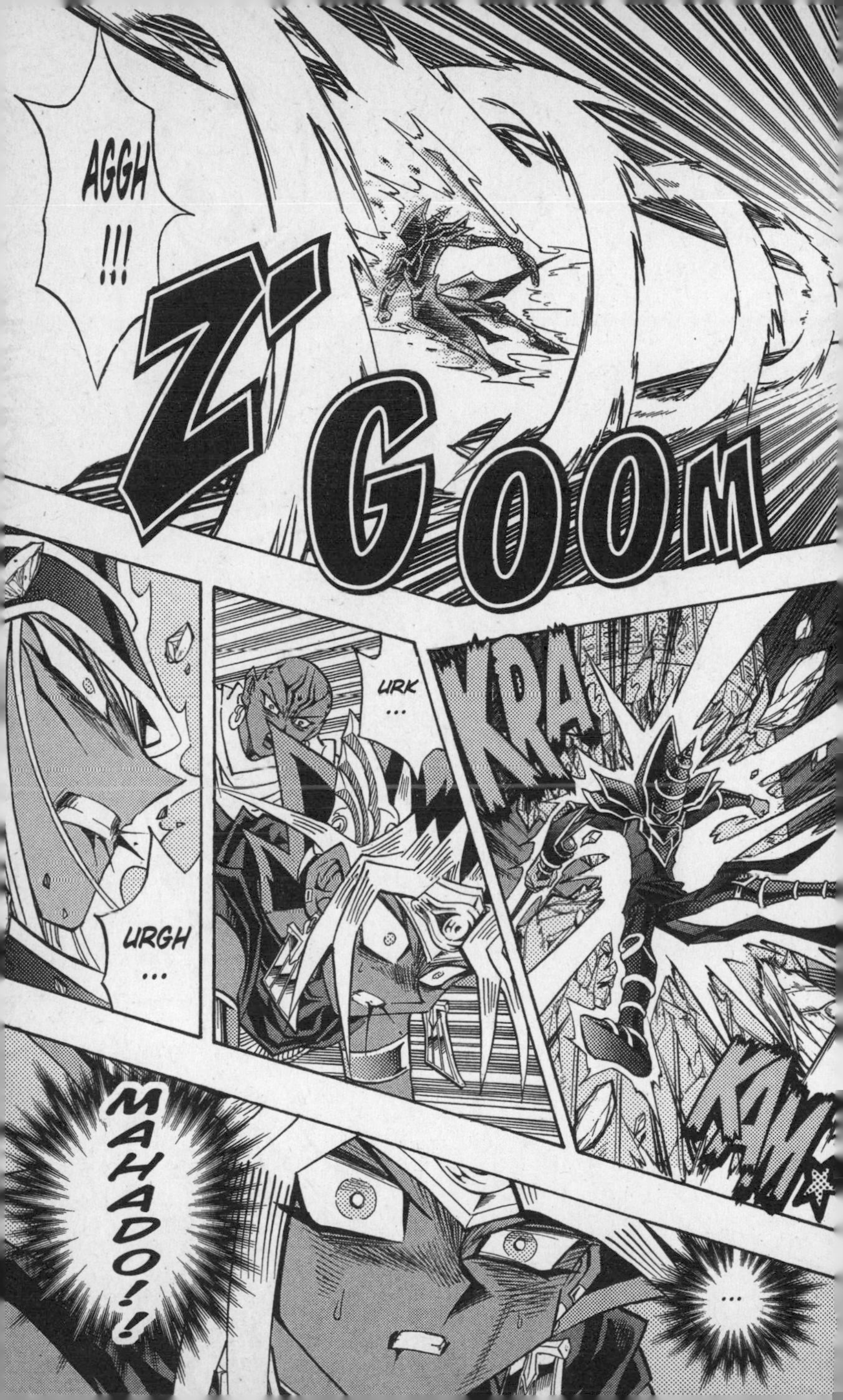
Z'GOOM
AGGH!!!
KRA
KAM
URK...
URGH...
MAHADO!!
...

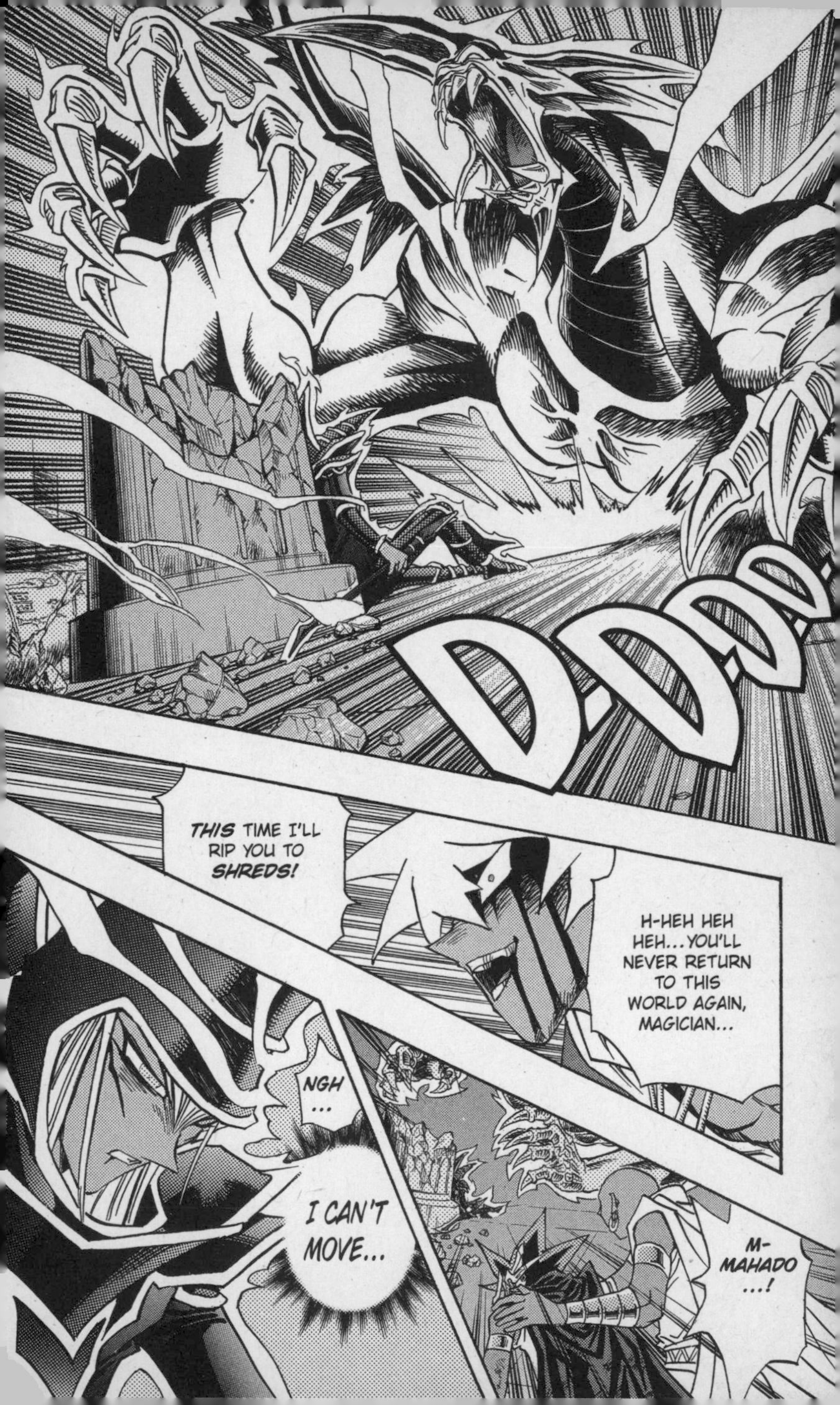
DDDD
THIS TIME I'LL RIP YOU TO SHREDS!
H-HEH HEH HEH...YOU'LL NEVER RETURN TO THIS WORLD AGAIN, MAGICIAN...
M-MAHADO...!
NGH...
I CAN'T MOVE...

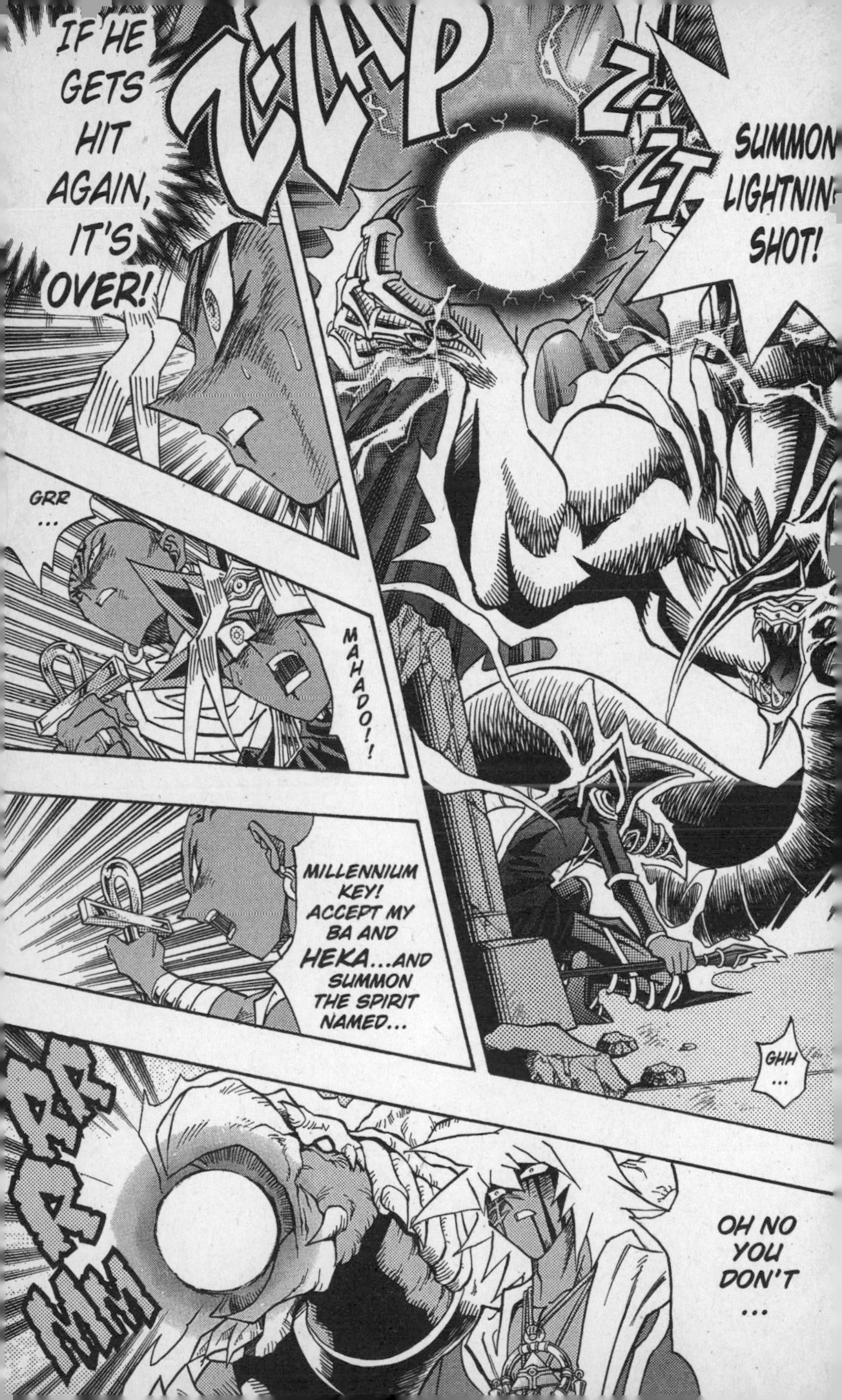
Z-ZAP
SUMMON LIGHTNING SHOT!
Z-ZT
IF HE GETS HIT AGAIN, IT'S OVER!
GRR...
MAHADO!!
GHH...
MILLENNIUM KEY! ACCEPT MY BA AND HEKA...AND SUMMON THE SPIRIT NAMED...
OH NO YOU DON'T...

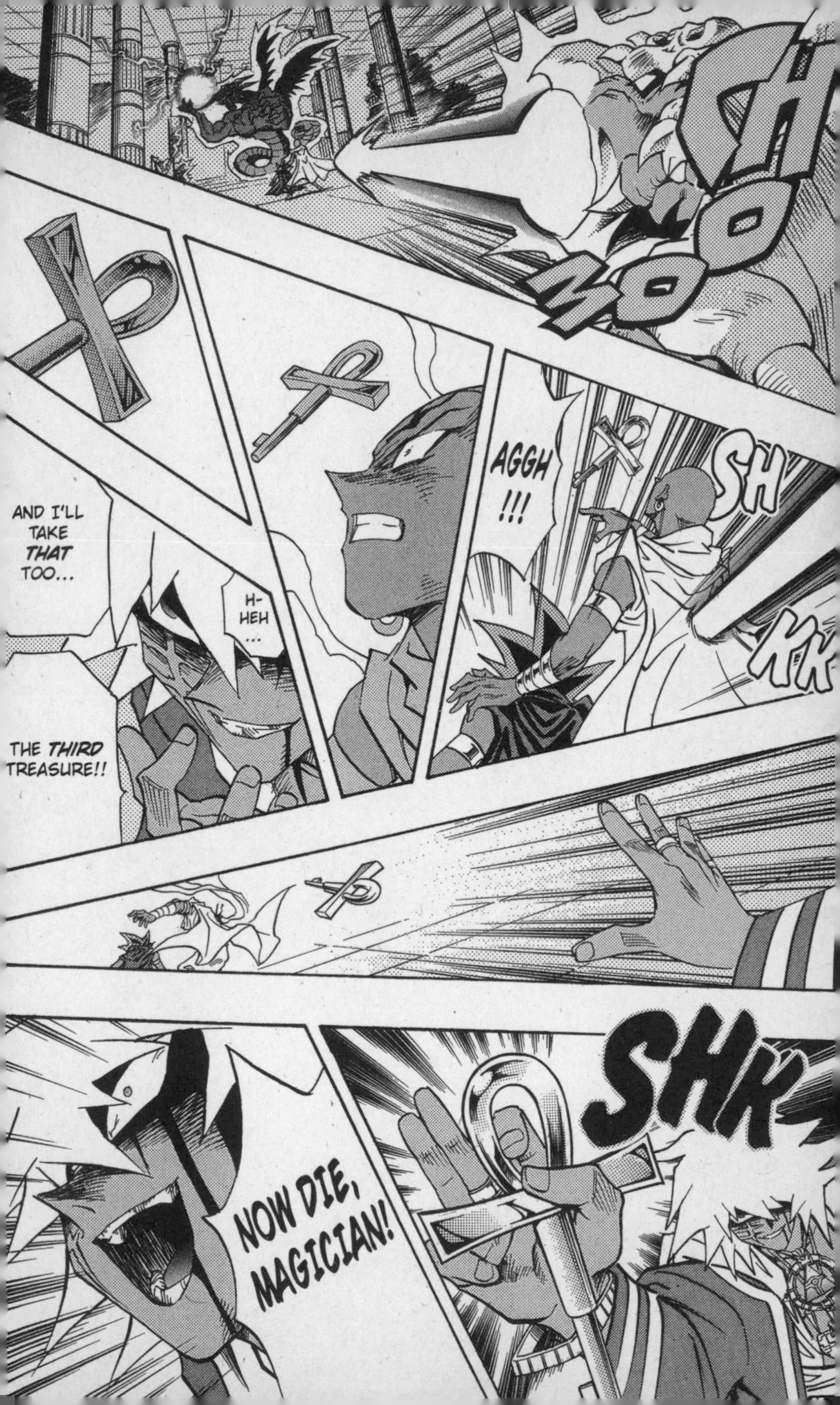
CHOOOM
SHKK
AGGH!!!
H-HEH...
AND I'LL TAKE *THAT* TOO...
THE *THIRD* TREASURE!!
SHK
NOW DIE, MAGICIAN!

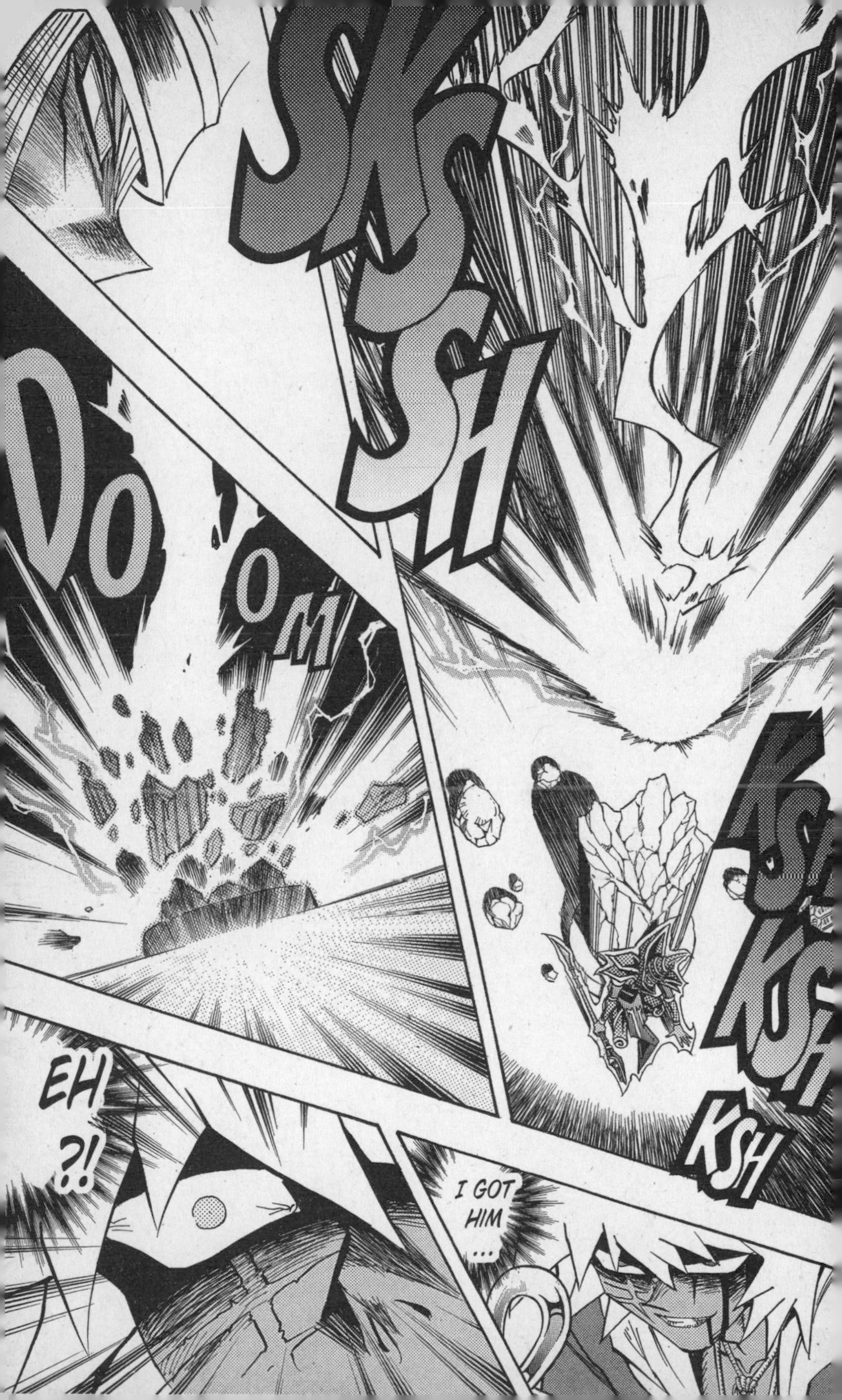
SKSSH
KSH
KSH
KSH
DOOM
I GOT HIM ...
EH ?!

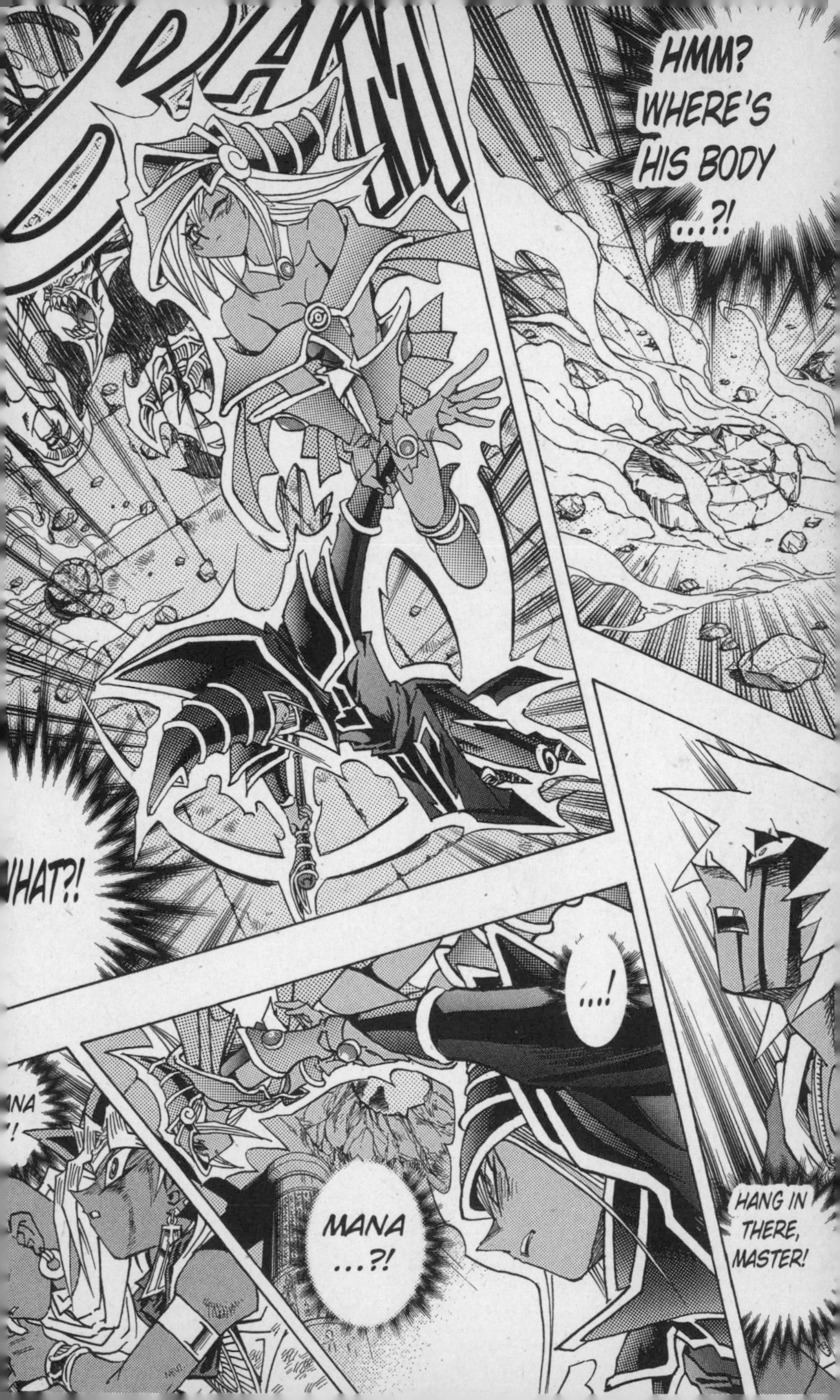
HMM? WHERE'S HIS BODY ...?!
WHAT?!
...!
HANG IN THERE, MASTER!
MANA ...?!
ANA ?!

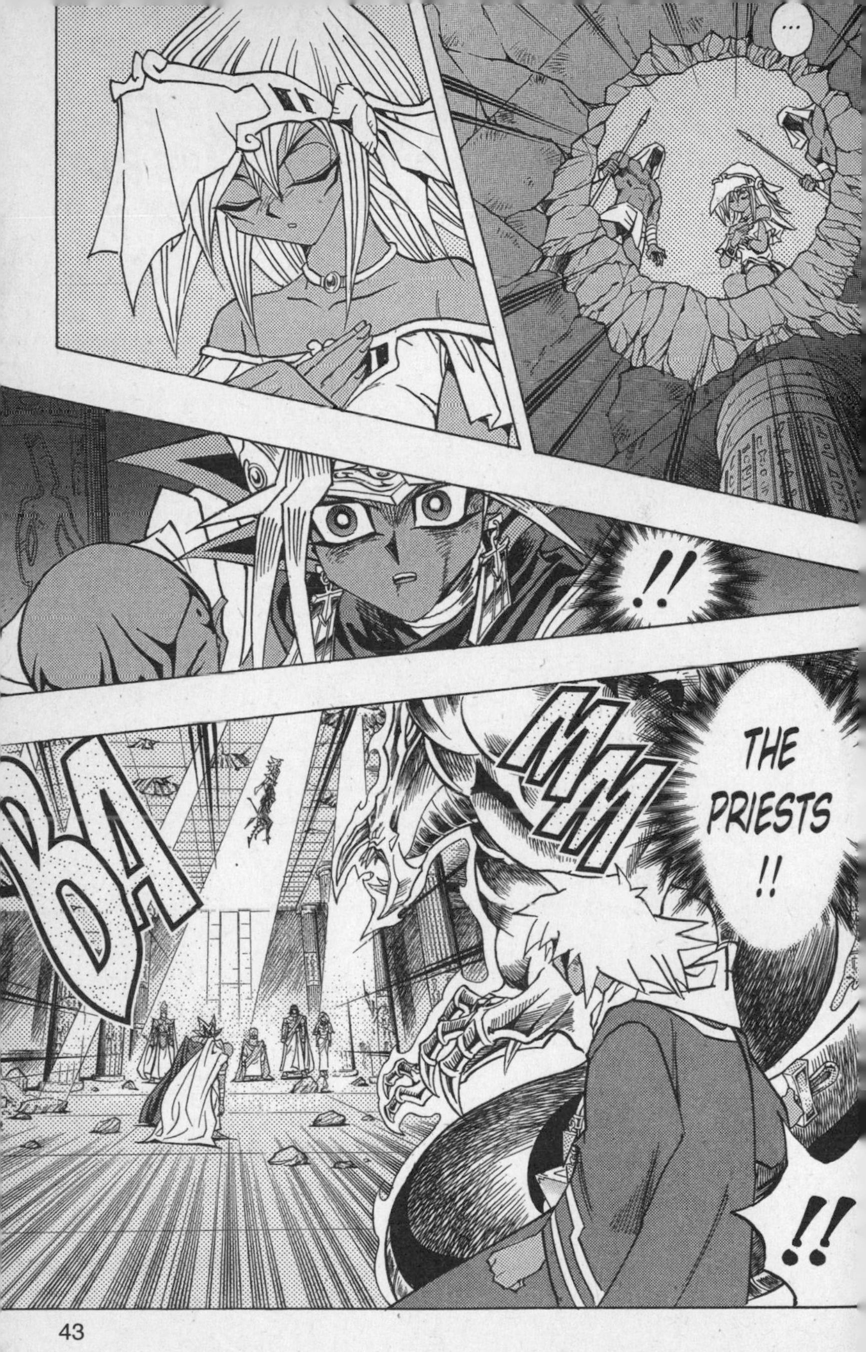
...
!!
THE PRIESTS !!
MM
BA
!!

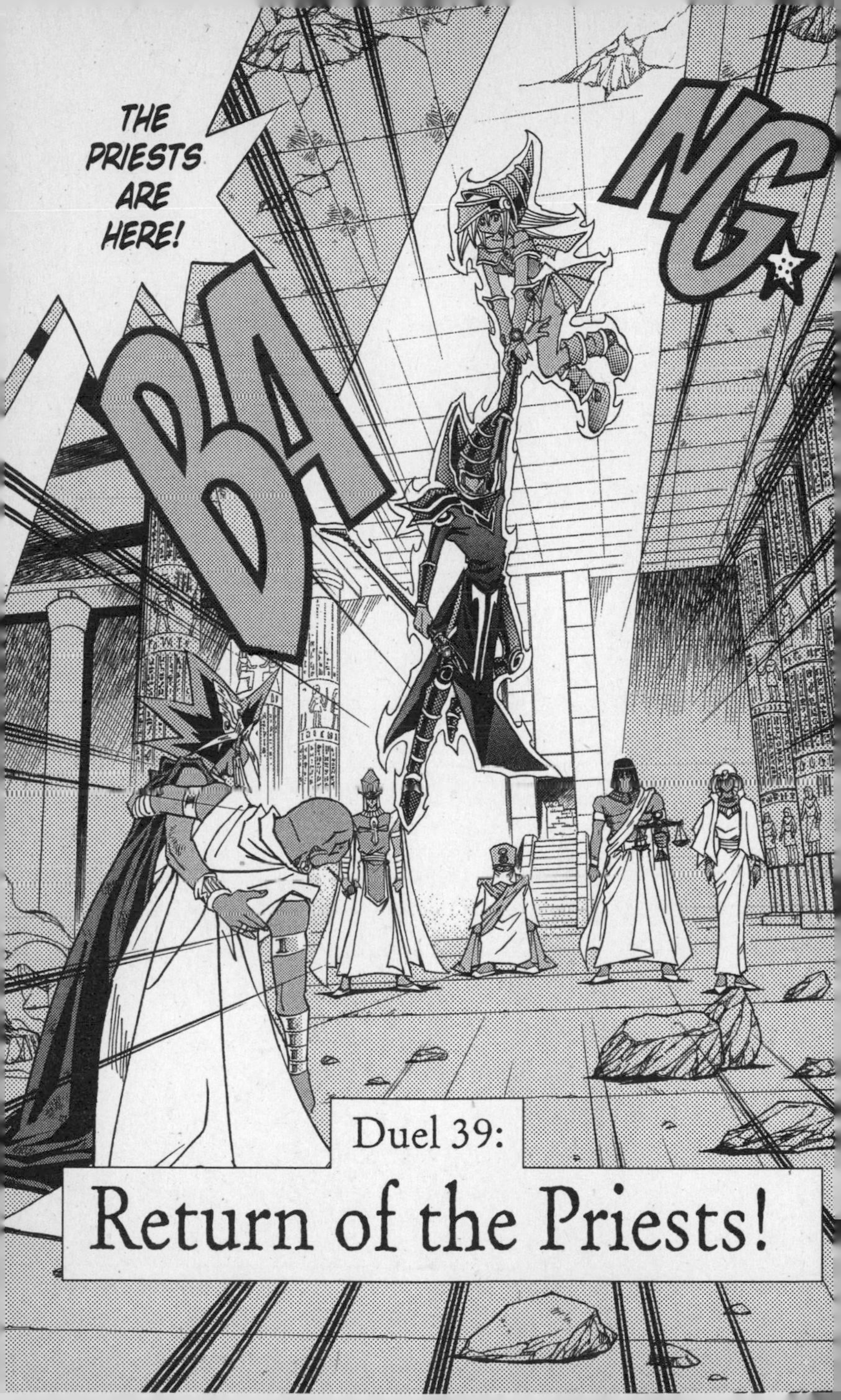
BANG
THE PRIESTS ARE HERE!
Duel 39:
Return of the Priests!

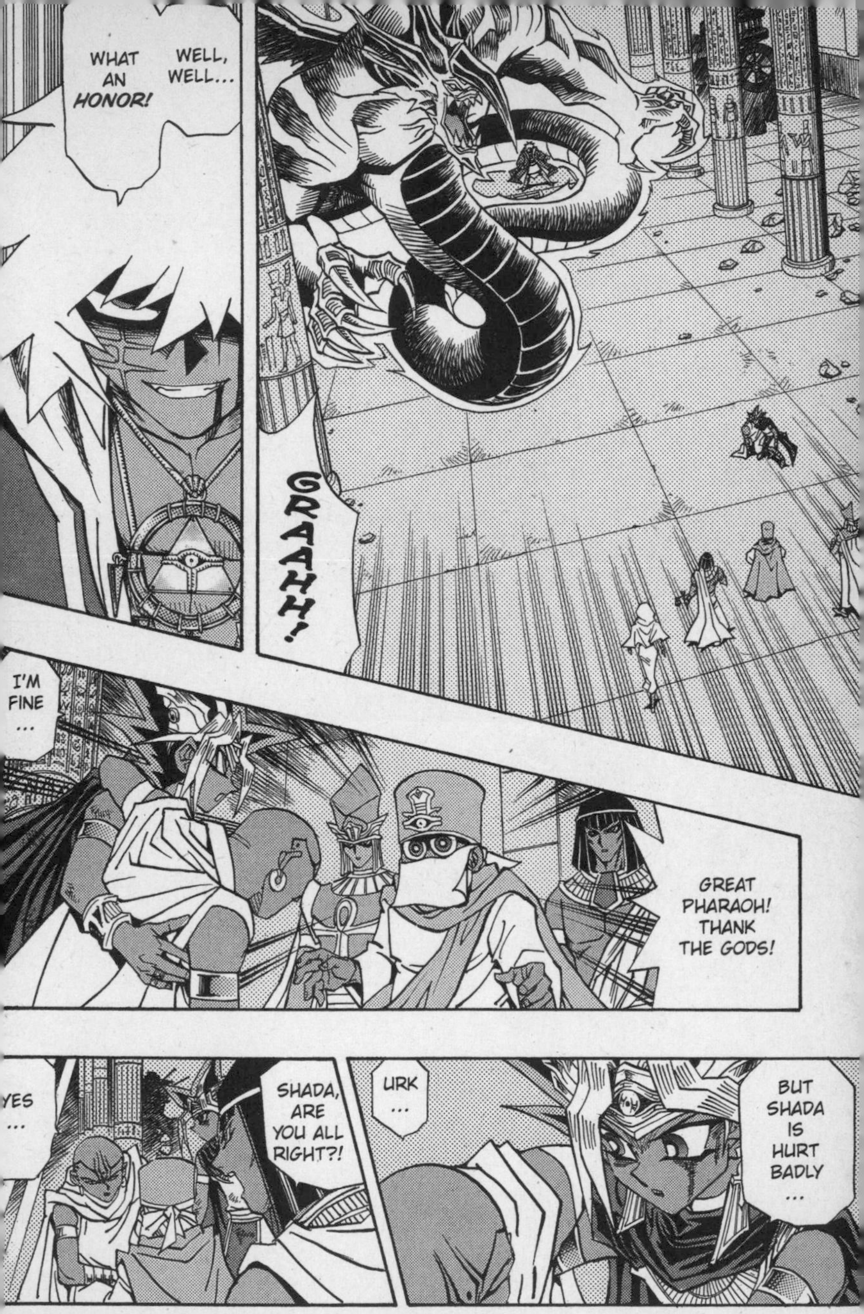

GRAAHH!
WELL, WELL...
WHAT AN HONOR!
GREAT PHARAOH! THANK THE GODS!
I'M FINE ...
BUT SHADA IS HURT BADLY ...
URK ...
SHADA, ARE YOU ALL RIGHT?!
YES ...

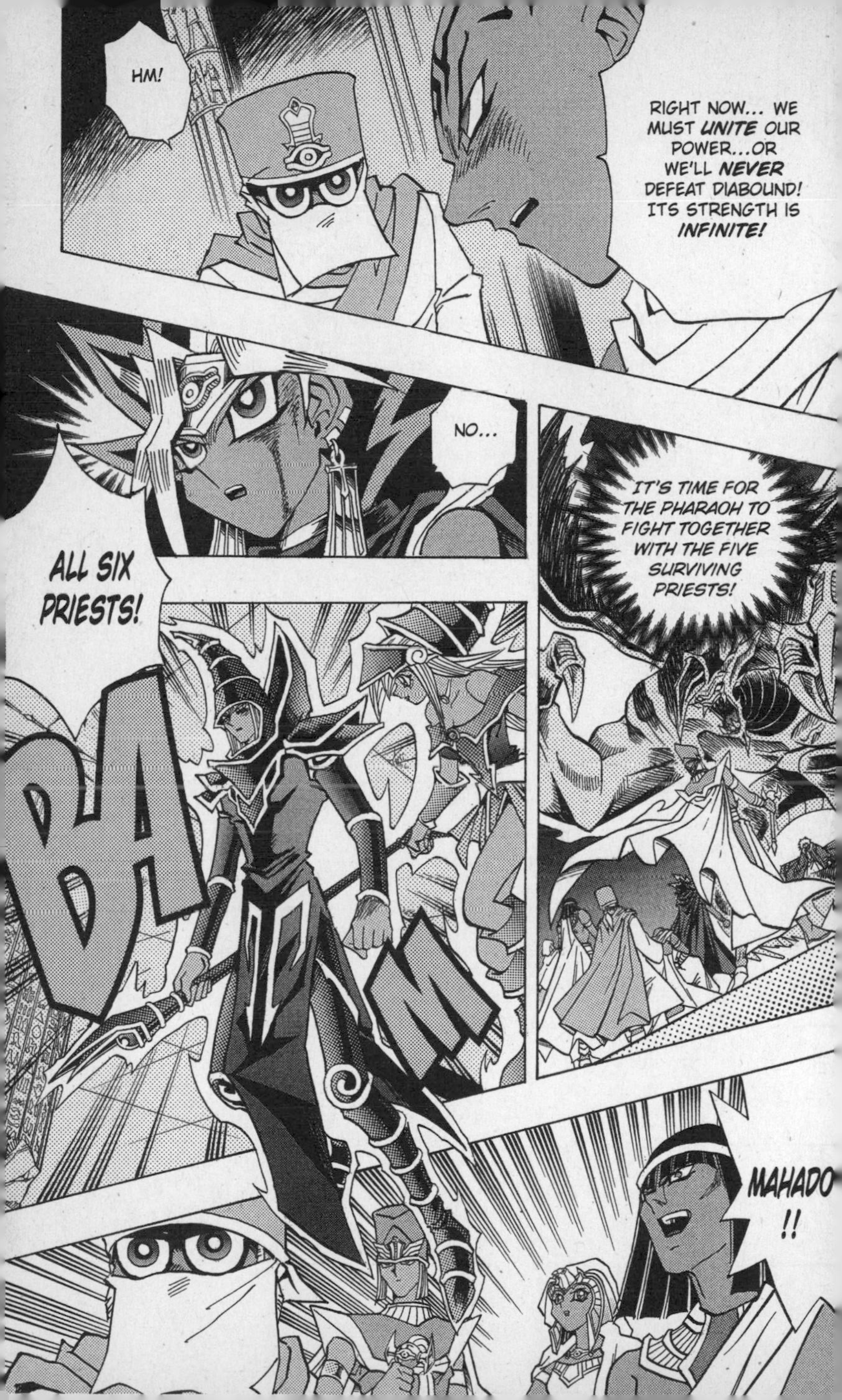
RIGHT NOW... WE MUST *UNITE* OUR POWER...OR WE'LL *NEVER* DEFEAT DIABOUND! ITS STRENGTH IS *INFINITE!*
HM!
IT'S TIME FOR THE PHARAOH TO FIGHT TOGETHER WITH THE FIVE SURVIVING PRIESTS!
NO...
ALL SIX PRIESTS!
BAM
MAHADO !!

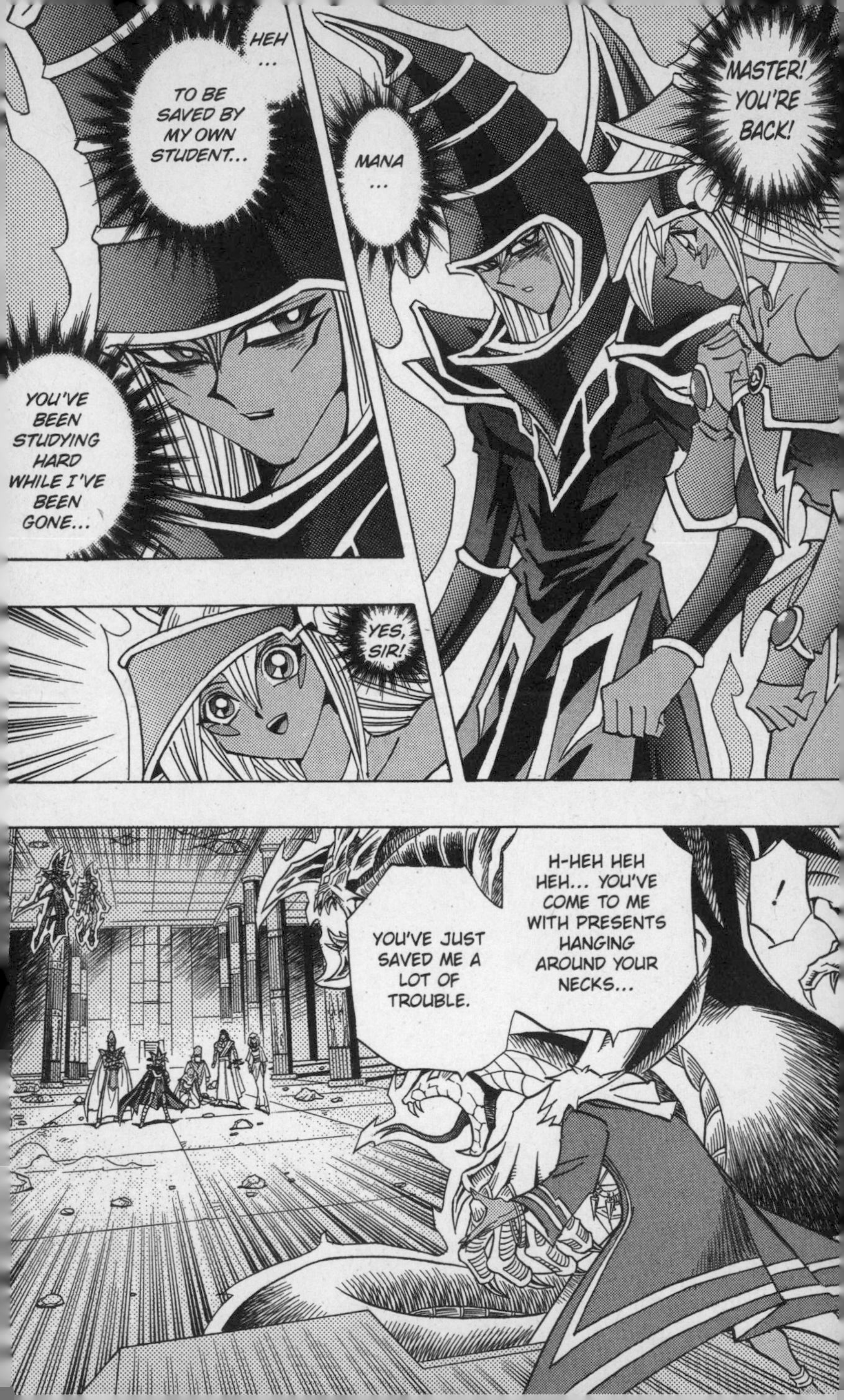
MASTER! YOU'RE BACK!
MANA ...
HEH ...
TO BE SAVED BY MY OWN STUDENT...
YOU'VE BEEN STUDYING HARD WHILE I'VE BEEN GONE...
YES, SIR!
!
H-HEH HEH HEH... YOU'VE COME TO ME WITH PRESENTS HANGING AROUND YOUR NECKS...
YOU'VE JUST SAVED ME A LOT OF TROUBLE.

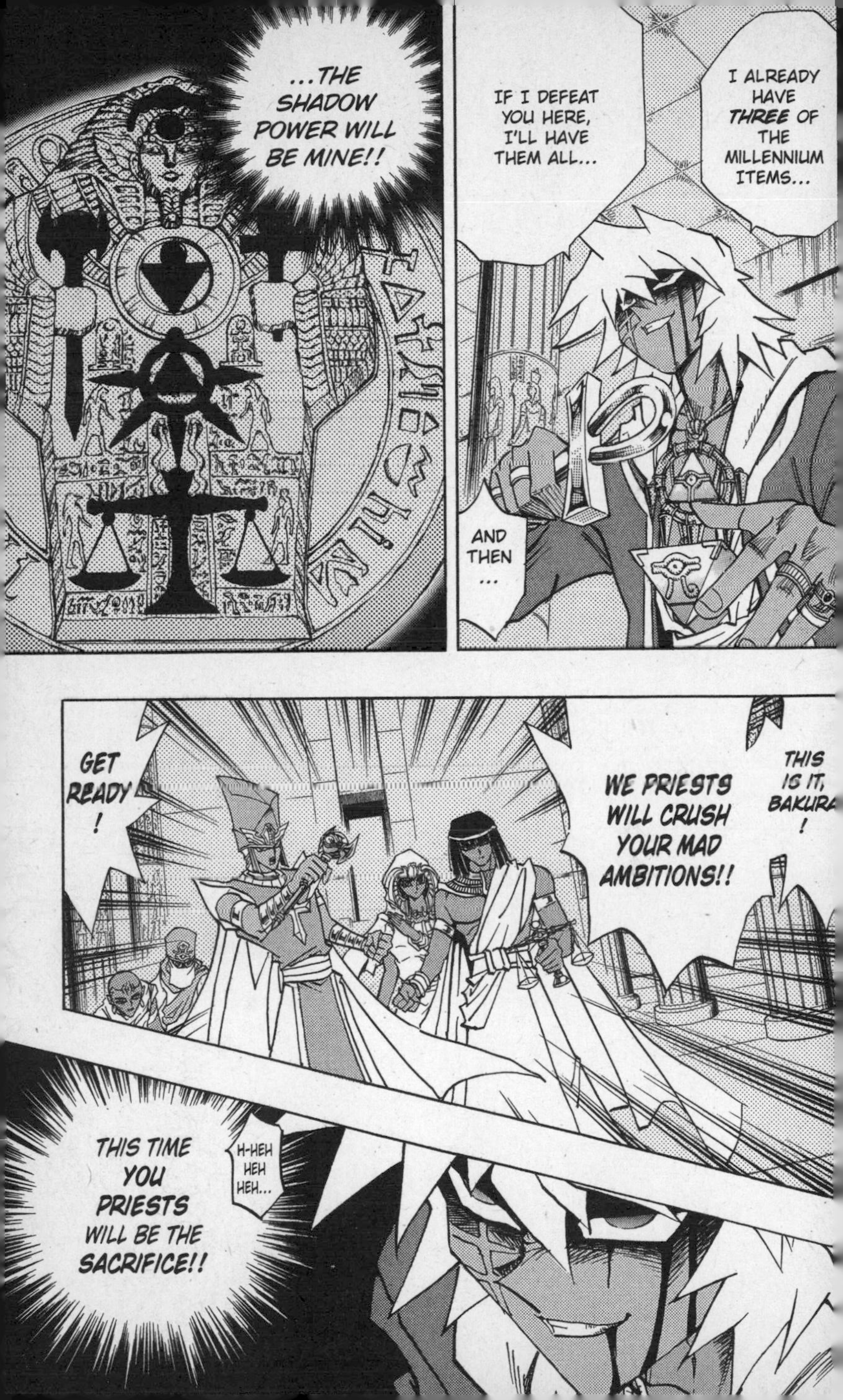
I ALREADY HAVE THREE OF THE MILLENNIUM ITEMS...
IF I DEFEAT YOU HERE, I'LL HAVE THEM ALL...
AND THEN...
...THE SHADOW POWER WILL BE MINE!!
THIS IS IT, BAKURA!
WE PRIESTS WILL CRUSH YOUR MAD AMBITIONS!!
GET READY!
H-HEH HEH HEH...
THIS TIME YOU PRIESTS WILL BE THE SACRIFICE!!

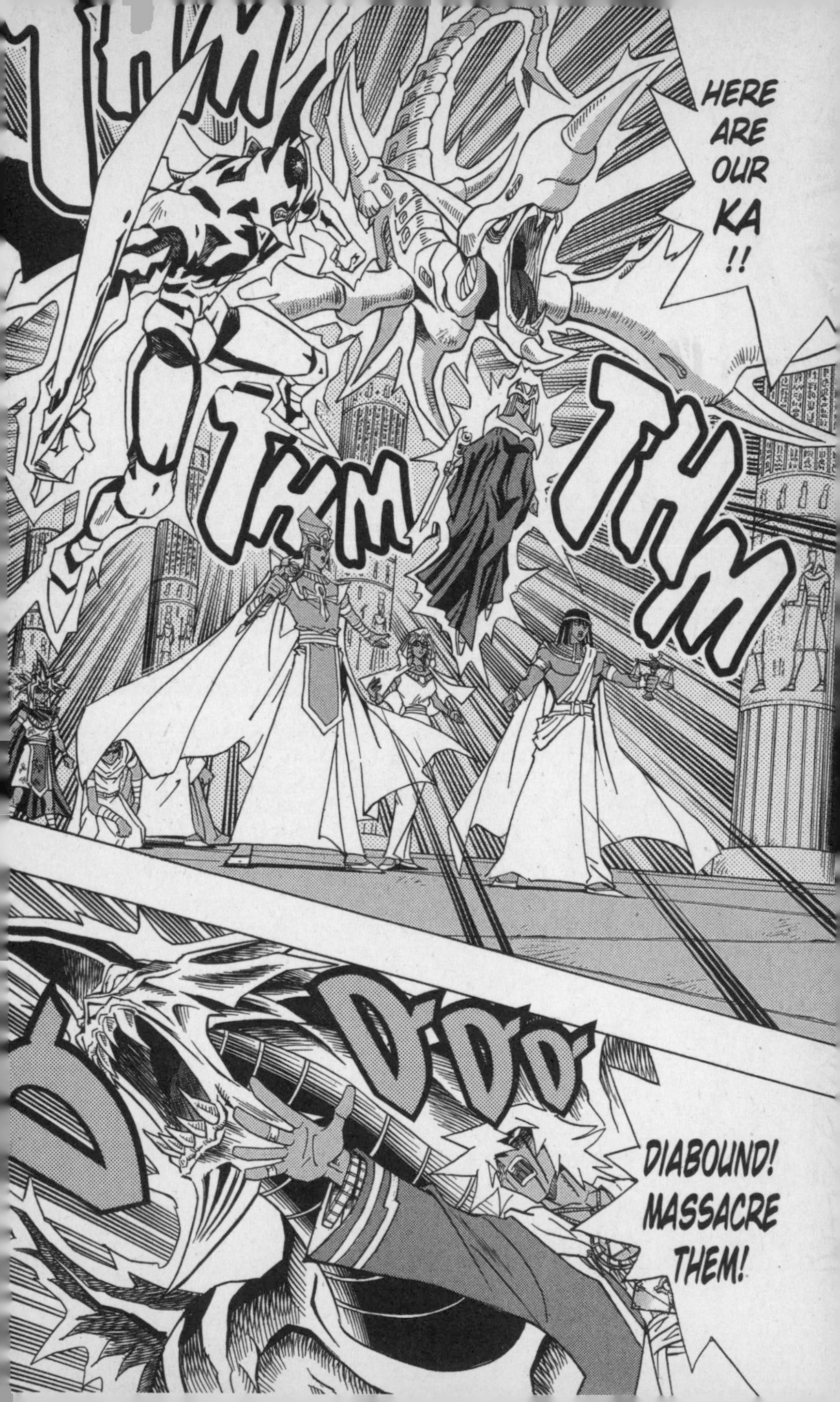
HERE ARE OUR KA !!
THM
THM
DIABOUND! MASSACRE THEM!

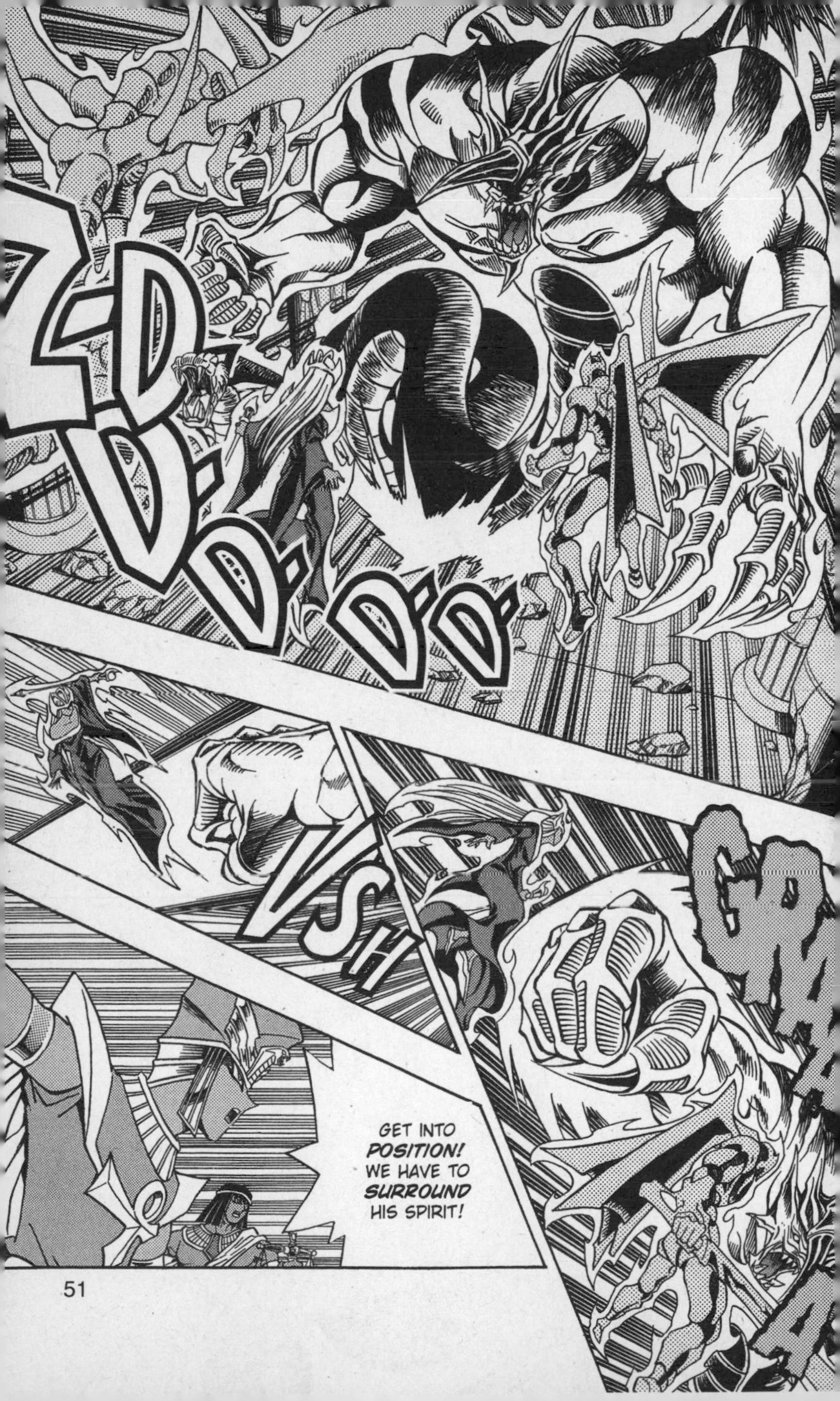
GET INTO *POSITION!* WE HAVE TO *SURROUND* HIS SPIRIT!

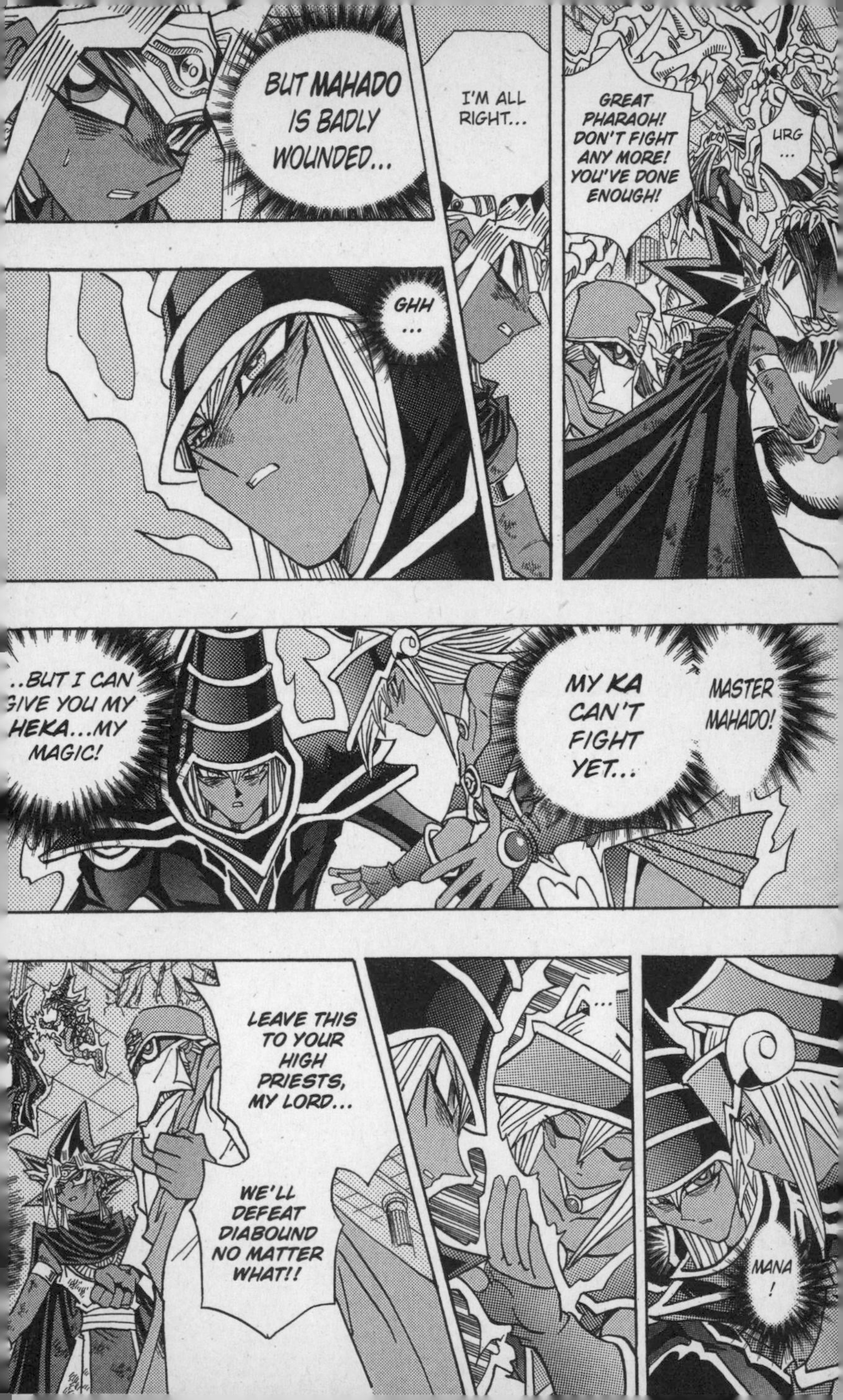
URG ...
GREAT PHARAOH! DON'T FIGHT ANY MORE! YOU'VE DONE ENOUGH!
I'M ALL RIGHT...
BUT MAHADO IS BADLY WOUNDED...
GHH ...
MASTER MAHADO!
MY KA CAN'T FIGHT YET...
..BUT I CAN GIVE YOU MY HEKA...MY MAGIC!
MANA !
...
LEAVE THIS TO YOUR HIGH PRIESTS, MY LORD...
WE'LL DEFEAT DIABOUND NO MATTER WHAT!!

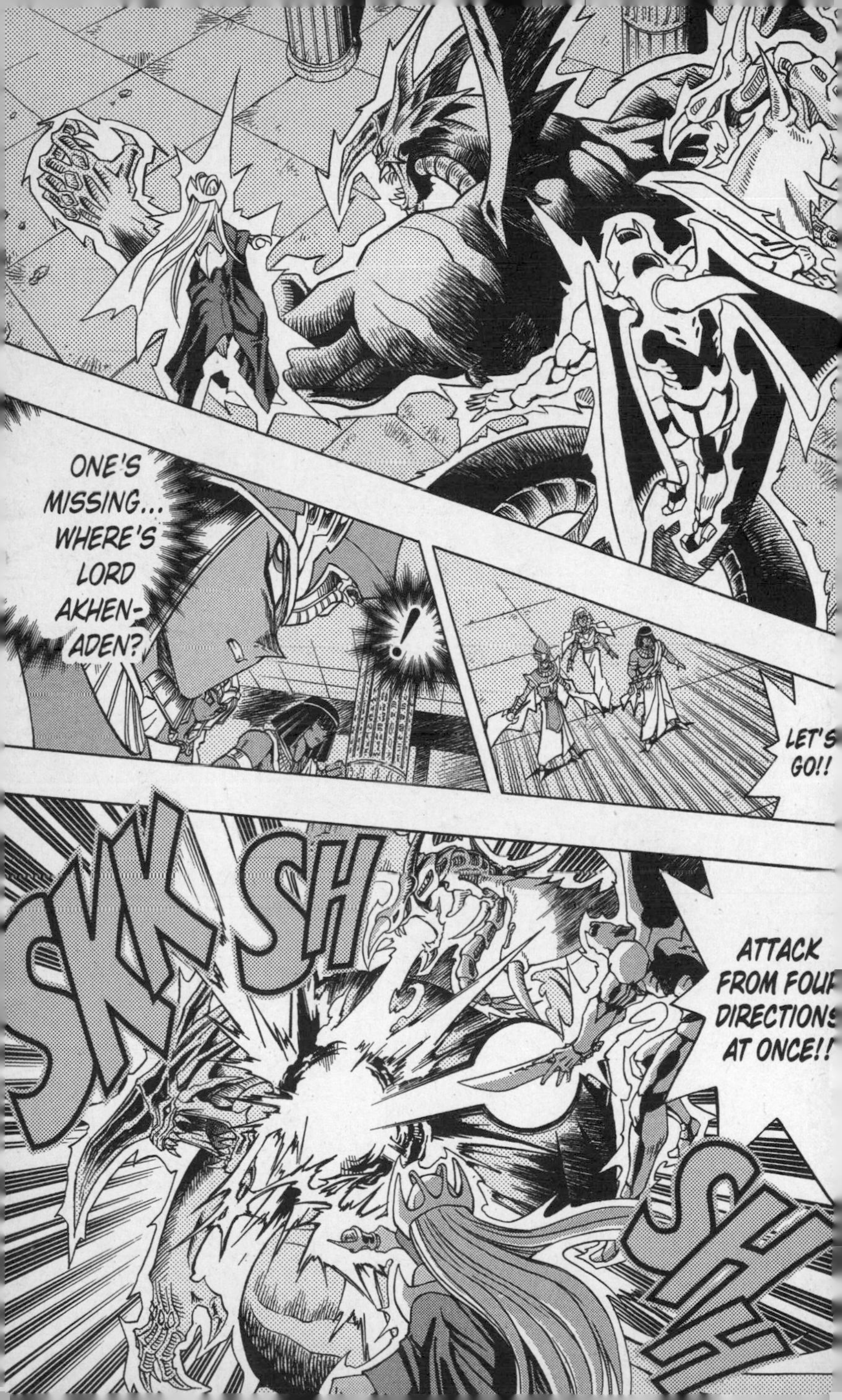
LET'S GO!!
ONE'S MISSING... WHERE'S LORD AKHEN-ADEN?
!
ATTACK FROM FOUR DIRECTIONS AT ONCE!!
SH

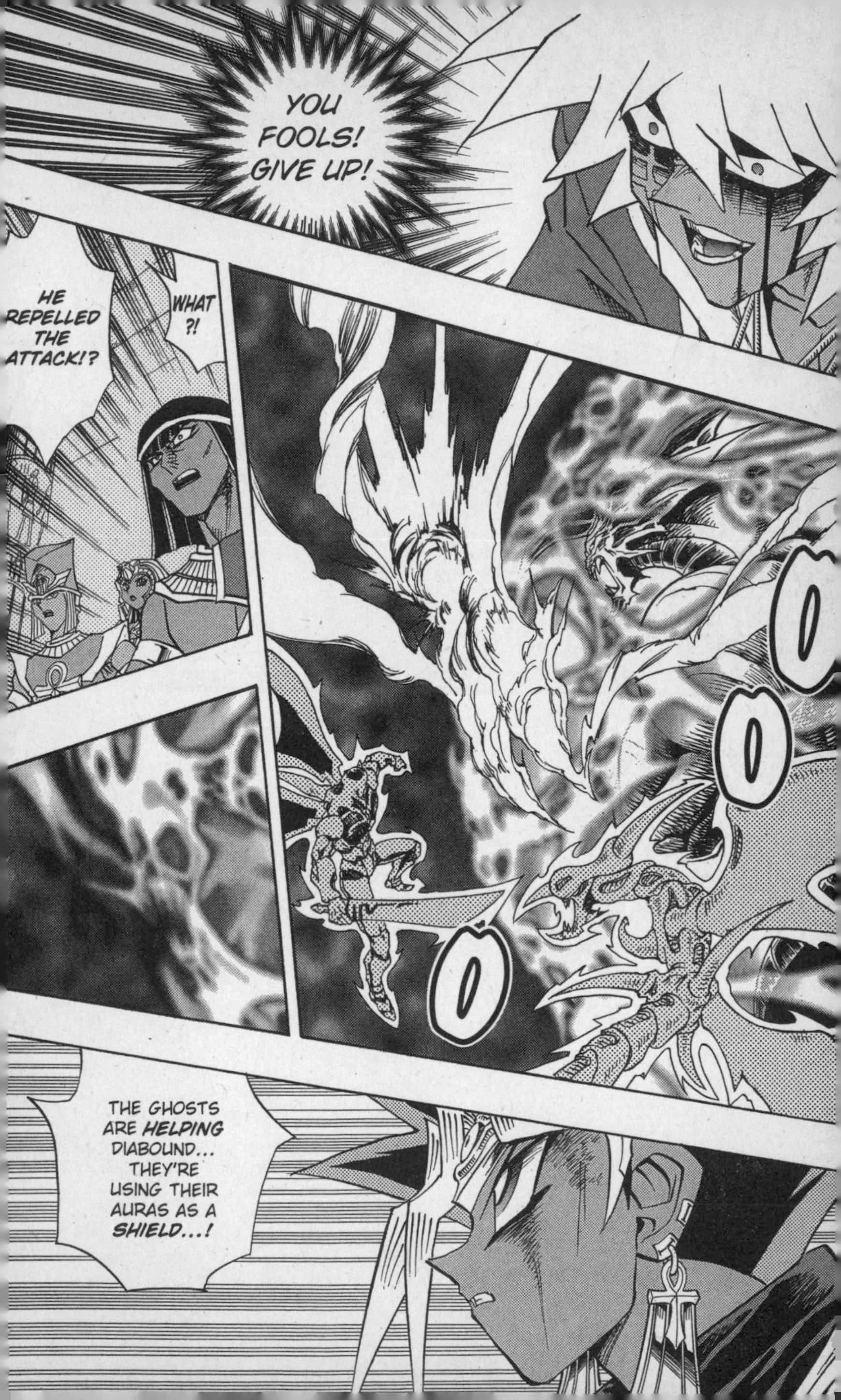
YOU FOOLS! GIVE UP!
WHAT ?!
HE REPELLED THE ATTACK!?
THE GHOSTS ARE HELPING DIABOUND... THEY'RE USING THEIR AURAS AS A SHIELD...!

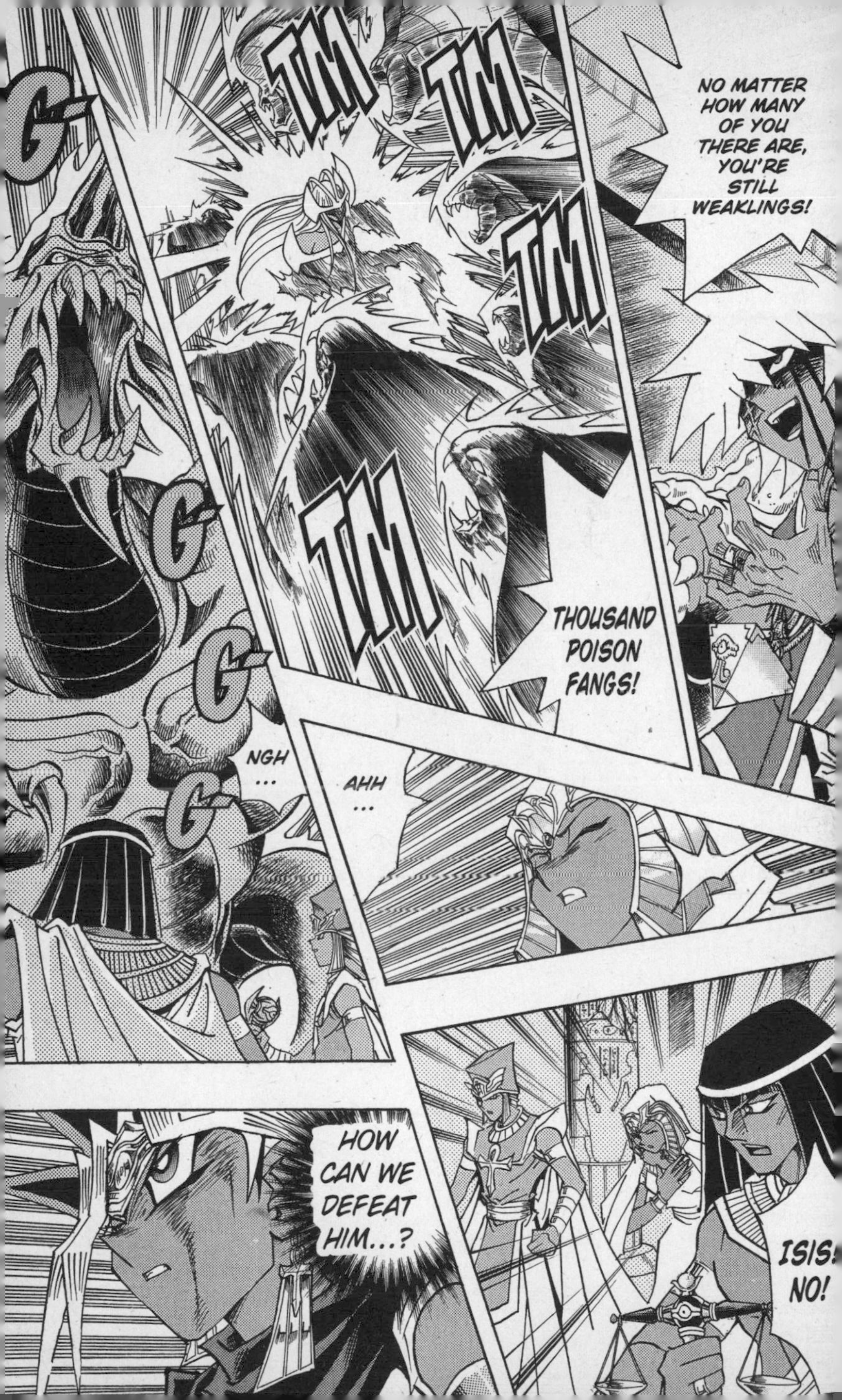
NO MATTER HOW MANY OF YOU THERE ARE, YOU'RE STILL WEAKLINGS!
THOUSAND POISON FANGS!
TM
TM
TM
TM
G
G
G
G
AHH ...
NGH ...
ISIS! NO!
HOW CAN WE DEFEAT HIM...?

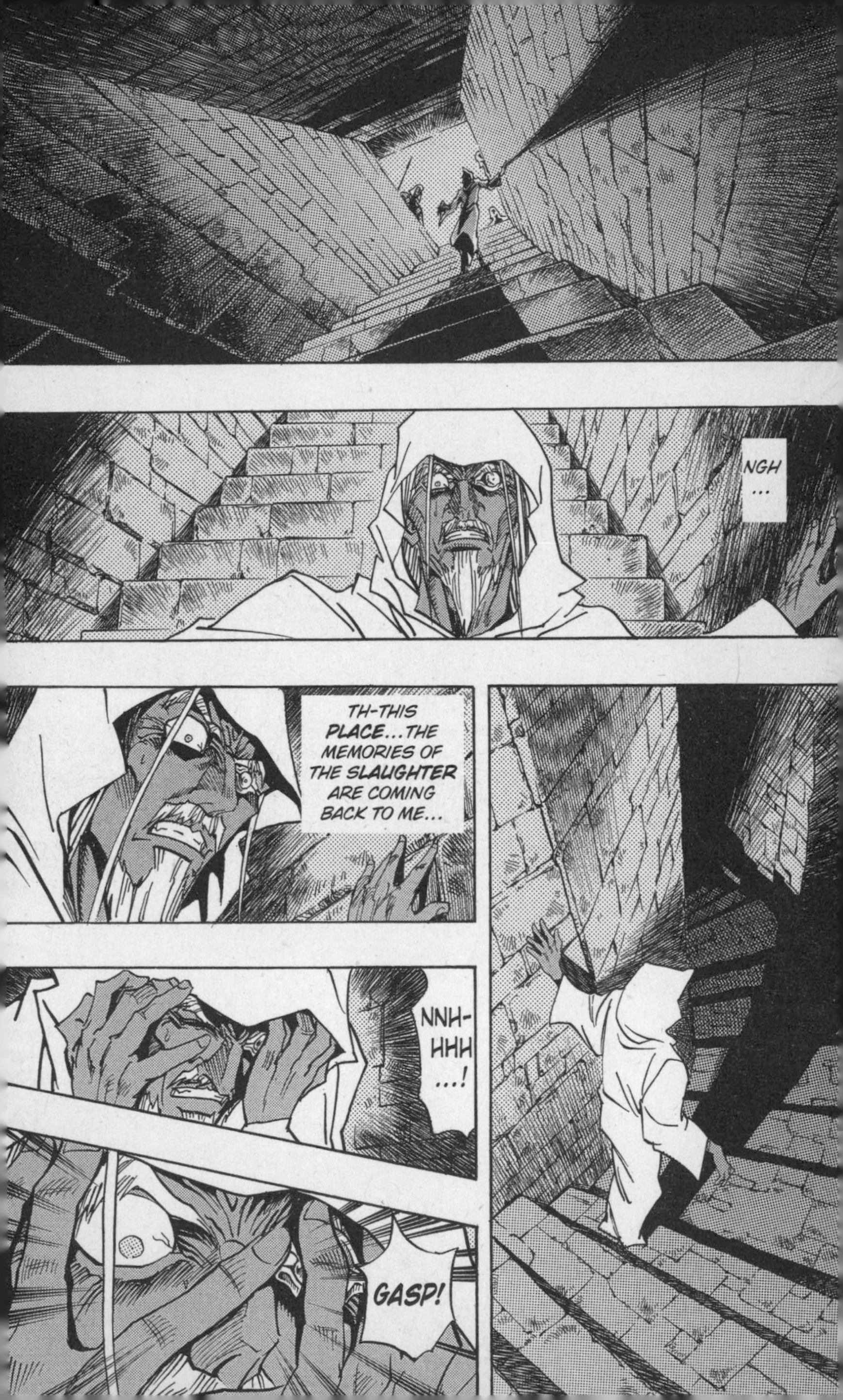
NGH ...
TH-THIS PLACE...THE MEMORIES OF THE SLAUGHTER ARE COMING BACK TO ME...
NNH-HHH ...!
GASP!

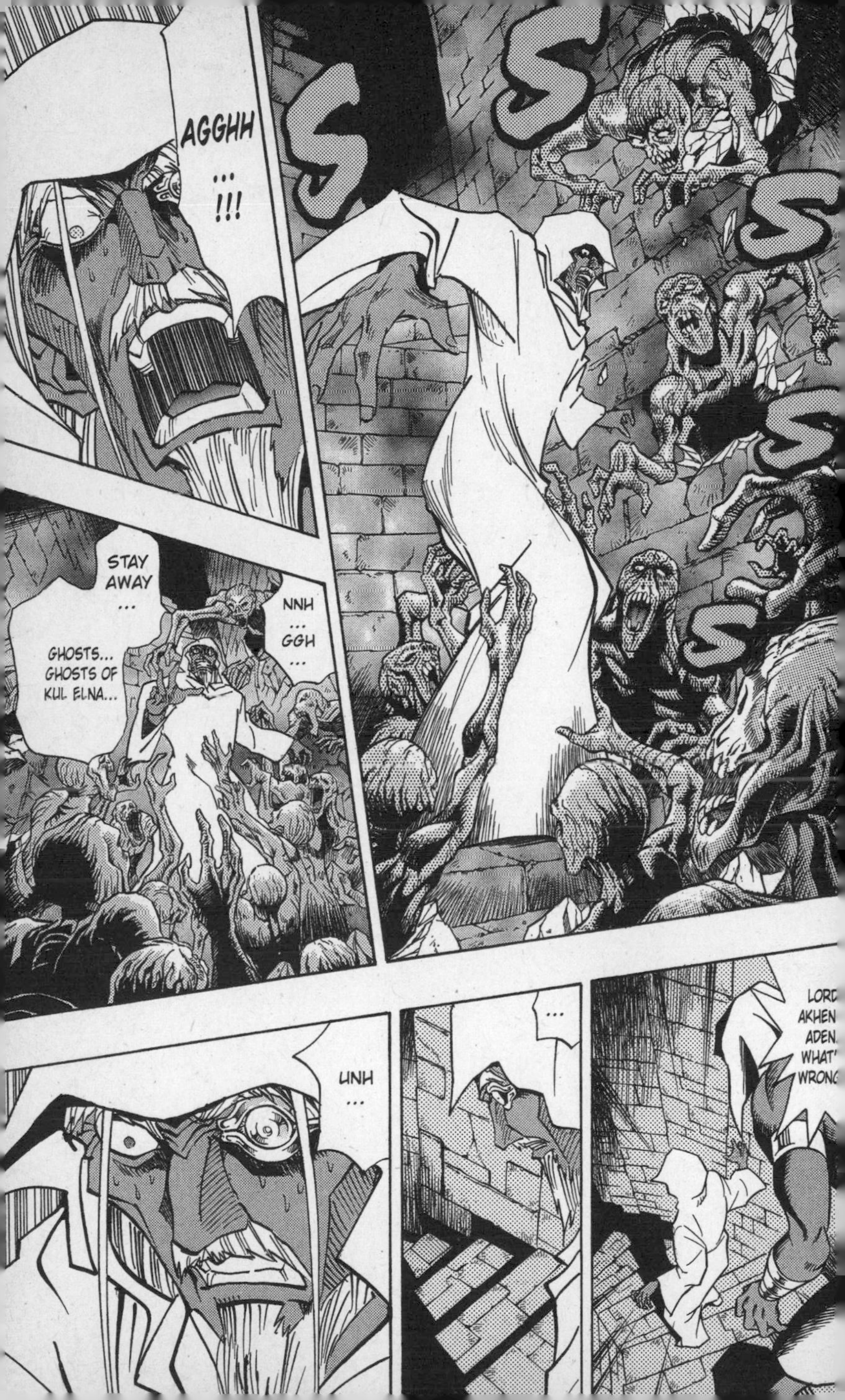
S S S S S
AGGHH ... !!!
NNH ... GGH ...
STAY AWAY ...
GHOSTS... GHOSTS OF KUL ELNA...
LORD AKHEN ADEN. WHAT' WRONG
...
UNH ...

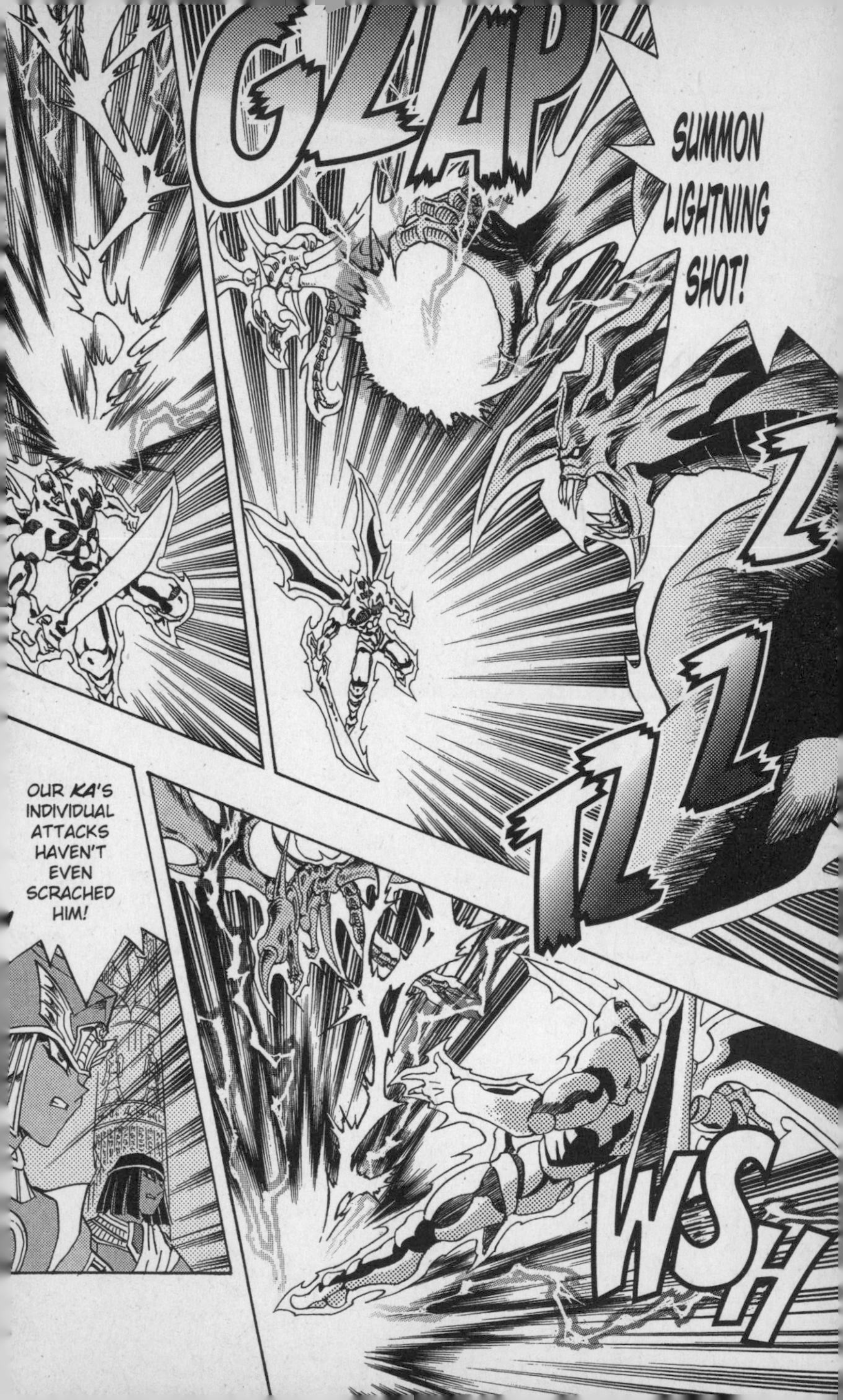
GZAP
SUMMON LIGHTNING SHOT!
ZZZ
WSH
OUR KA'S INDIVIDUAL ATTACKS HAVEN'T EVEN SCRACHED HIM!

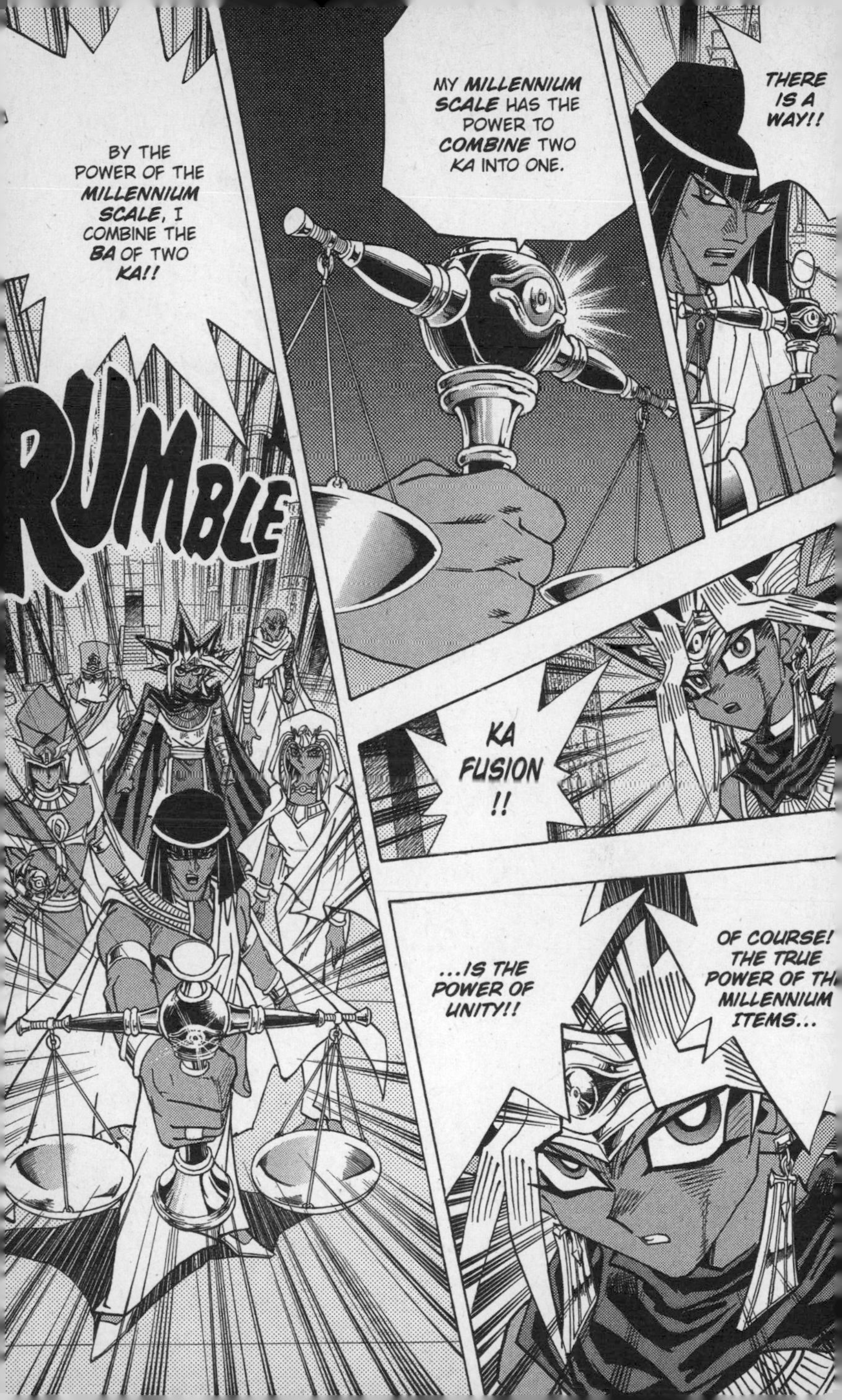

THERE IS A WAY!!
MY MILLENNIUM SCALE HAS THE POWER TO COMBINE TWO KA INTO ONE.
KA FUSION !!
OF COURSE! THE TRUE POWER OF TH MILLENNIUM ITEMS...
...IS THE POWER OF UNITY!!
BY THE POWER OF THE MILLENNIUM SCALE, I COMBINE THE BA OF TWO KA!!
RUMBLE

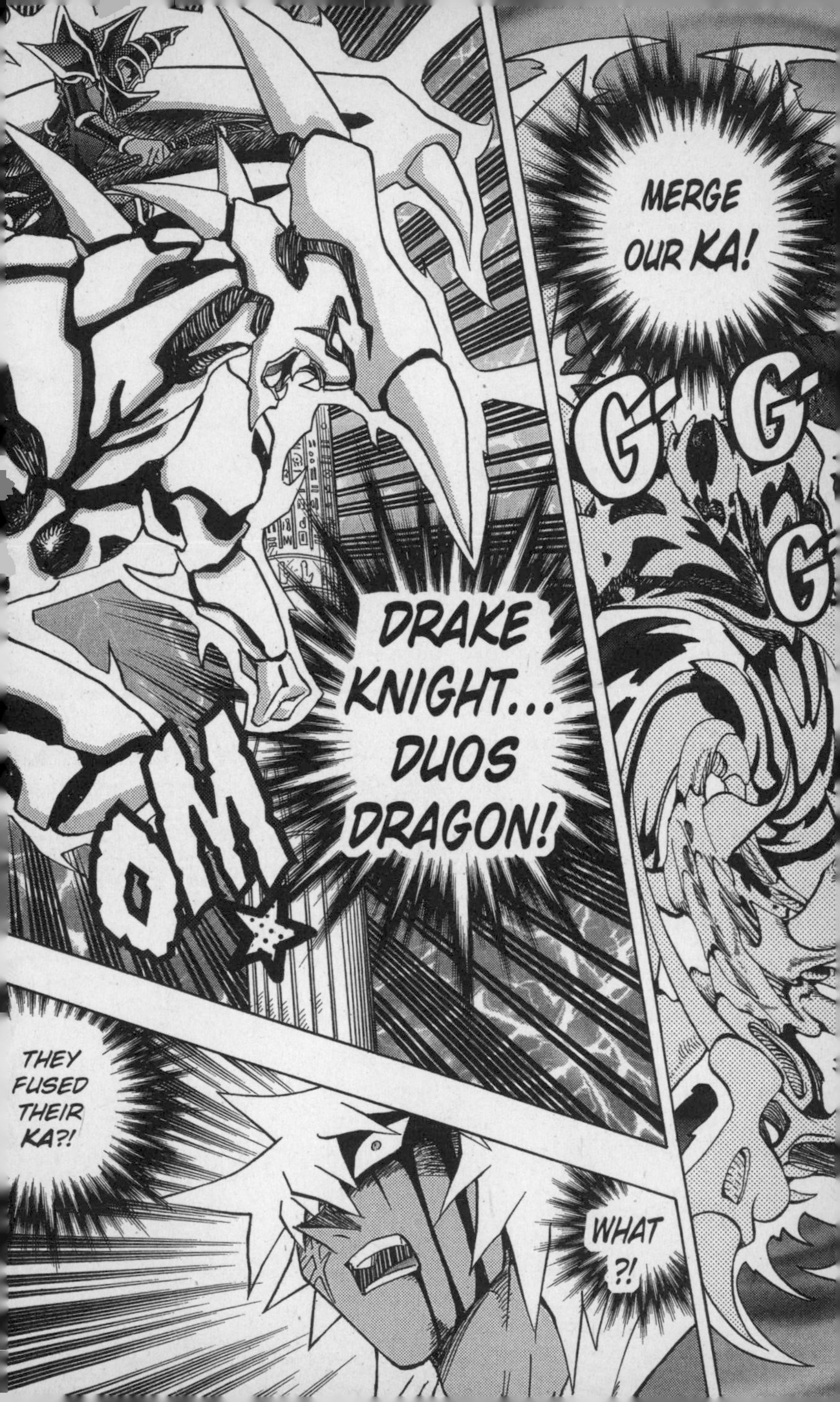
MERGE OUR KA!
G-G-G
DRAKE KNIGHT... DUOS DRAGON!
OM
WHAT ?!
THEY FUSED THEIR KA?!

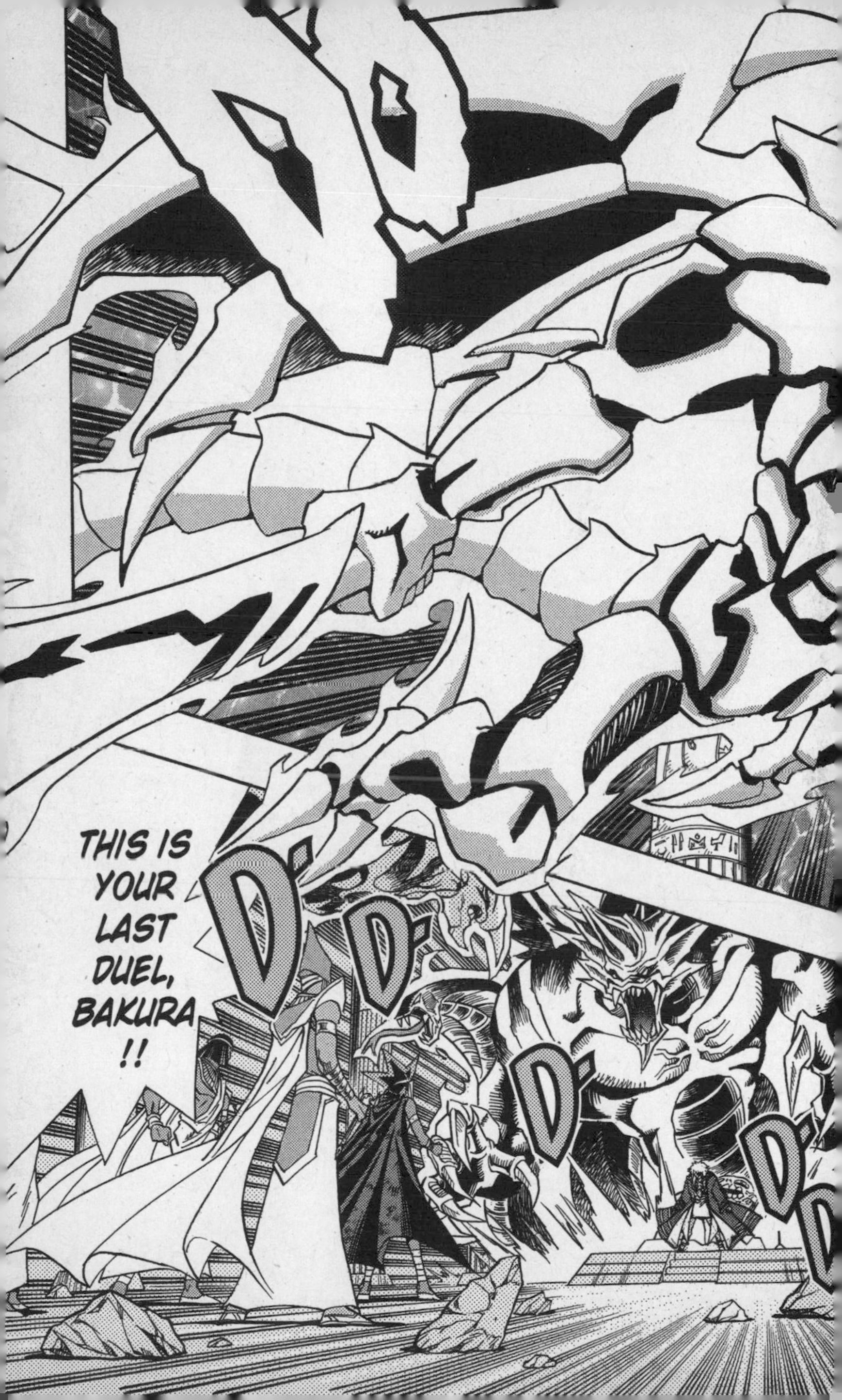
THIS IS YOUR LAST DUEL, BAKURA!!
D
D
D
D
D

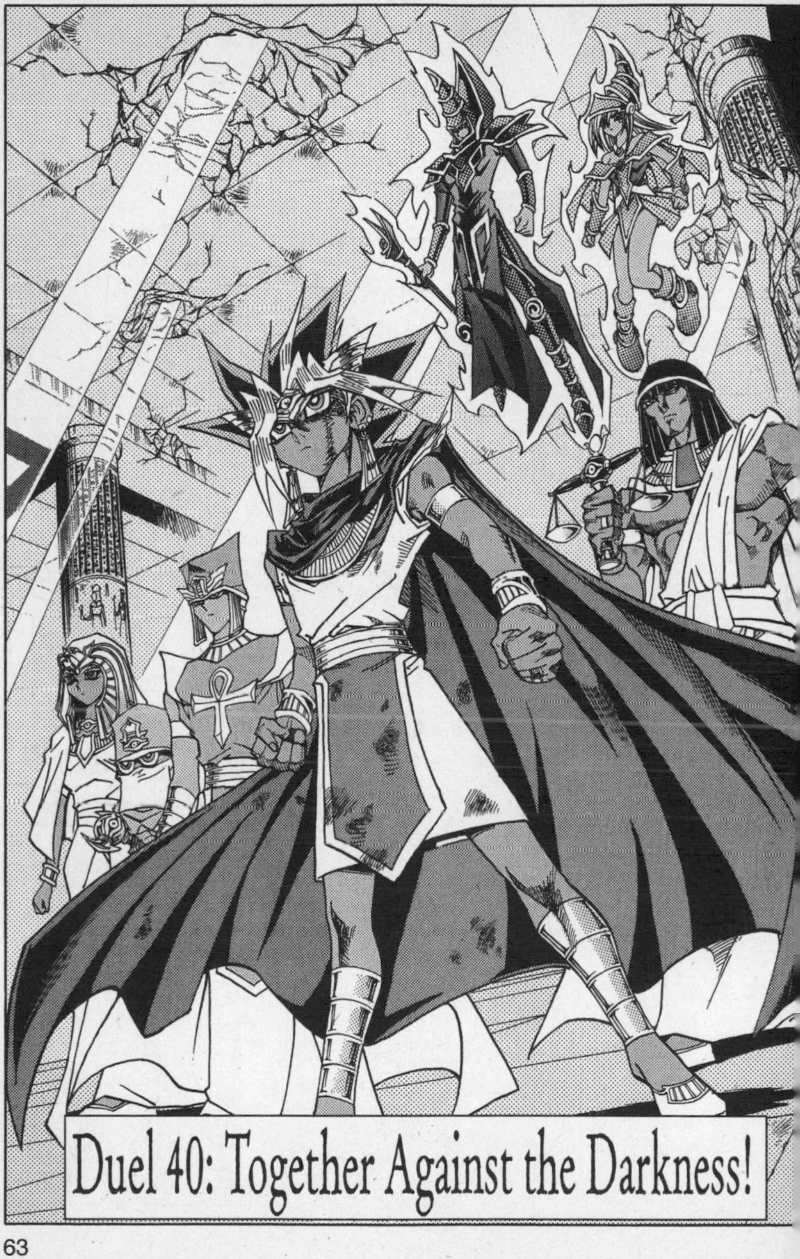
Duel 40: Together Against the Darkness!

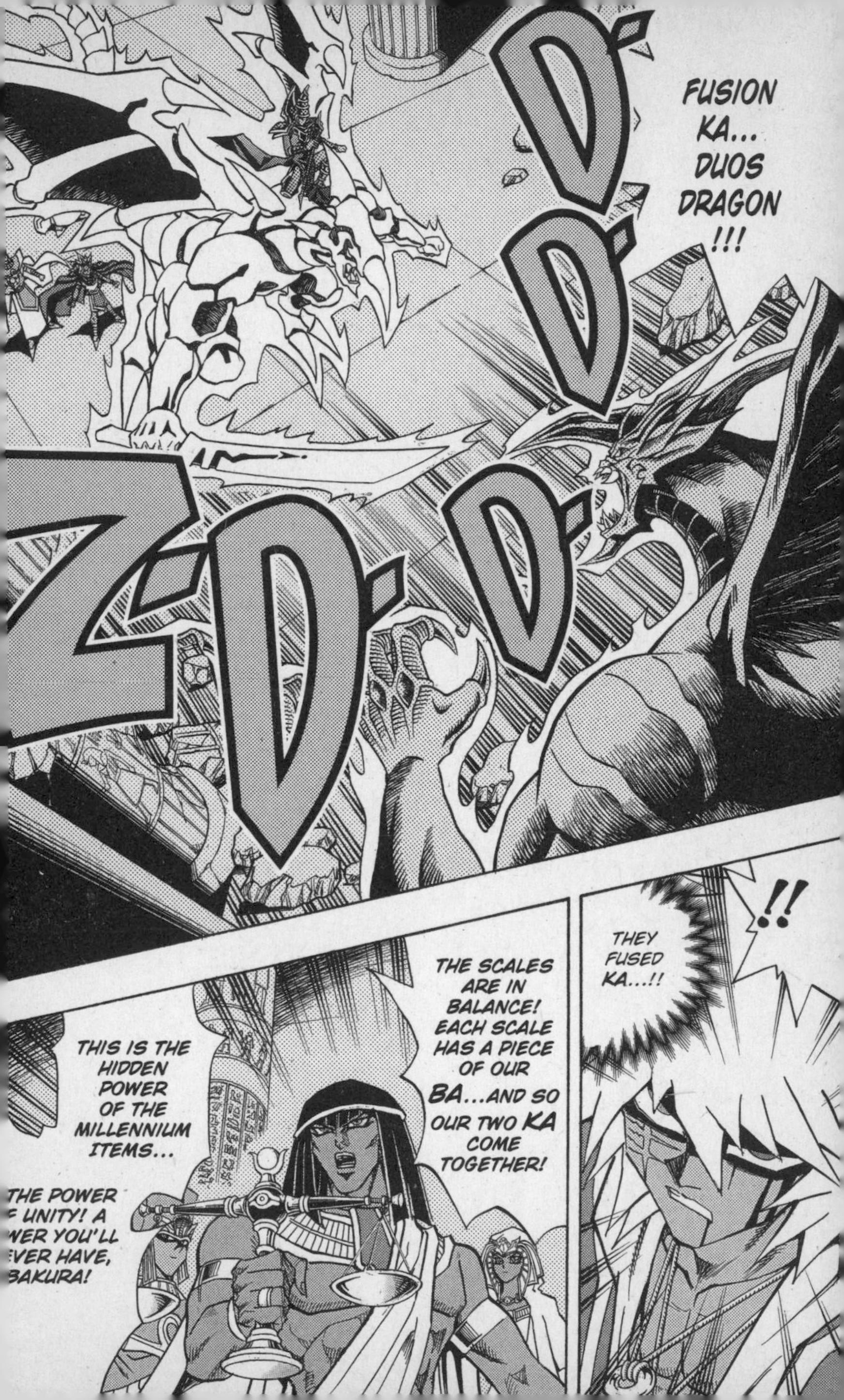

DDDDD
FUSION KA... DUOS DRAGON !!!
!!
THEY FUSED KA...!!
THE SCALES ARE IN BALANCE! EACH SCALE HAS A PIECE OF OUR BA...AND SO OUR TWO KA COME TOGETHER!
THIS IS THE HIDDEN POWER OF THE MILLENNIUM ITEMS...
THE POWER F UNITY! A WER YOU'LL EVER HAVE, BAKURA!

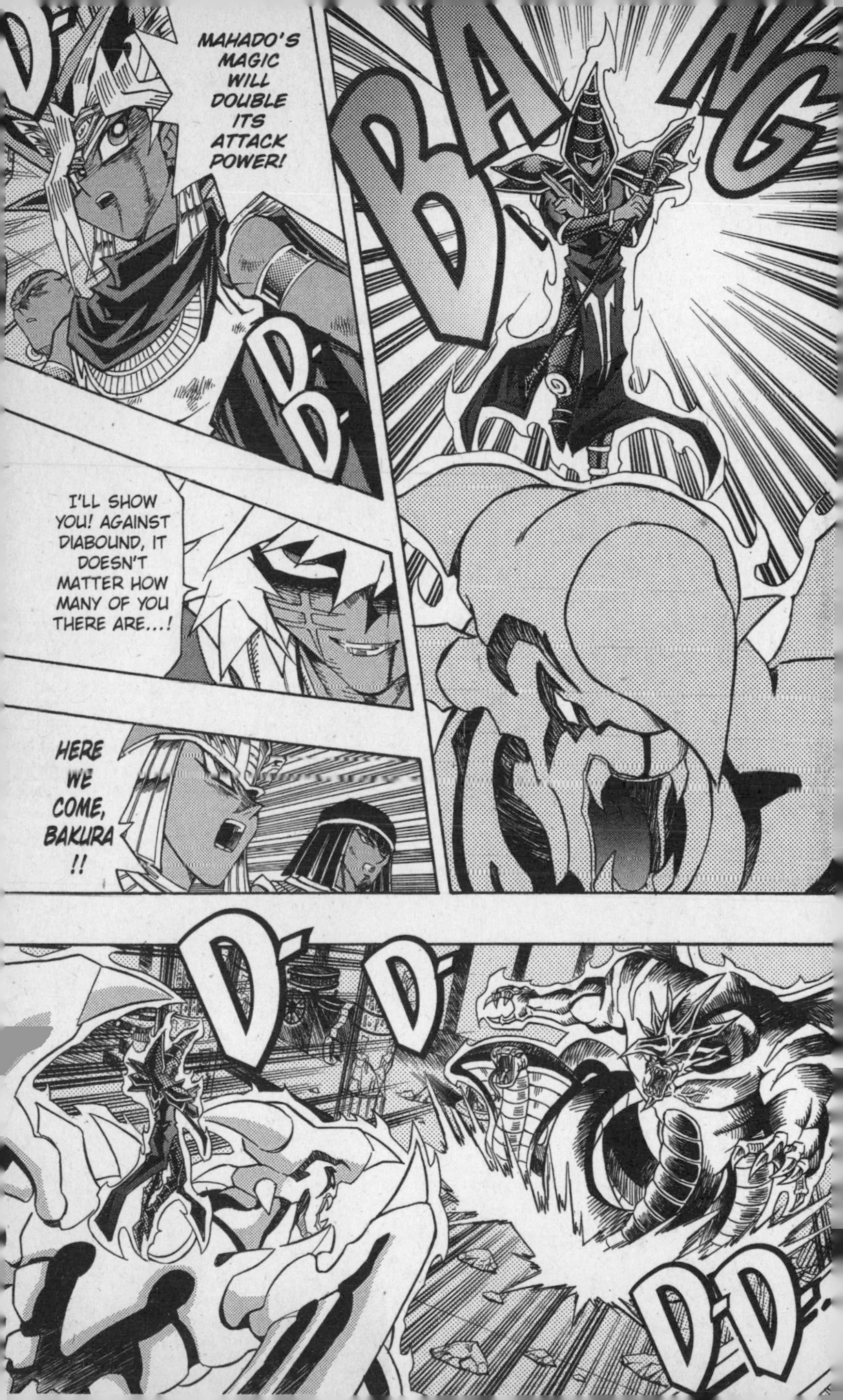
BANG
MAHADO'S MAGIC WILL DOUBLE ITS ATTACK POWER!
I'LL SHOW YOU! AGAINST DIABOUND, IT DOESN'T MATTER HOW MANY OF YOU THERE ARE...!
HERE WE COME, BAKURA !!

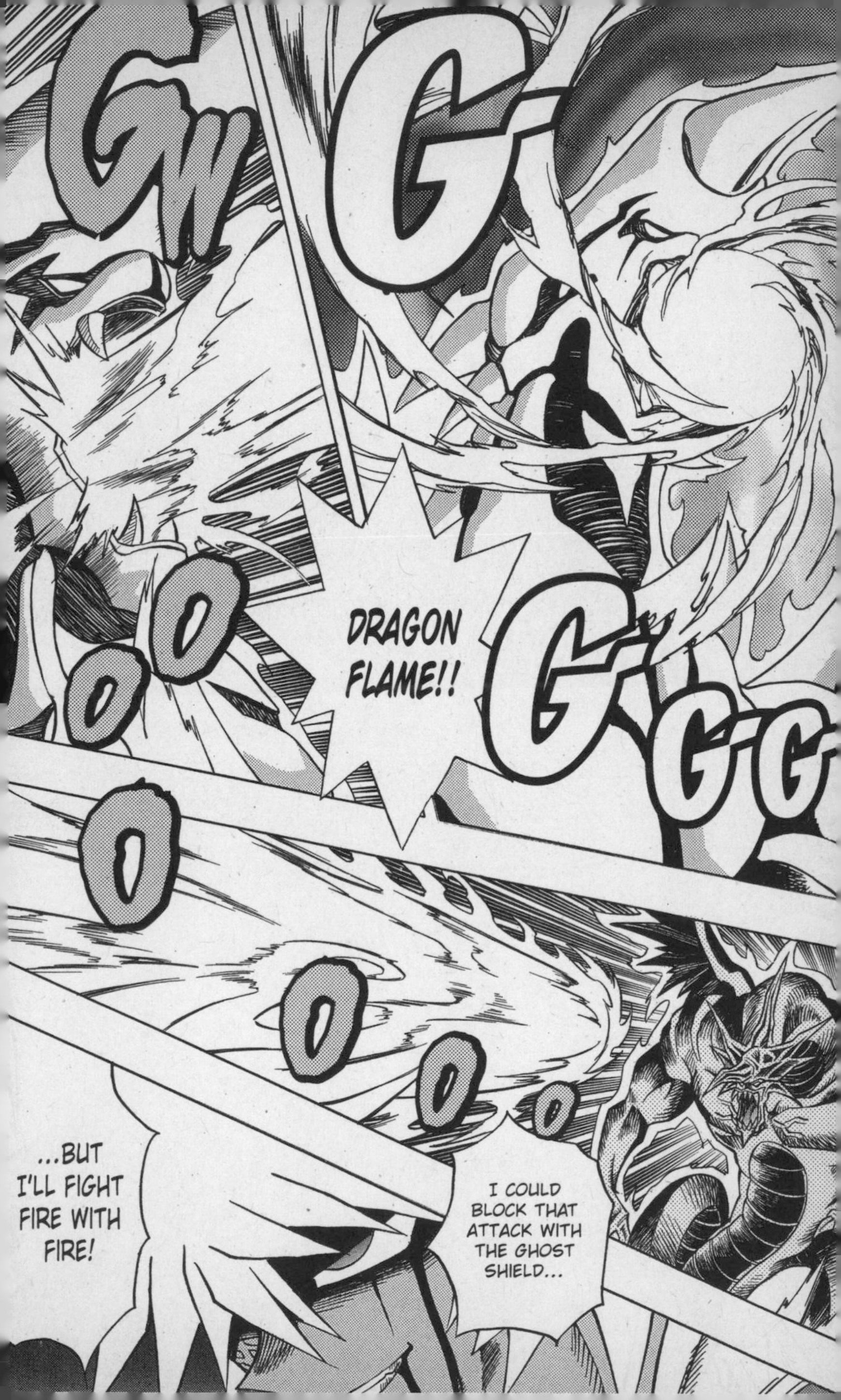
GWGG
GGG
DRAGON FLAME!!
OOOO
I COULD BLOCK THAT ATTACK WITH THE GHOST SHIELD...
...BUT I'LL FIGHT FIRE WITH FIRE!
OOOO

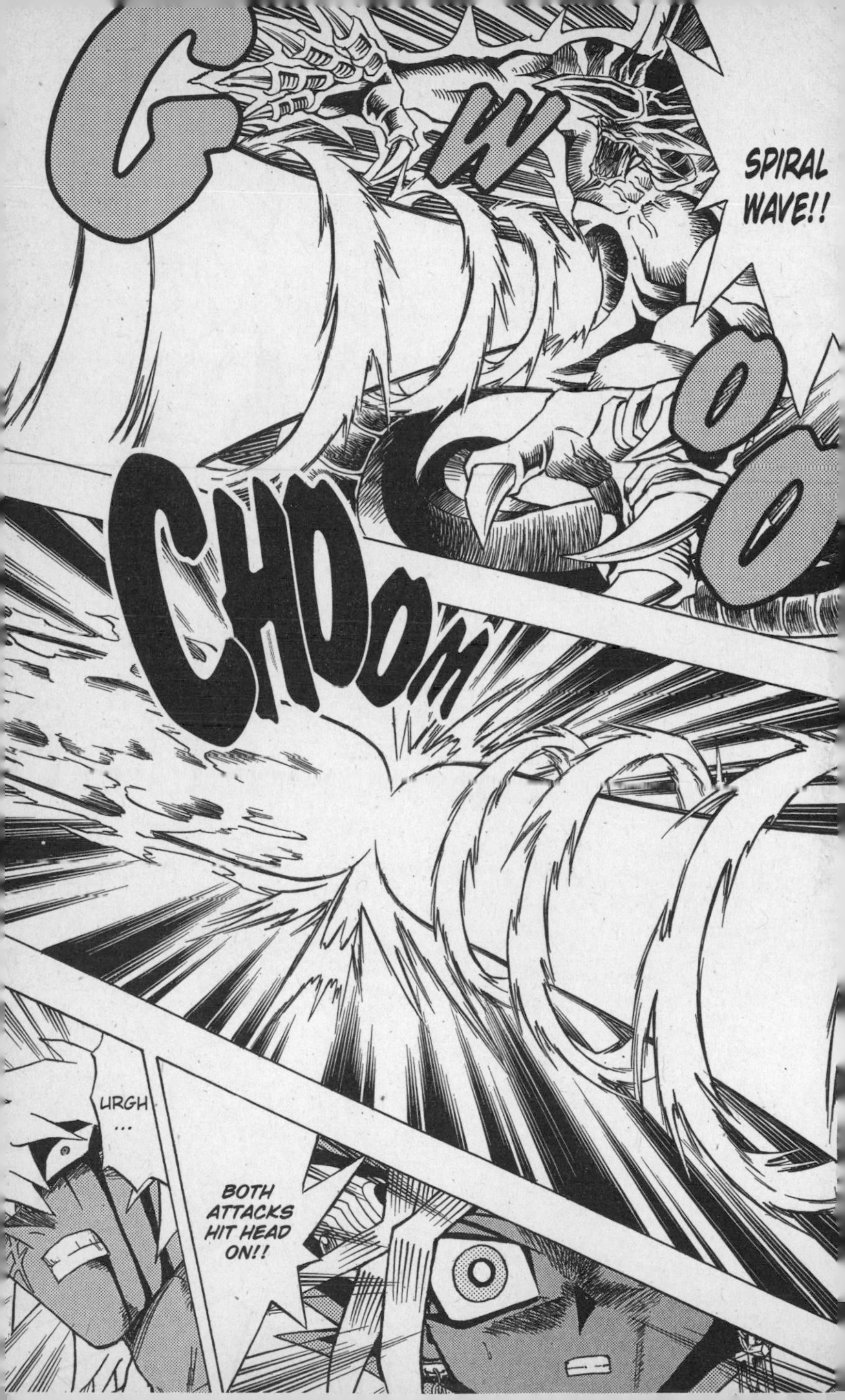
SPIRAL WAVE!!
GWOO
CHOOM
BOTH ATTACKS HIT HEAD ON!!
URGH ...

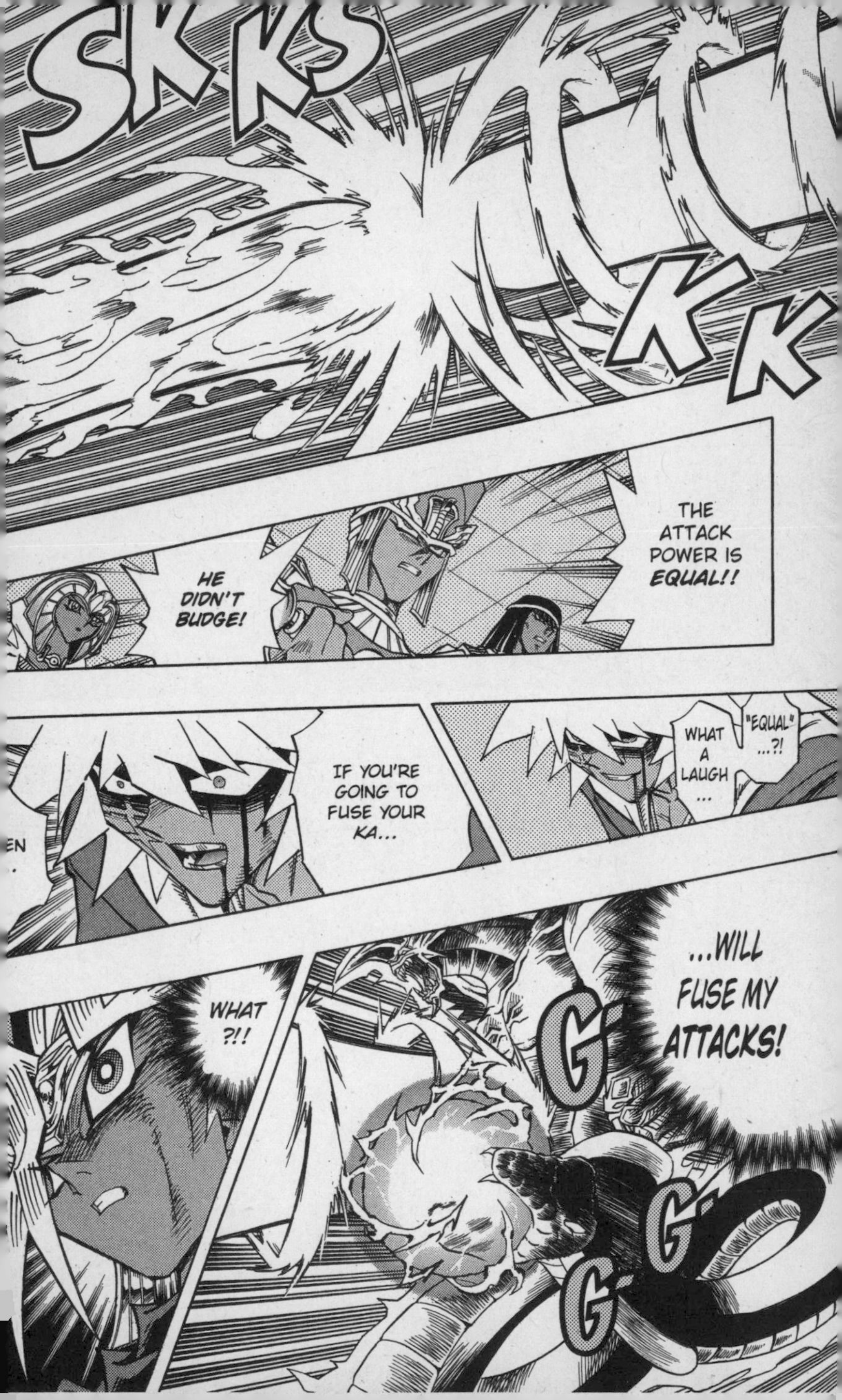
SKKS
KK
THE ATTACK POWER IS EQUAL!!
HE DIDN'T BUDGE!
"EQUAL" ...?!
WHAT A LAUGH ...
IF YOU'RE GOING TO FUSE YOUR KA...
...WILL FUSE MY ATTACKS!
G
GGG
WHAT ?!!

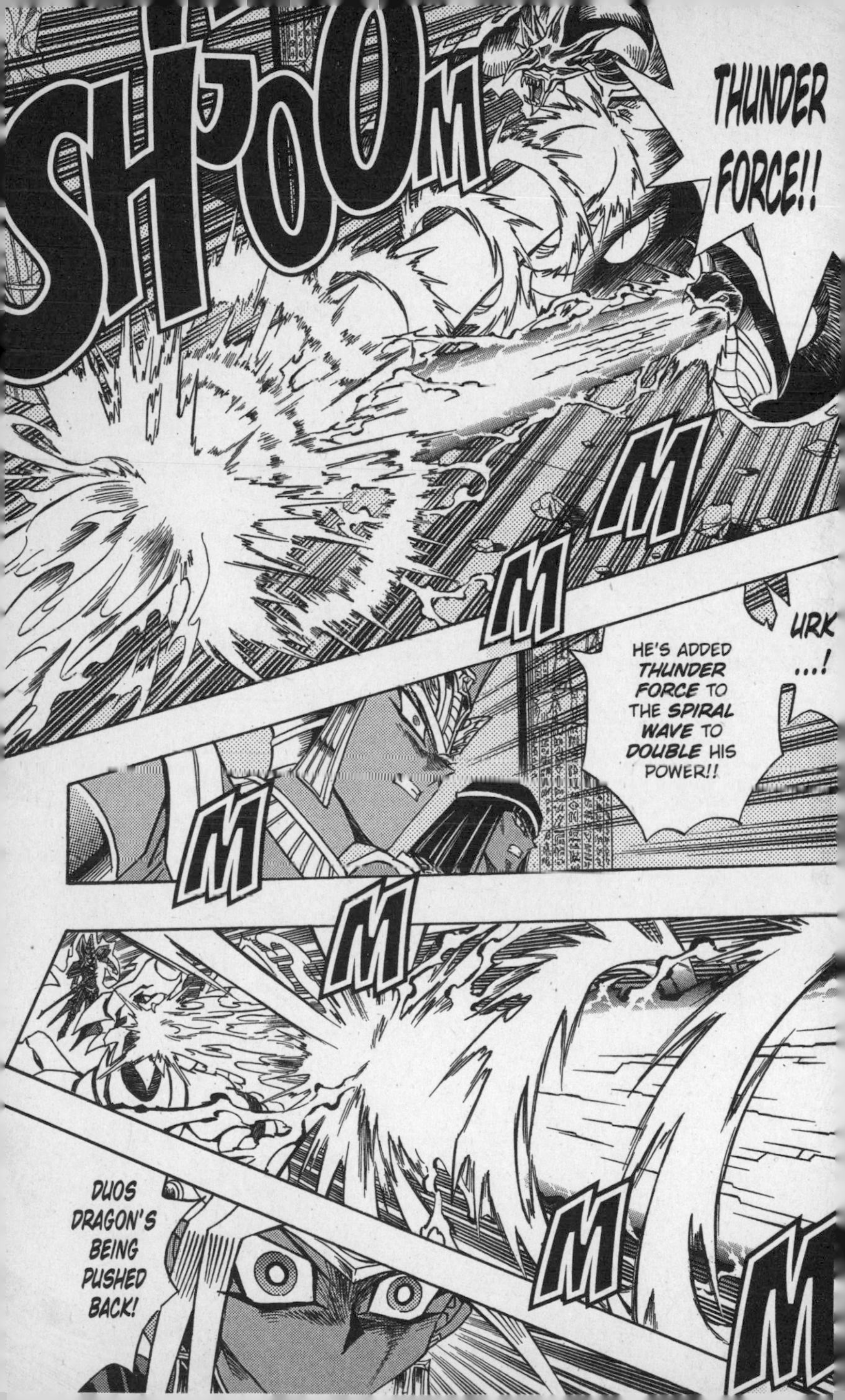
THUNDER FORCE!!
SHOOMM
MMM
URK ...!
HE'S ADDED THUNDER FORCE TO THE SPIRAL WAVE TO DOUBLE HIS POWER!!
M
M
MM
DUOS DRAGON'S BEING PUSHED BACK!

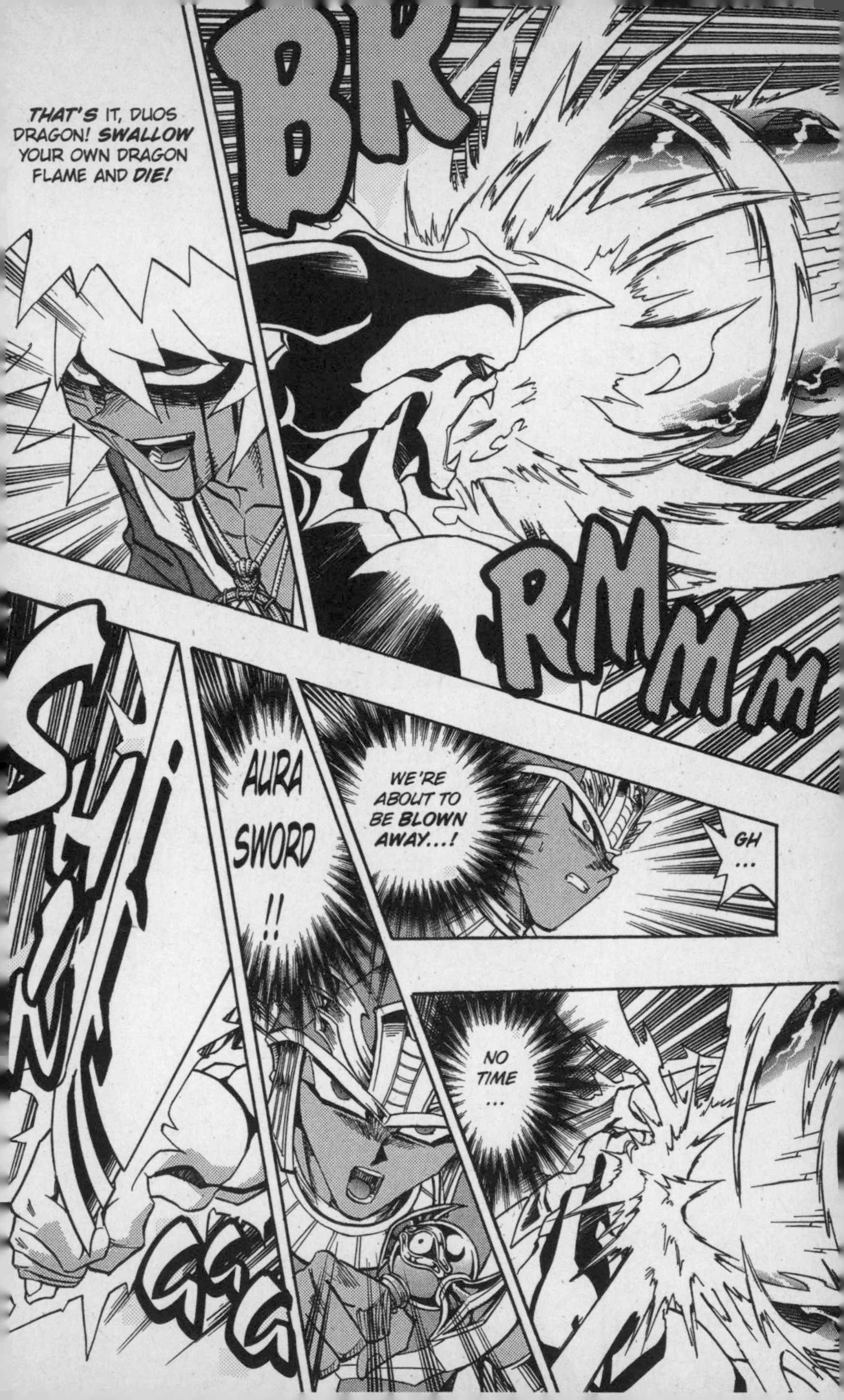
BR
RMMM
THAT'S IT, DUOS DRAGON! SWALLOW YOUR OWN DRAGON FLAME AND DIE!
GH ...
WE'RE ABOUT TO BE BLOWN AWAY...!
AURA SWORD !!
NO TIME ...
GGG

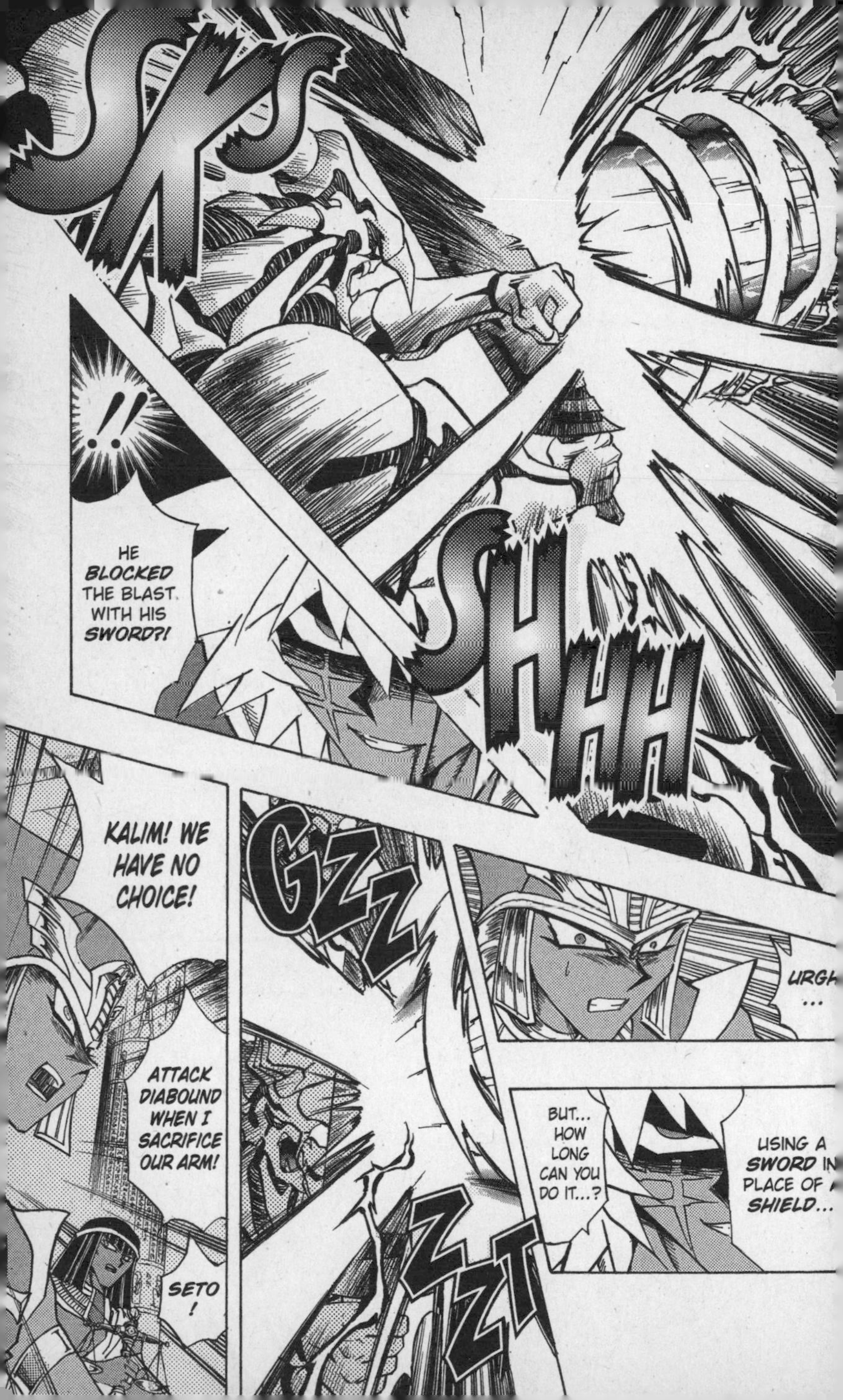
SKS
!!
HE BLOCKED THE BLAST WITH HIS SWORD?!
SHHH
URGH...
GZZ
KALIM! WE HAVE NO CHOICE!
ATTACK DIABOUND WHEN I SACRIFICE OUR ARM!
SETO!
USING A SWORD IN PLACE OF A SHIELD...
BUT... HOW LONG CAN YOU DO IT...?
ZZT

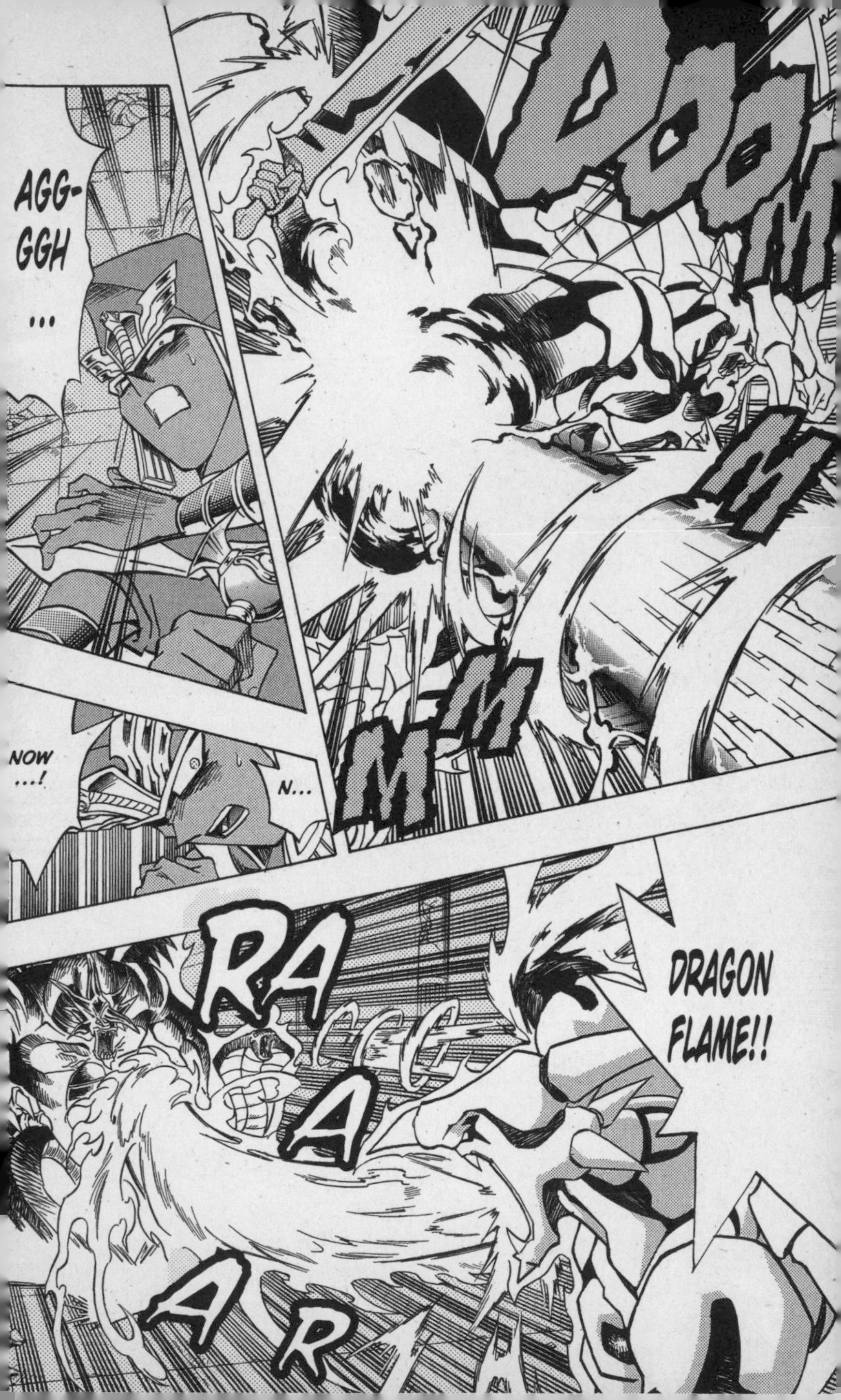
DOOMMMM
AGG-GGH ...
N...
NOW ...!
DRAGON FLAME!!
RAAAR

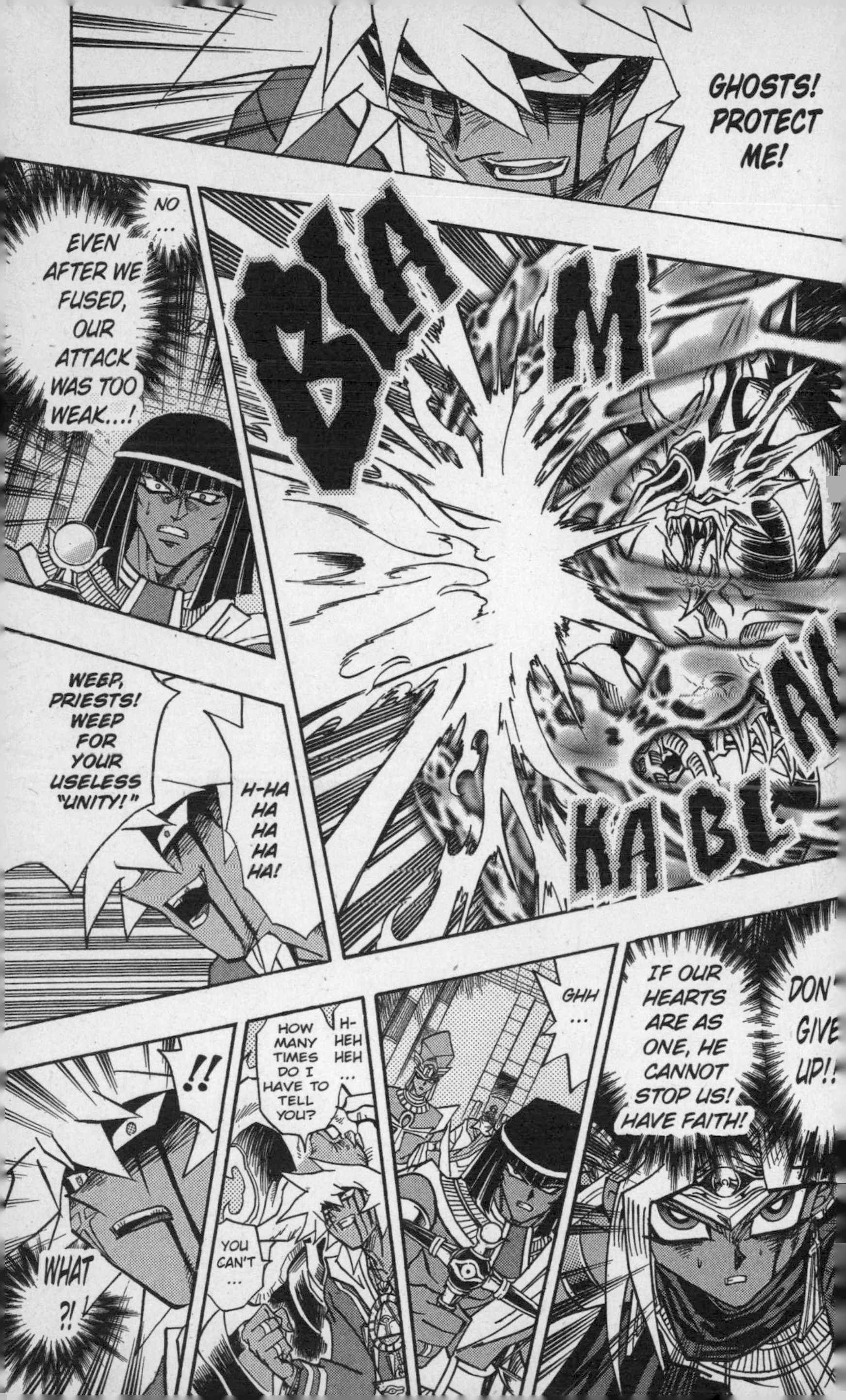
GHOSTS! PROTECT ME!
BLAM
KA BL
NO...
EVEN AFTER WE FUSED, OUR ATTACK WAS TOO WEAK...!
WEEP, PRIESTS! WEEP FOR YOUR USELESS "UNITY!"
H-HA HA HA HA HA!
DON'T GIVE UP!!
IF OUR HEARTS ARE AS ONE, HE CANNOT STOP US! HAVE FAITH!
GHH...
H-HEH HEH...
HOW MANY TIMES DO I HAVE TO TELL YOU?
YOU CAN'T...
!!
WHAT?!

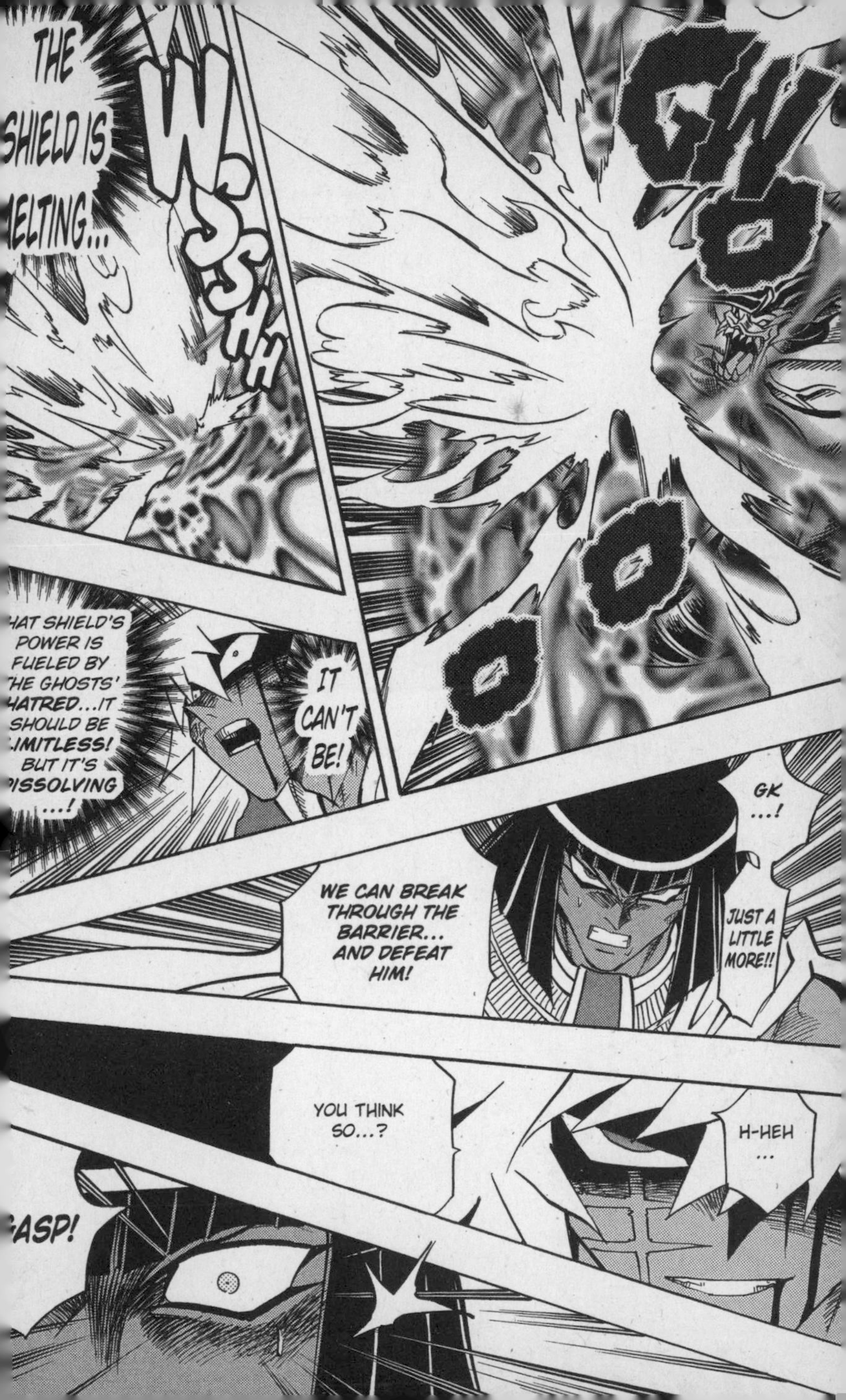
GWOOO
THE SHIELD IS MELTING...
WSSHH
IT CAN'T BE!
HAT SHIELD'S POWER IS FUELED BY THE GHOSTS' HATRED...IT SHOULD BE LIMITLESS! BUT IT'S DISSOLVING ...!
GK ...!
JUST A LITTLE MORE!!
WE CAN BREAK THROUGH THE BARRIER... AND DEFEAT HIM!
H-HEH ...
YOU THINK SO...?
GASP!

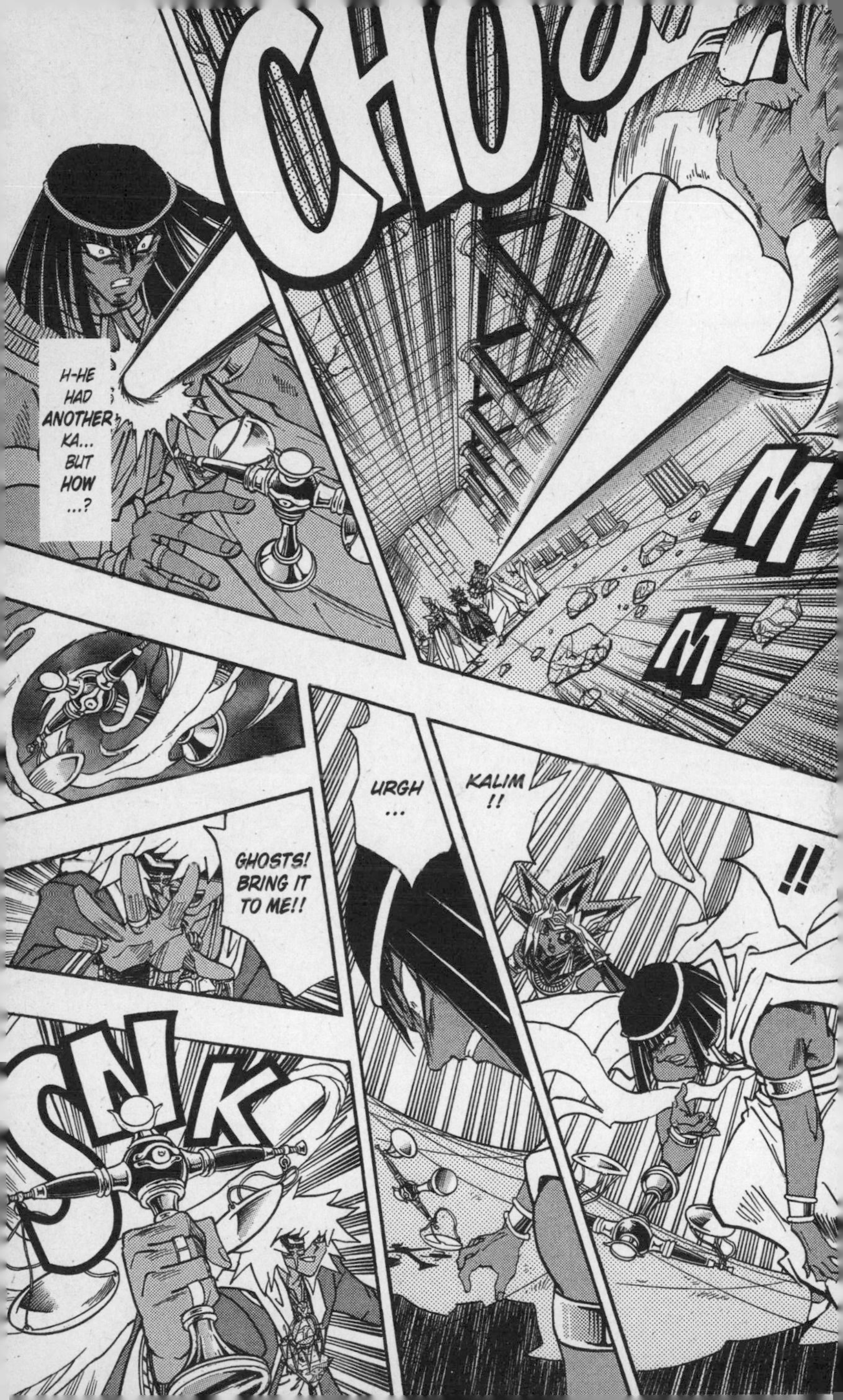
CHOO
M M
H-HE HAD ANOTHER KA... BUT HOW ...?
KALIM !!
!!
URGH ...
GHOSTS! BRING IT TO ME!!
NK

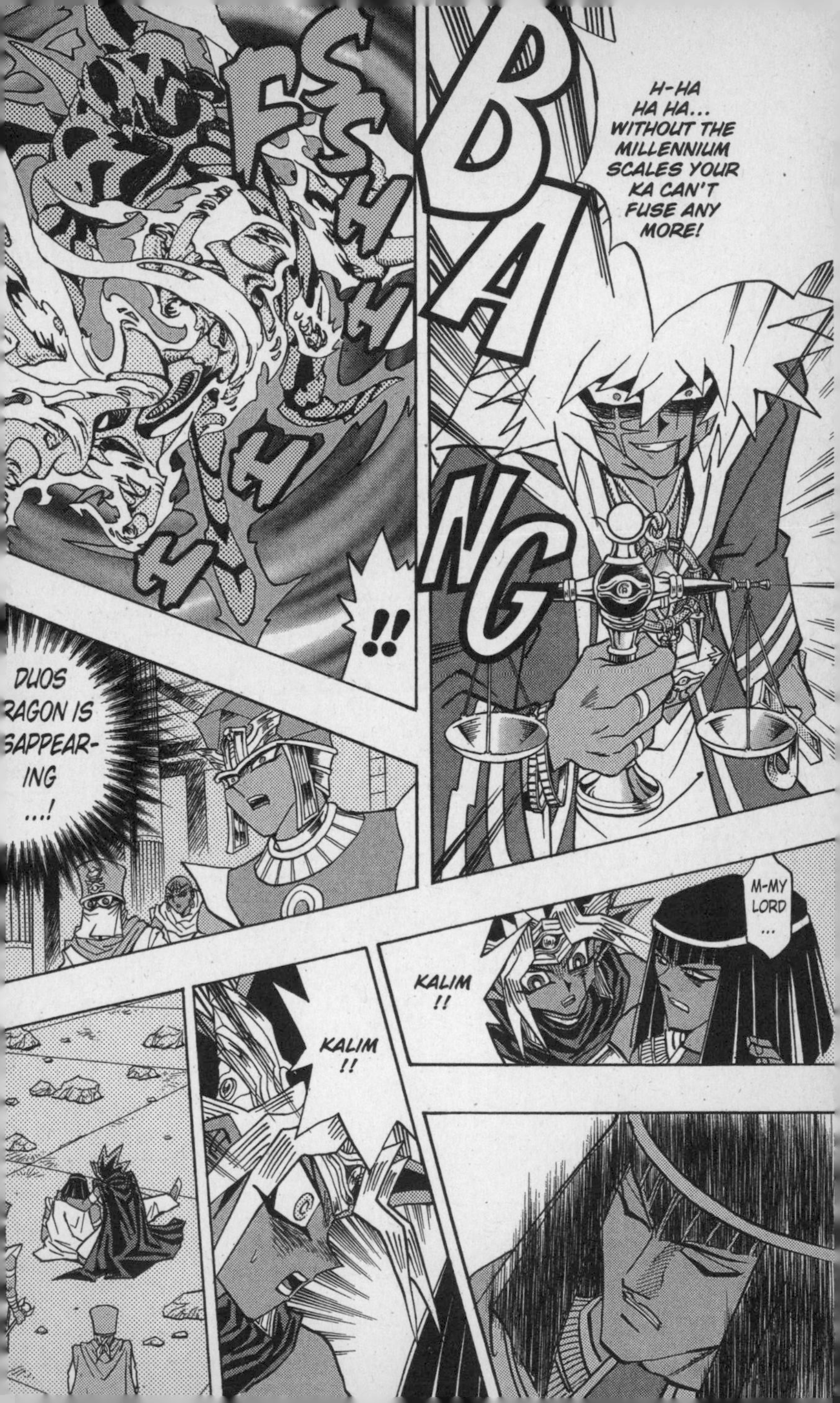
BANG
H-HA HA HA... WITHOUT THE MILLENNIUM SCALES YOUR KA CAN'T FUSE ANY MORE!
FSSHHHH
!!
DUOS RAGON IS SAPPEAR-ING ...!
M-MY LORD ...
KALIM !!
KALIM !!

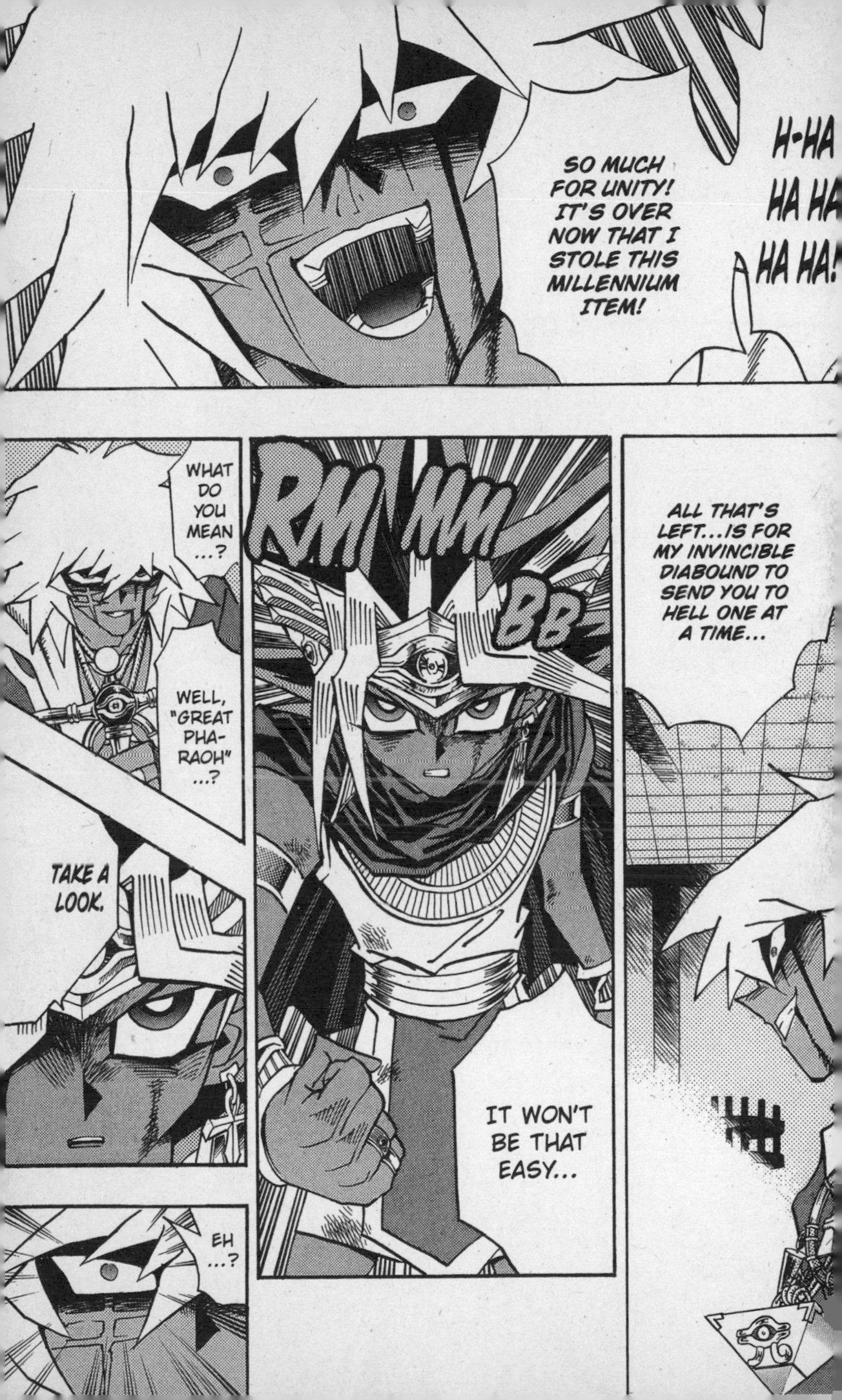
H-HA HA HA HA HA!
SO MUCH FOR UNITY! IT'S OVER NOW THAT I STOLE THIS MILLENNIUM ITEM!
ALL THAT'S LEFT...IS FOR MY INVINCIBLE DIABOUND TO SEND YOU TO HELL ONE AT A TIME...
RMMMMBB
IT WON'T BE THAT EASY...
WHAT DO YOU MEAN ...?
WELL, "GREAT PHARAOH" ...?
TAKE A LOOK.
EH ...?

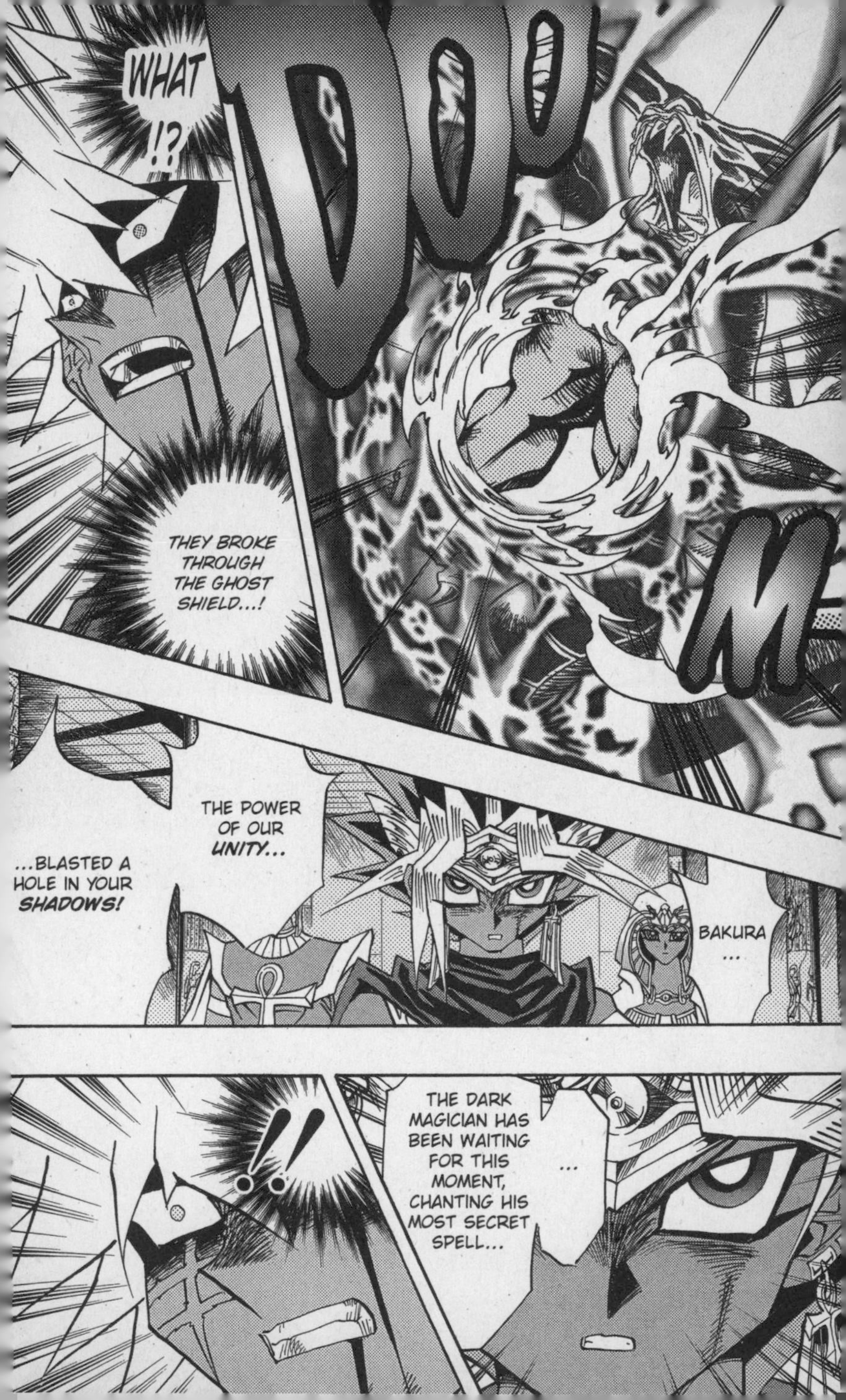
DOOO
M
WHAT !?
THEY BROKE THROUGH THE GHOST SHIELD...!
THE POWER OF OUR *UNITY*...
...BLASTED A HOLE IN YOUR *SHADOWS!*
BAKURA ...
...
THE DARK MAGICIAN HAS BEEN WAITING FOR THIS MOMENT, CHANTING HIS MOST SECRET SPELL...
!!

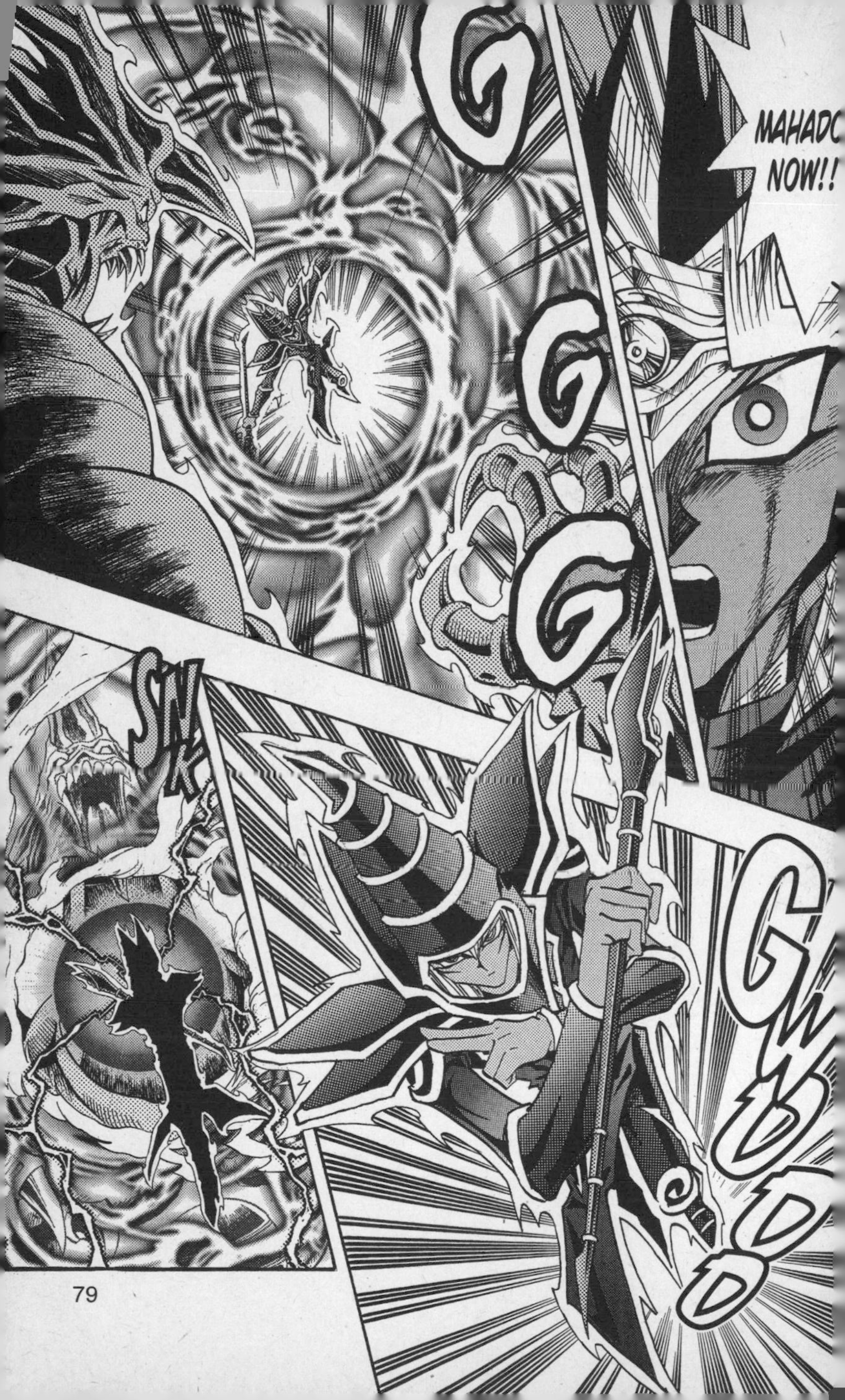
MAHADO
NOW!!
GGG
SNK
GWOOD

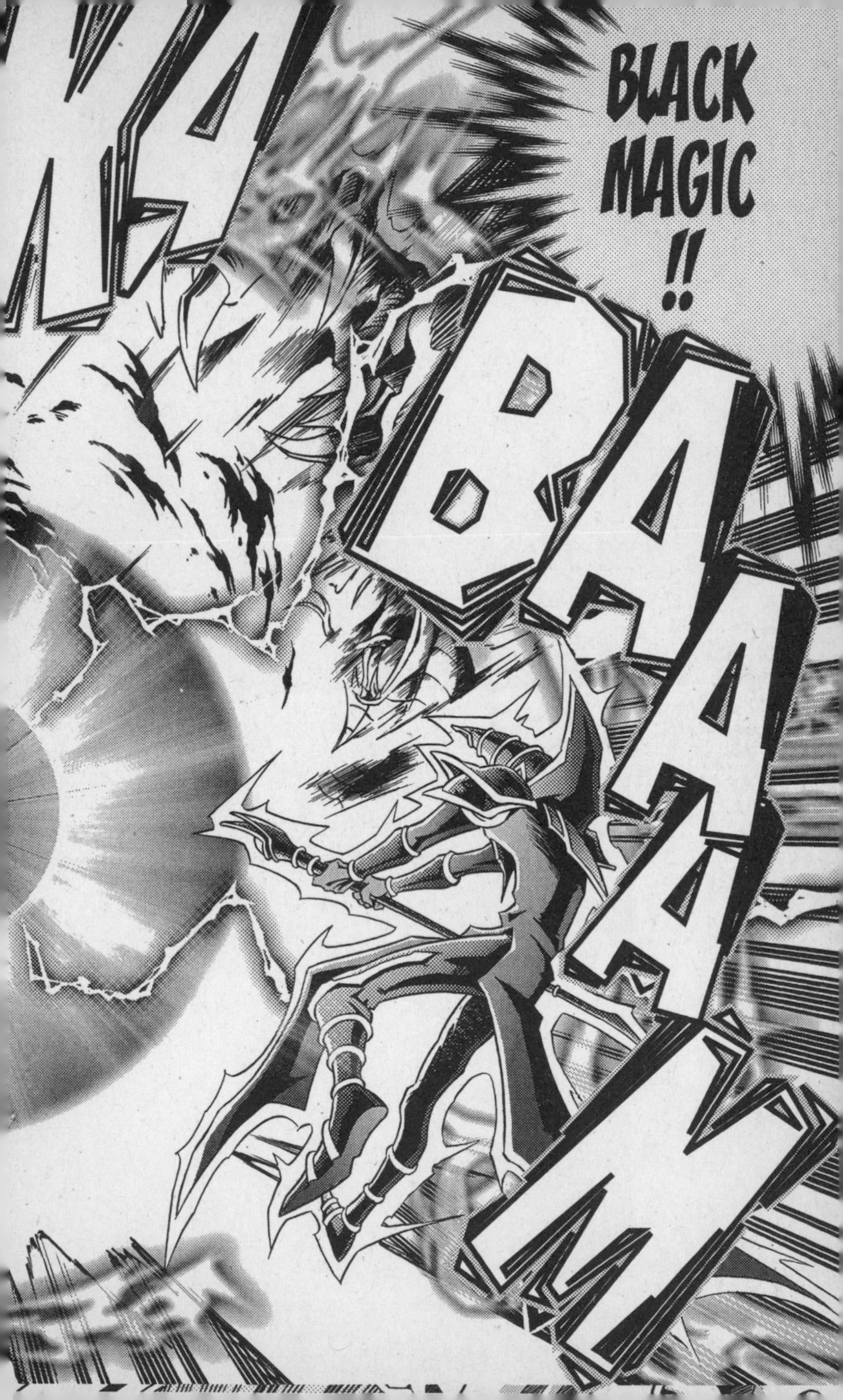
BLACK MAGIC!!

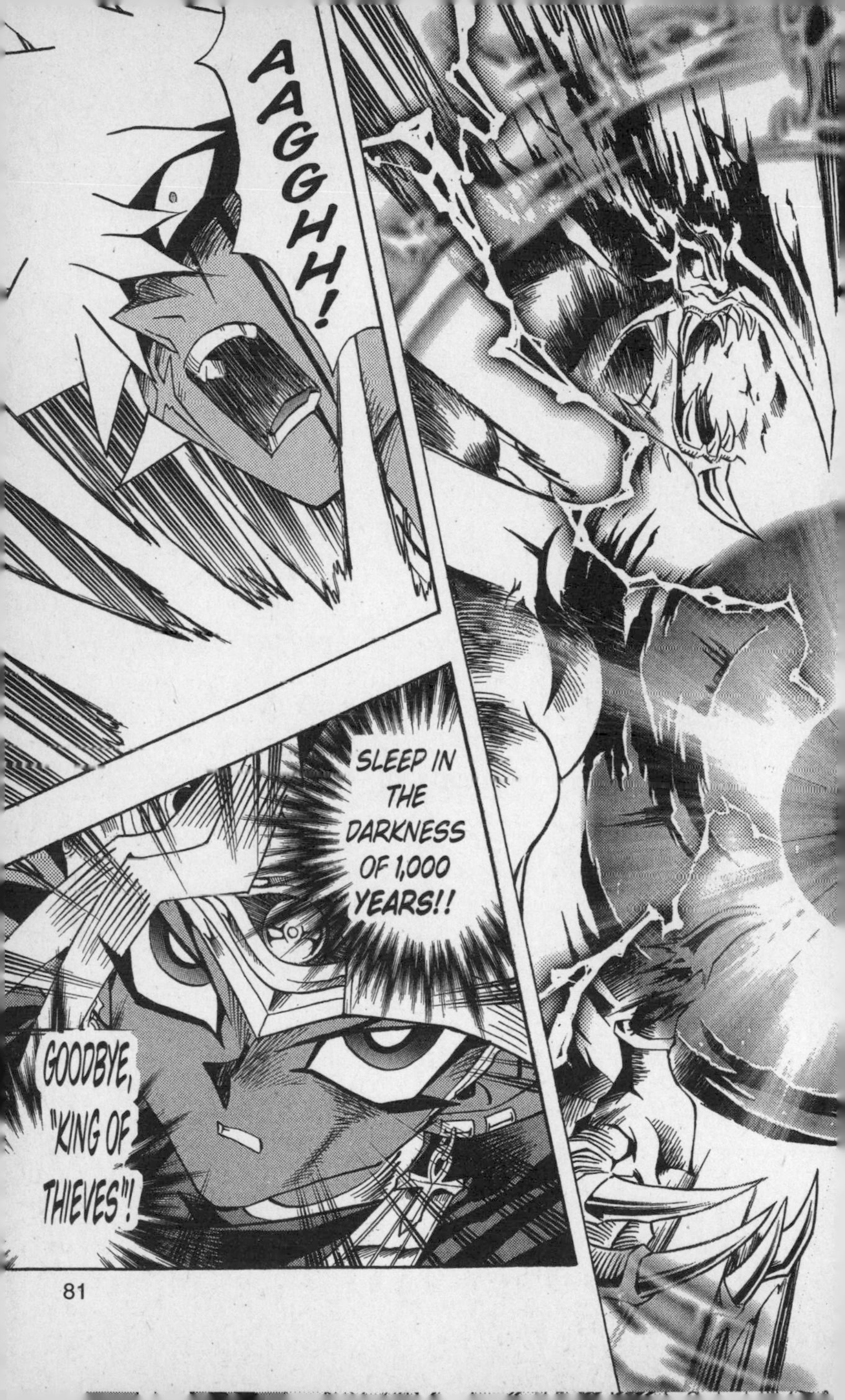
AAGGHH!
SLEEP IN THE DARKNESS OF 1,000 YEARS!!
GOODBYE, "KING OF THIEVES"!

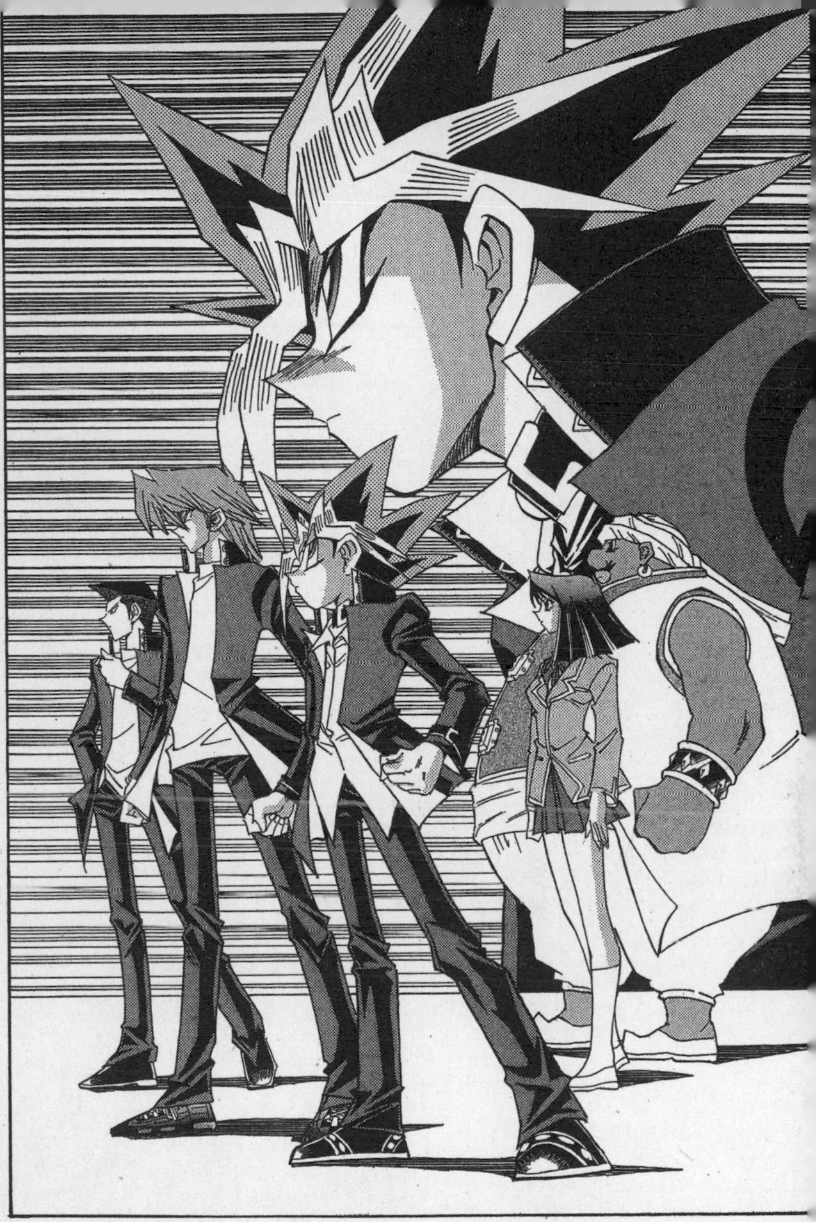

Duel 41: The Pawns of Memory!

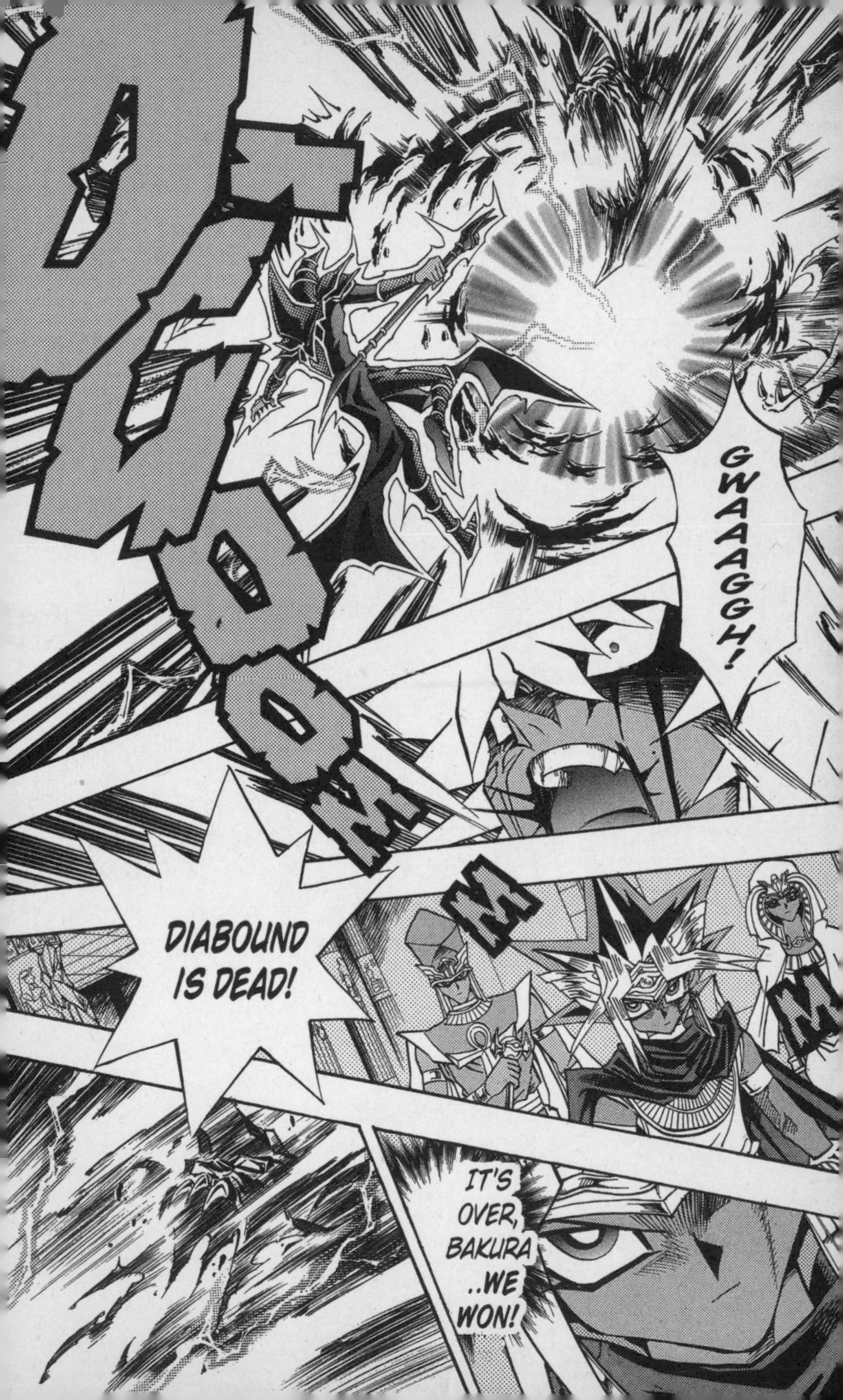
GWAAAAGGH!
BOOOMMM
DIABOUND IS DEAD!
IT'S OVER, BAKURA ...WE WON!

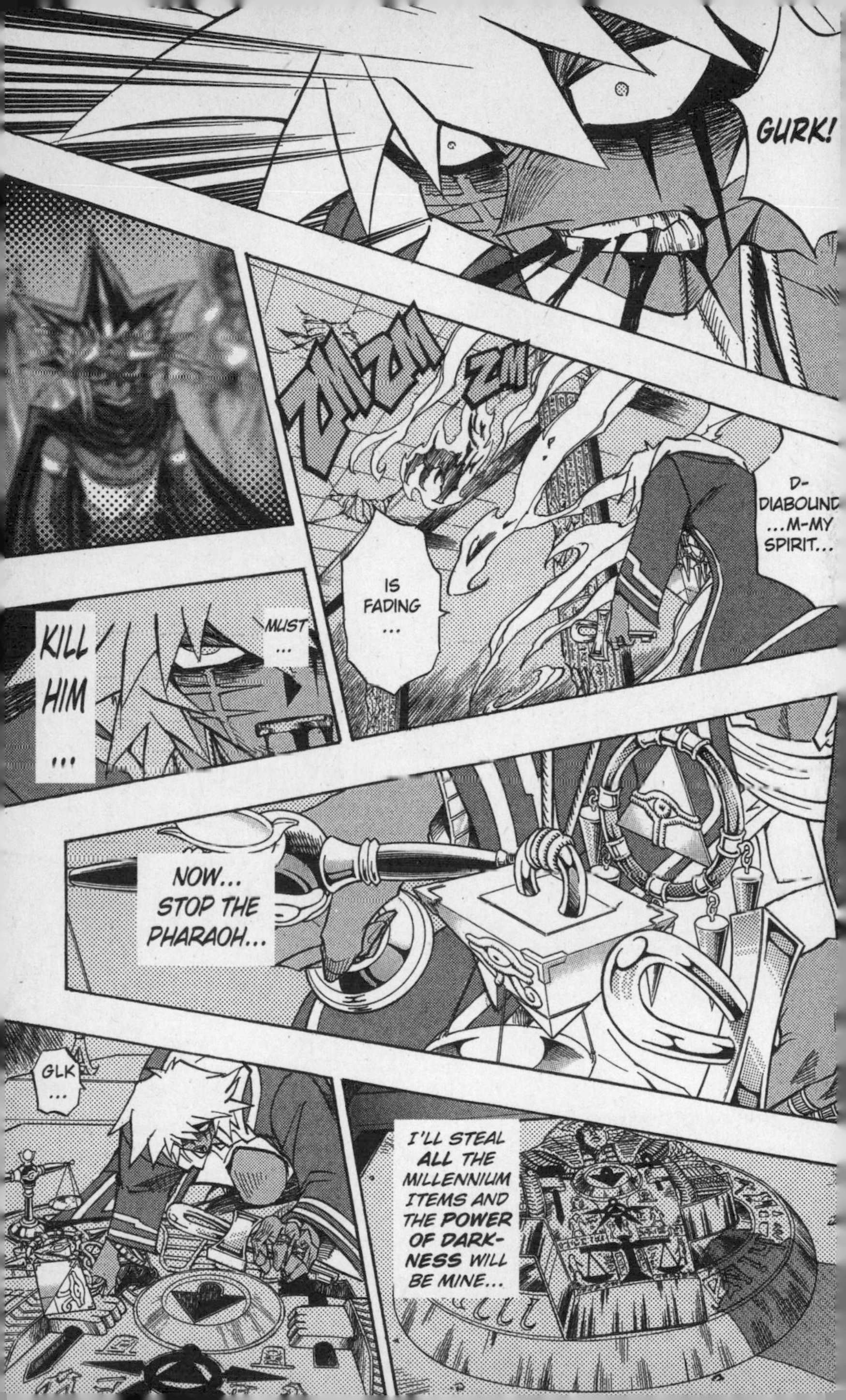
GURK!
ZAM ZAM
ZAM
D-DIABOUND ...M-MY SPIRIT...
IS FADING ...
MUST ...
KILL HIM ...
NOW... STOP THE PHARAOH...
I'LL STEAL ALL THE MILLENNIUM ITEMS AND THE POWER OF DARKNESS WILL BE MINE...
GLK ...

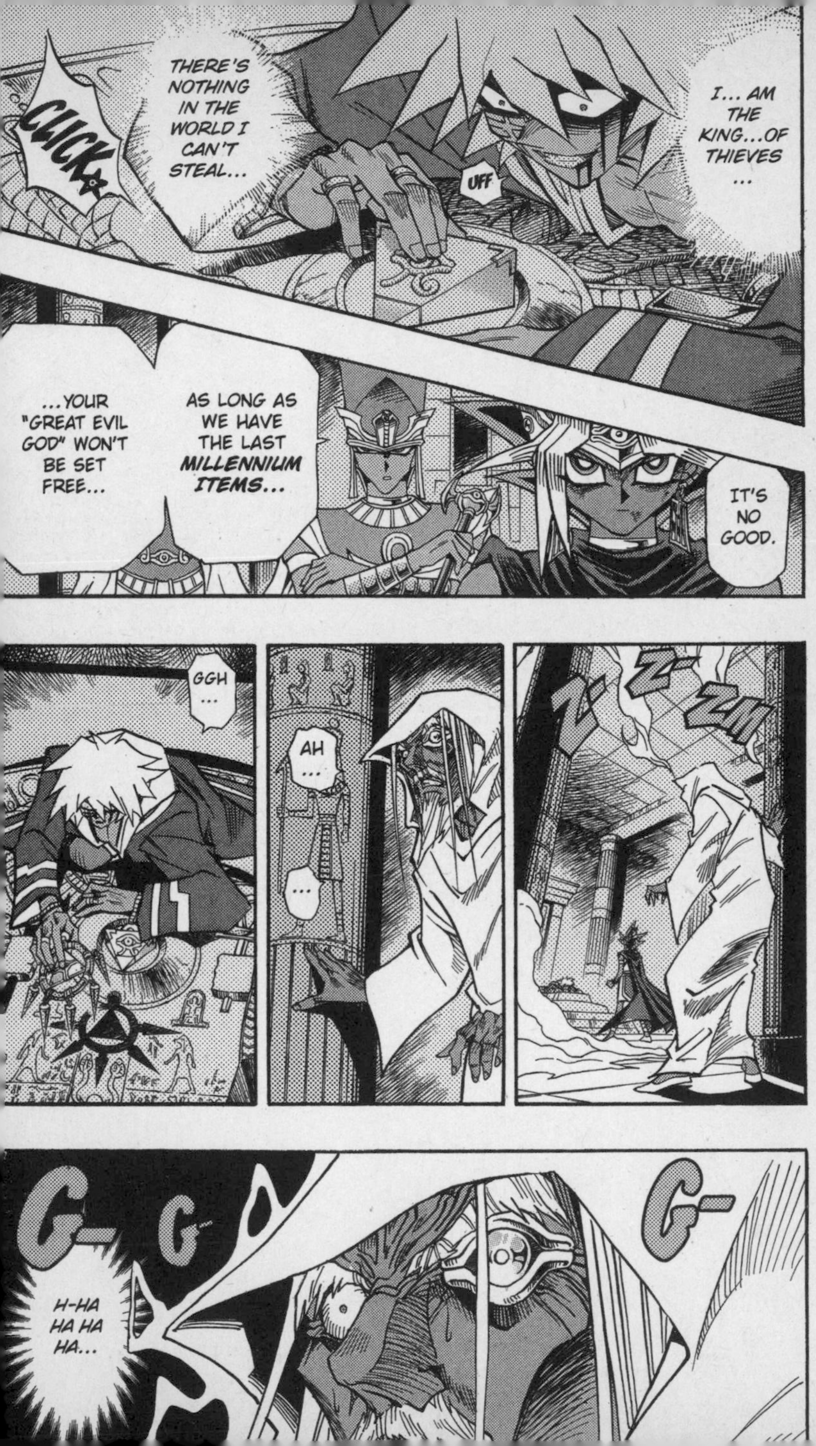
I... AM THE KING...OF THIEVES ...
UFF
THERE'S NOTHING IN THE WORLD I CAN'T STEAL...
CLICK
IT'S NO GOOD.
AS LONG AS WE HAVE THE LAST MILLENNIUM ITEMS...
...YOUR "GREAT EVIL GOD" WON'T BE SET FREE...
Z- Z- ZM
AH ...
...
GGH ...
G- G G-
H-HA HA HA HA...

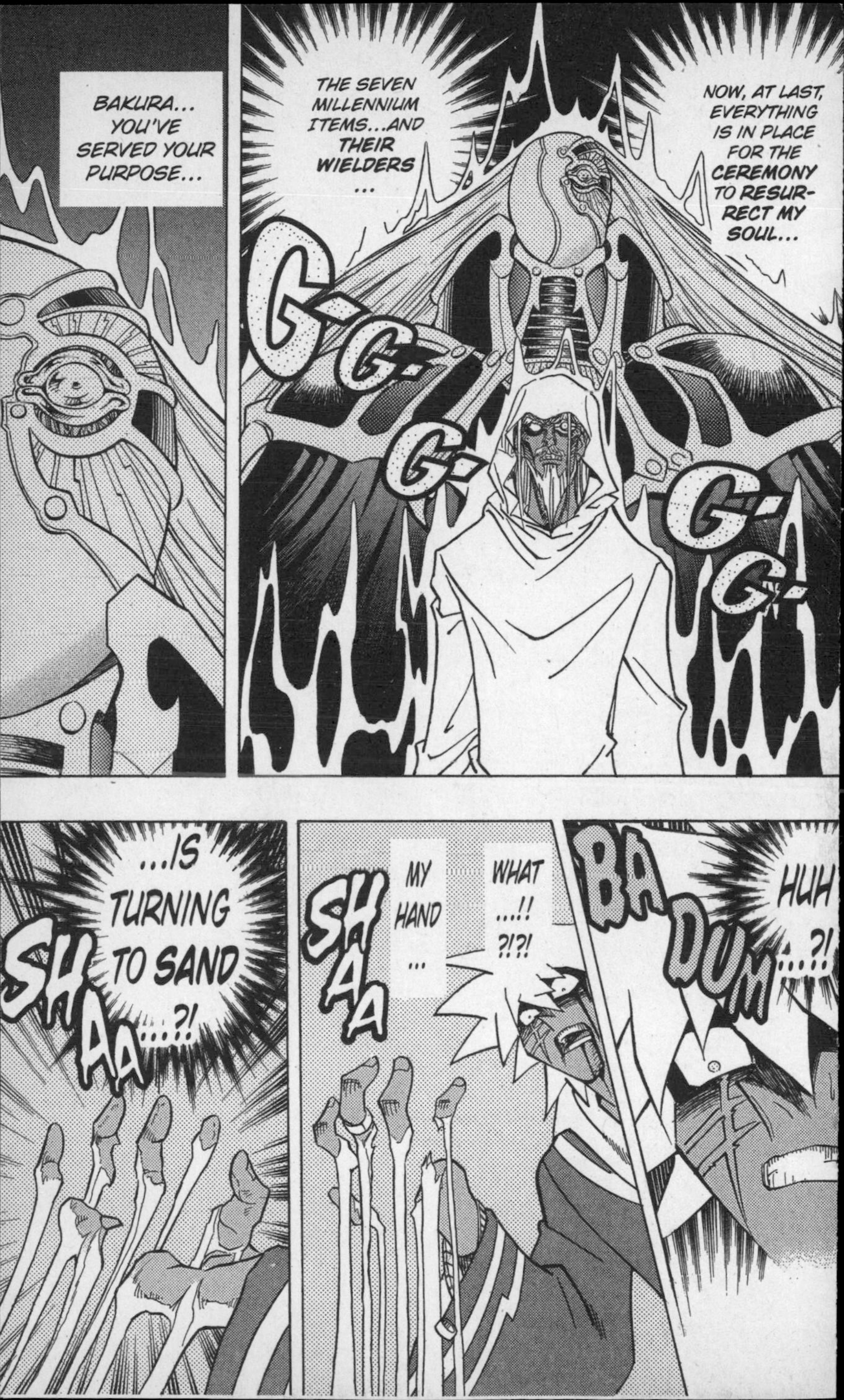
NOW, AT LAST, EVERYTHING IS IN PLACE FOR THE CEREMONY TO RESURRECT MY SOUL...
THE SEVEN MILLENNIUM ITEMS...AND THEIR WIELDERS...
G-G-G-
G-G-
BAKURA... YOU'VE SERVED YOUR PURPOSE...
HUH...?!
BA-DUM
WHAT...!! ?!?!
MY HAND...
SHAAA
...IS TURNING TO SAND...?!
SHAA

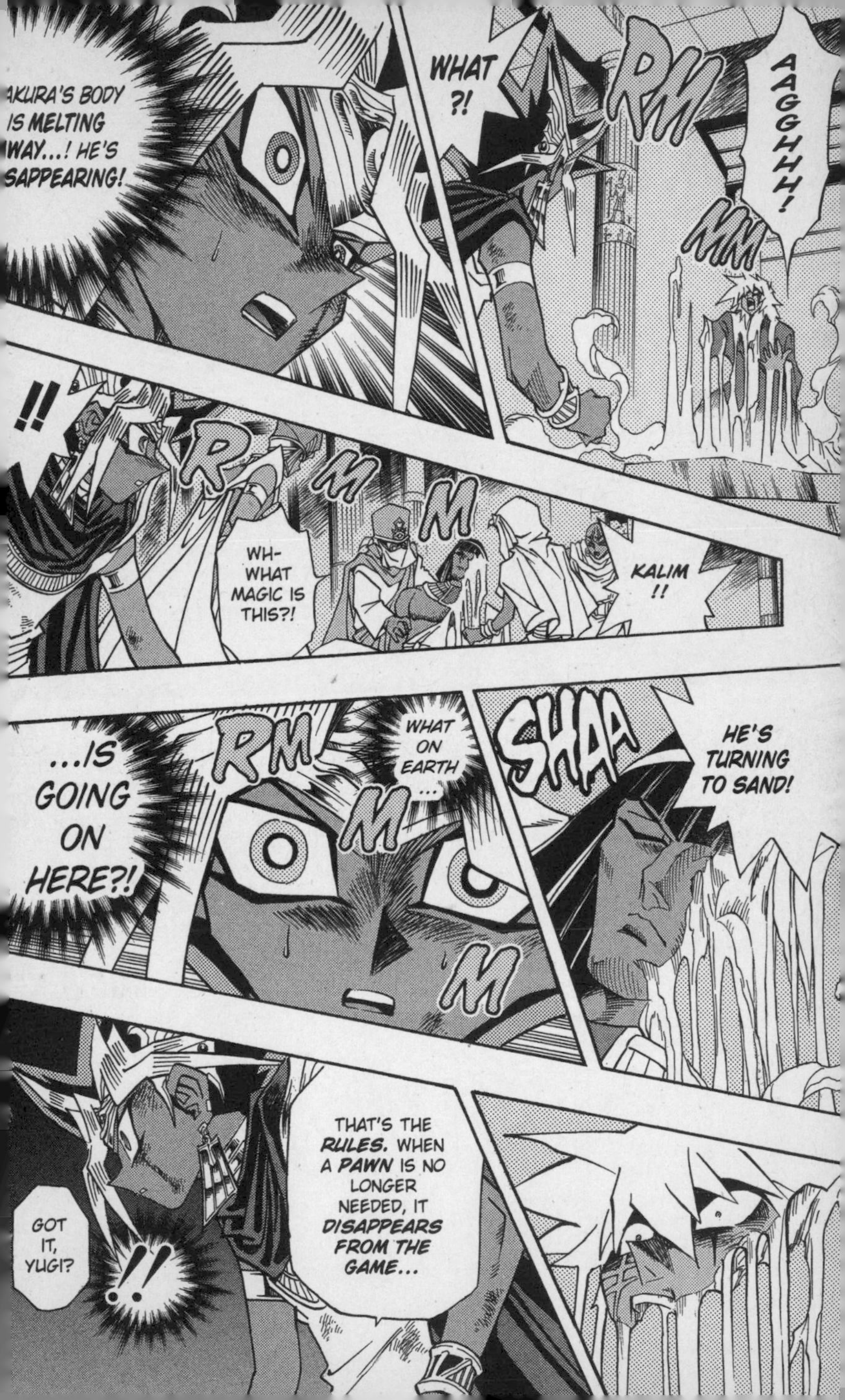
AAGGHHH!
RM
MM
WHAT ?!
AKURA'S BODY IS MELTING WAY...! HE'S SAPPEARING!
KALIM !!
WH- WHAT MAGIC IS THIS?!
RMMM
!!
SHAA
HE'S TURNING TO SAND!
WHAT ON EARTH...
RMMM
...IS GOING ON HERE?!
THAT'S THE RULES. WHEN A PAWN IS NO LONGER NEEDED, IT DISAPPEARS FROM THE GAME...
!!
GOT IT, YUGI?

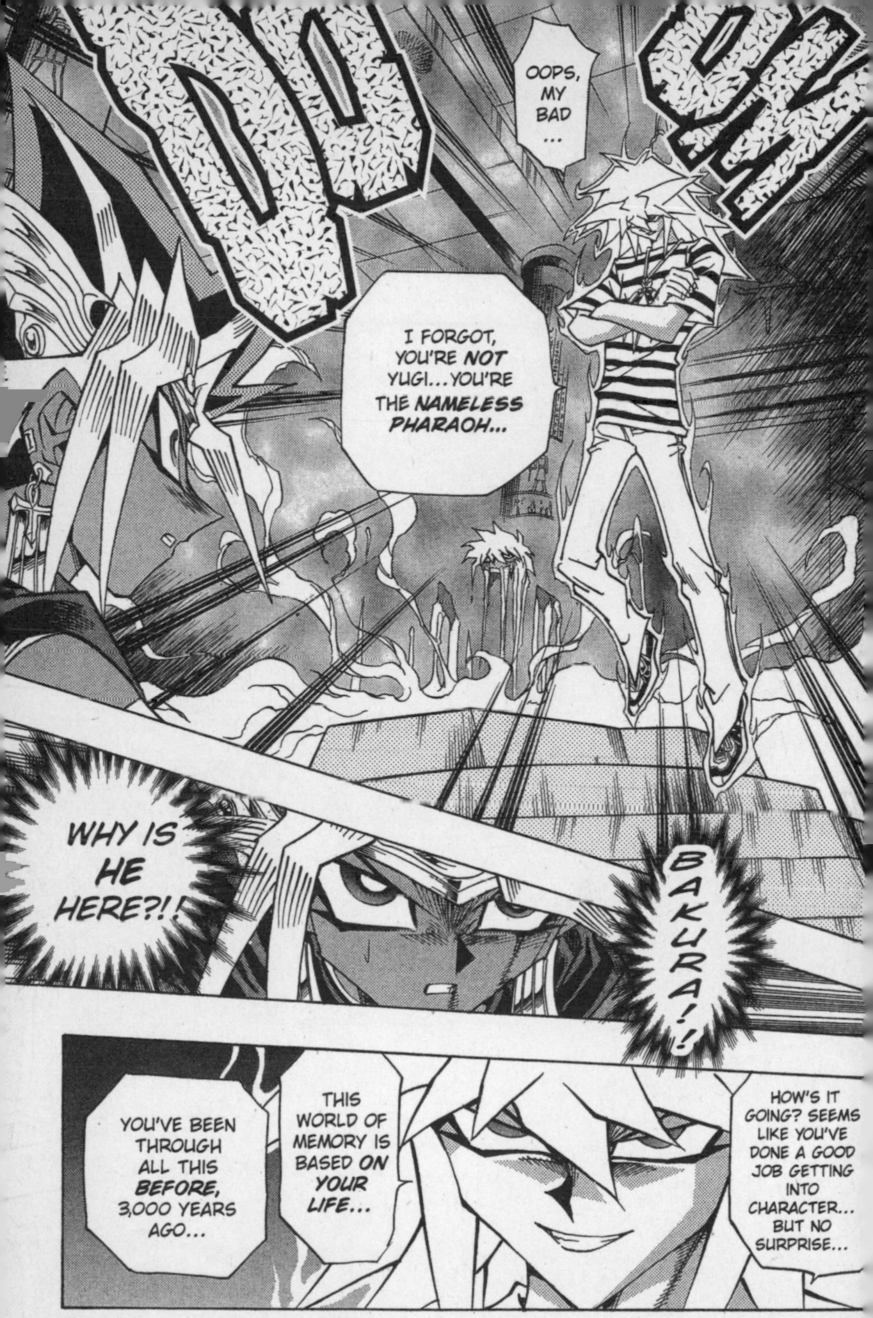
OOPS, MY BAD...
I FORGOT, YOU'RE NOT YUGI... YOU'RE THE NAMELESS PHARAOH...
BAKURA!!
WHY IS HE HERE?!!
HOW'S IT GOING? SEEMS LIKE YOU'VE DONE A GOOD JOB GETTING INTO CHARACTER... BUT NO SURPRISE...
THIS WORLD OF MEMORY IS BASED ON YOUR LIFE...
YOU'VE BEEN THROUGH ALL THIS BEFORE, 3,000 YEARS AGO...

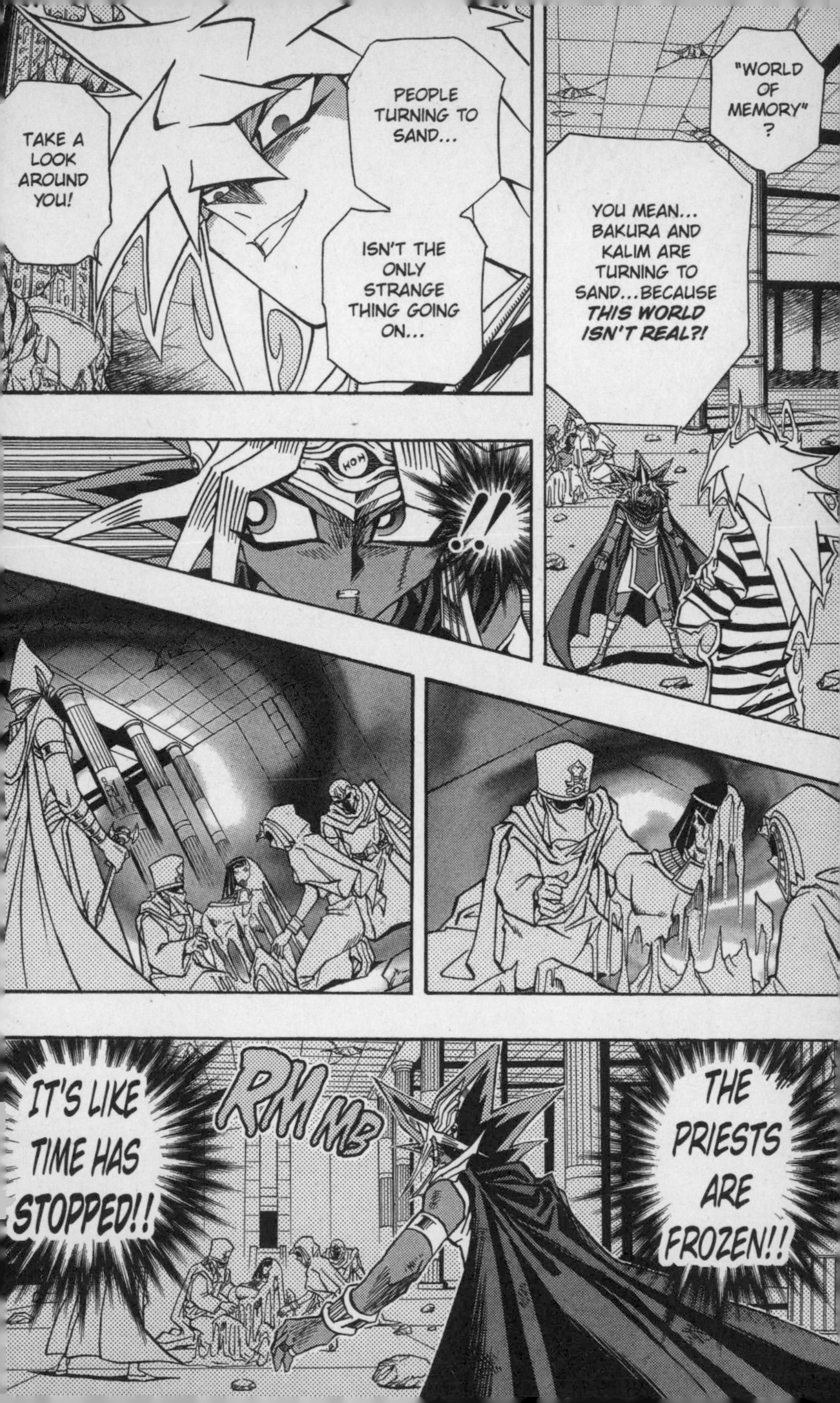
"WORLD OF MEMORY"?
YOU MEAN... BAKURA AND KALIM ARE TURNING TO SAND...BECAUSE ***THIS WORLD ISN'T REAL?!***
PEOPLE TURNING TO SAND...
ISN'T THE ONLY STRANGE THING GOING ON...
TAKE A LOOK AROUND YOU!
!!
THE PRIESTS ARE FROZEN!!
IT'S LIKE TIME HAS STOPPED!!

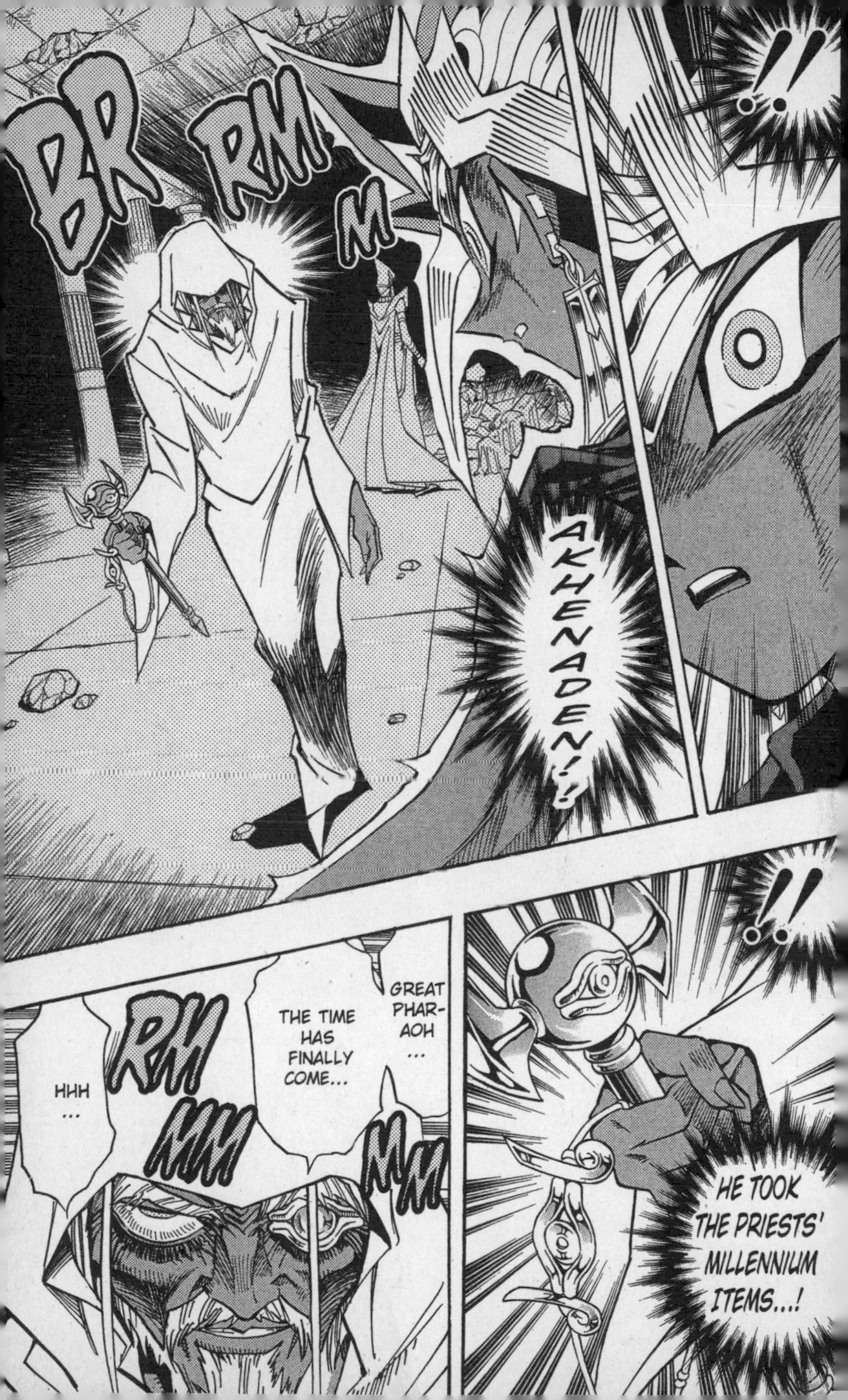

!!
AKHENADEN!!
BRRMM
!!
HE TOOK THE PRIESTS' MILLENNIUM ITEMS...!
GREAT PHARAOH...
THE TIME HAS FINALLY COME...
RMMMMM
HHH...

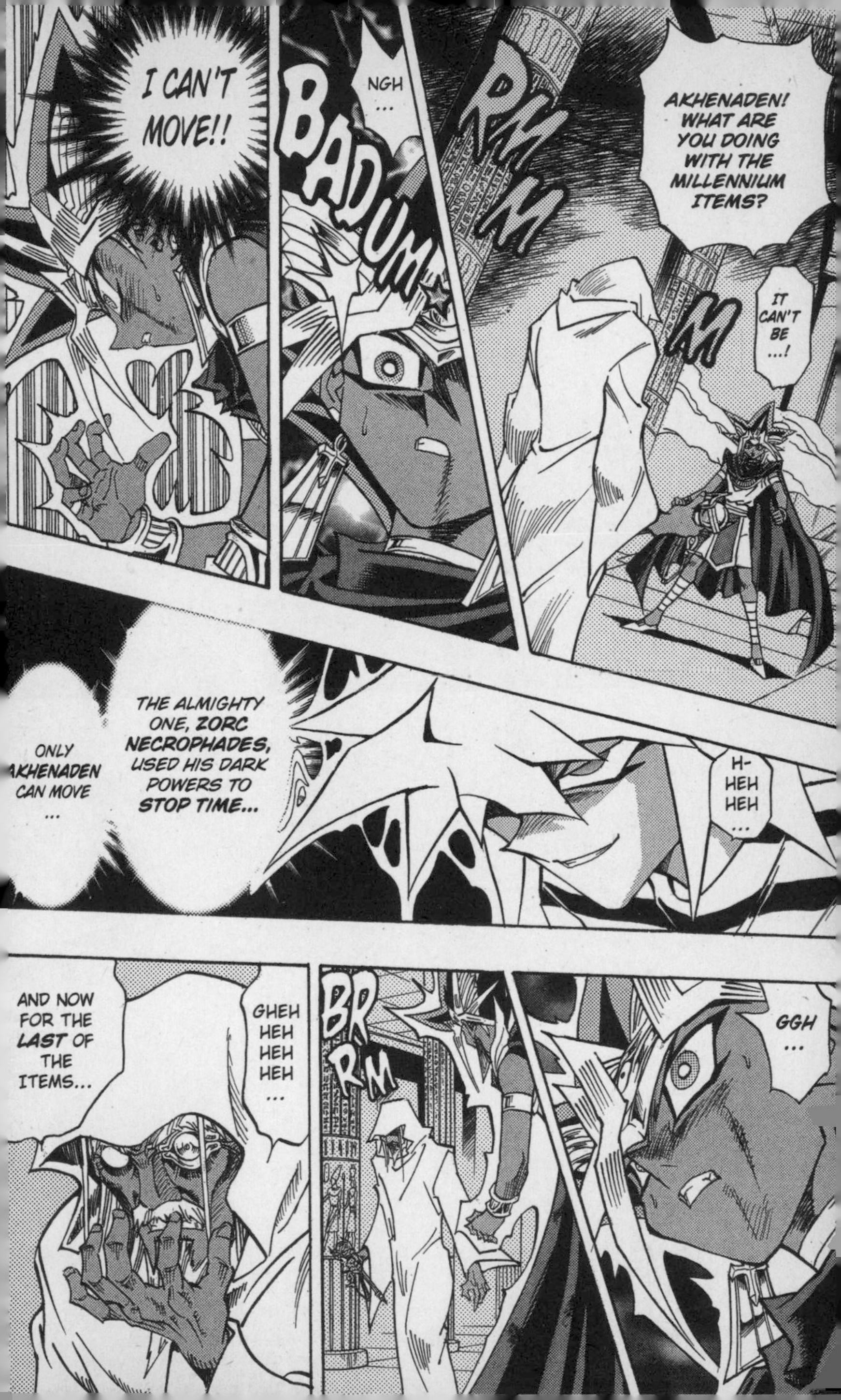
AKHENADEN! WHAT ARE YOU DOING WITH THE MILLENNIUM ITEMS?
RMMM
IT CAN'T BE ...!
NGH ...
BADUM
I CAN'T MOVE!!
H-HEH HEH ...
THE ALMIGHTY ONE, ZORC NECROPHADES, USED HIS DARK POWERS TO STOP TIME...
ONLY AKHENADEN CAN MOVE ...
GGH ...
BRRM
GHEH HEH HEH HEH ...
AND NOW FOR THE LAST OF THE ITEMS...

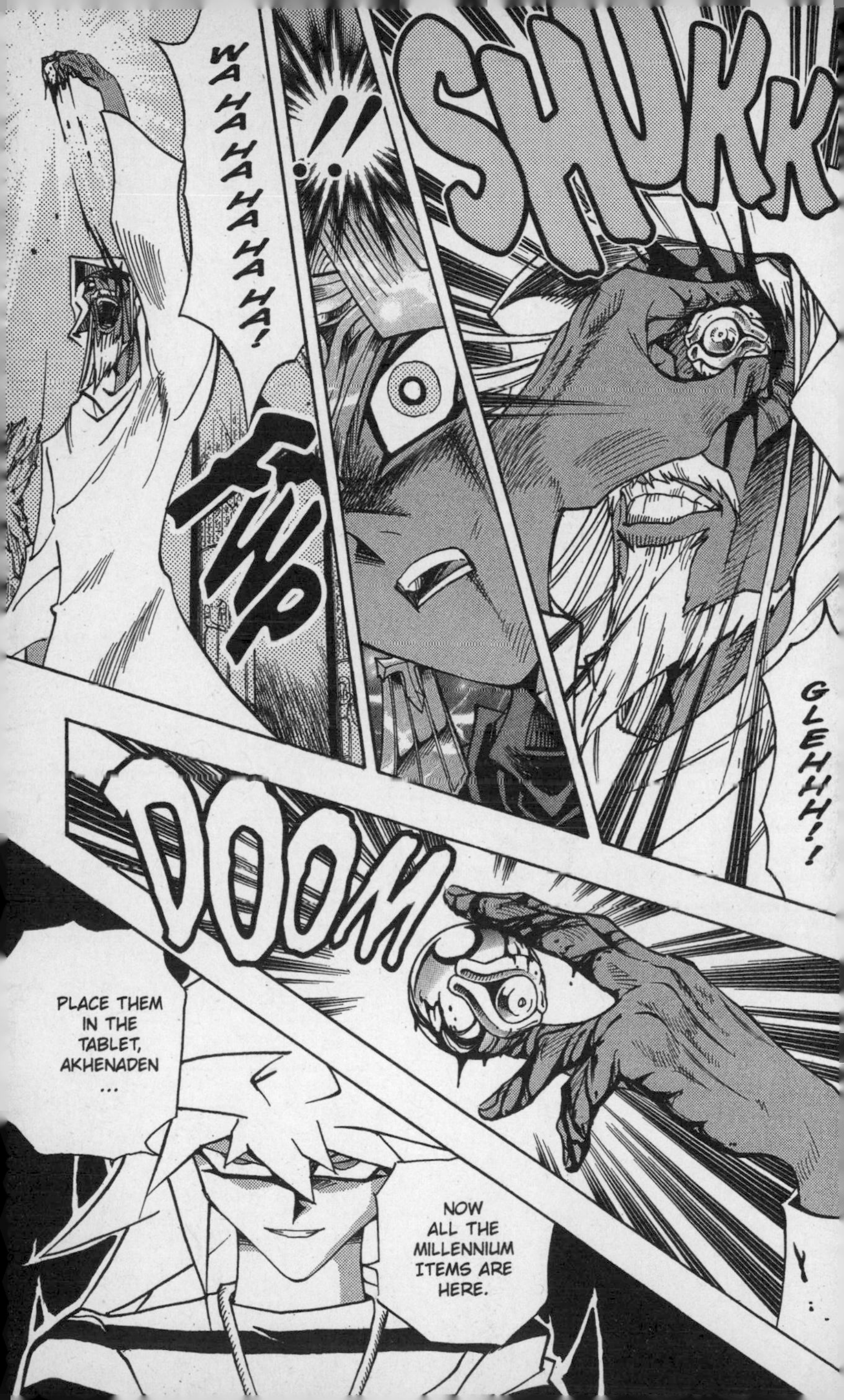
SHUKK
GLEHHH!!
!!
TWIP
WAHAHAHAHAHAHAHA!
DOOM
NOW ALL THE MILLENNIUM ITEMS ARE HERE.
PLACE THEM IN THE TABLET, AKHENADEN ...

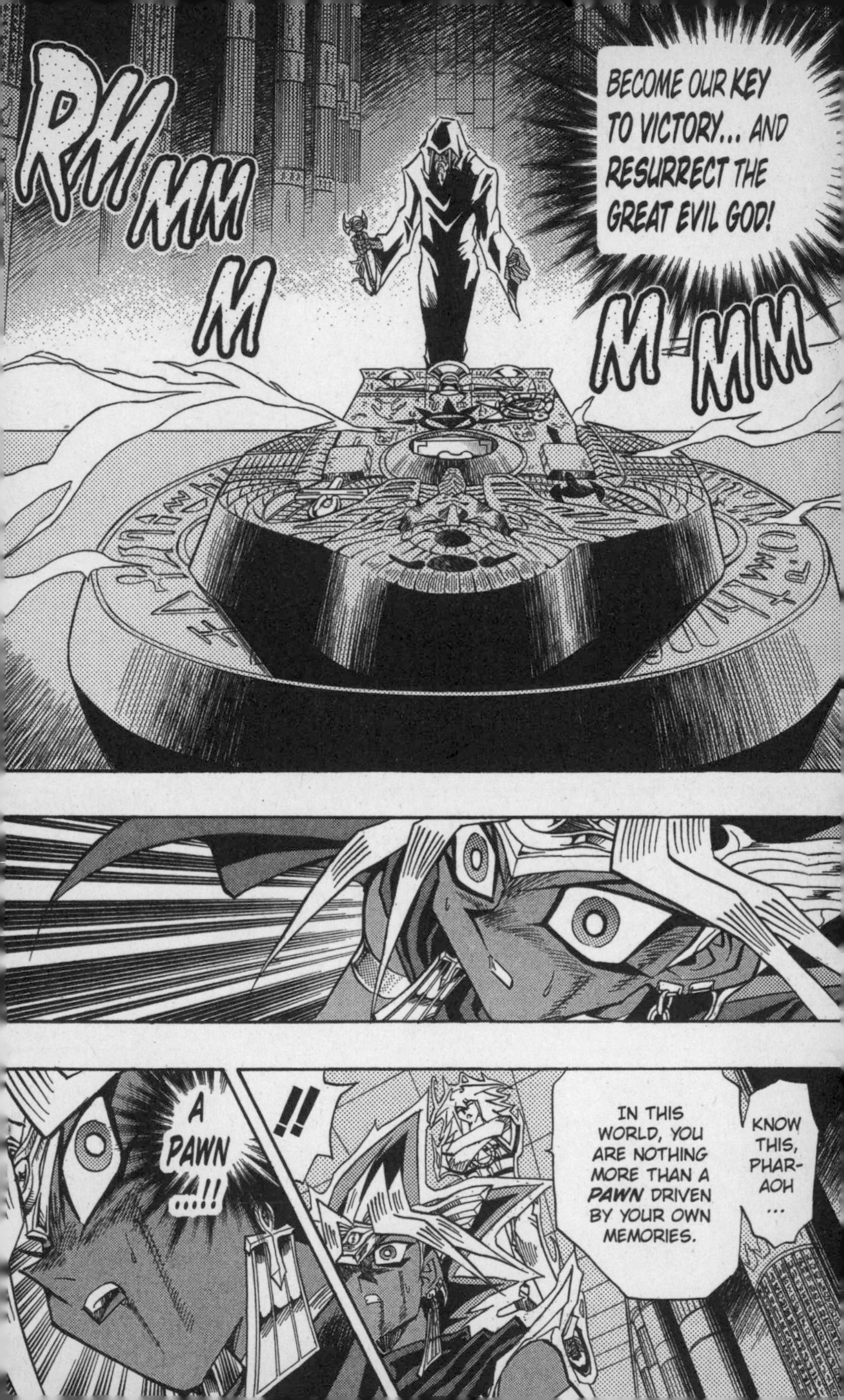
BECOME OUR KEY TO VICTORY... AND RESURRECT THE GREAT EVIL GOD!
RMMMMM M
M-MM
KNOW THIS, PHARAOH...
IN THIS WORLD, YOU ARE NOTHING MORE THAN A PAWN DRIVEN BY YOUR OWN MEMORIES.
!!
A PAWN...!!

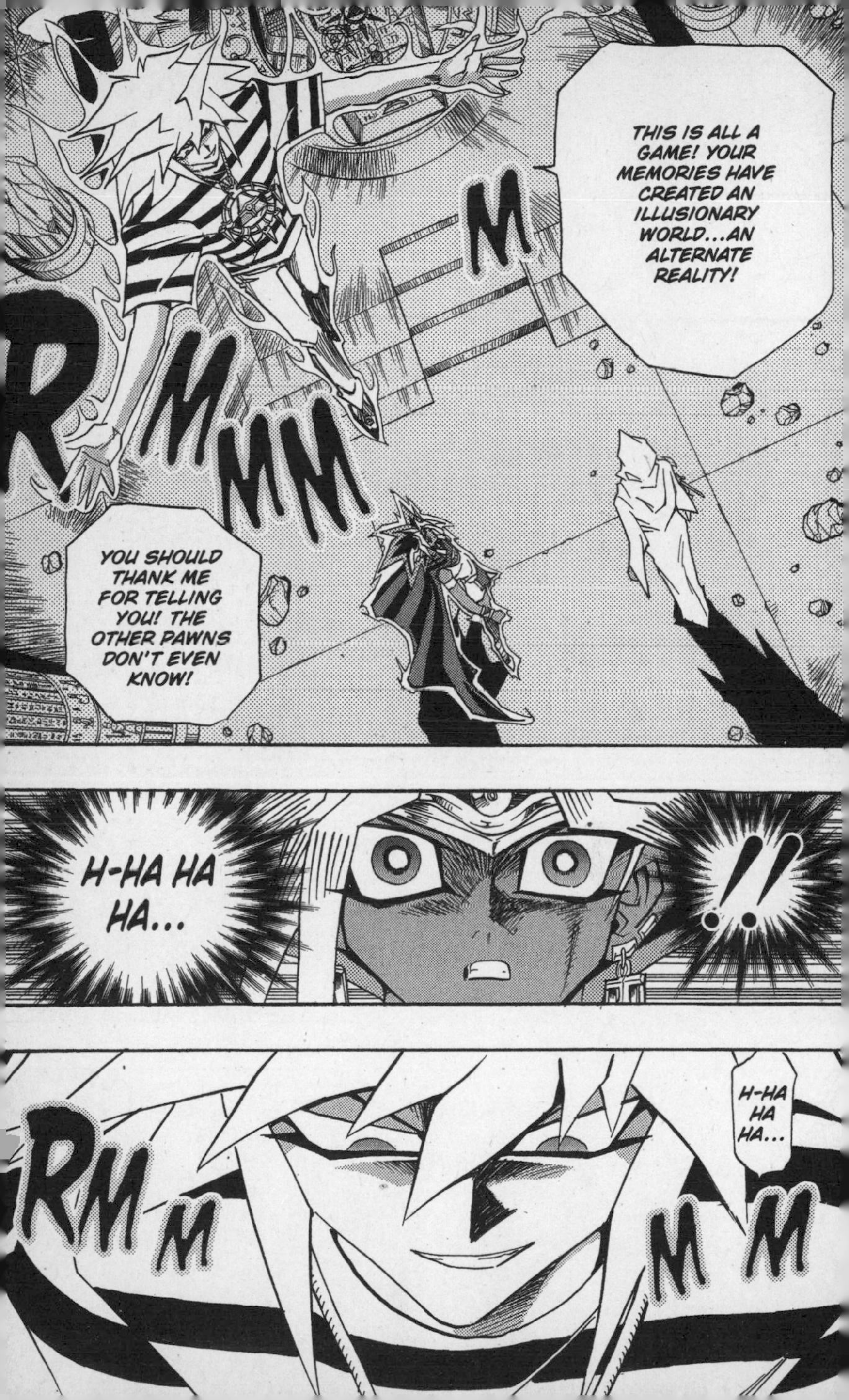
THIS IS ALL A GAME! YOUR MEMORIES HAVE CREATED AN ILLUSIONARY WORLD...AN ALTERNATE REALITY!
RMMMMM
YOU SHOULD THANK ME FOR TELLING YOU! THE OTHER PAWNS DON'T EVEN KNOW!
!!
H-HA HA HA...
H-HA HA HA...
RMMMM

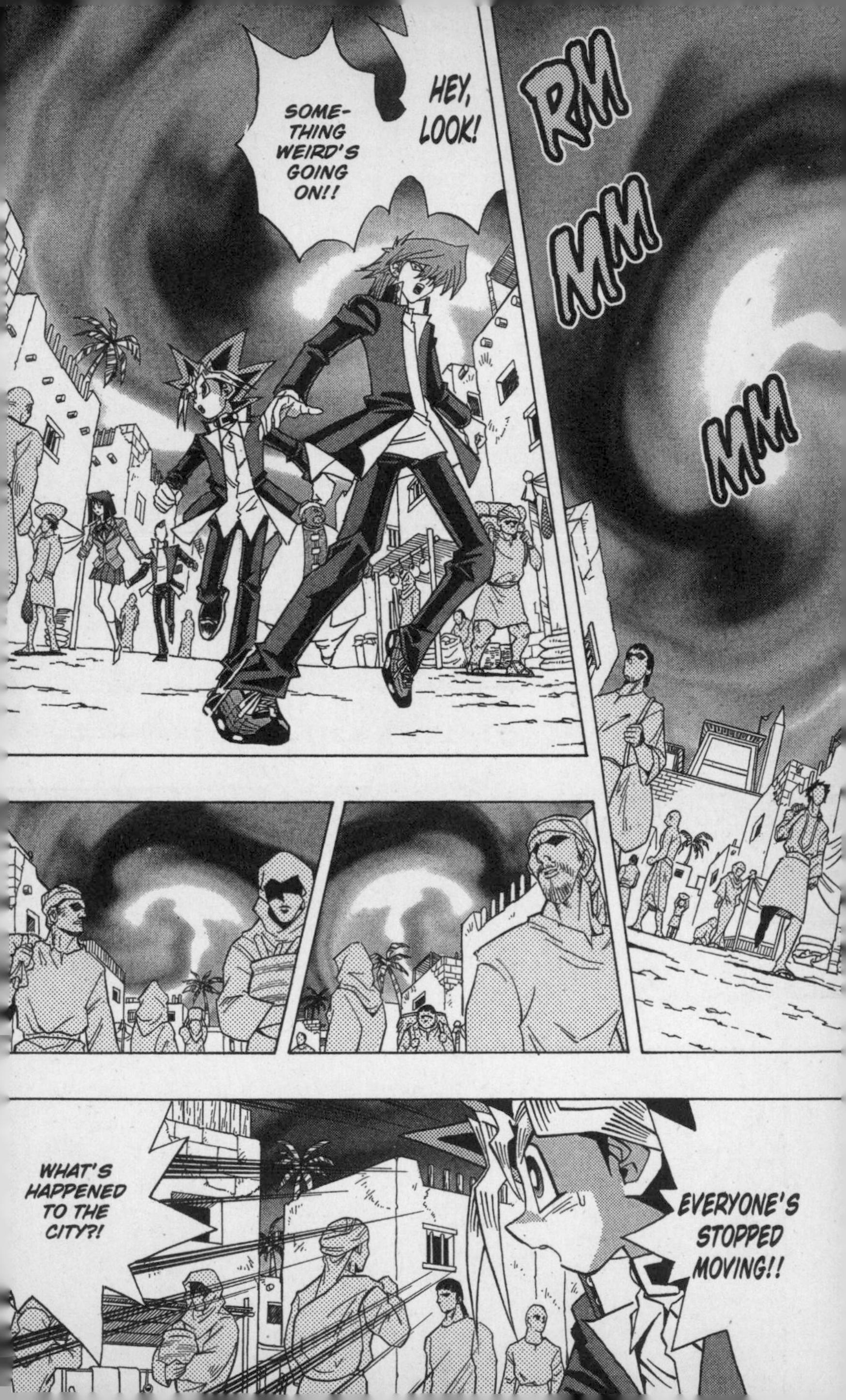
RMMMMMM
HEY, LOOK!
SOME-THING WEIRD'S GOING ON!!
EVERYONE'S STOPPED MOVING!!
WHAT'S HAPPENED TO THE CITY?!

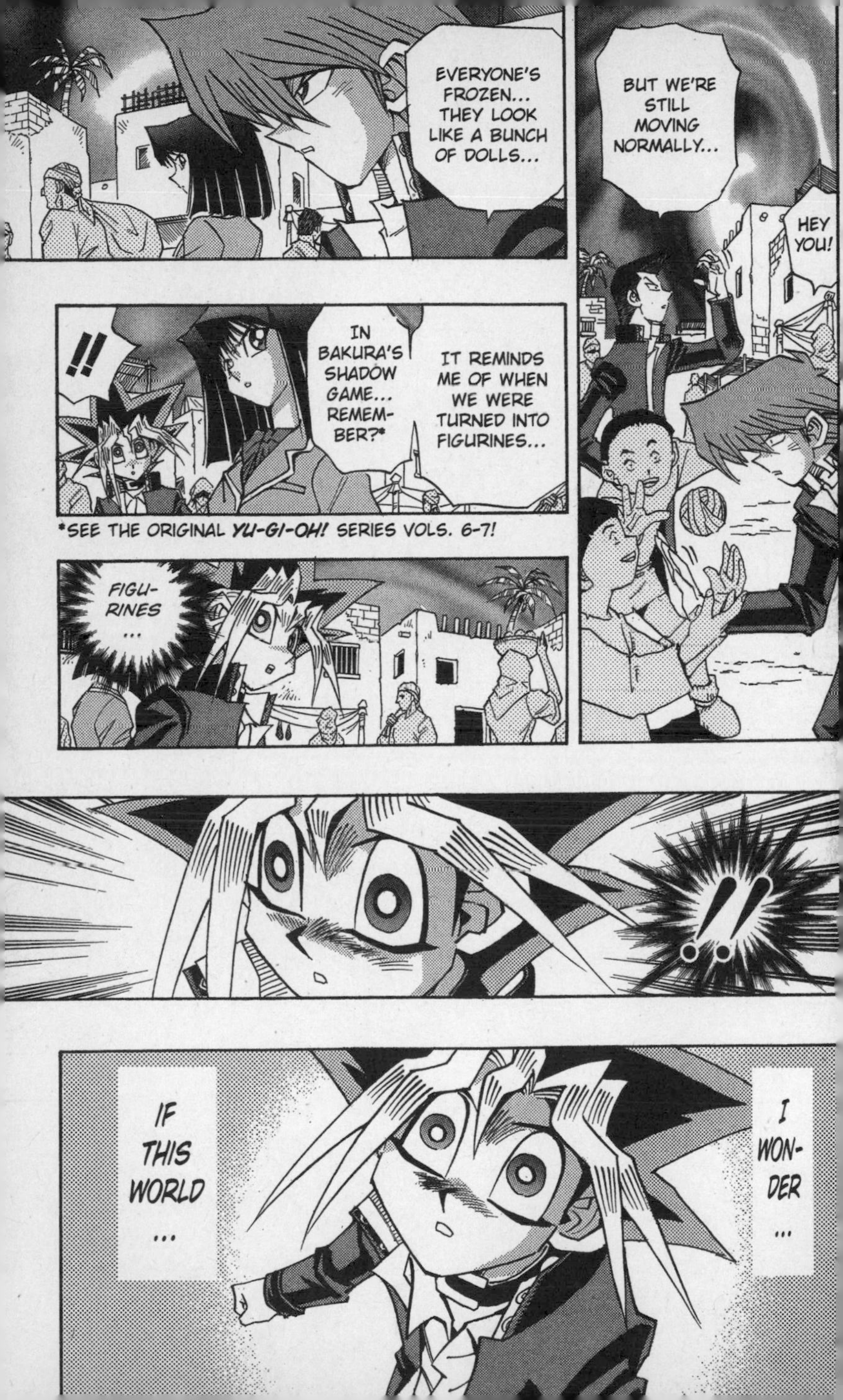
BUT WE'RE STILL MOVING NORMALLY...
HEY YOU!
EVERYONE'S FROZEN... THEY LOOK LIKE A BUNCH OF DOLLS...
IT REMINDS ME OF WHEN WE WERE TURNED INTO FIGURINES...
IN BAKURA'S SHADOW GAME... REMEMBER?*
!!
*SEE THE ORIGINAL YU-GI-OH! SERIES VOLS. 6-7!
FIGURINES...
!!
I WONDER...
IF THIS WORLD...

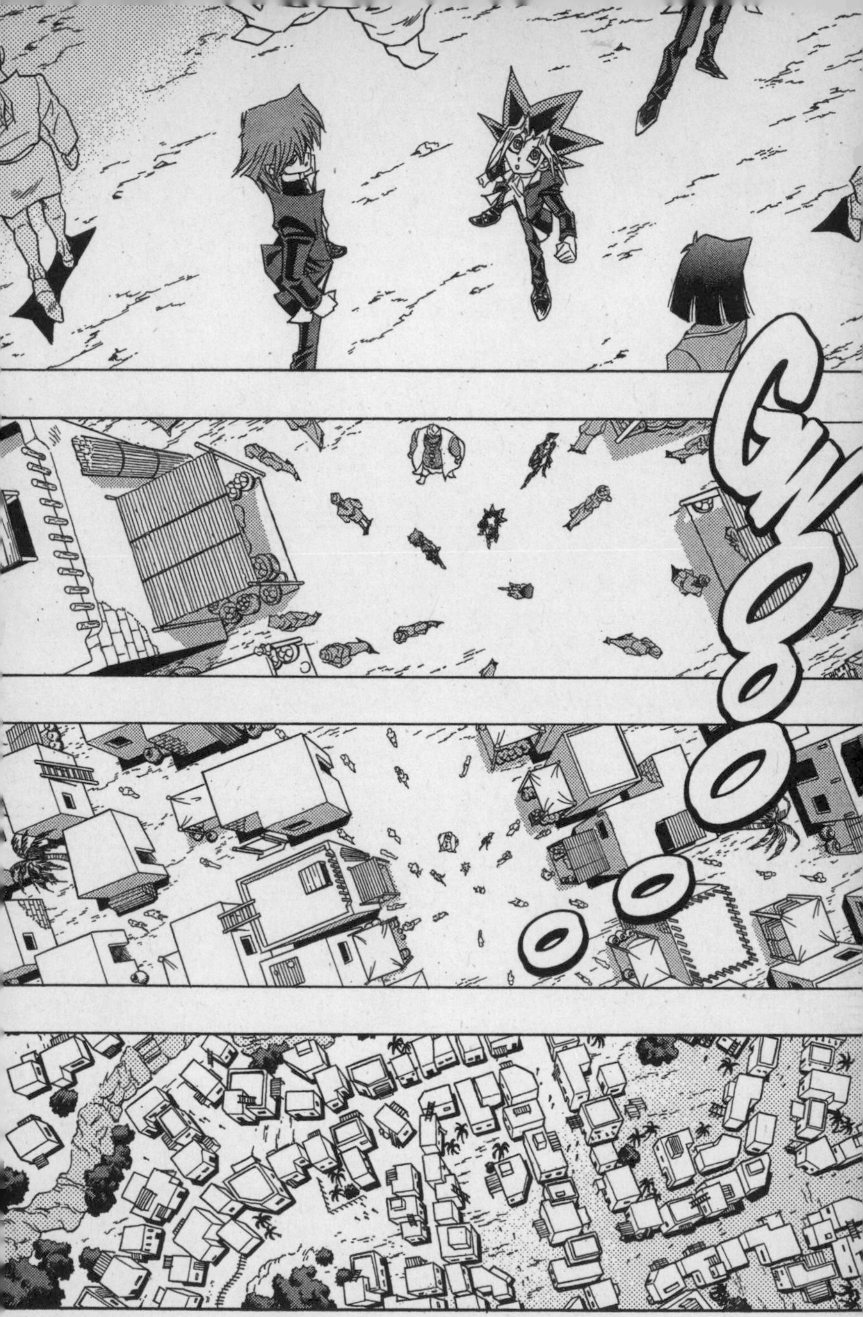
GWOOOOO

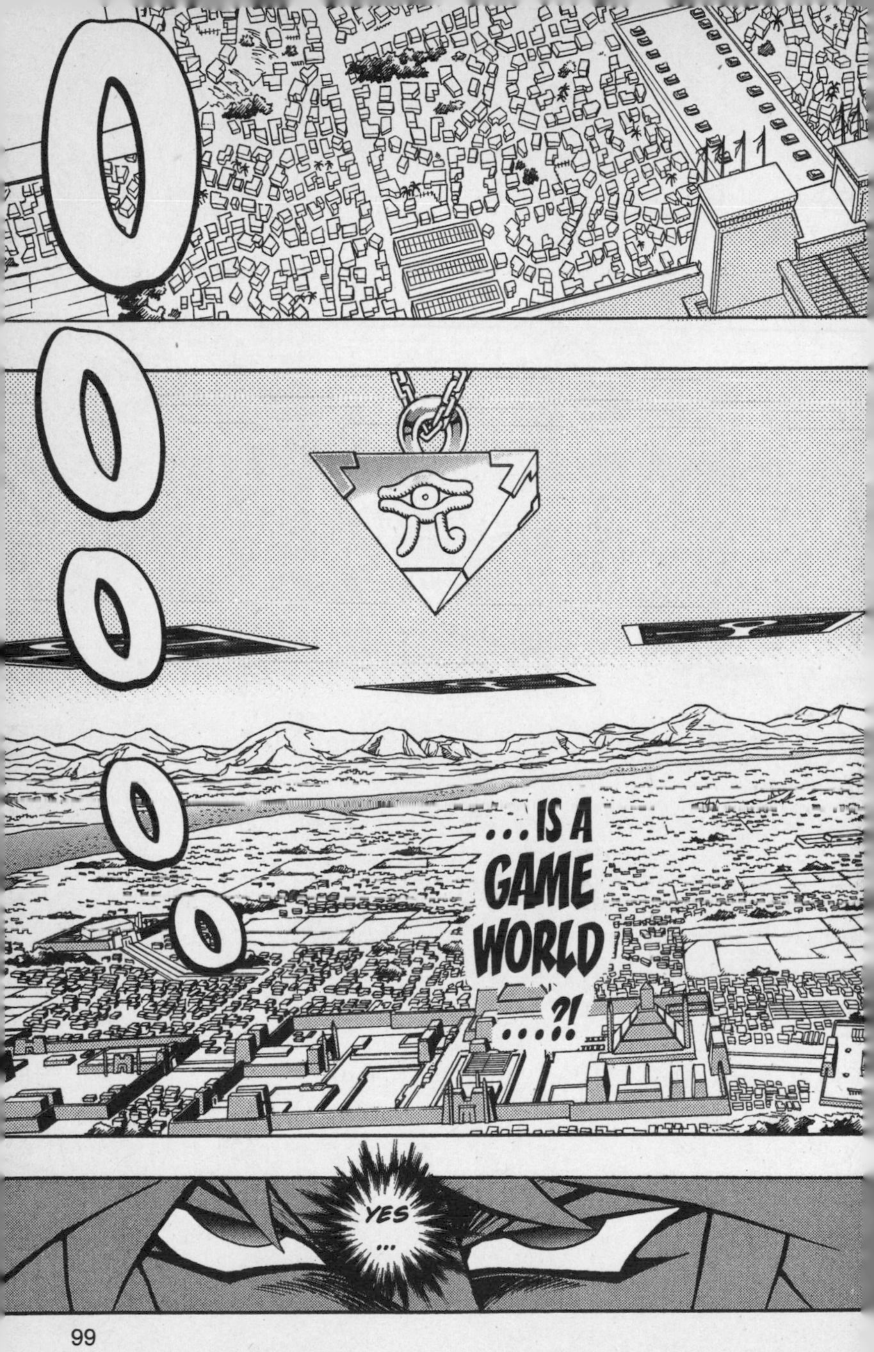
...IS A GAME WORLD ...?!
YES ...

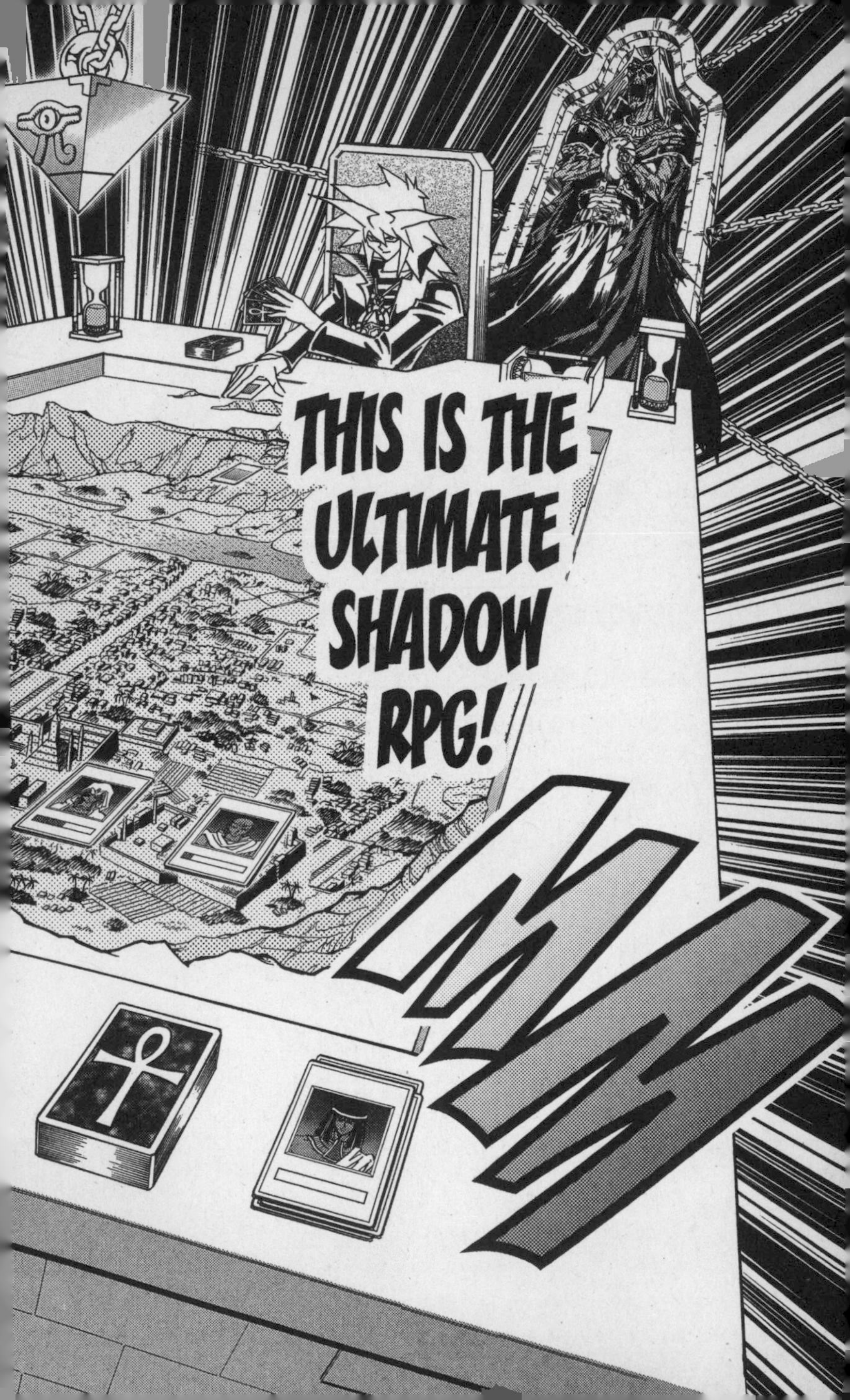
THIS IS THE ULTIMATE SHADOW RPG!

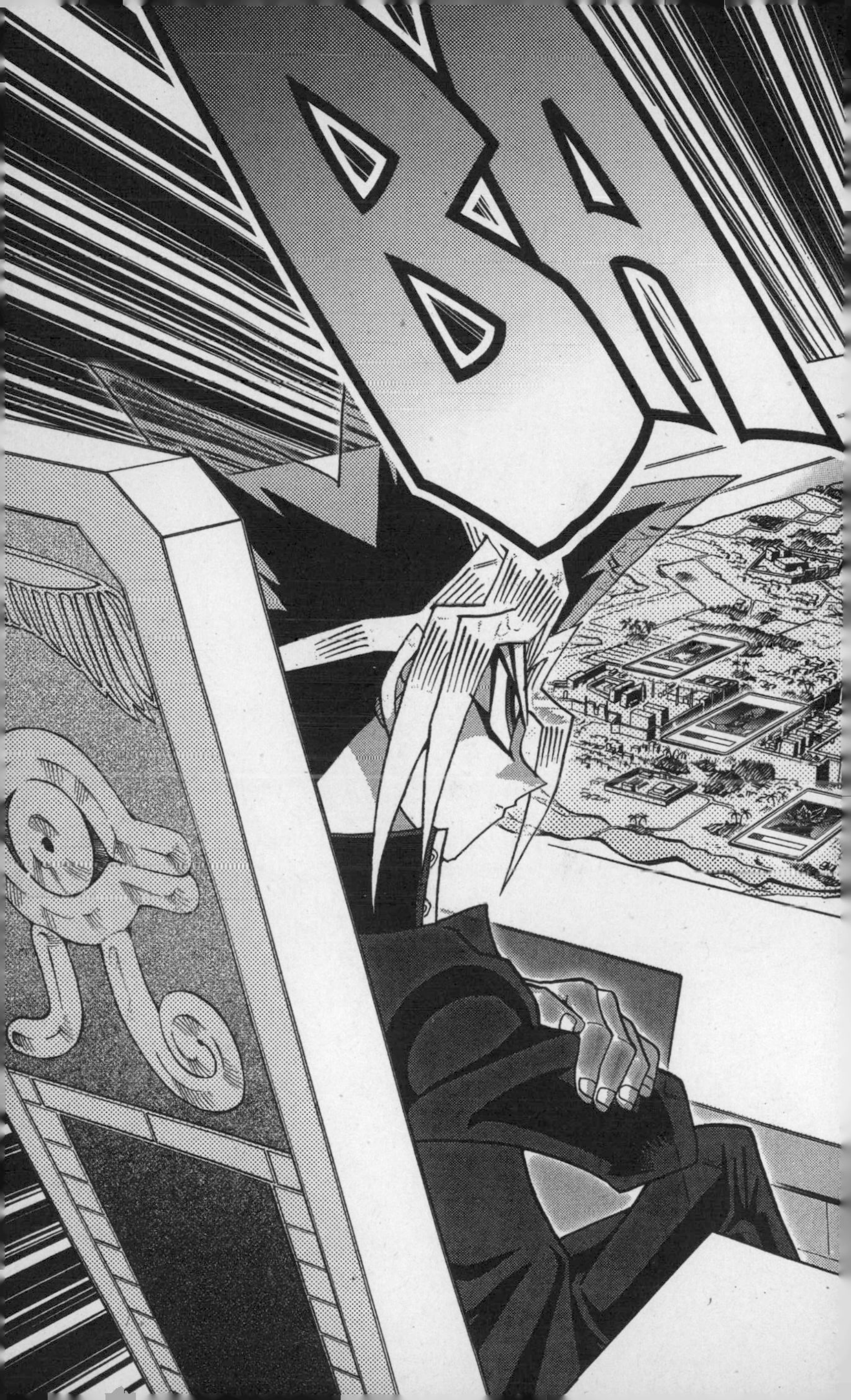

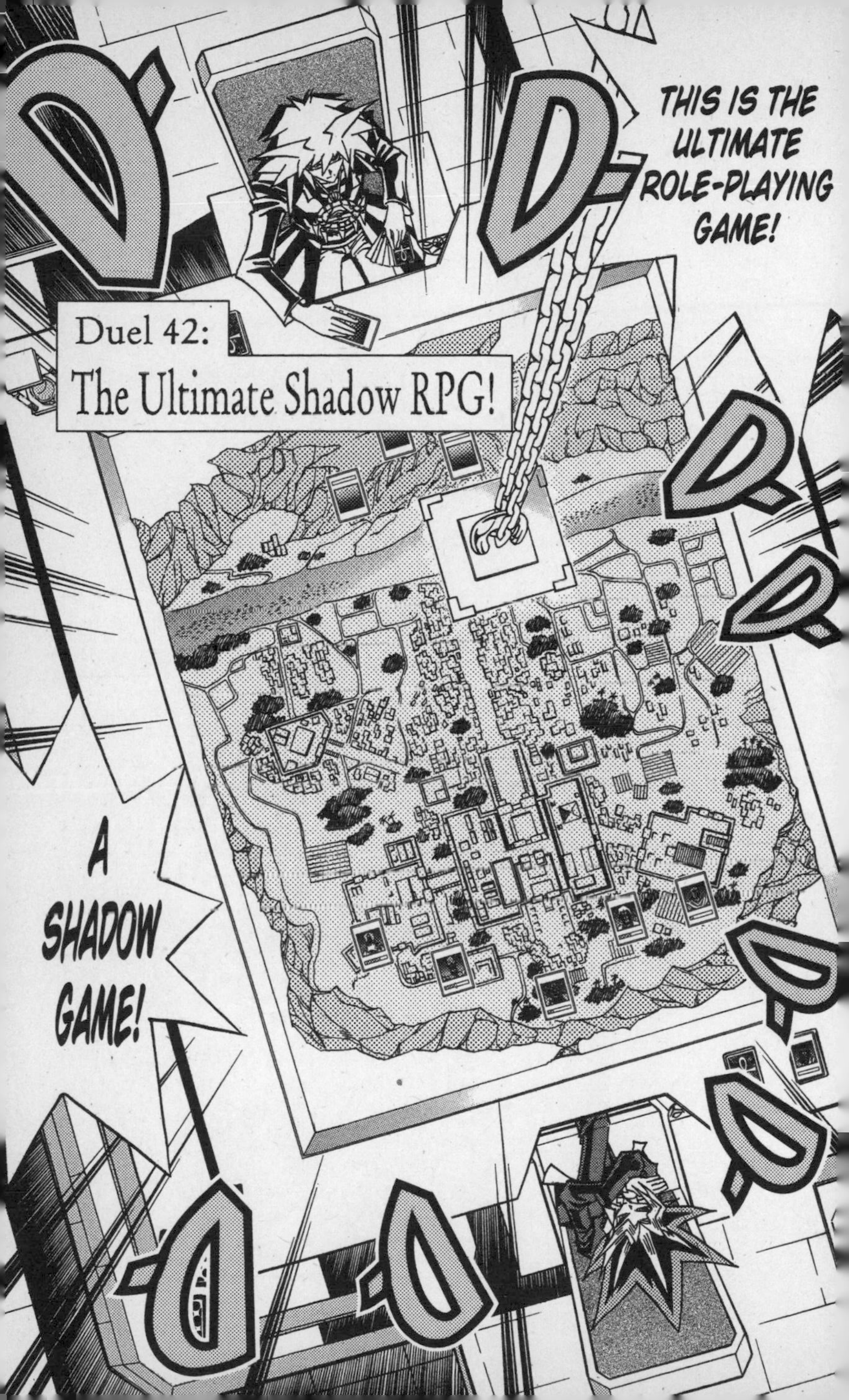
THIS IS THE ULTIMATE ROLE-PLAYING GAME!
Duel 42:
The Ultimate Shadow RPG!
A SHADOW GAME!

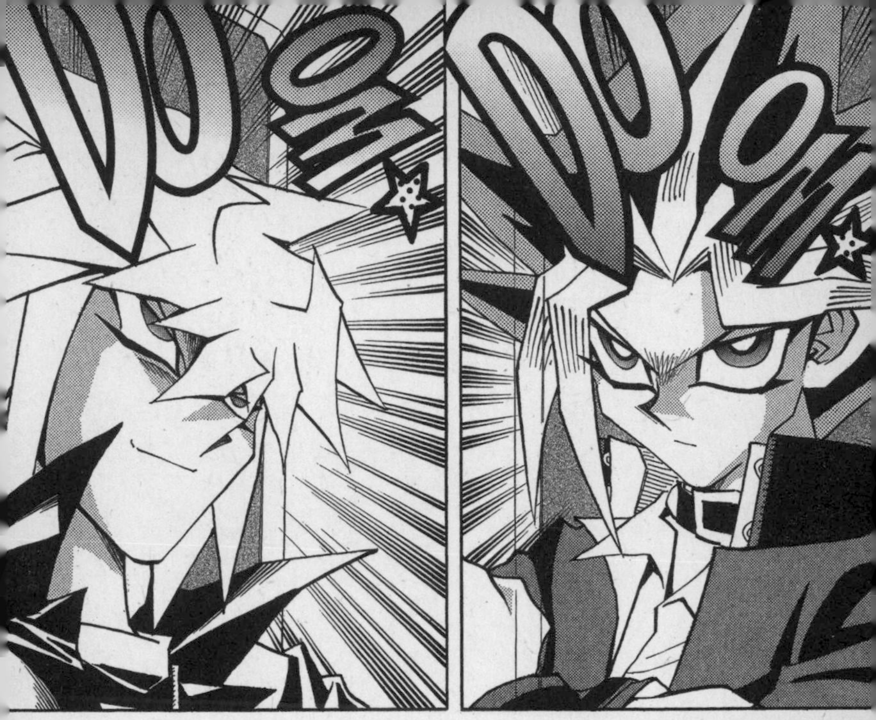

Duel 42: The Ultimate Shadow RPG!

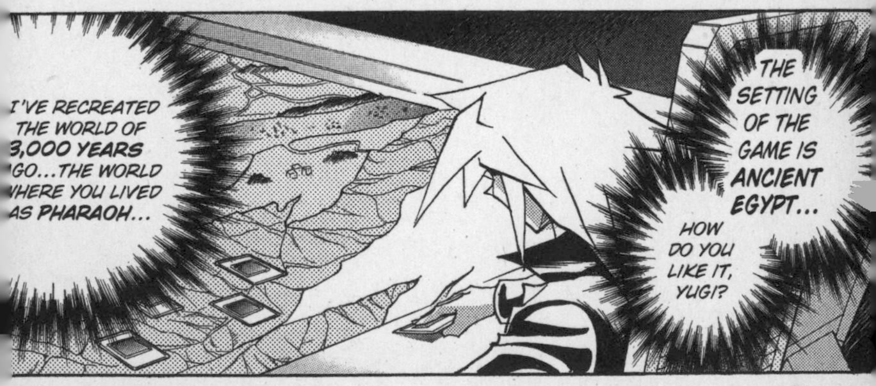
THE SETTING OF THE GAME IS ANCIENT EGYPT...
HOW DO YOU LIKE IT, YUGI?
I'VE RECREATED THE WORLD OF 3,000 YEARS AGO...THE WORLD WHERE YOU LIVED AS PHARAOH...

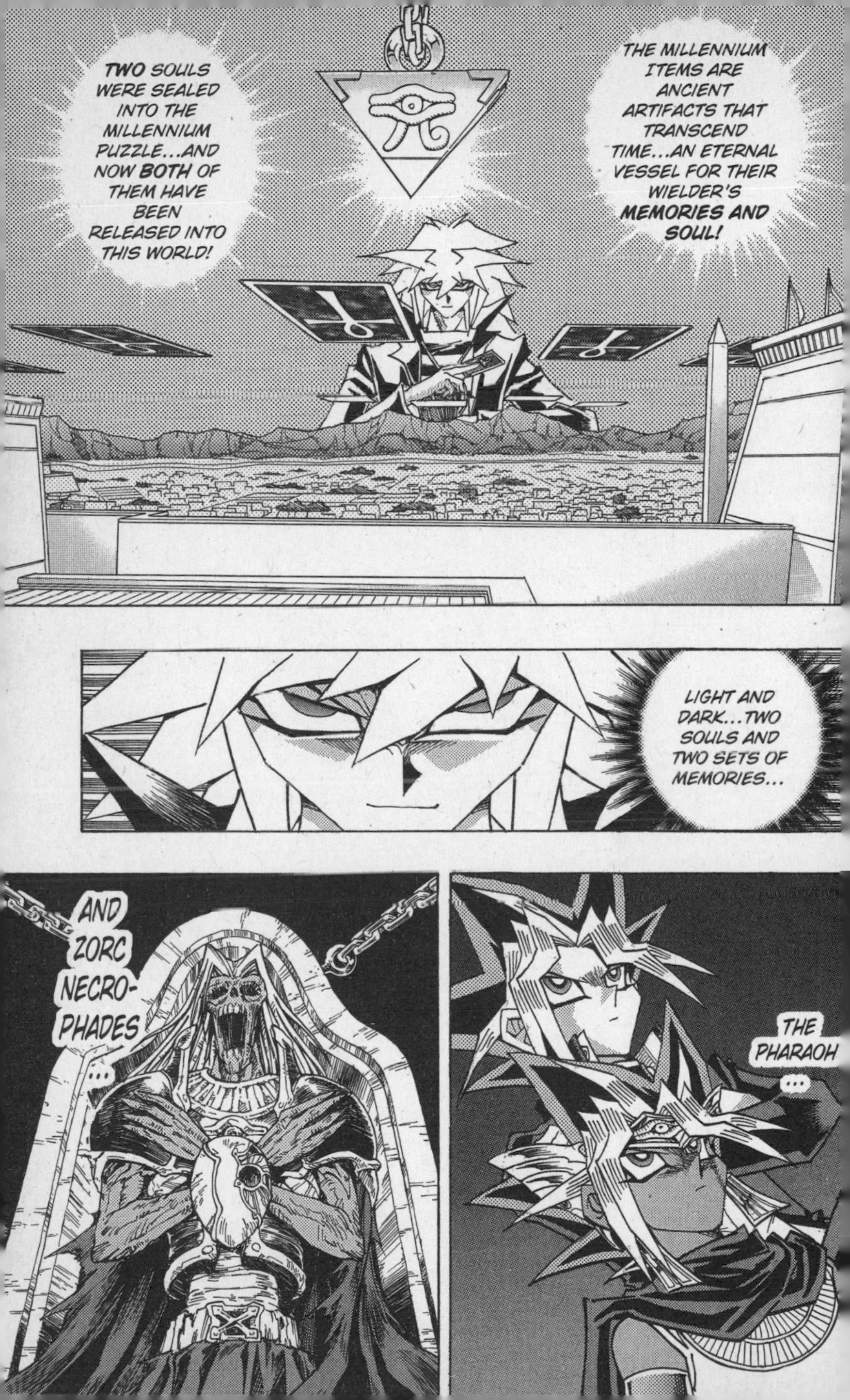
THE MILLENNIUM ITEMS ARE ANCIENT ARTIFACTS THAT TRANSCEND TIME...AN ETERNAL VESSEL FOR THEIR WIELDER'S MEMORIES AND SOUL!
TWO SOULS WERE SEALED INTO THE MILLENNIUM PUZZLE...AND NOW BOTH OF THEM HAVE BEEN RELEASED INTO THIS WORLD!
LIGHT AND DARK...TWO SOULS AND TWO SETS OF MEMORIES...
THE PHARAOH ...
AND ZORC NECRO-PHADES ...

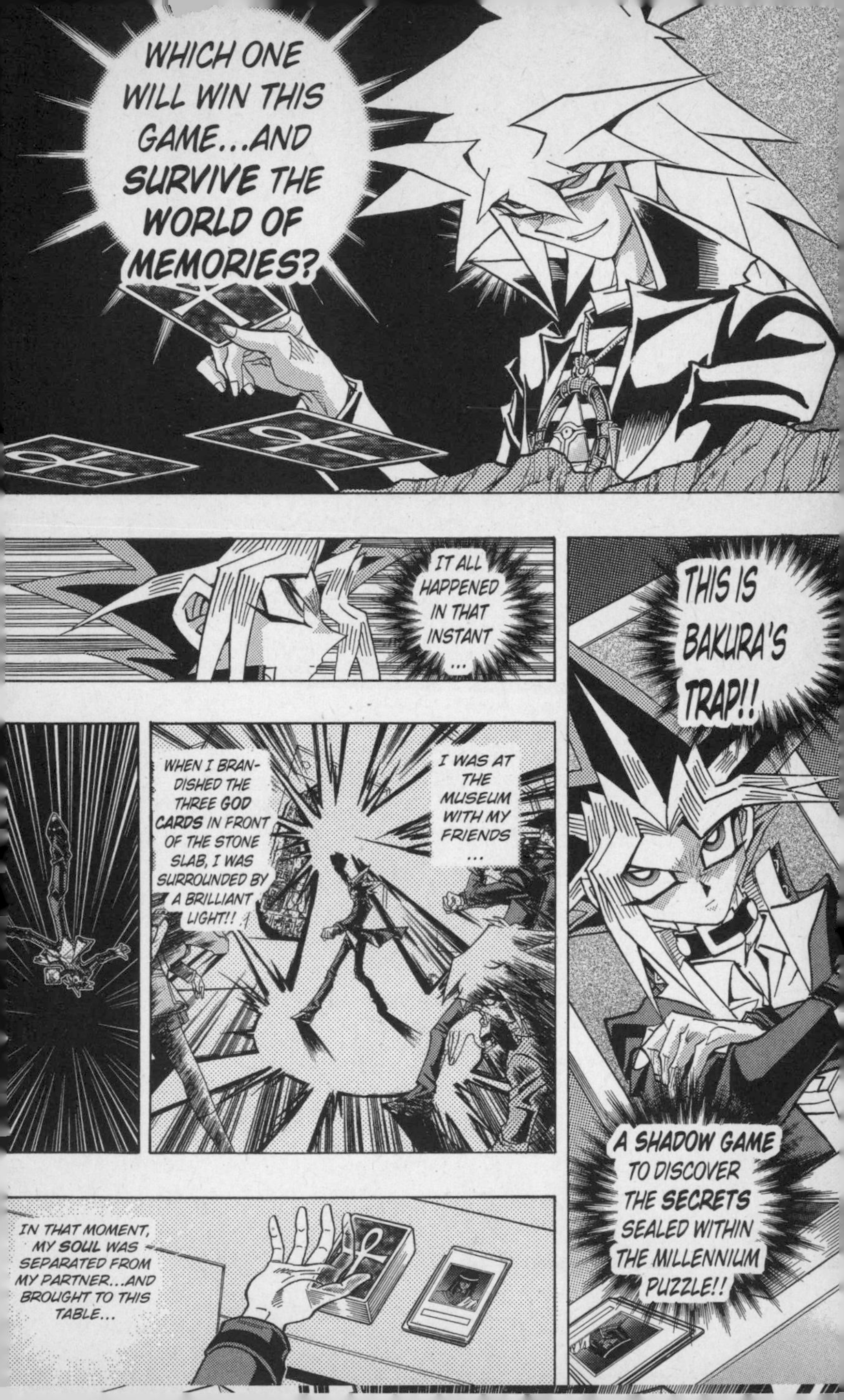
WHICH ONE WILL WIN THIS GAME...AND SURVIVE THE WORLD OF MEMORIES?
THIS IS BAKURA'S TRAP!!
A SHADOW GAME TO DISCOVER THE SECRETS SEALED WITHIN THE MILLENNIUM PUZZLE!!
IT ALL HAPPENED IN THAT INSTANT...
I WAS AT THE MUSEUM WITH MY FRIENDS...
WHEN I BRANDISHED THE THREE GOD CARDS IN FRONT OF THE STONE SLAB, I WAS SURROUNDED BY A BRILLIANT LIGHT!!
IN THAT MOMENT, MY SOUL WAS SEPARATED FROM MY PARTNER...AND BROUGHT TO THIS TABLE...

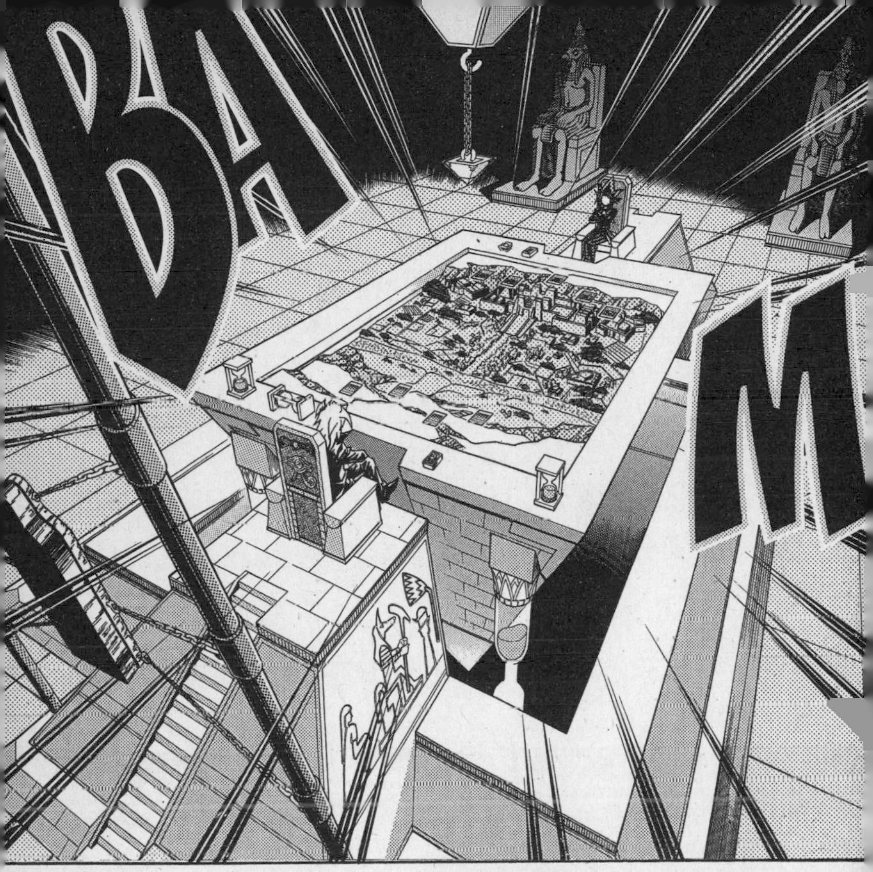

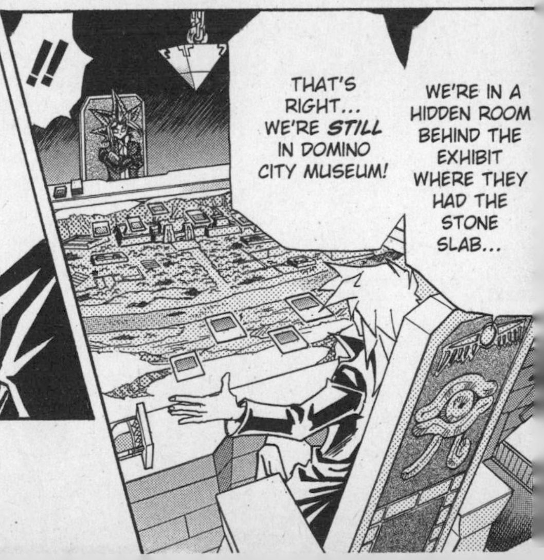
!!
THAT'S RIGHT... WE'RE STILL IN DOMINO CITY MUSEUM!
WE'RE IN A HIDDEN ROOM BEHIND THE EXHIBIT WHERE THEY HAD THE STONE SLAB...

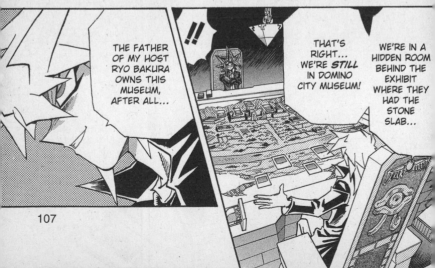

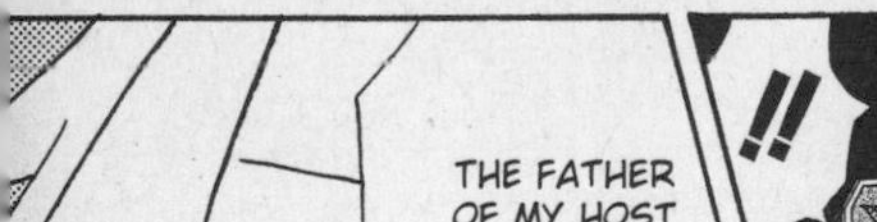
THE FATHER OF MY HOST RYO BAKURA OWNS THIS MUSEUM, AFTER ALL...

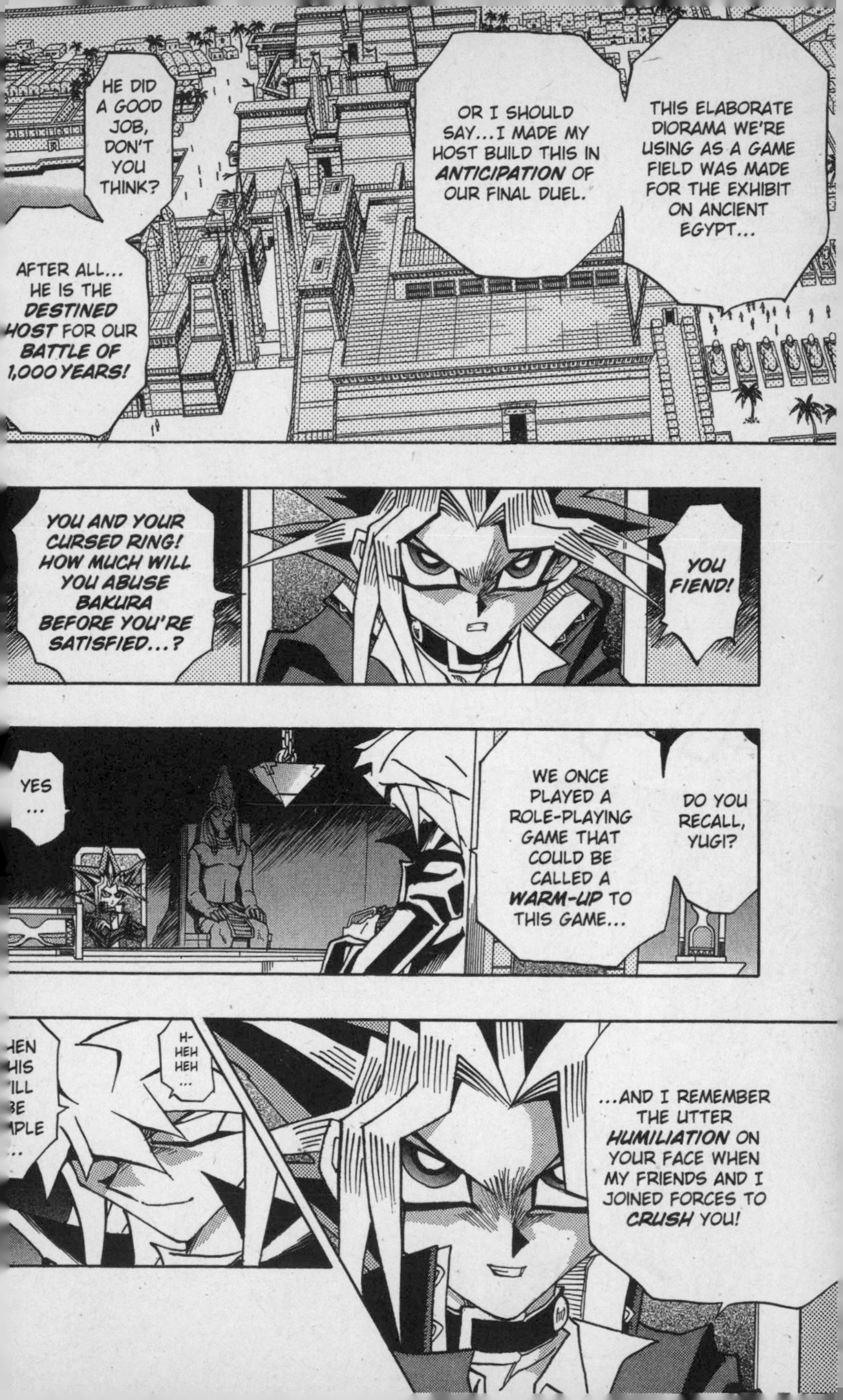
THIS ELABORATE DIORAMA WE'RE USING AS A GAME FIELD WAS MADE FOR THE EXHIBIT ON ANCIENT EGYPT...
OR I SHOULD SAY...I MADE MY HOST BUILD THIS IN *ANTICIPATION* OF OUR FINAL DUEL.
HE DID A GOOD JOB, DON'T YOU THINK?
AFTER ALL... HE IS THE *DESTINED HOST* FOR OUR *BATTLE OF 1,000 YEARS!*
YOU FIEND!
YOU AND YOUR CURSED RING! HOW MUCH WILL YOU ABUSE BAKURA BEFORE YOU'RE SATISFIED...?
DO YOU RECALL, YUGI?
WE ONCE PLAYED A ROLE-PLAYING GAME THAT COULD BE CALLED A *WARM-UP* TO THIS GAME...
YES ...
...AND I REMEMBER THE UTTER *HUMILIATION* ON YOUR FACE WHEN MY FRIENDS AND I JOINED FORCES TO *CRUSH* YOU!
H-HEH HEH ...
HEN THIS ILL BE MPLE ...

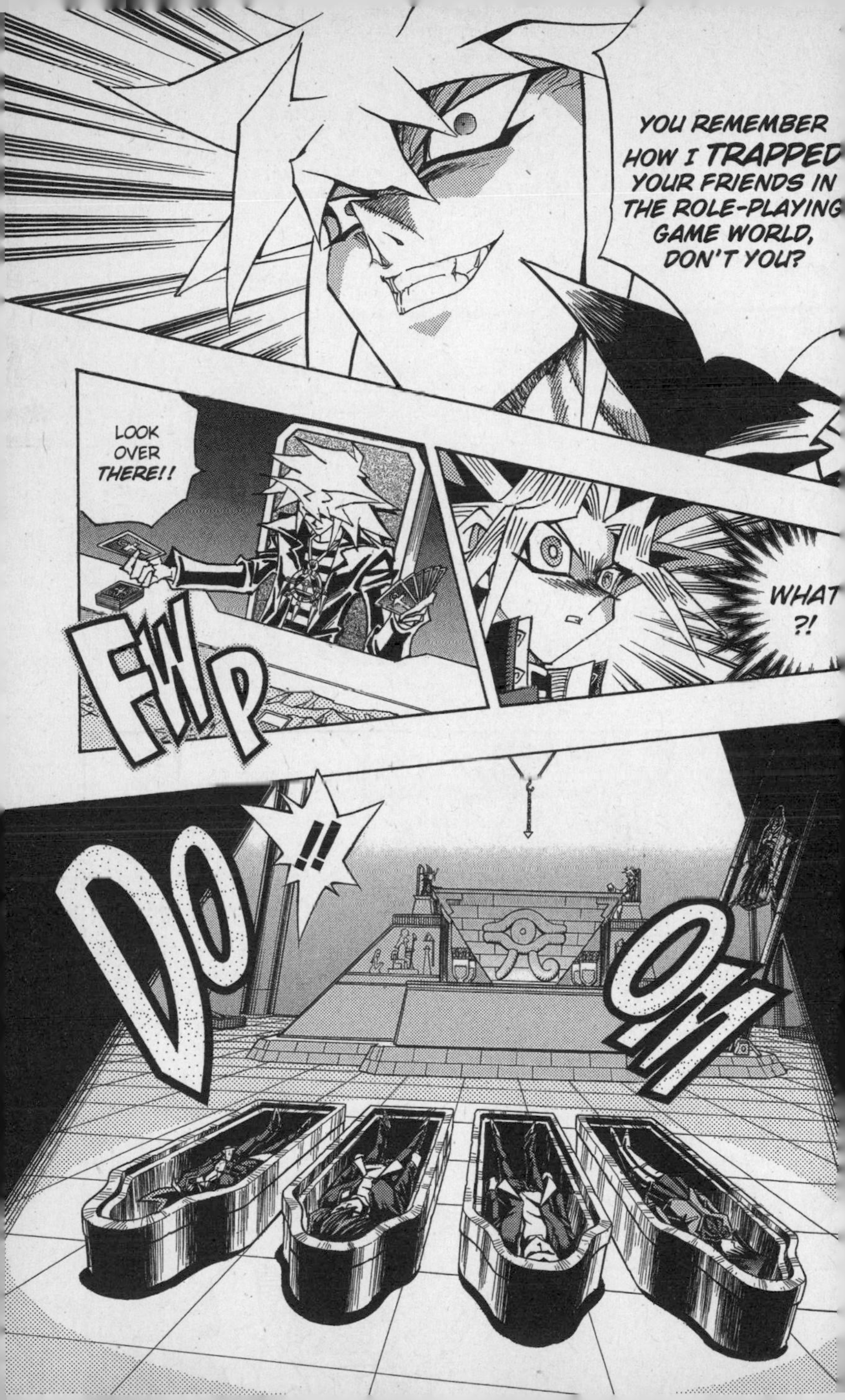
YOU REMEMBER HOW I TRAPPED YOUR FRIENDS IN THE ROLE-PLAYING GAME WORLD, DON'T YOU?
WHAT ?!
LOOK OVER THERE!!
FWP
DOOM
!!

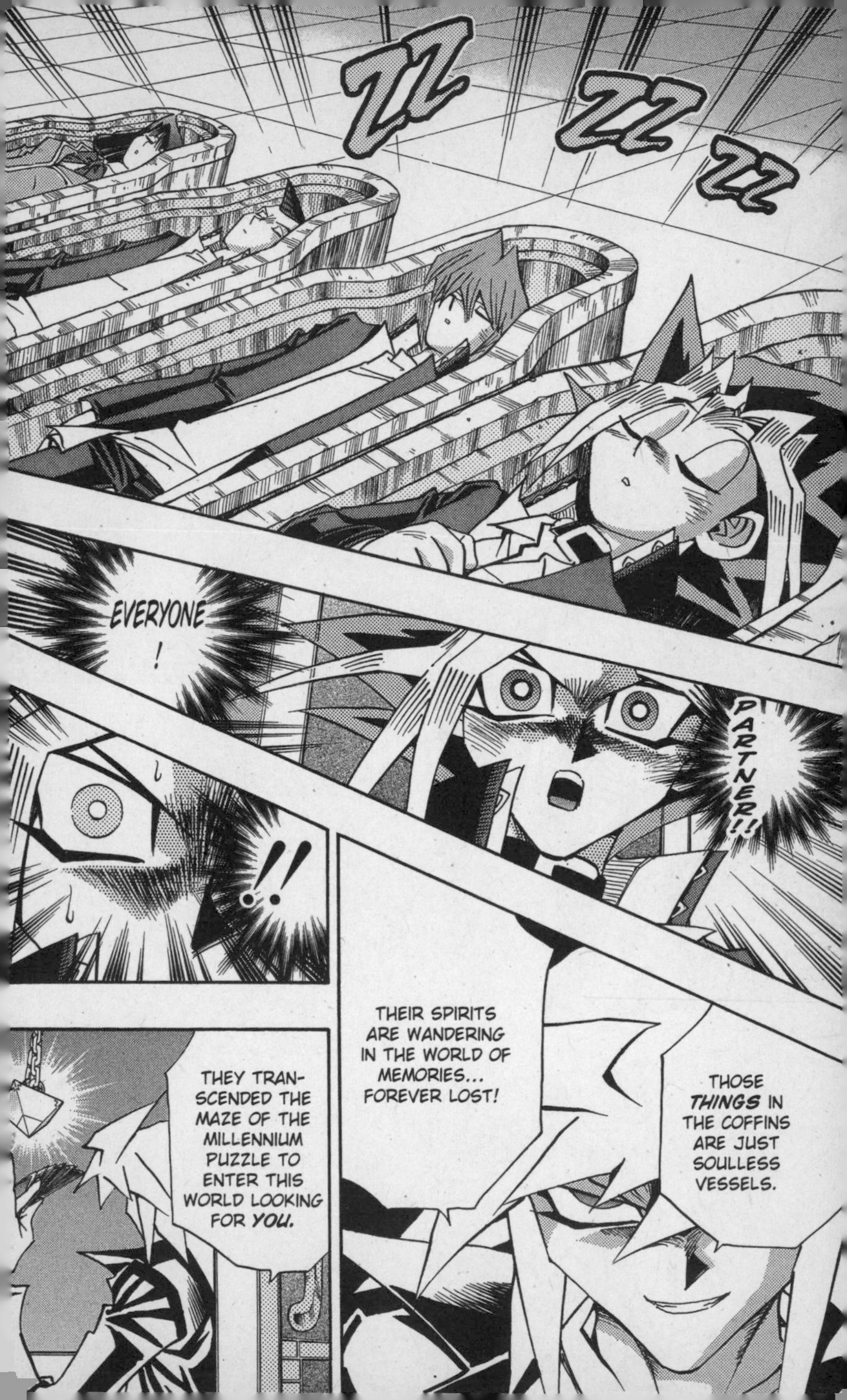
ZZ
ZZ
ZZ
EVERYONE!
PARTNER!!
!!
THOSE *THINGS* IN THE COFFINS ARE JUST SOULLESS VESSELS.
THEIR SPIRITS ARE WANDERING IN THE WORLD OF MEMORIES... FOREVER LOST!
THEY TRAN-SCENDED THE MAZE OF THE MILLENNIUM PUZZLE TO ENTER THIS WORLD LOOKING FOR *YOU*.

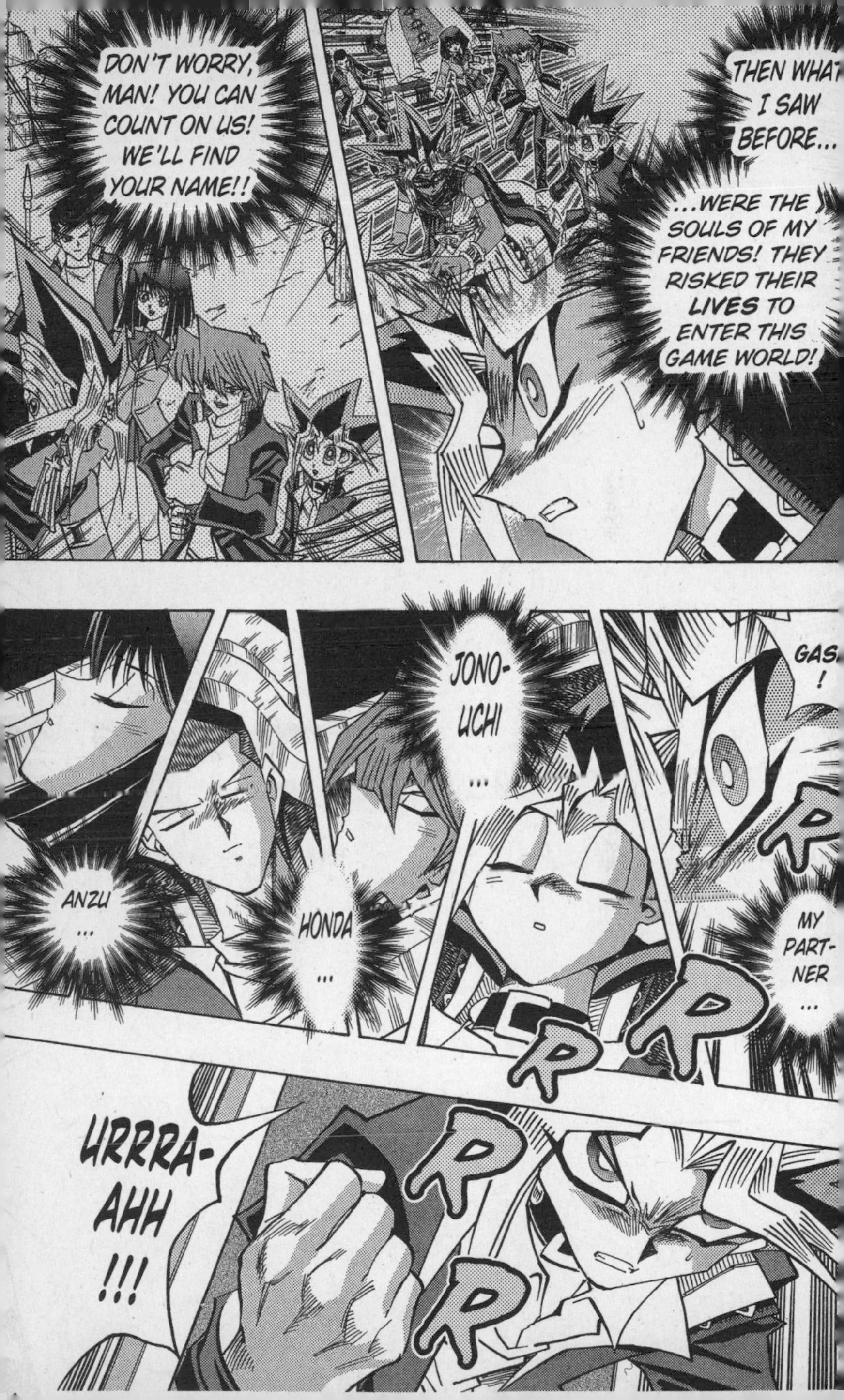
THEN WHAT I SAW BEFORE...
...WERE THE SOULS OF MY FRIENDS! THEY RISKED THEIR LIVES TO ENTER THIS GAME WORLD!
DON'T WORRY, MAN! YOU CAN COUNT ON US! WE'LL FIND YOUR NAME!!
GAS!
MY PART-NER...
JONO-UCHI...
HONDA...
ANZU...
R R R R R R
URRRA-AHH!!!

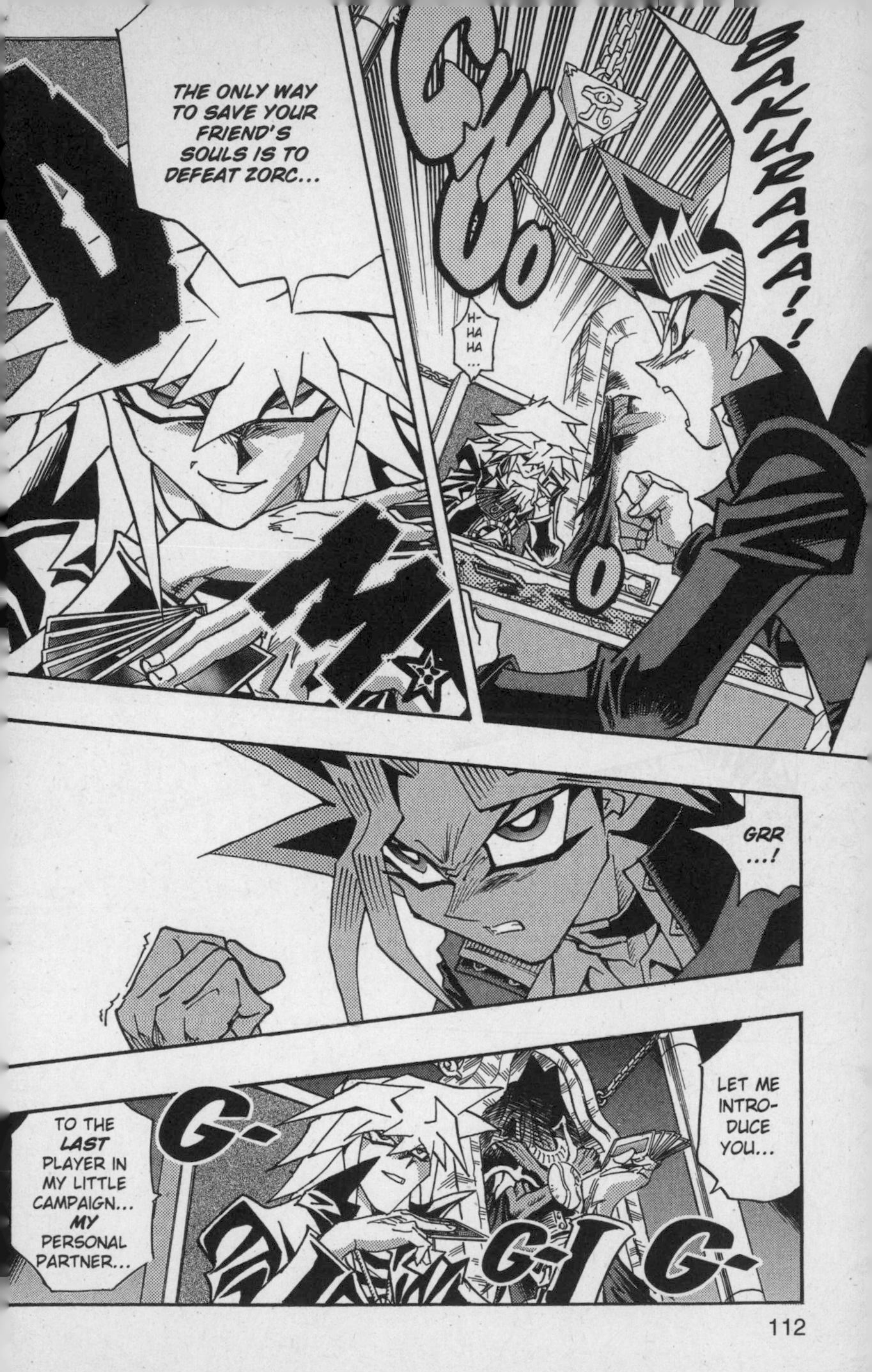
BAKURAAAA!!
H-HA HA...
THE ONLY WAY TO SAVE YOUR FRIEND'S SOULS IS TO DEFEAT ZORC...
GRR...!
LET ME INTRO-DUCE YOU...
TO THE LAST PLAYER IN MY LITTLE CAMPAIGN... MY PERSONAL PARTNER...
G-
G-I
G-

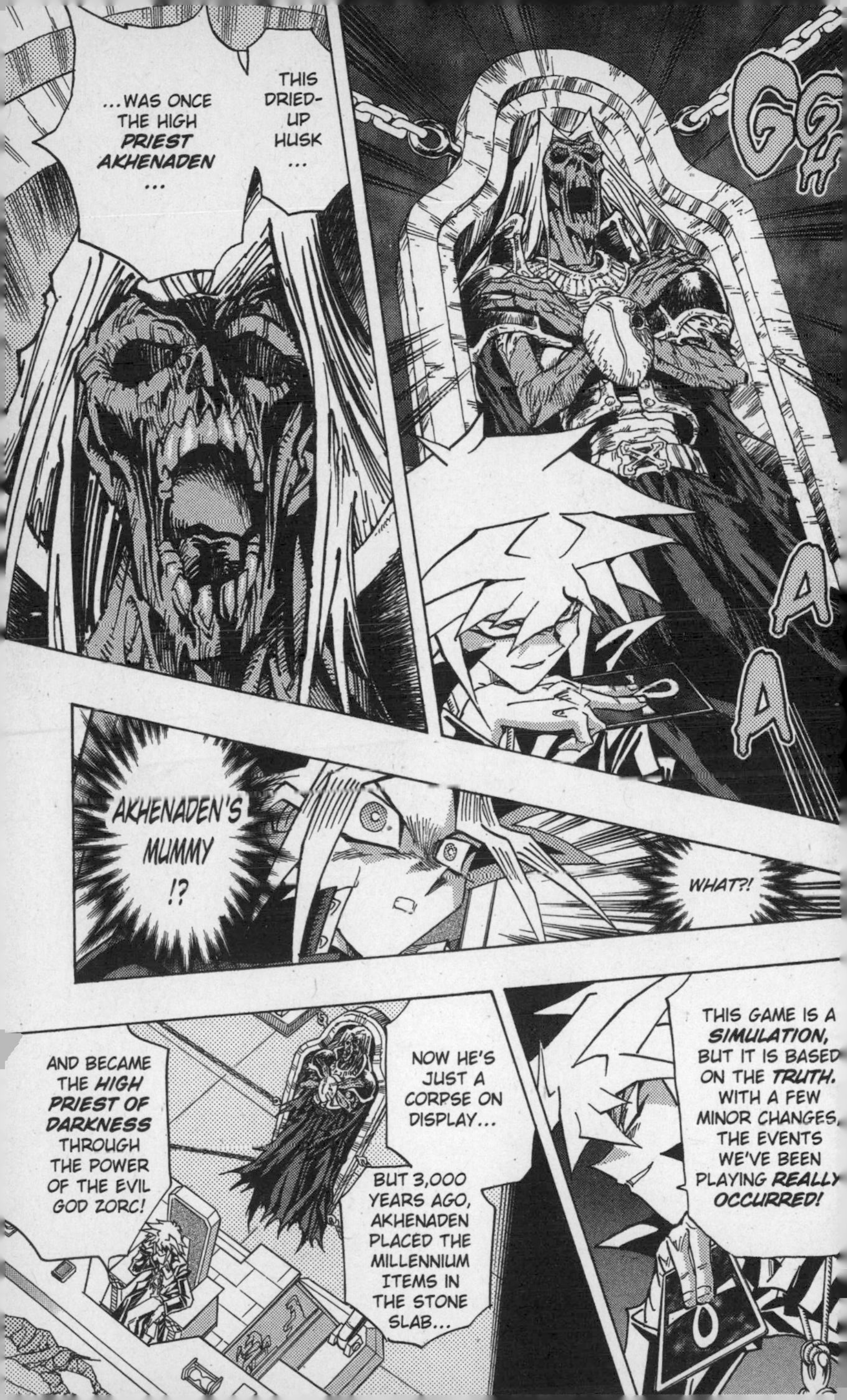
GG
A
A
THIS DRIED-UP HUSK...
...WAS ONCE THE HIGH *PRIEST AKHENADEN*...
WHAT?!
AKHENADEN'S MUMMY!?
THIS GAME IS A *SIMULATION*, BUT IT IS BASED ON THE *TRUTH*. WITH A FEW MINOR CHANGES, THE EVENTS WE'VE BEEN PLAYING *REALLY OCCURRED!*
NOW HE'S JUST A CORPSE ON DISPLAY...
BUT 3,000 YEARS AGO, AKHENADEN PLACED THE MILLENNIUM ITEMS IN THE STONE SLAB...
AND BECAME THE *HIGH PRIEST OF DARKNESS* THROUGH THE POWER OF THE EVIL GOD ZORC!

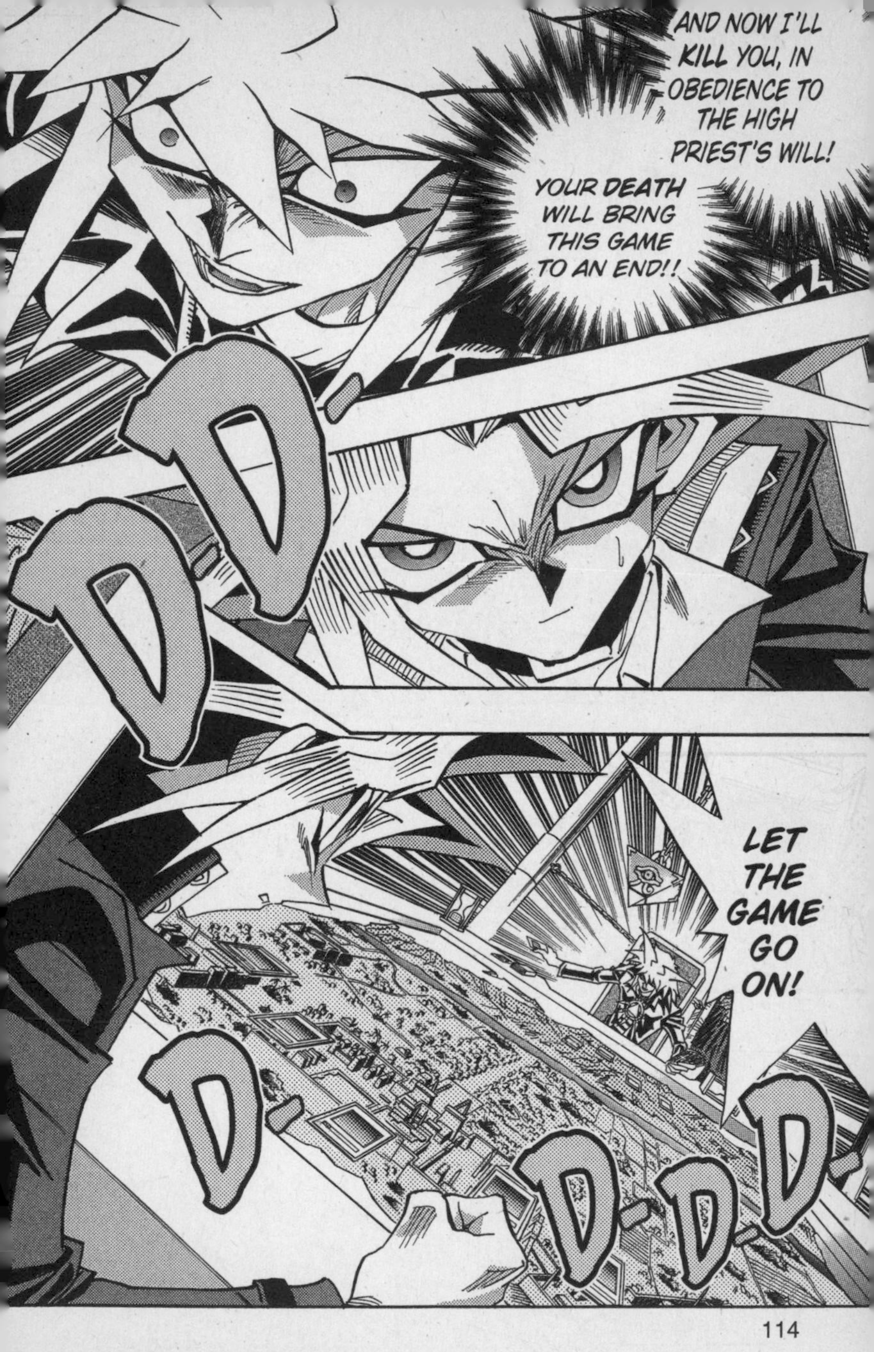
AND NOW I'LL KILL YOU, IN OBEDIENCE TO THE HIGH PRIEST'S WILL!
YOUR DEATH WILL BRING THIS GAME TO AN END!!
DD
LET THE GAME GO ON!
D-D-D-D-

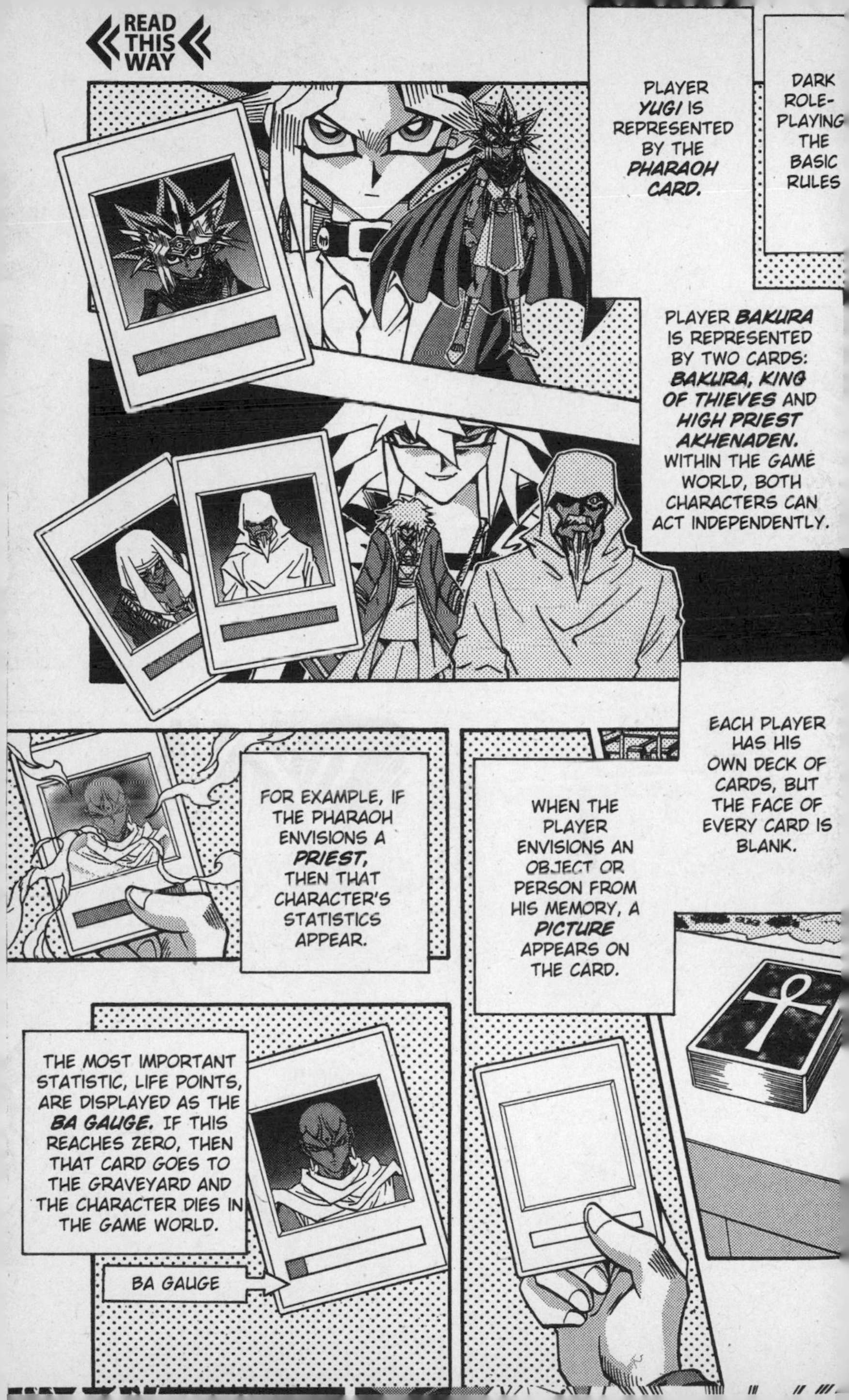
READ THIS WAY
DARK ROLE-PLAYING THE BASIC RULES
PLAYER YUGI IS REPRESENTED BY THE PHARAOH CARD.
PLAYER BAKURA IS REPRESENTED BY TWO CARDS: BAKURA, KING OF THIEVES AND HIGH PRIEST AKHENADEN. WITHIN THE GAME WORLD, BOTH CHARACTERS CAN ACT INDEPENDENTLY.
EACH PLAYER HAS HIS OWN DECK OF CARDS, BUT THE FACE OF EVERY CARD IS BLANK.
WHEN THE PLAYER ENVISIONS AN OBJECT OR PERSON FROM HIS MEMORY, A PICTURE APPEARS ON THE CARD.
FOR EXAMPLE, IF THE PHARAOH ENVISIONS A PRIEST, THEN THAT CHARACTER'S STATISTICS APPEAR.
THE MOST IMPORTANT STATISTIC, LIFE POINTS, ARE DISPLAYED AS THE BA GAUGE. IF THIS REACHES ZERO, THEN THAT CARD GOES TO THE GRAVEYARD AND THE CHARACTER DIES IN THE GAME WORLD.
BA GAUGE

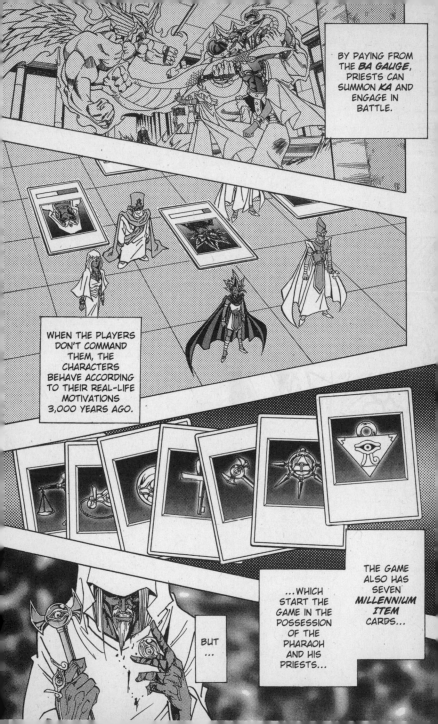

BY PAYING FROM THE *BA GAUGE*, PRIESTS CAN SUMMON *KA* AND ENGAGE IN BATTLE.

WHEN THE PLAYERS DON'T COMMAND THEM, THE CHARACTERS BEHAVE ACCORDING TO THEIR REAL-LIFE MOTIVATIONS 3,000 YEARS AGO.

THE GAME ALSO HAS SEVEN *MILLENNIUM ITEM* CARDS...

...WHICH START THE GAME IN THE POSSESSION OF THE PHARAOH AND HIS PRIESTS...

BUT ...

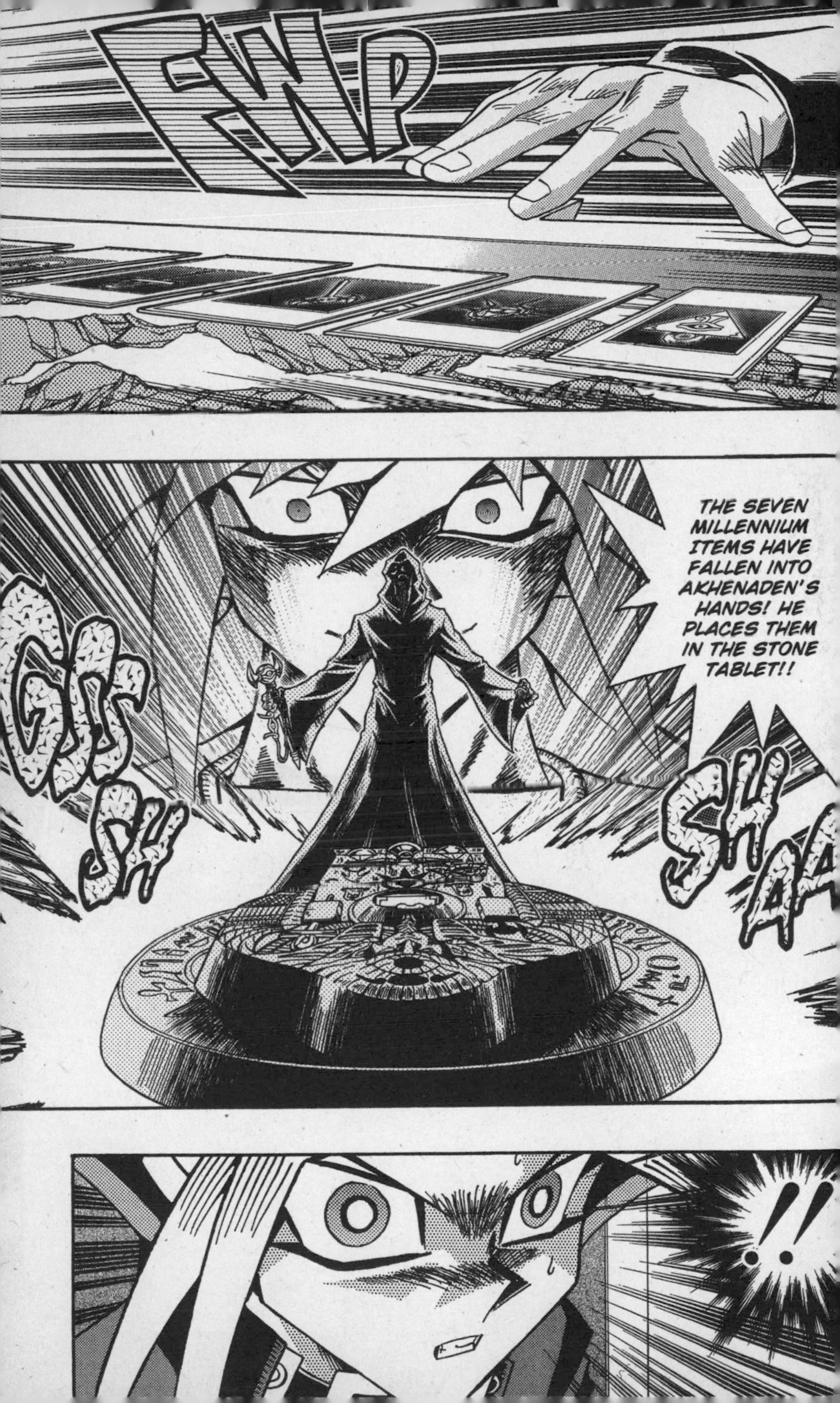
FWIP
THE SEVEN MILLENNIUM ITEMS HAVE FALLEN INTO AKHENADEN'S HANDS! HE PLACES THEM IN THE STONE TABLET!!
SHAA
!!

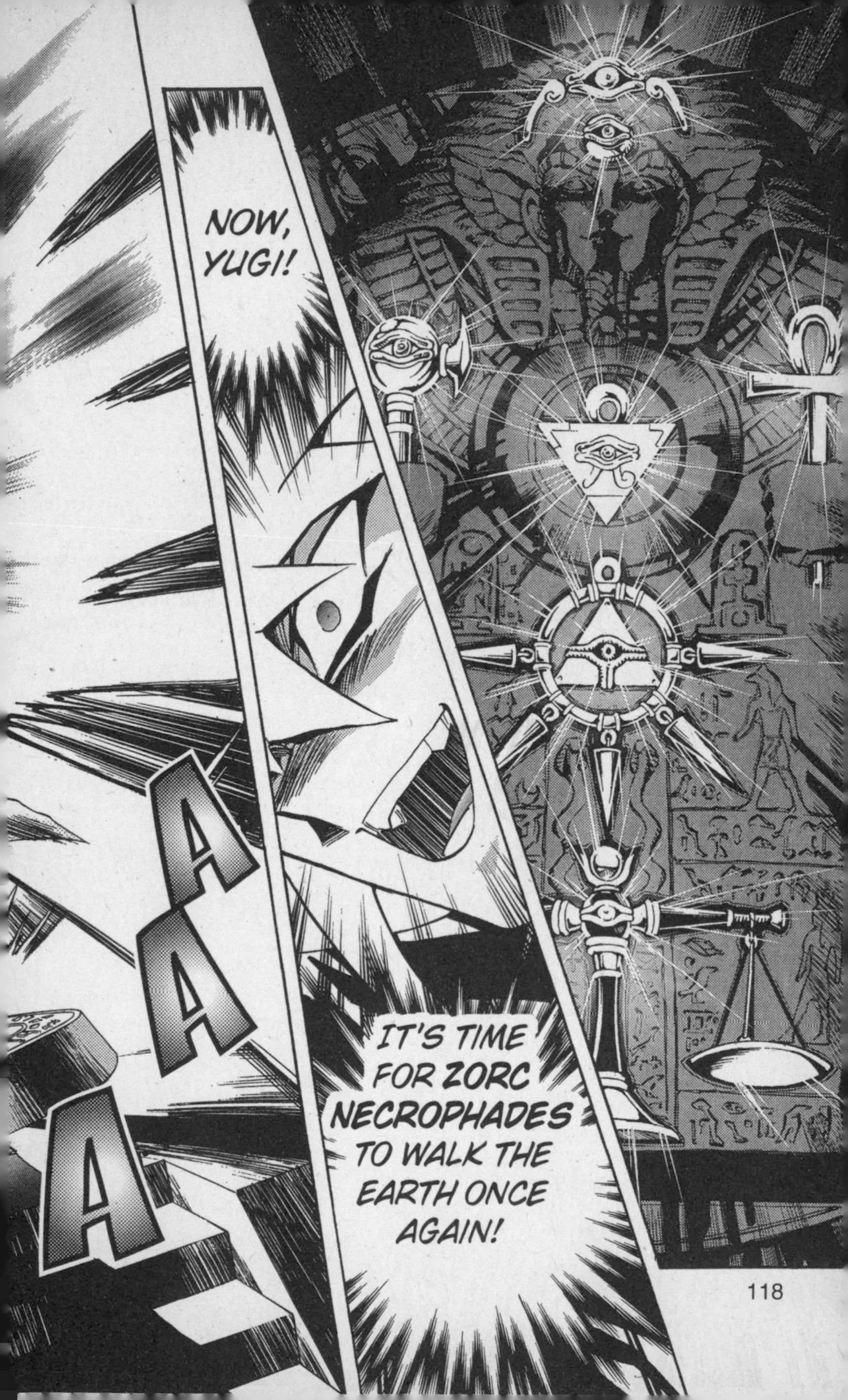
NOW, YUGI!
IT'S TIME FOR ZORC NECROPHADES TO WALK THE EARTH ONCE AGAIN!
AAA

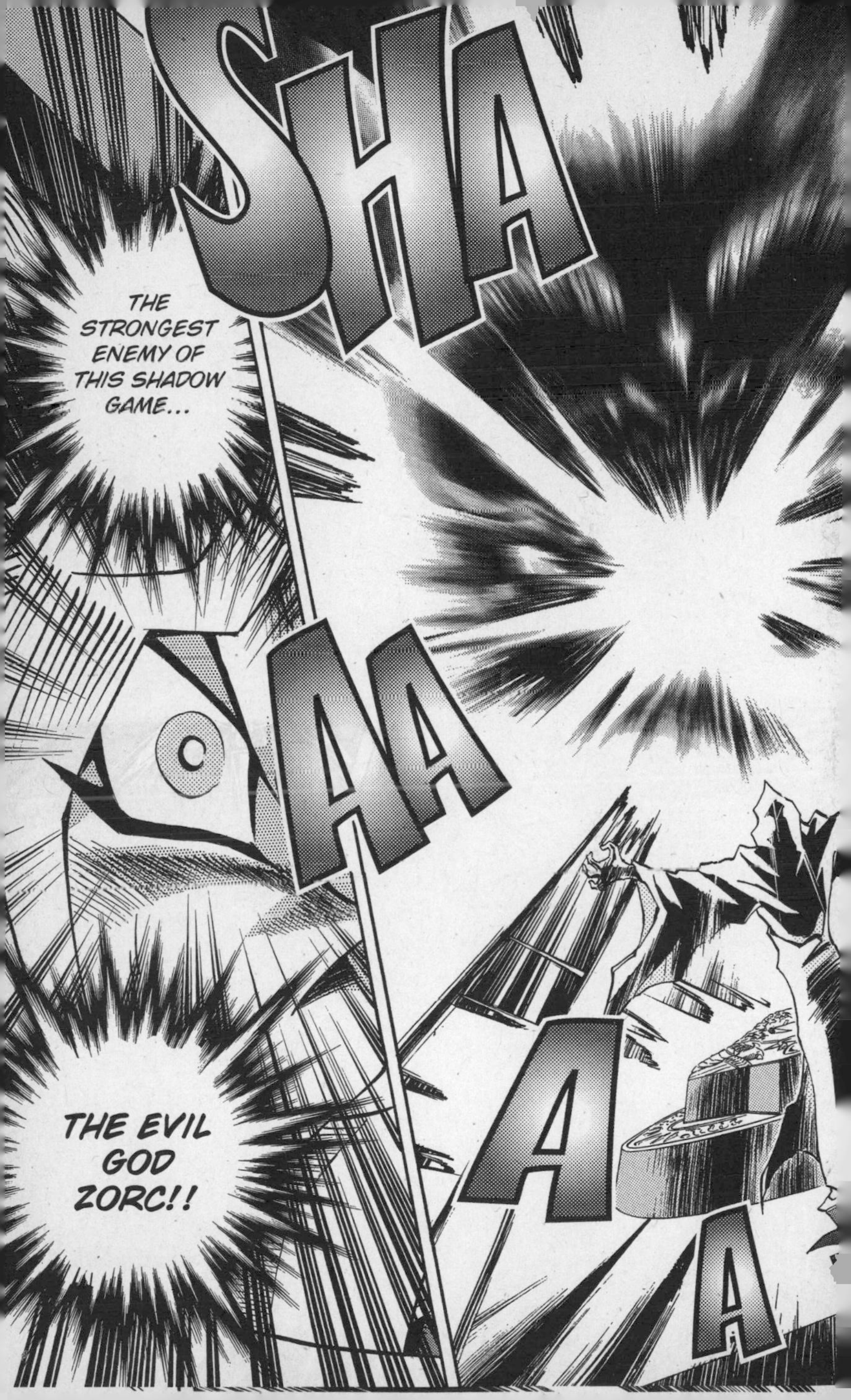
SHAAAAA
THE STRONGEST ENEMY OF THIS SHADOW GAME...
THE EVIL GOD ZORC!!

Duel 43: The Dark God Awakes!

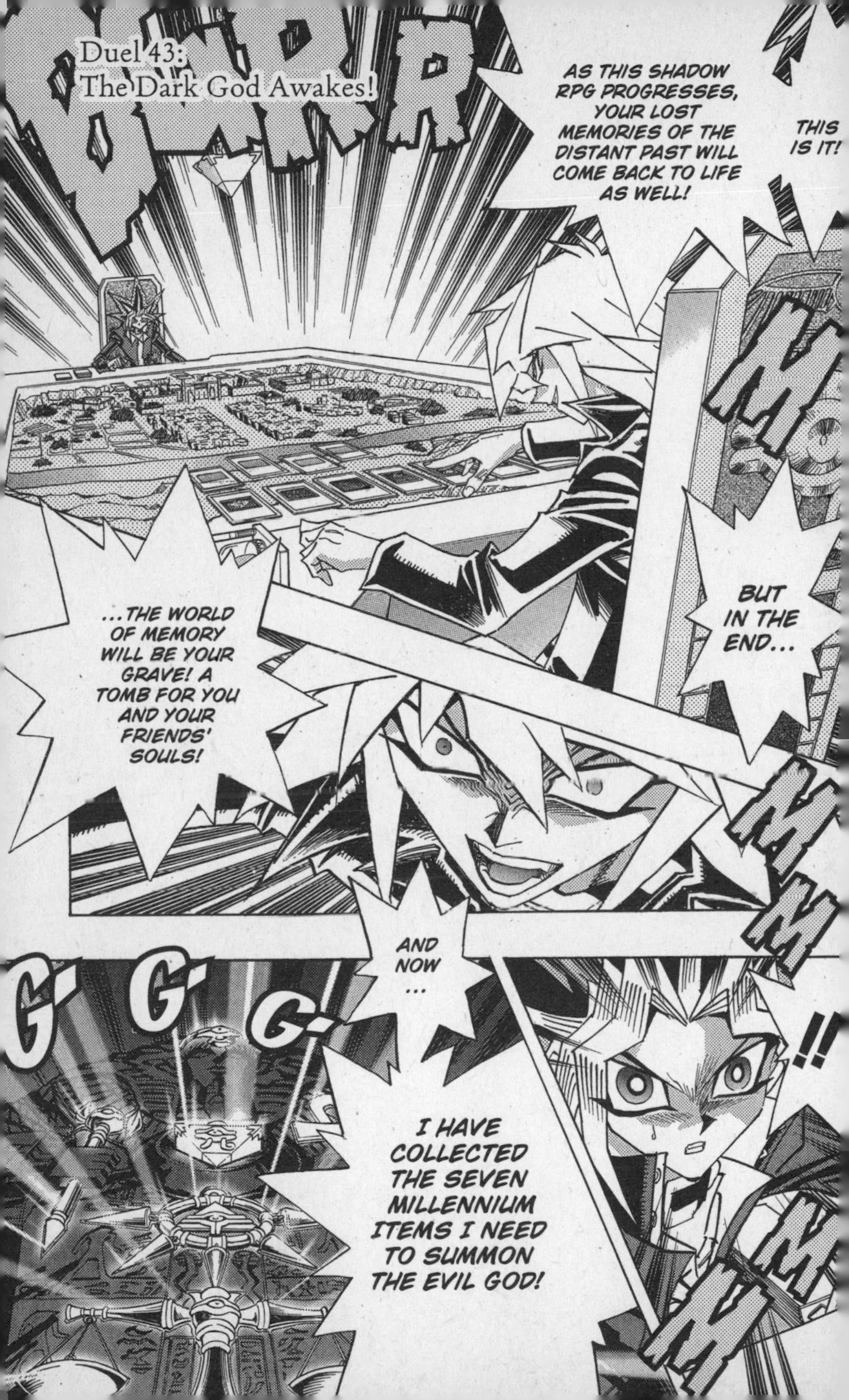
THIS IS IT!
AS THIS SHADOW RPG PROGRESSES, YOUR LOST MEMORIES OF THE DISTANT PAST WILL COME BACK TO LIFE AS WELL!
BUT IN THE END...
...THE WORLD OF MEMORY WILL BE YOUR GRAVE! A TOMB FOR YOU AND YOUR FRIENDS' SOULS!
!!
AND NOW...
I HAVE COLLECTED THE SEVEN MILLENNIUM ITEMS I NEED TO SUMMON THE EVIL GOD!

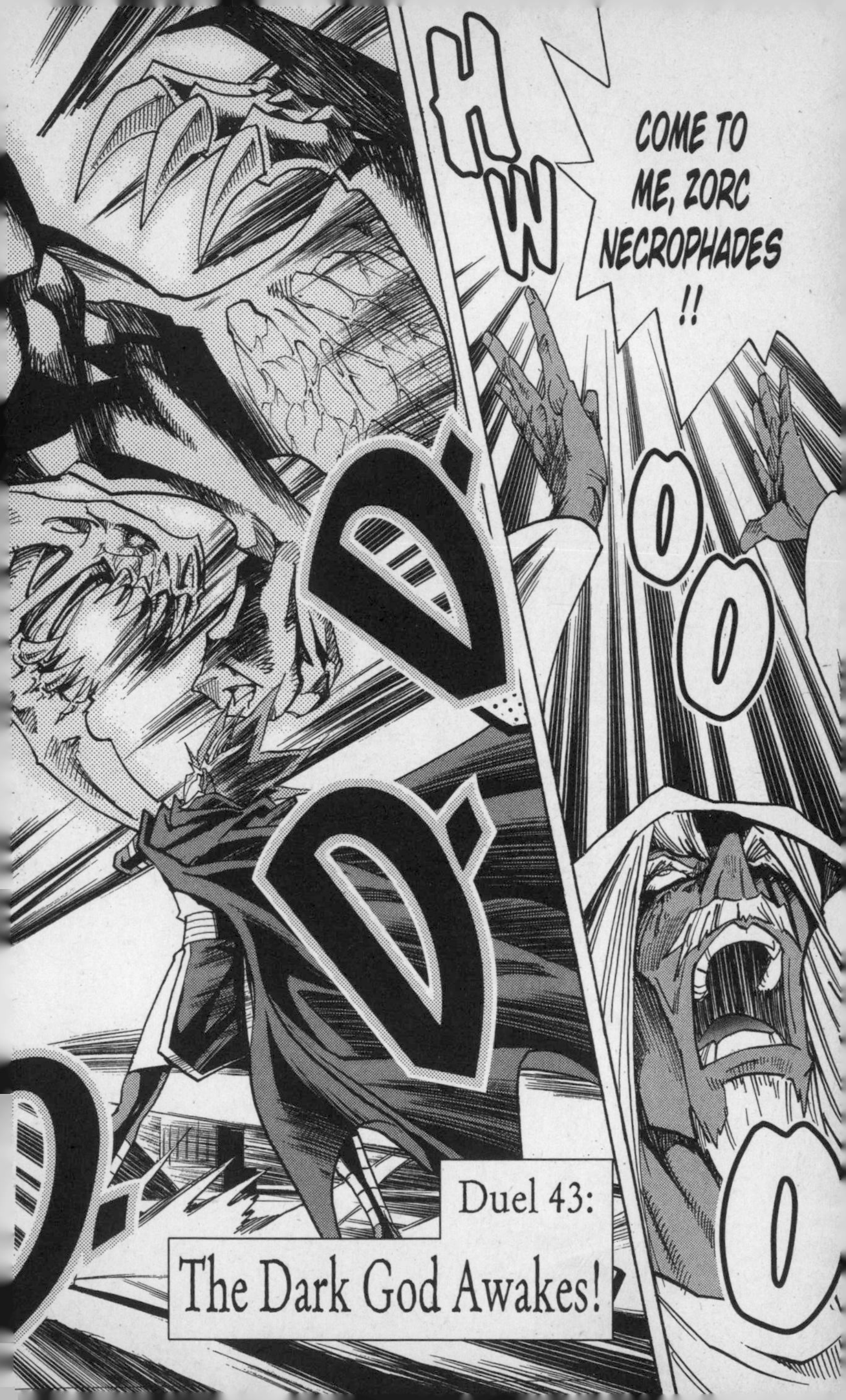
COME TO ME, ZORC NECROPHADES !!
HWN
OOOO
DDD
Duel 43:
The Dark God Awakes!

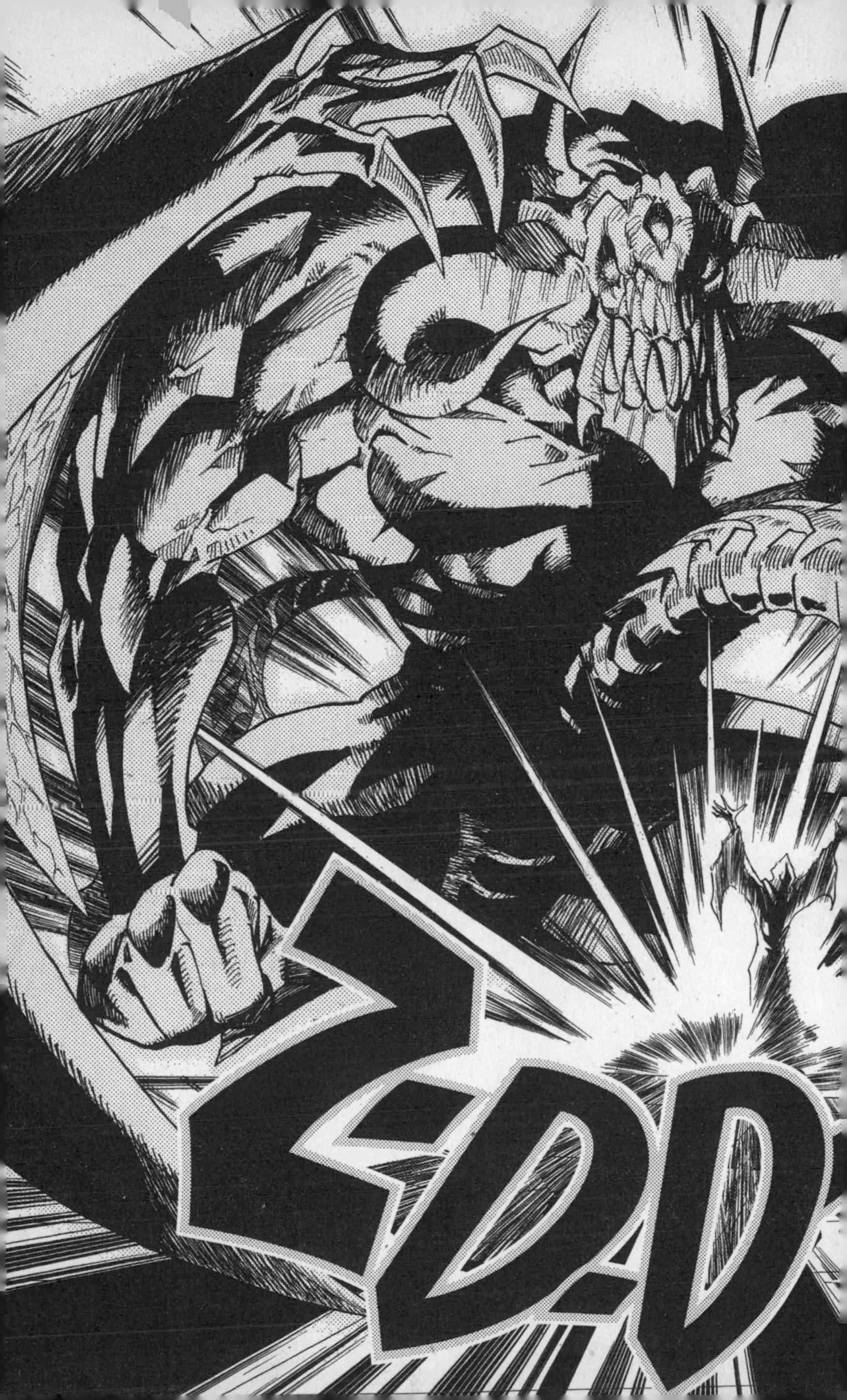
ZDD

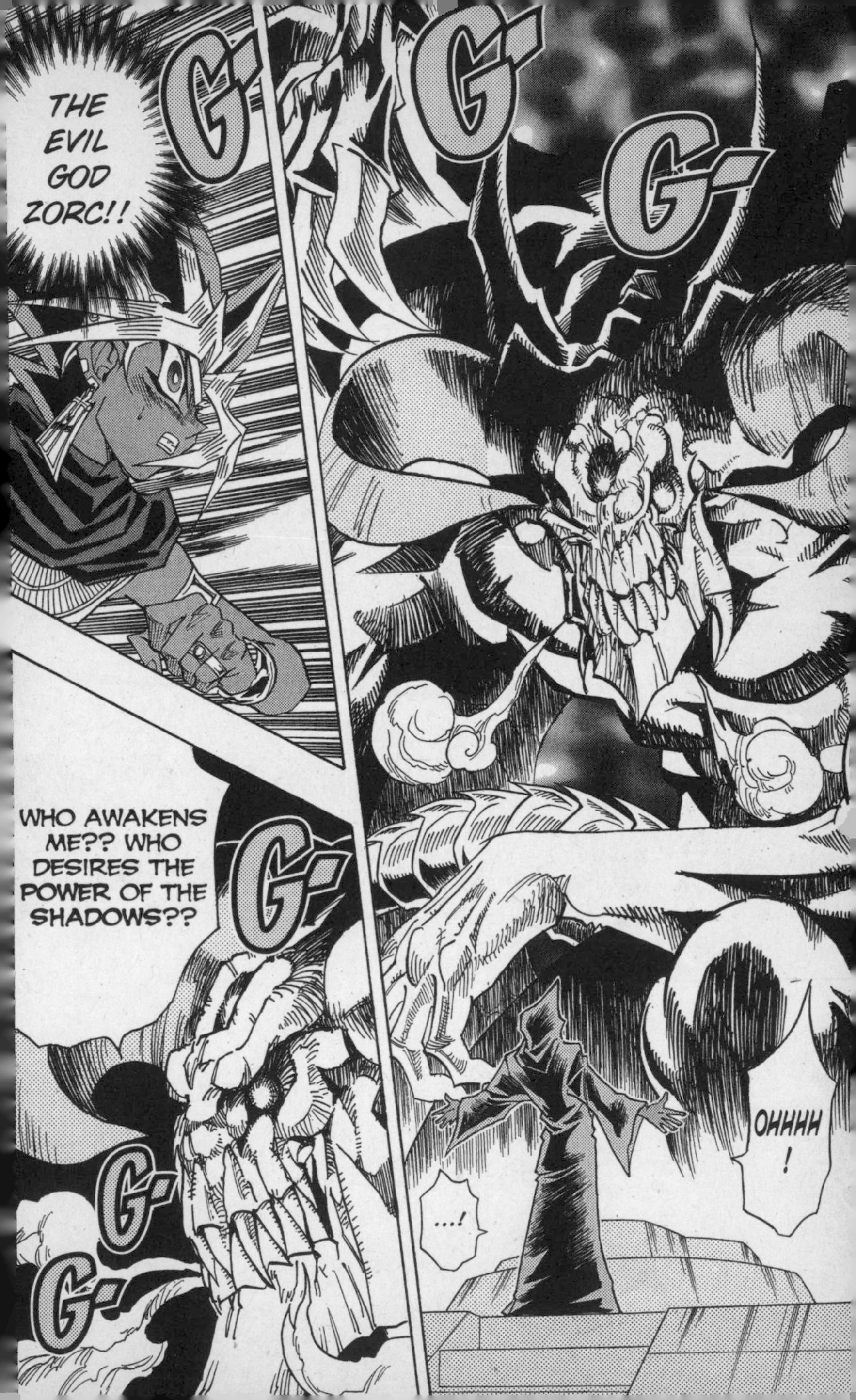
G-
G-
G-
OHHHH!
...!
THE EVIL GOD ZORC!!
WHO AWAKENS ME?? WHO DESIRES THE POWER OF THE SHADOWS??
G-
G-
G-

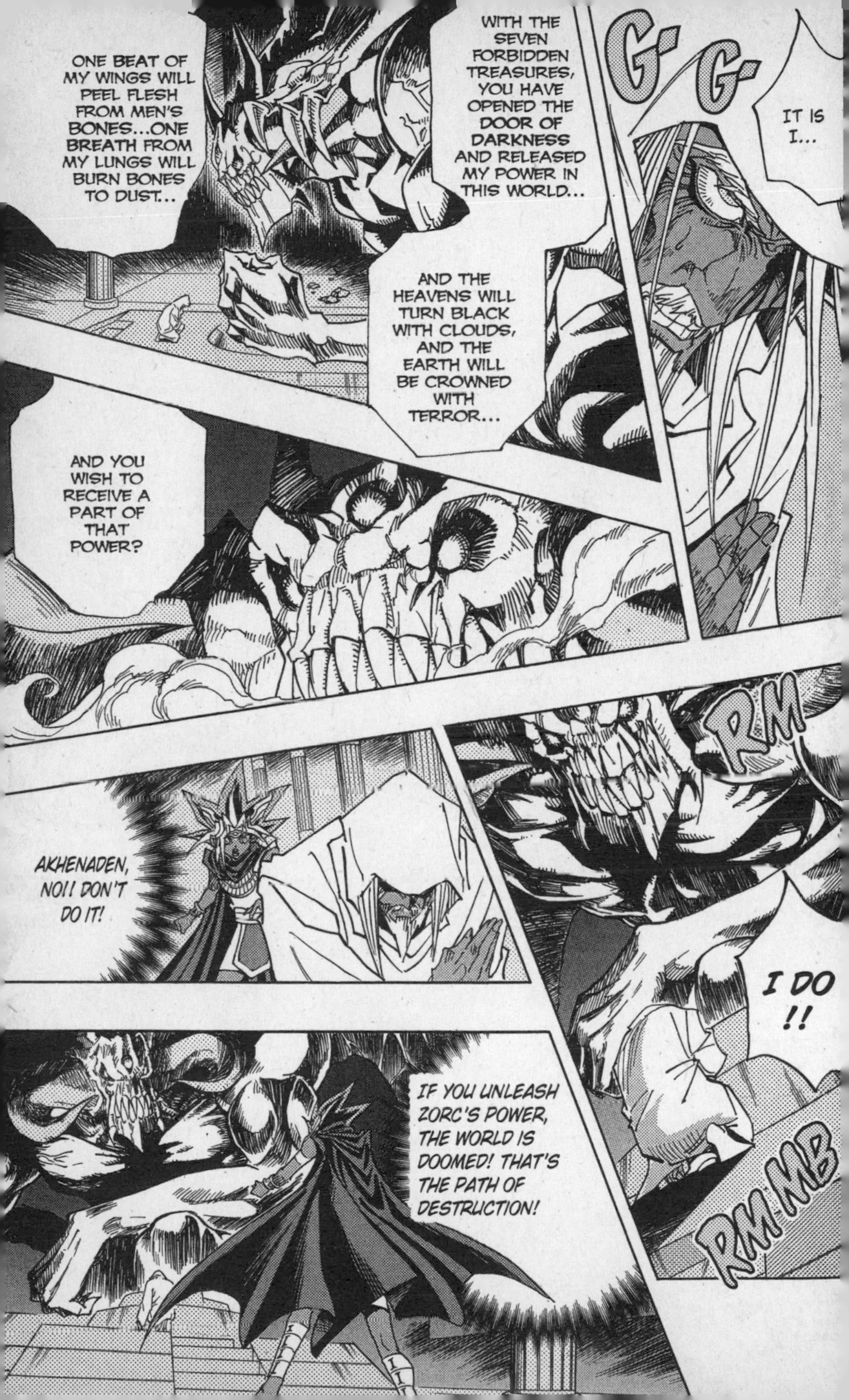
G-G-
IT IS I...
WITH THE SEVEN FORBIDDEN TREASURES, YOU HAVE OPENED THE DOOR OF DARKNESS AND RELEASED MY POWER IN THIS WORLD...
ONE BEAT OF MY WINGS WILL PEEL FLESH FROM MEN'S BONES...ONE BREATH FROM MY LUNGS WILL BURN BONES TO DUST...
AND THE HEAVENS WILL TURN BLACK WITH CLOUDS, AND THE EARTH WILL BE CROWNED WITH TERROR...
AND YOU WISH TO RECEIVE A PART OF THAT POWER?
RM
I DO !!
RMMB
AKHENADEN, NO!! DON'T DO IT!
IF YOU UNLEASH ZORC'S POWER, THE WORLD IS DOOMED! THAT'S THE PATH OF DESTRUCTION!

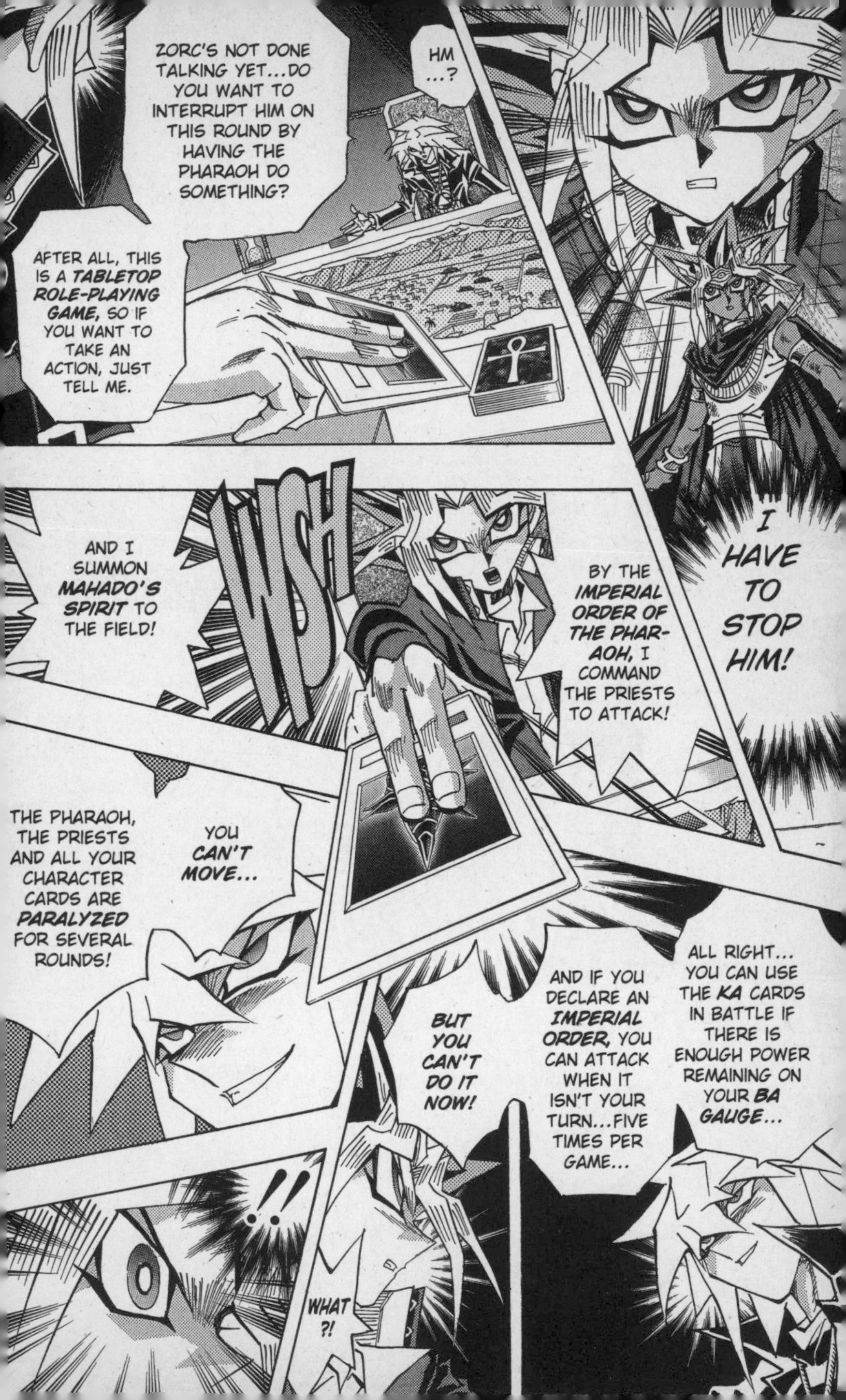
HM ...?
ZORC'S NOT DONE TALKING YET...DO YOU WANT TO INTERRUPT HIM ON THIS ROUND BY HAVING THE PHARAOH DO SOMETHING?
AFTER ALL, THIS IS A TABLETOP ROLE-PLAYING GAME, SO IF YOU WANT TO TAKE AN ACTION, JUST TELL ME.
I HAVE TO STOP HIM!
BY THE IMPERIAL ORDER OF THE PHARAOH, I COMMAND THE PRIESTS TO ATTACK!
WSH
AND I SUMMON MAHADO'S SPIRIT TO THE FIELD!
ALL RIGHT... YOU CAN USE THE KA CARDS IN BATTLE IF THERE IS ENOUGH POWER REMAINING ON YOUR BA GAUGE...
AND IF YOU DECLARE AN IMPERIAL ORDER, YOU CAN ATTACK WHEN IT ISN'T YOUR TURN...FIVE TIMES PER GAME...
BUT YOU CAN'T DO IT NOW!
YOU CAN'T MOVE...
THE PHARAOH, THE PRIESTS AND ALL YOUR CHARACTER CARDS ARE PARALYZED FOR SEVERAL ROUNDS!
WHAT ?!
!!

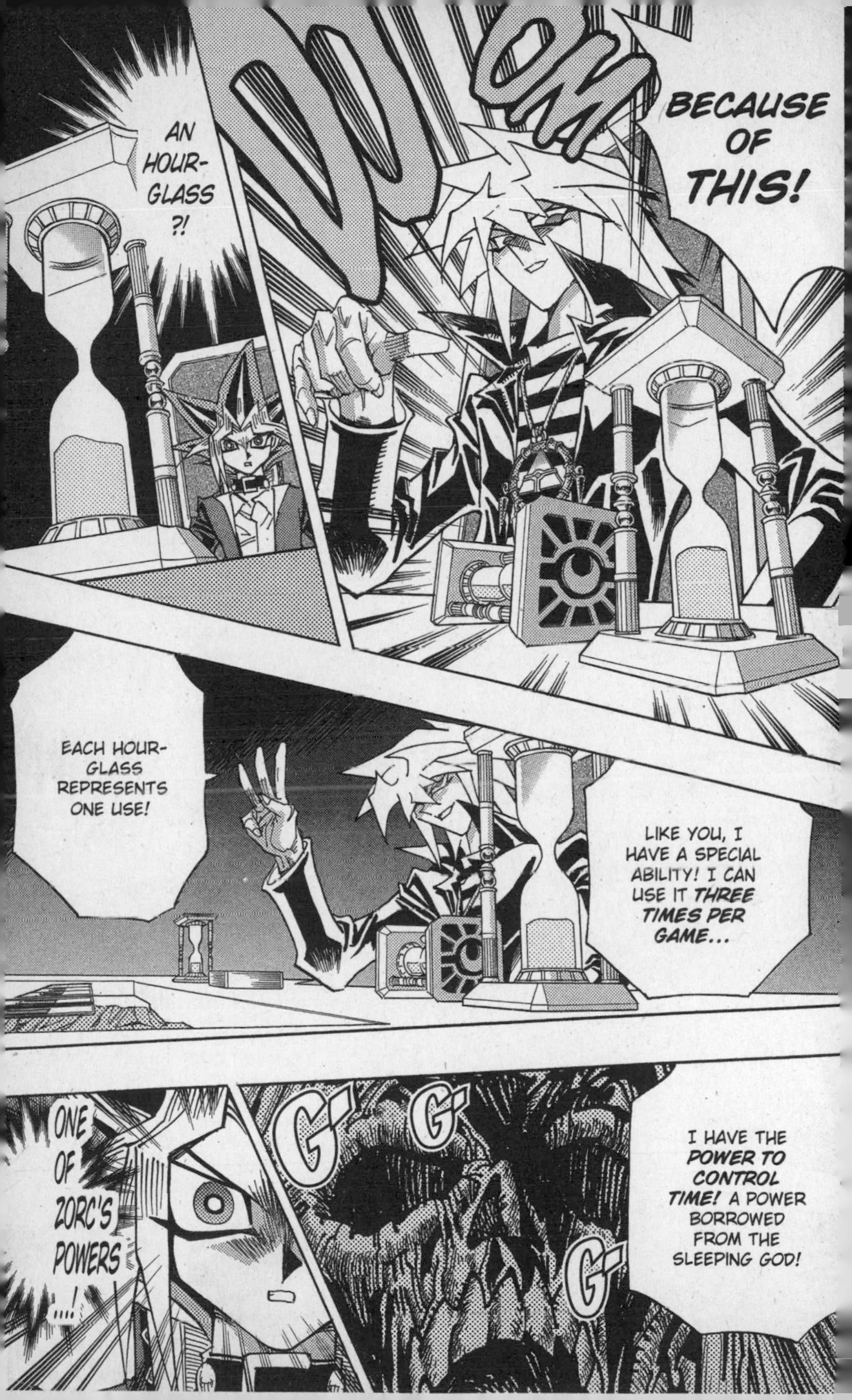
BECAUSE OF THIS!
AN HOUR-GLASS ?!
LIKE YOU, I HAVE A SPECIAL ABILITY! I CAN USE IT *THREE TIMES PER GAME...*
EACH HOUR-GLASS REPRESENTS ONE USE!
I HAVE THE *POWER TO CONTROL TIME!* A POWER BORROWED FROM THE SLEEPING GOD!
G G G
ONE OF ZORC'S POWERS ...!

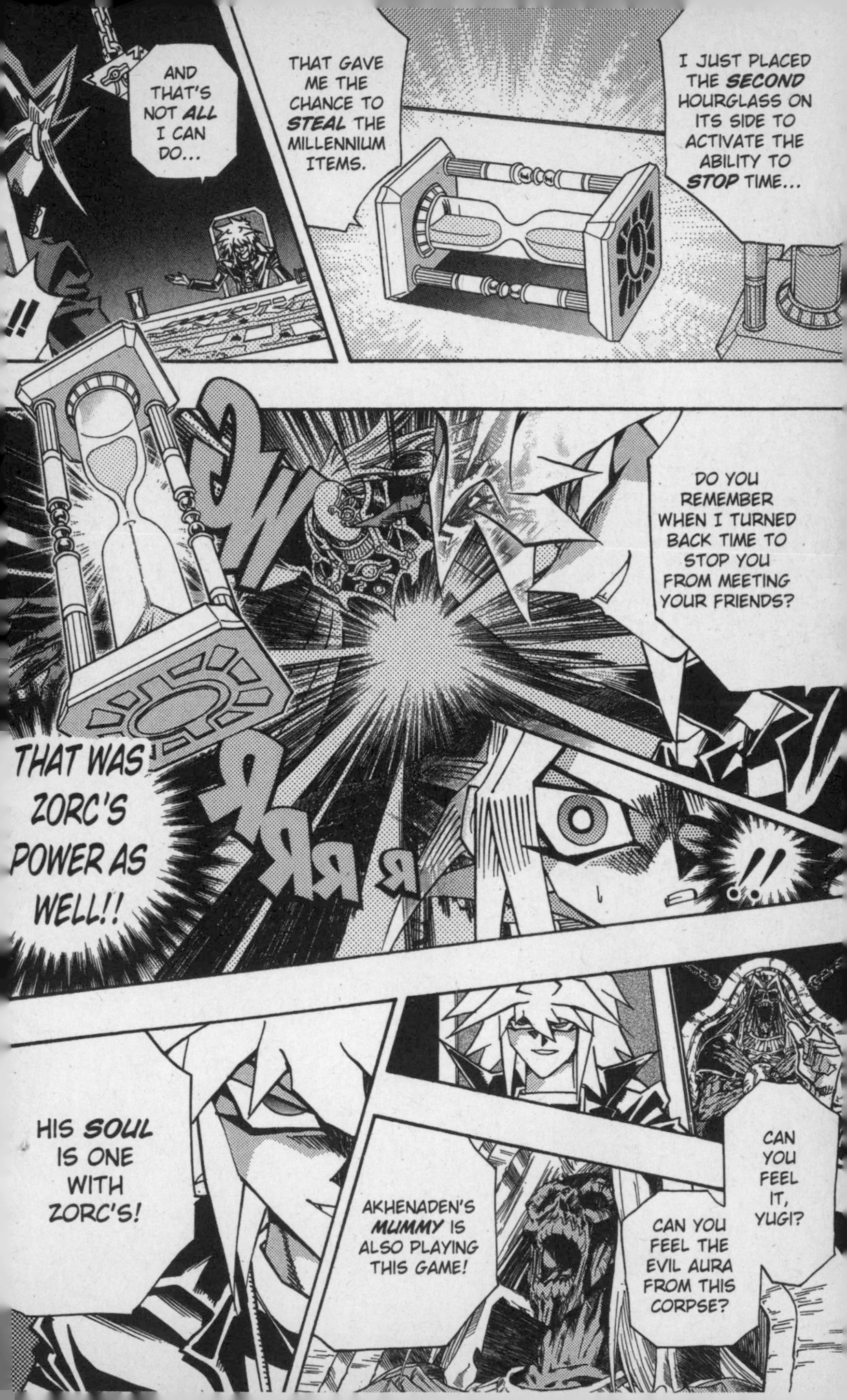
I JUST PLACED THE *SECOND* HOURGLASS ON ITS SIDE TO ACTIVATE THE ABILITY TO *STOP* TIME...
THAT GAVE ME THE CHANCE TO *STEAL* THE MILLENNIUM ITEMS.
AND THAT'S NOT *ALL* I CAN DO...
!!
DO YOU REMEMBER WHEN I TURNED BACK TIME TO STOP YOU FROM MEETING YOUR FRIENDS?
!!
THAT WAS ZORC'S POWER AS WELL!!
CAN YOU FEEL IT, YUGI?
CAN YOU FEEL THE EVIL AURA FROM THIS CORPSE?
AKHENADEN'S *MUMMY* IS ALSO PLAYING THIS GAME!
HIS *SOUL* IS ONE WITH ZORC'S!

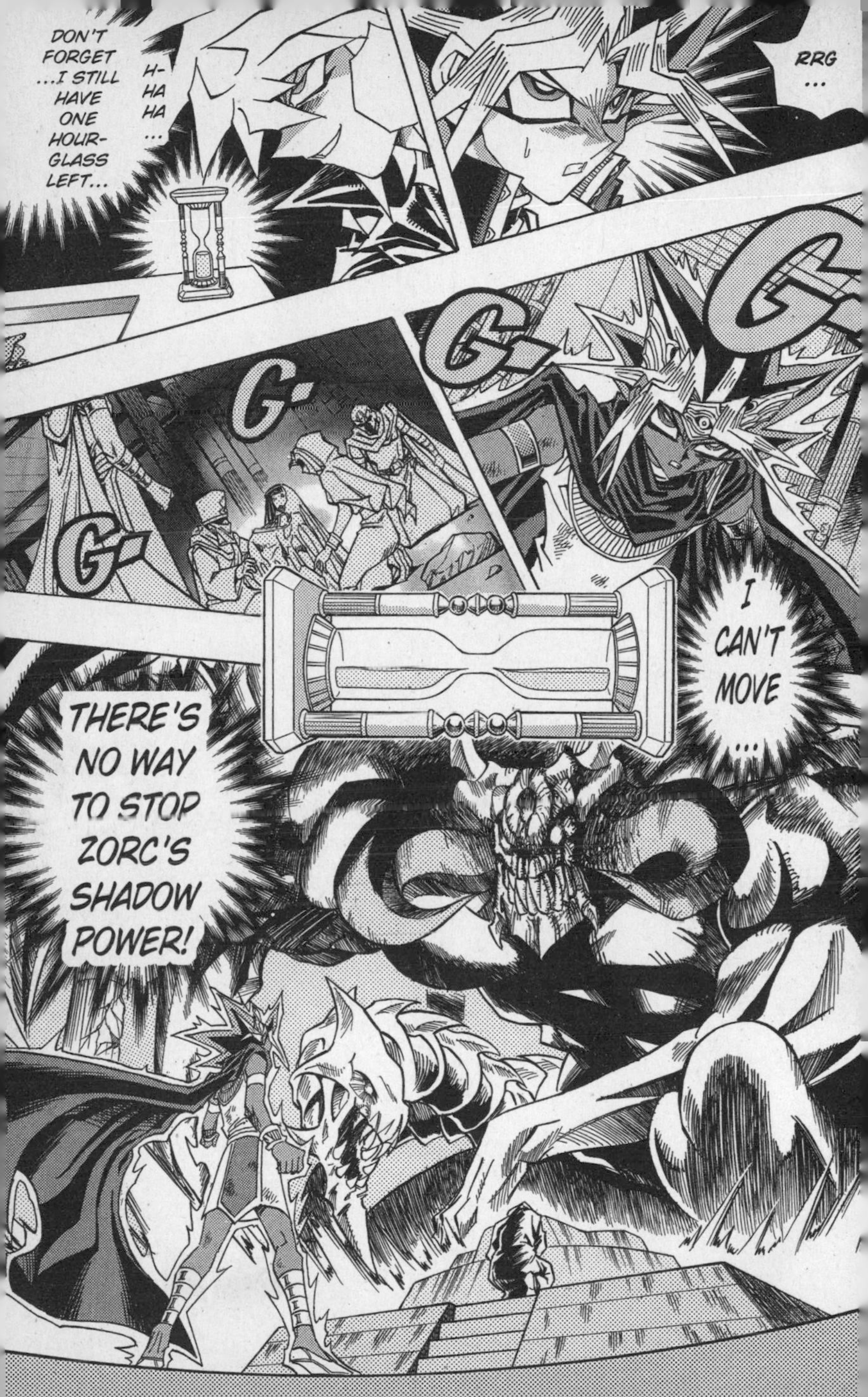

RRG ...
DON'T FORGET ...I STILL HAVE ONE HOUR-GLASS LEFT...
H-HA HA ...
G
G-
G-
G-
I CAN'T MOVE ...
THERE'S NO WAY TO STOP ZORC'S SHADOW POWER!

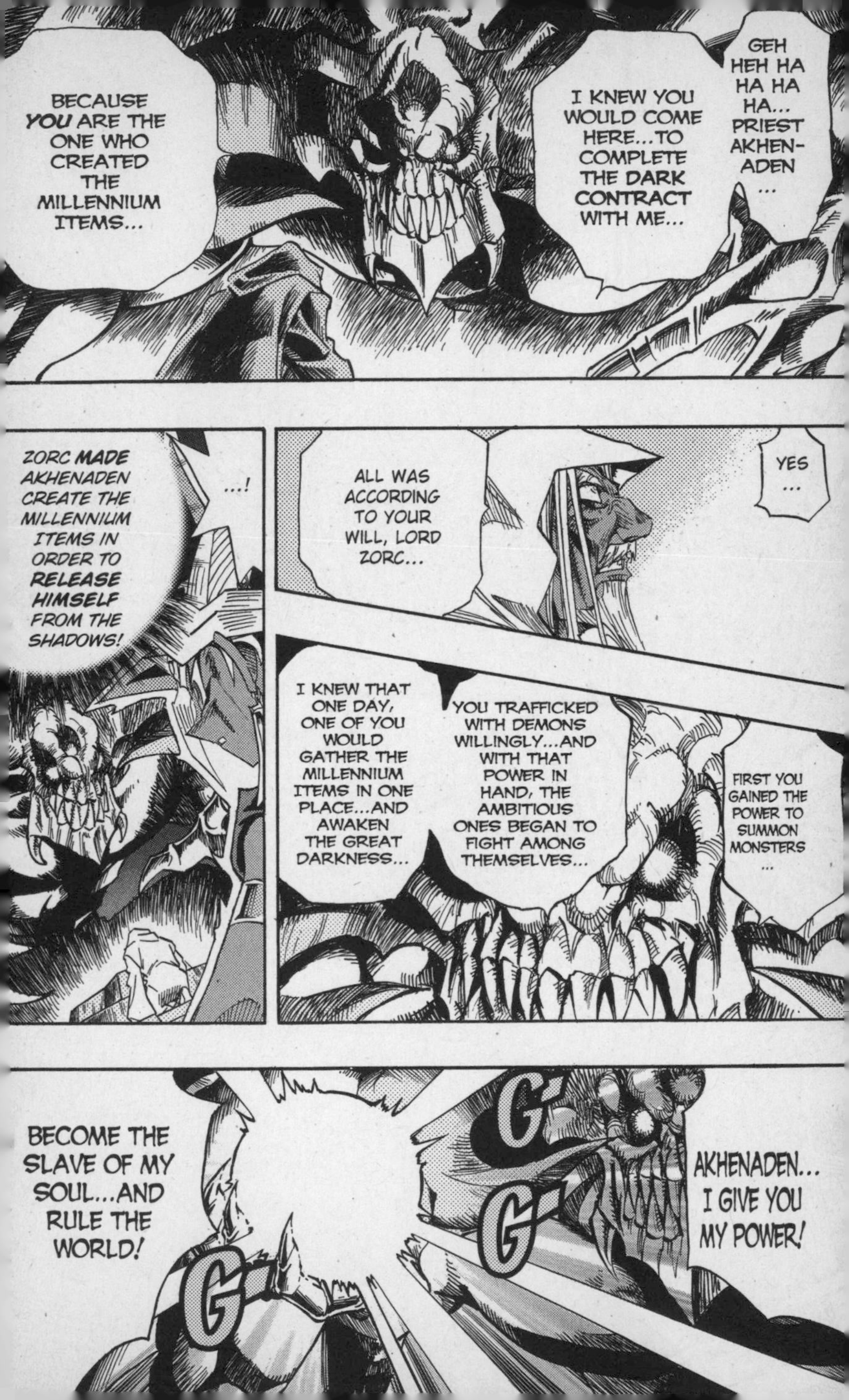

GEH HEH HA HA HA HA... PRIEST AKHEN-ADEN ...
I KNEW YOU WOULD COME HERE...TO COMPLETE THE DARK CONTRACT WITH ME...
BECAUSE YOU ARE THE ONE WHO CREATED THE MILLENNIUM ITEMS...
YES ...
ALL WAS ACCORDING TO YOUR WILL, LORD ZORC...
FIRST YOU GAINED THE POWER TO SUMMON MONSTERS ...
YOU TRAFFICKED WITH DEMONS WILLINGLY...AND WITH THAT POWER IN HAND, THE AMBITIOUS ONES BEGAN TO FIGHT AMONG THEMSELVES...
I KNEW THAT ONE DAY, ONE OF YOU WOULD GATHER THE MILLENNIUM ITEMS IN ONE PLACE...AND AWAKEN THE GREAT DARKNESS...
...!
ZORC MADE AKHENADEN CREATE THE MILLENNIUM ITEMS IN ORDER TO RELEASE HIMSELF FROM THE SHADOWS!
AKHENADEN... I GIVE YOU MY POWER!
G
G
G
BECOME THE SLAVE OF MY SOUL...AND RULE THE WORLD!

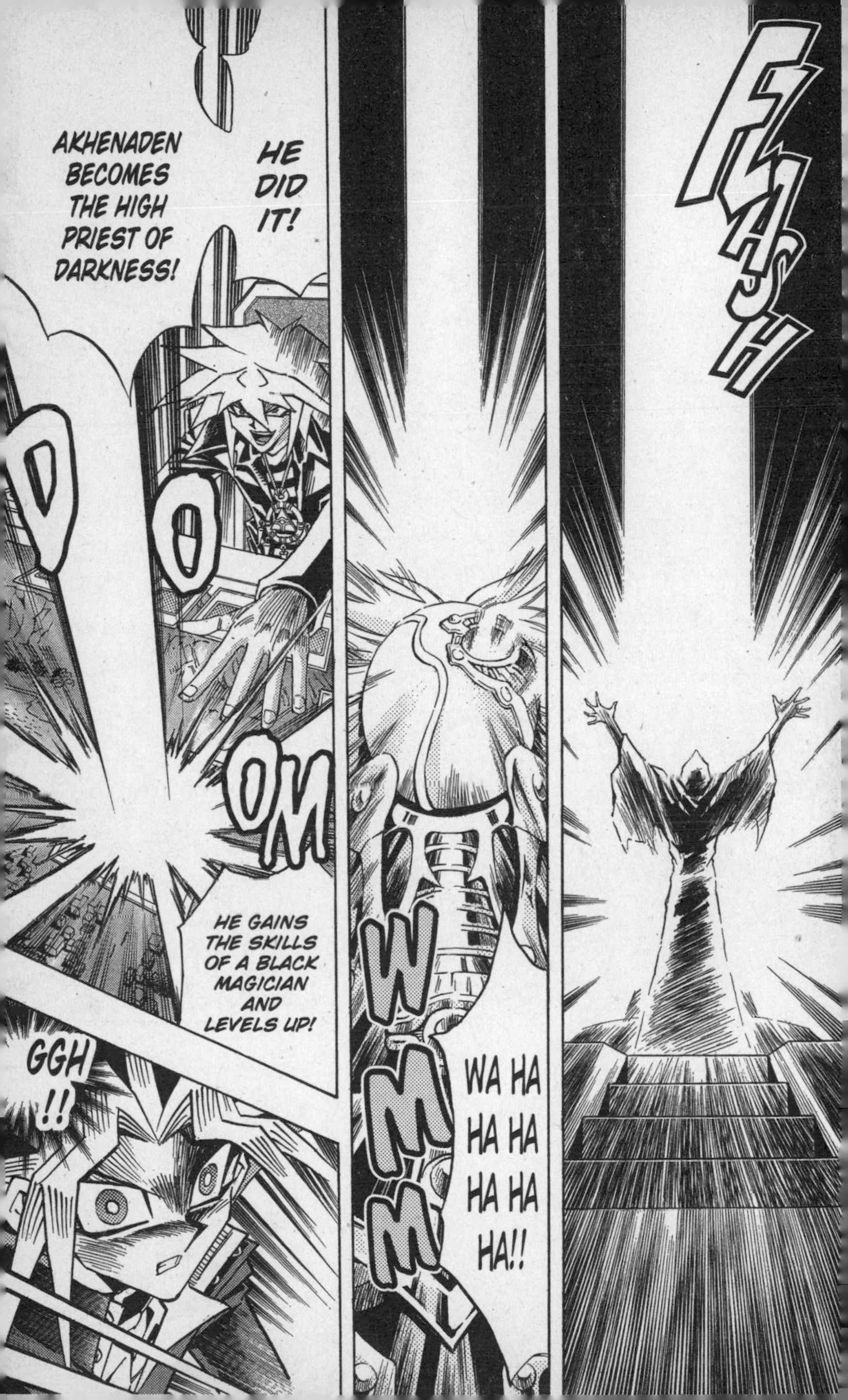
FLASH
WA HA HA HA HA HA HA HA!!
WWMMM
HE DID IT!
AKHENADEN BECOMES THE HIGH PRIEST OF DARKNESS!
DOOM
HE GAINS THE SKILLS OF A BLACK MAGICIAN AND LEVELS UP!
GGH!!

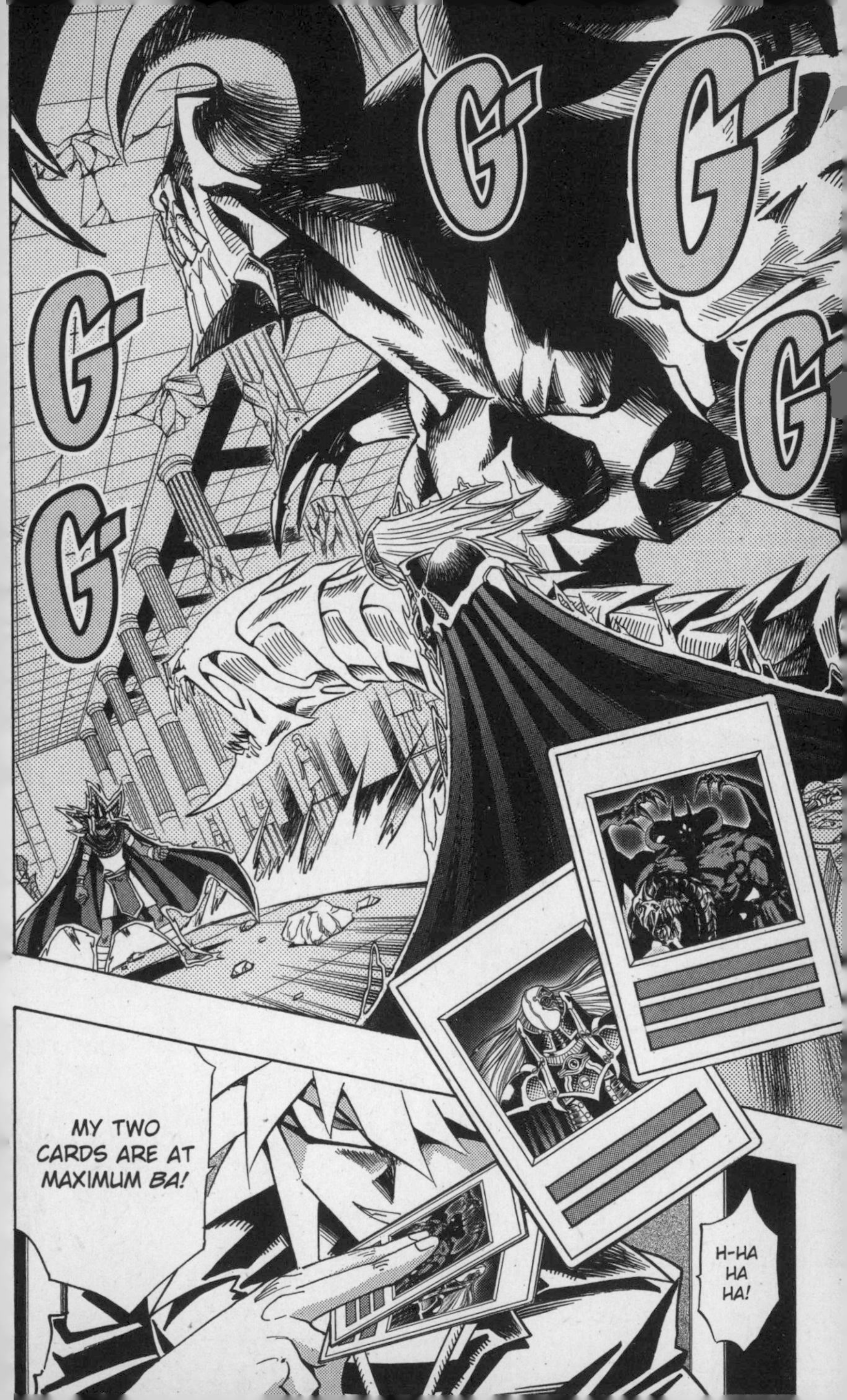
G-G-G-G-G-
H-HA HA HA!
MY TWO CARDS ARE AT MAXIMUM BA!

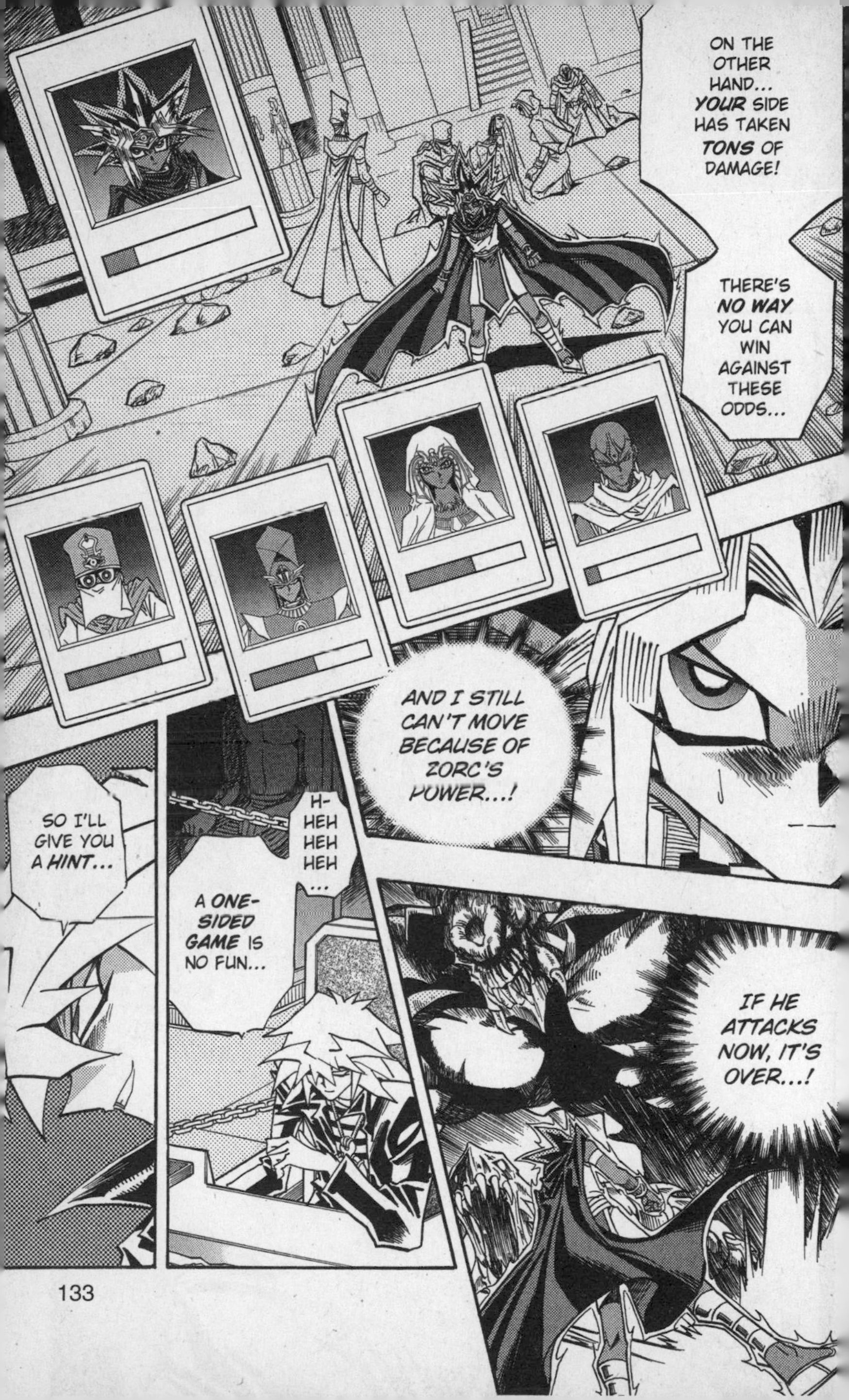
ON THE OTHER HAND... ***YOUR*** SIDE HAS TAKEN ***TONS*** OF DAMAGE!
THERE'S ***NO WAY*** YOU CAN WIN AGAINST THESE ODDS...
AND I STILL CAN'T MOVE BECAUSE OF ZORC'S POWER...!
IF HE ATTACKS NOW, IT'S OVER...!
H-HEH HEH HEH...
A ***ONE-SIDED GAME*** IS NO FUN...
SO I'LL GIVE YOU A ***HINT***...

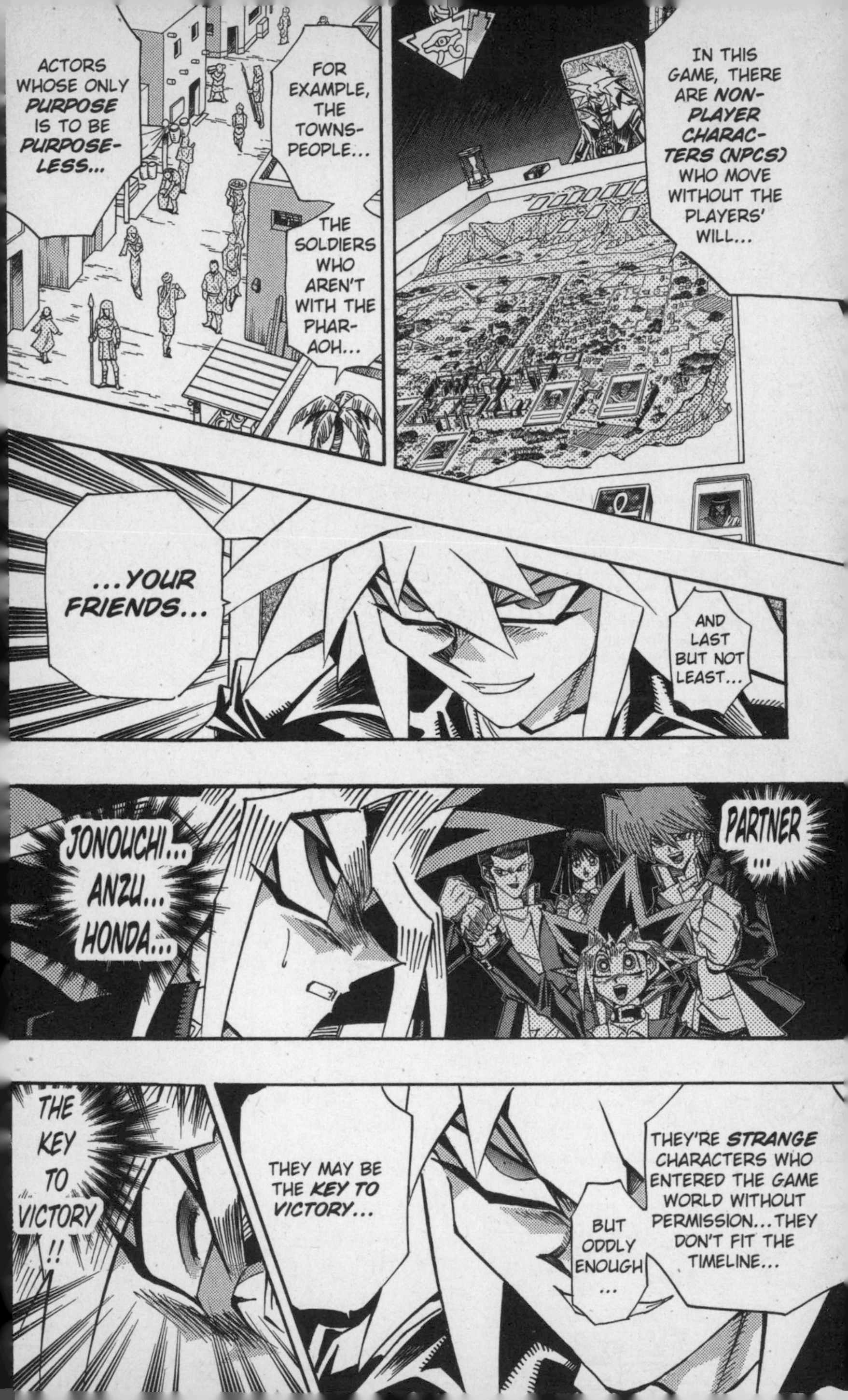
IN THIS GAME, THERE ARE NON-PLAYER CHARACTERS (NPCS) WHO MOVE WITHOUT THE PLAYERS' WILL...
FOR EXAMPLE, THE TOWNSPEOPLE...
THE SOLDIERS WHO AREN'T WITH THE PHARAOH...
ACTORS WHOSE ONLY PURPOSE IS TO BE PURPOSELESS...
AND LAST BUT NOT LEAST...
...YOUR FRIENDS...
PARTNER...
JONOUCHI... ANZU... HONDA...
THEY'RE STRANGE CHARACTERS WHO ENTERED THE GAME WORLD WITHOUT PERMISSION...THEY DON'T FIT THE TIMELINE...
BUT ODDLY ENOUGH...
THEY MAY BE THE KEY TO VICTORY...
THE KEY TO VICTORY!!

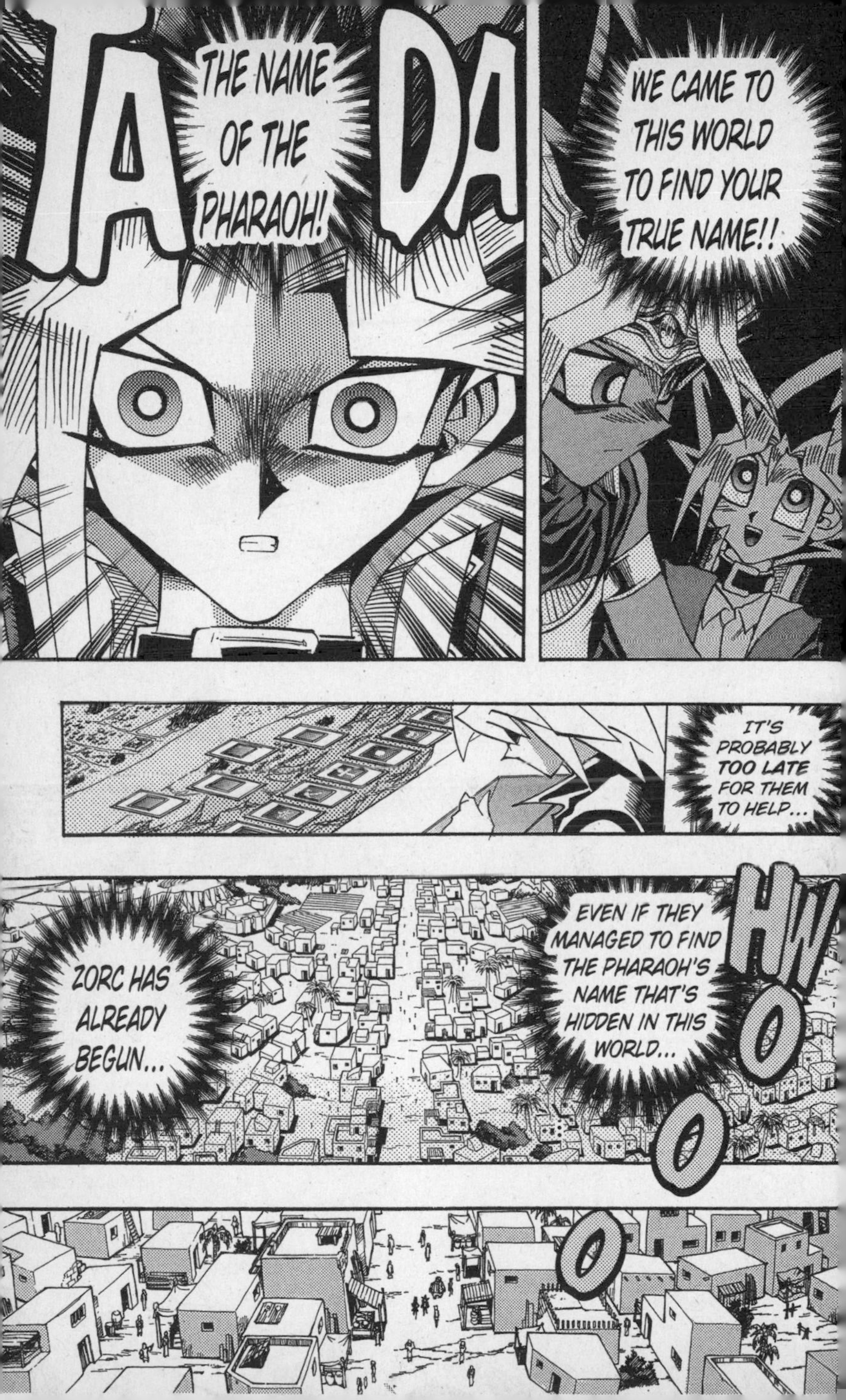
WE CAME TO THIS WORLD TO FIND YOUR TRUE NAME!!
DA
THE NAME OF THE PHARAOH!
A
IT'S PROBABLY TOO LATE FOR THEM TO HELP...
HW
O
EVEN IF THEY MANAGED TO FIND THE PHARAOH'S NAME THAT'S HIDDEN IN THIS WORLD...
ZORC HAS ALREADY BEGUN...
O
O

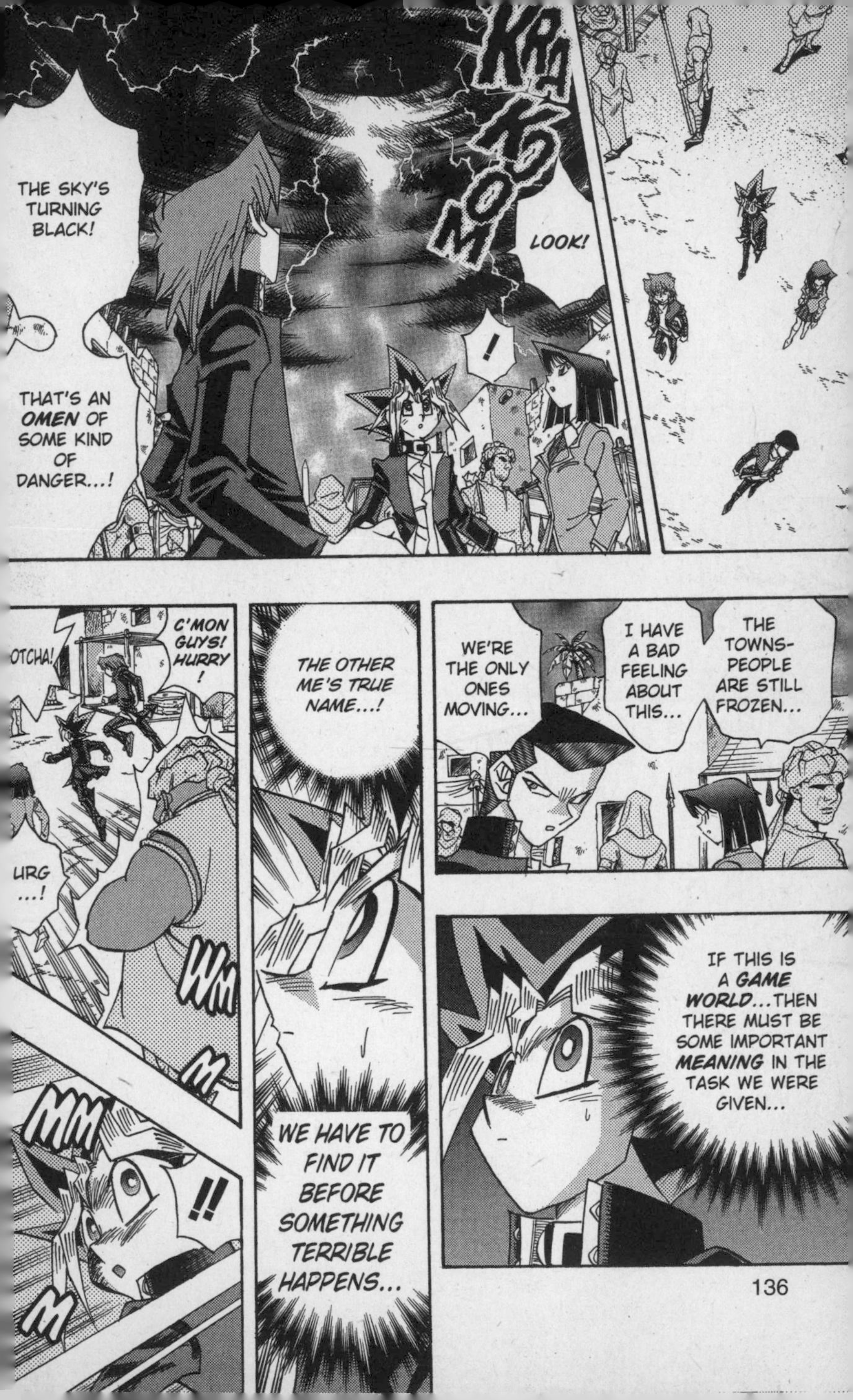
KRABOOM
LOOK!
!
THE SKY'S TURNING BLACK!
THAT'S AN OMEN OF SOME KIND OF DANGER...!
THE TOWNSPEOPLE ARE STILL FROZEN...
I HAVE A BAD FEELING ABOUT THIS...
WE'RE THE ONLY ONES MOVING...
IF THIS IS A GAME WORLD...THEN THERE MUST BE SOME IMPORTANT MEANING IN THE TASK WE WERE GIVEN...
THE OTHER ME'S TRUE NAME...!
WE HAVE TO FIND IT BEFORE SOMETHING TERRIBLE HAPPENS...
C'MON GUYS! HURRY!
OTCHA!
URG...!
WMMMMM
!!

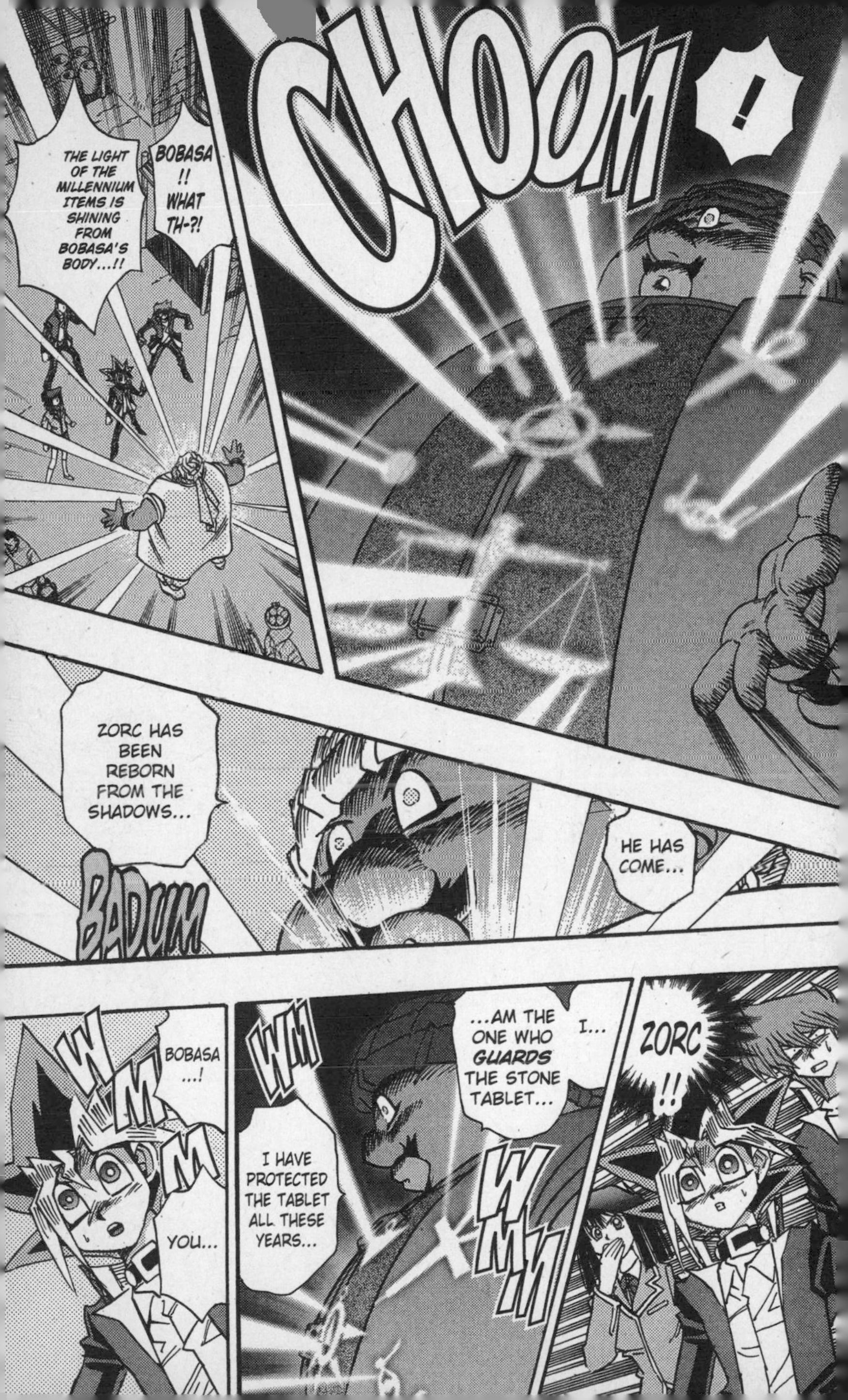
CHOOM
!
BOBASA!! WHAT TH-?!
THE LIGHT OF THE MILLENNIUM ITEMS IS SHINING FROM BOBASA'S BODY...!!
ZORC HAS BEEN REBORN FROM THE SHADOWS...
HE HAS COME...
BADUM
ZORC!!
I...
...AM THE ONE WHO GUARDS THE STONE TABLET...
WM
I HAVE PROTECTED THE TABLET ALL THESE YEARS...
WMN
BOBASA...!
WMMM
YOU...

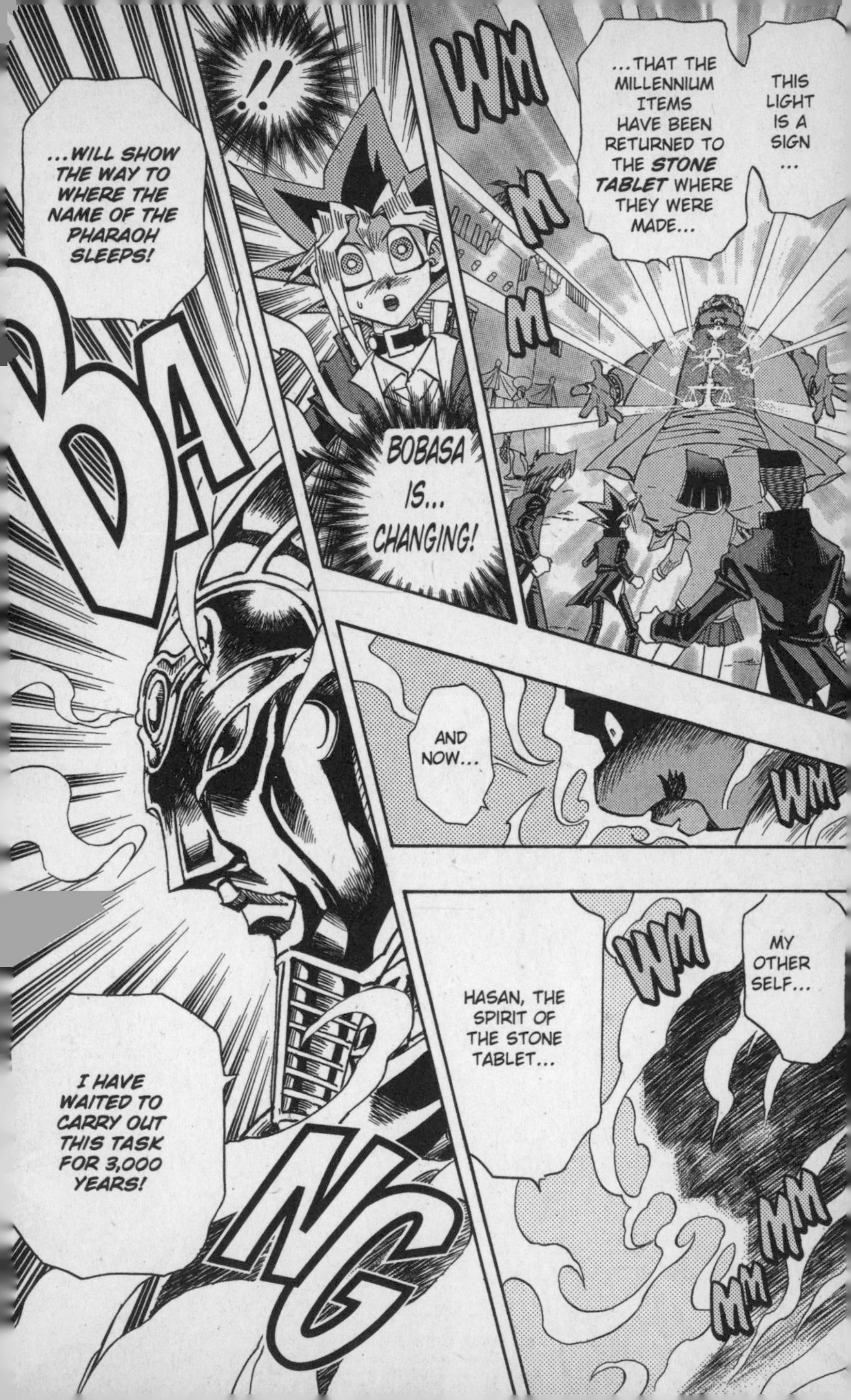
THIS LIGHT IS A SIGN...
...THAT THE MILLENNIUM ITEMS HAVE BEEN RETURNED TO THE STONE TABLET WHERE THEY WERE MADE...
WM
M
M
!!
BOBASA IS... CHANGING!
AND NOW...
WM
MY OTHER SELF...
HASAN, THE SPIRIT OF THE STONE TABLET...
WM
MMMM
...WILL SHOW THE WAY TO WHERE THE NAME OF THE PHARAOH SLEEPS!
BADA
I HAVE WAITED TO CARRY OUT THIS TASK FOR 3,000 YEARS!
NG

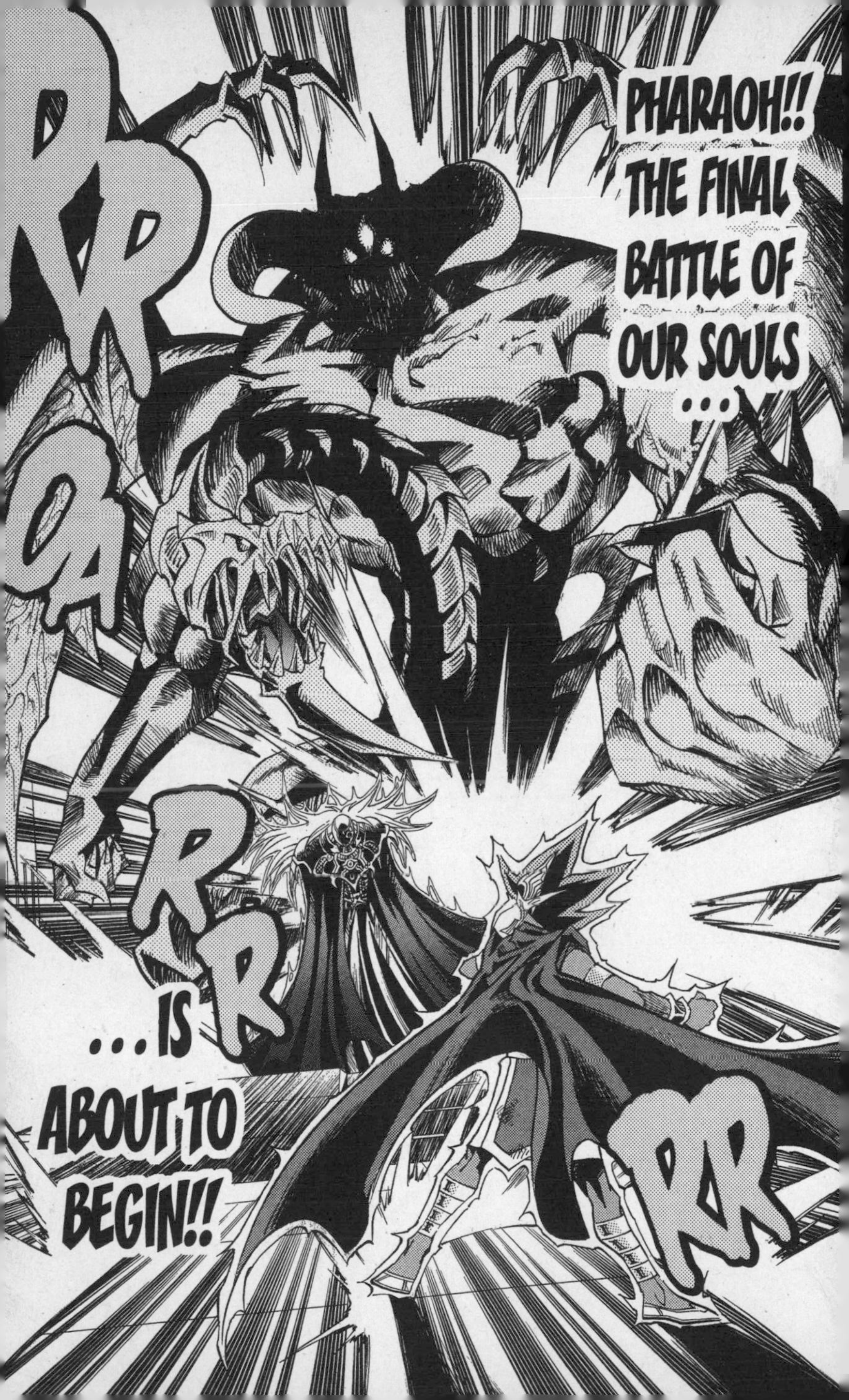
PHARAOH!! THE FINAL BATTLE OF OUR SOULS ...
...IS ABOUT TO BEGIN!!
RRRRRRR

Duel 44: The Mysterious NPC!

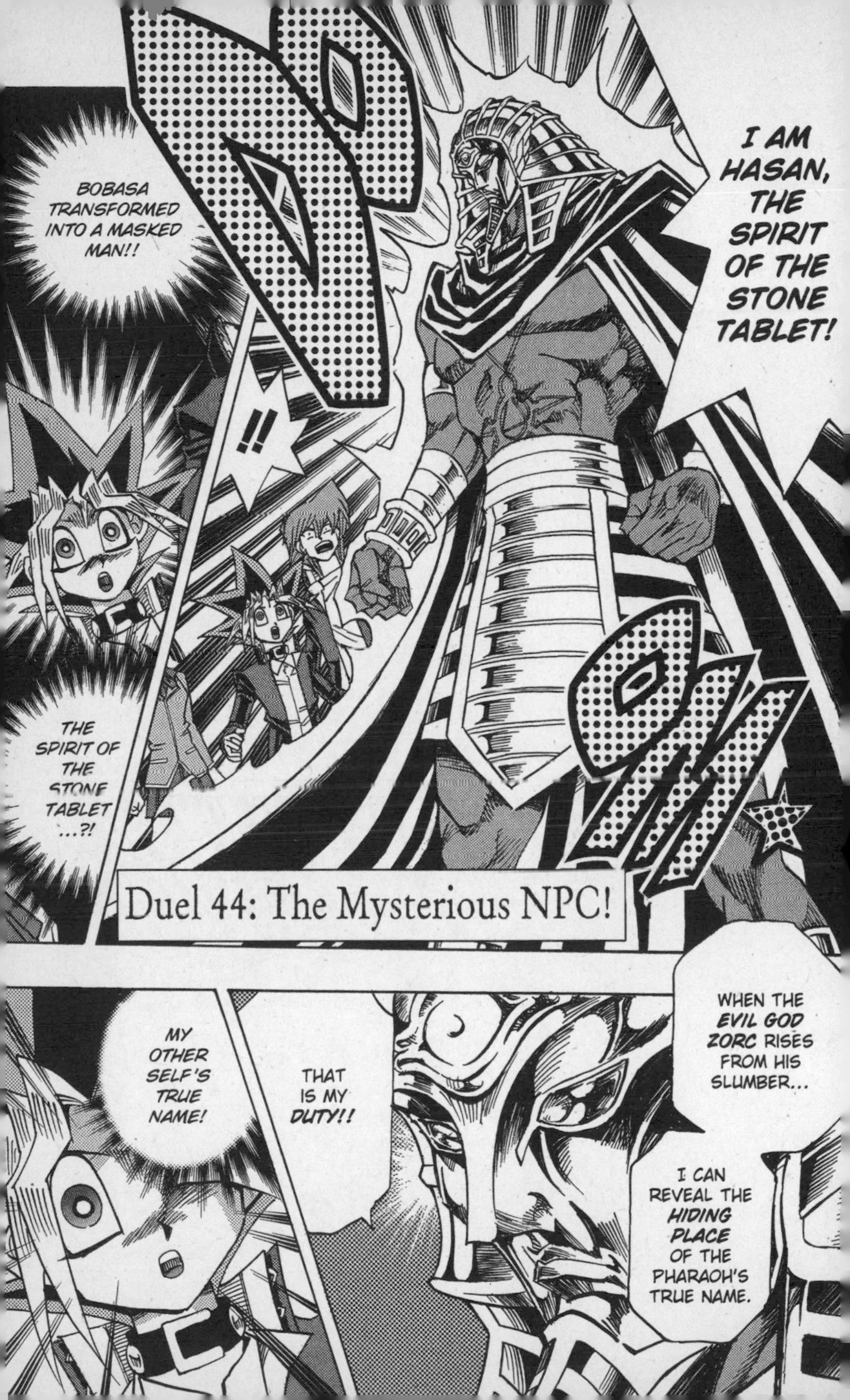
I AM HASAN, THE SPIRIT OF THE STONE TABLET!
!!
BOBASA TRANSFORMED INTO A MASKED MAN!!
THE SPIRIT OF THE STONE TABLET ...?!
WHEN THE *EVIL GOD ZORC* RISES FROM HIS SLUMBER...
I CAN REVEAL THE *HIDING PLACE* OF THE PHARAOH'S TRUE NAME.
THAT IS MY *DUTY!!*
MY OTHER SELF'S TRUE NAME!

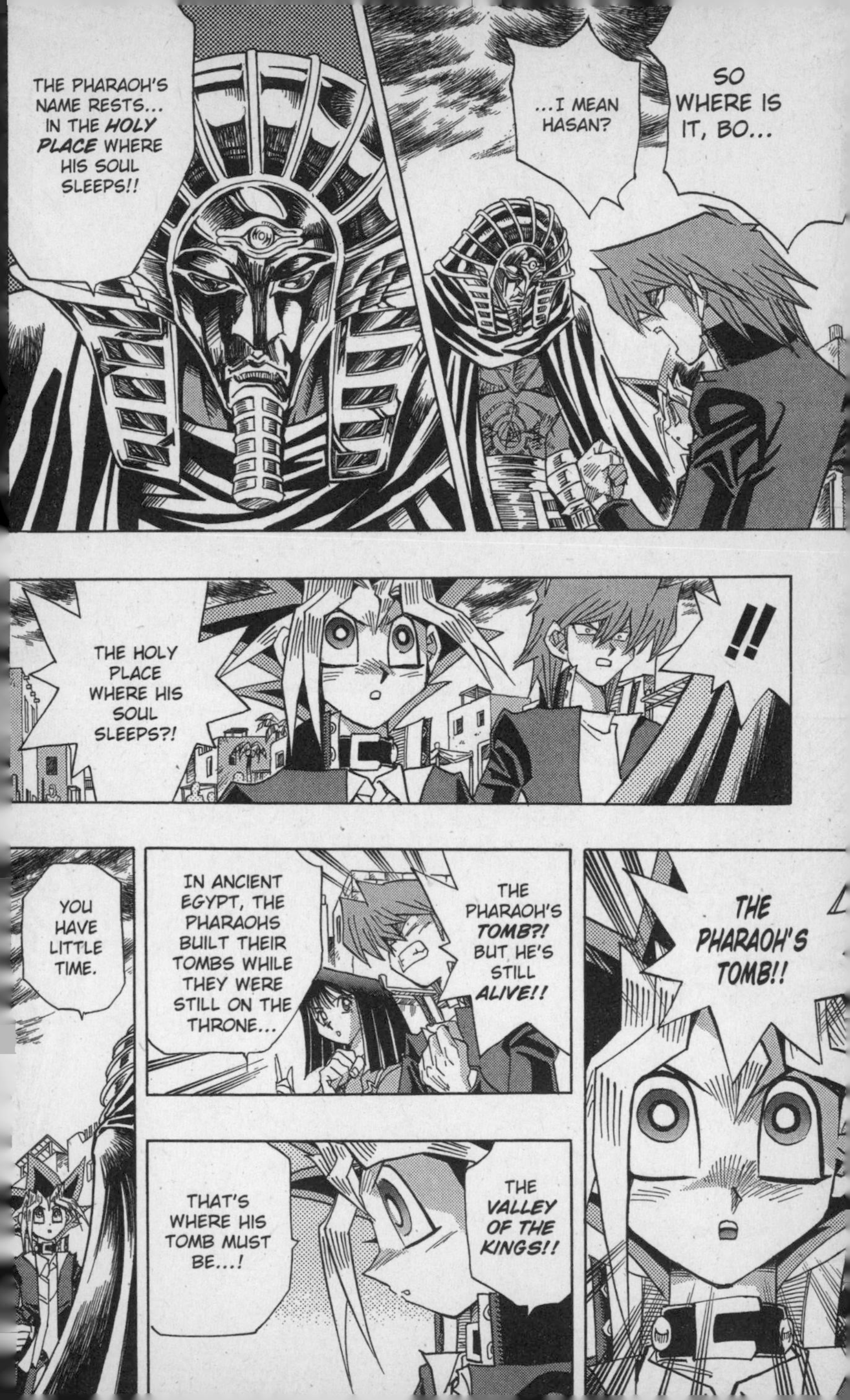
SO WHERE IS IT, BO...
...I MEAN HASAN?
THE PHARAOH'S NAME RESTS... IN THE HOLY PLACE WHERE HIS SOUL SLEEPS!!
!!
THE HOLY PLACE WHERE HIS SOUL SLEEPS?!
THE PHARAOH'S TOMB!!
THE PHARAOH'S TOMB?! BUT HE'S STILL ALIVE!!
IN ANCIENT EGYPT, THE PHARAOHS BUILT THEIR TOMBS WHILE THEY WERE STILL ON THE THRONE...
THE VALLEY OF THE KINGS!!
THAT'S WHERE HIS TOMB MUST BE...!
YOU HAVE LITTLE TIME.

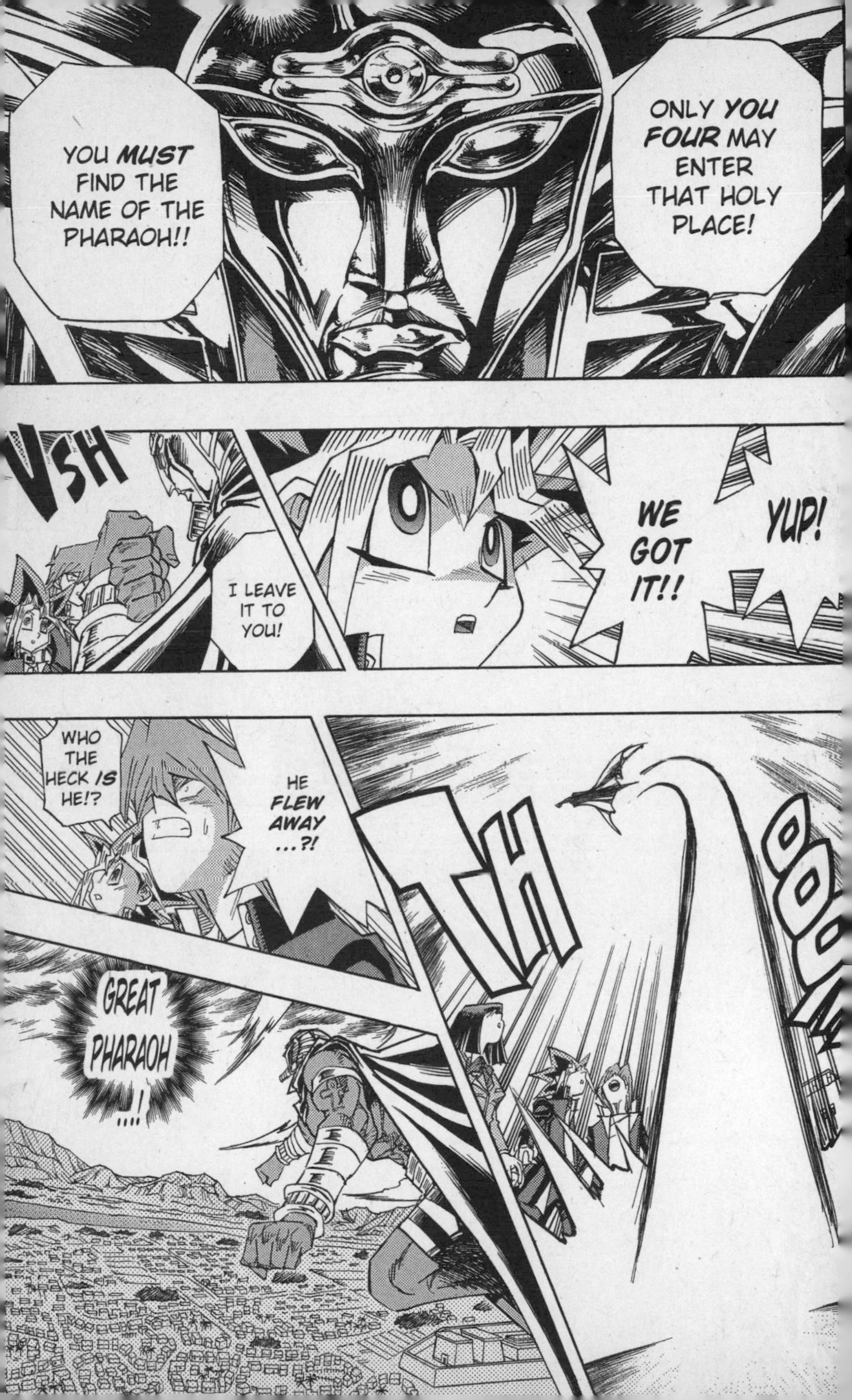
ONLY YOU FOUR MAY ENTER THAT HOLY PLACE!
YOU MUST FIND THE NAME OF THE PHARAOH!!
YUP!
WE GOT IT!!
I LEAVE IT TO YOU!
VSH
OOOOM
VSH
HE FLEW AWAY...?!
WHO THE HECK IS HE!?
GREAT PHARAOH...!

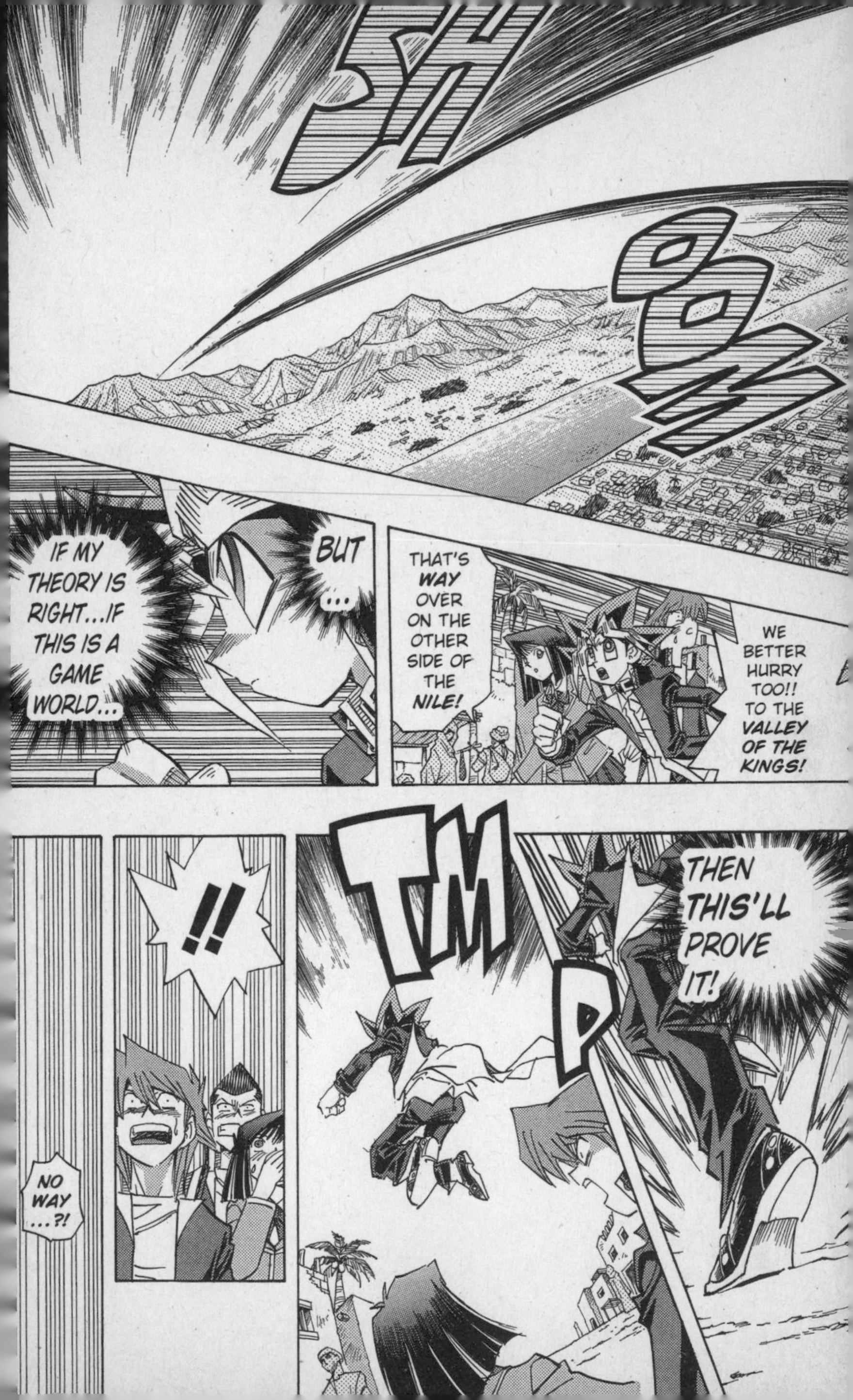
SH
OOM
WE BETTER HURRY TOO!! TO THE VALLEY OF THE KINGS!
THAT'S WAY OVER ON THE OTHER SIDE OF THE NILE!
BUT ...
IF MY THEORY IS RIGHT...IF THIS IS A GAME WORLD...
THEN THIS'LL PROVE IT!
TMP
!!
NO WAY ...?!

Duel 44: The Mysterious NPC!

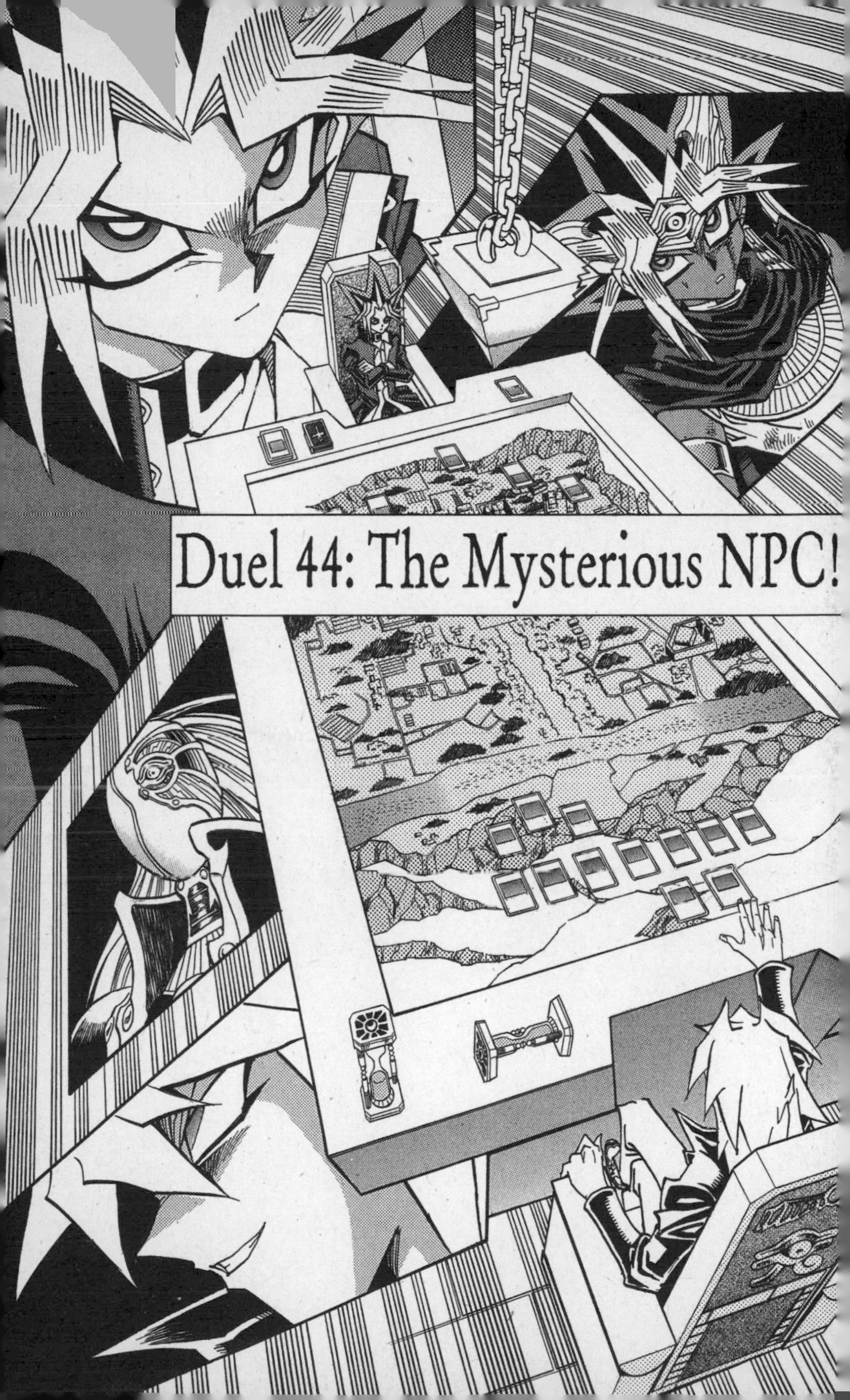

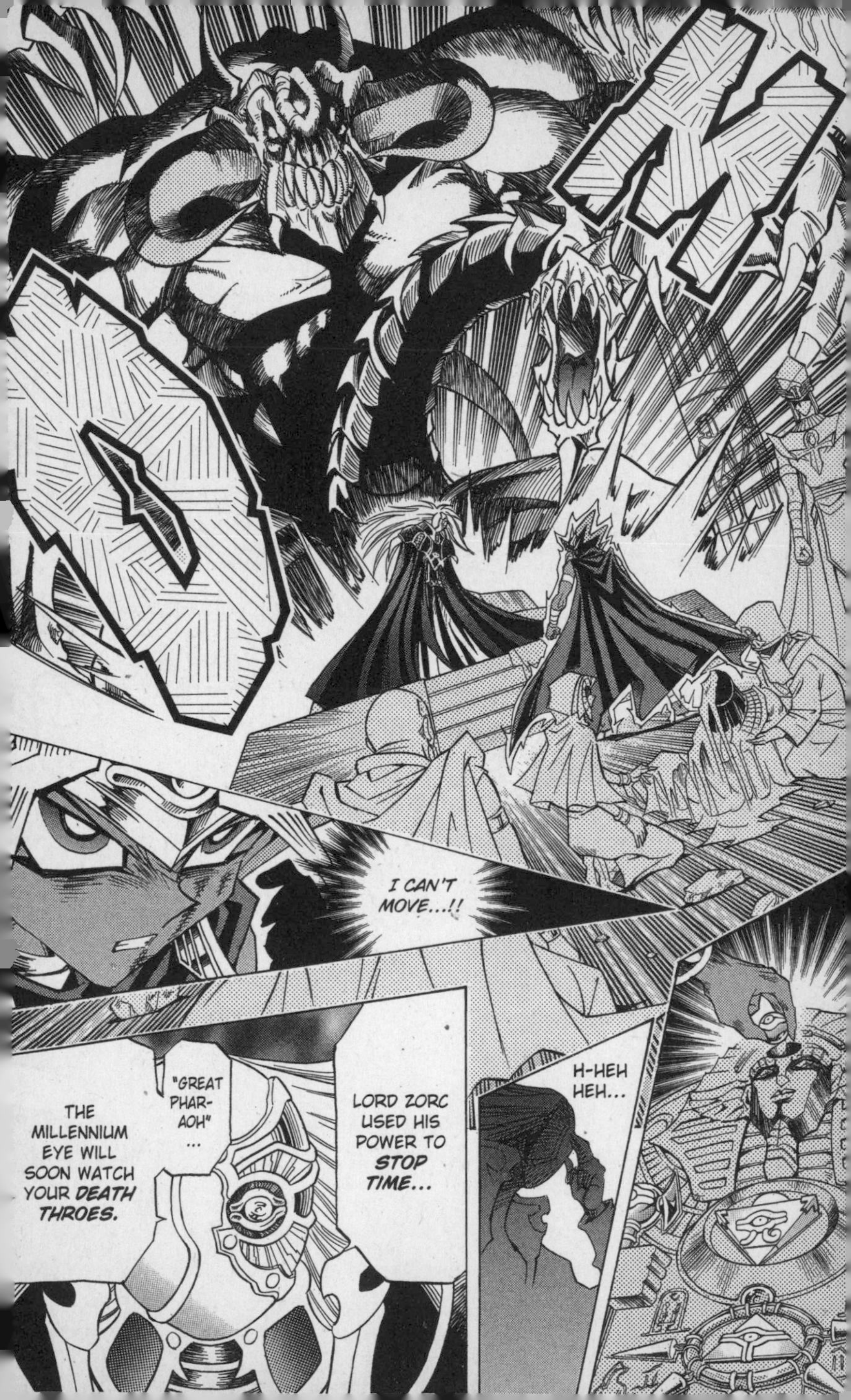
I CAN'T MOVE...!!
H-HEH HEH...
LORD ZORC USED HIS POWER TO STOP TIME...
"GREAT PHARAOH" ...
THE MILLENNIUM EYE WILL SOON WATCH YOUR DEATH THROES.

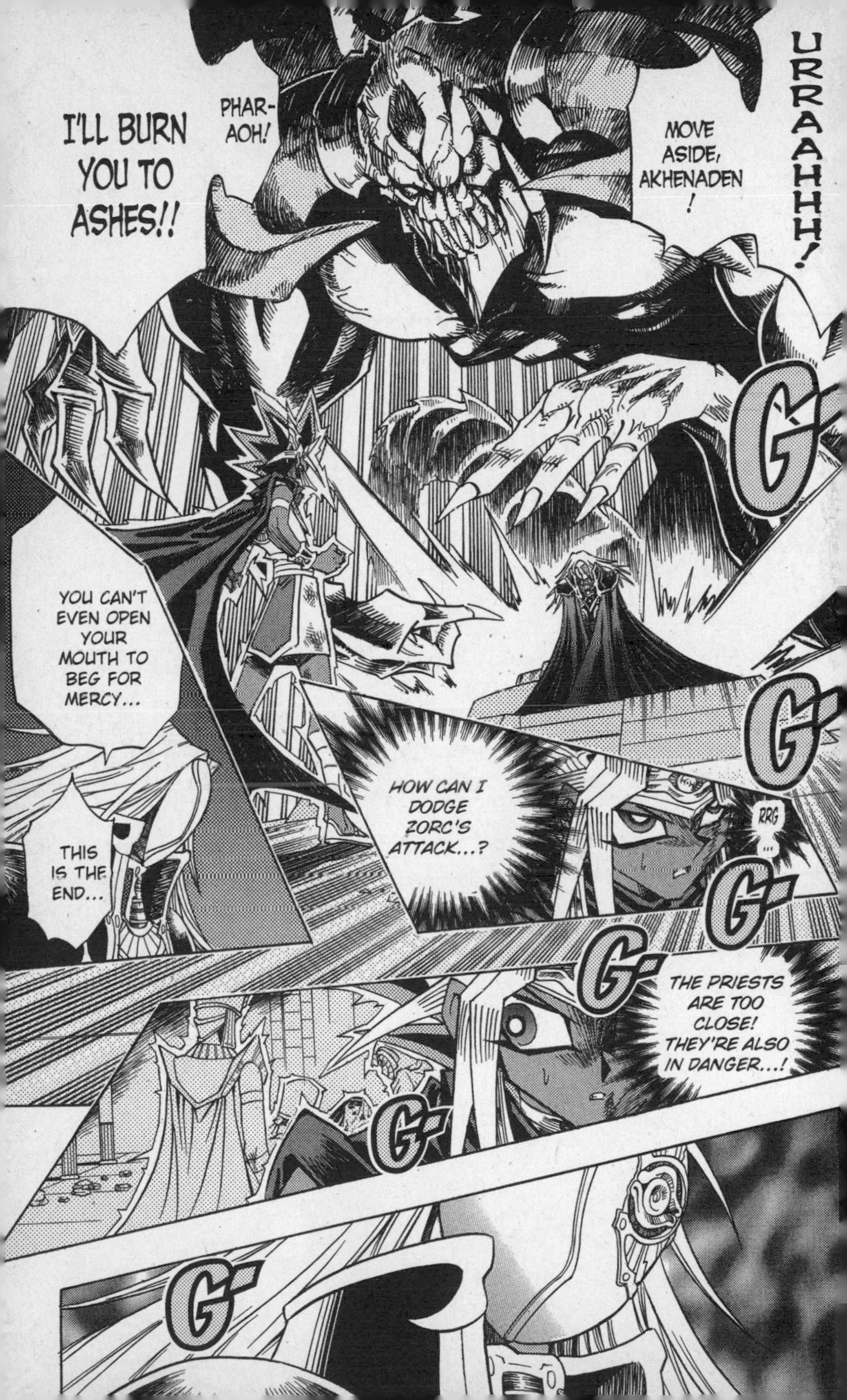
URRAAHHH!
MOVE ASIDE, AKHENADEN!
PHAR-AOH!
I'LL BURN YOU TO ASHES!!
G
YOU CAN'T EVEN OPEN YOUR MOUTH TO BEG FOR MERCY...
G
RRG...
HOW CAN I DODGE ZORC'S ATTACK...?
G
THIS IS THE END...
G
THE PRIESTS ARE TOO CLOSE! THEY'RE ALSO IN DANGER...!
G
G

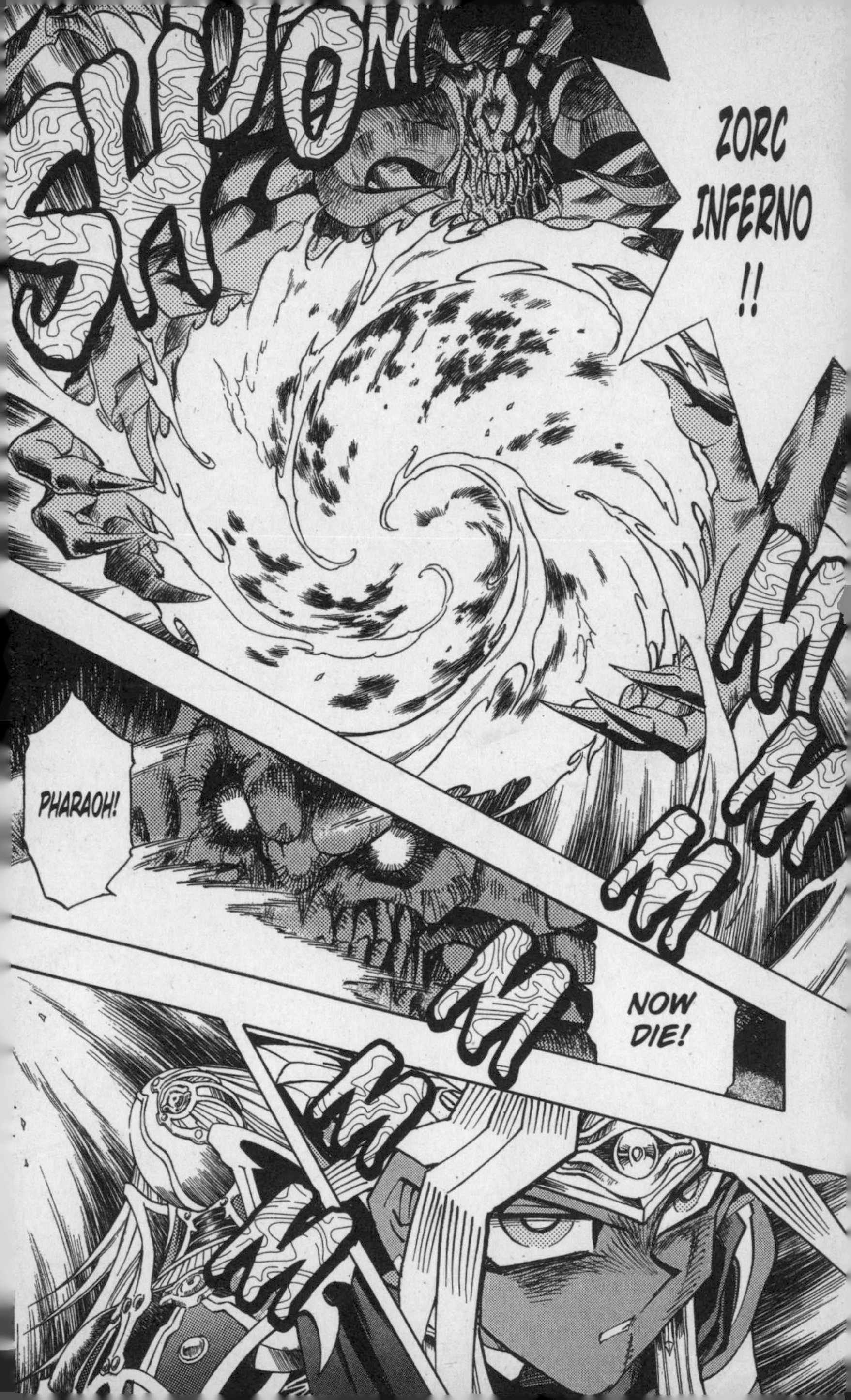
ZORC INFERNO!!
PHARAOH!
NOW DIE!

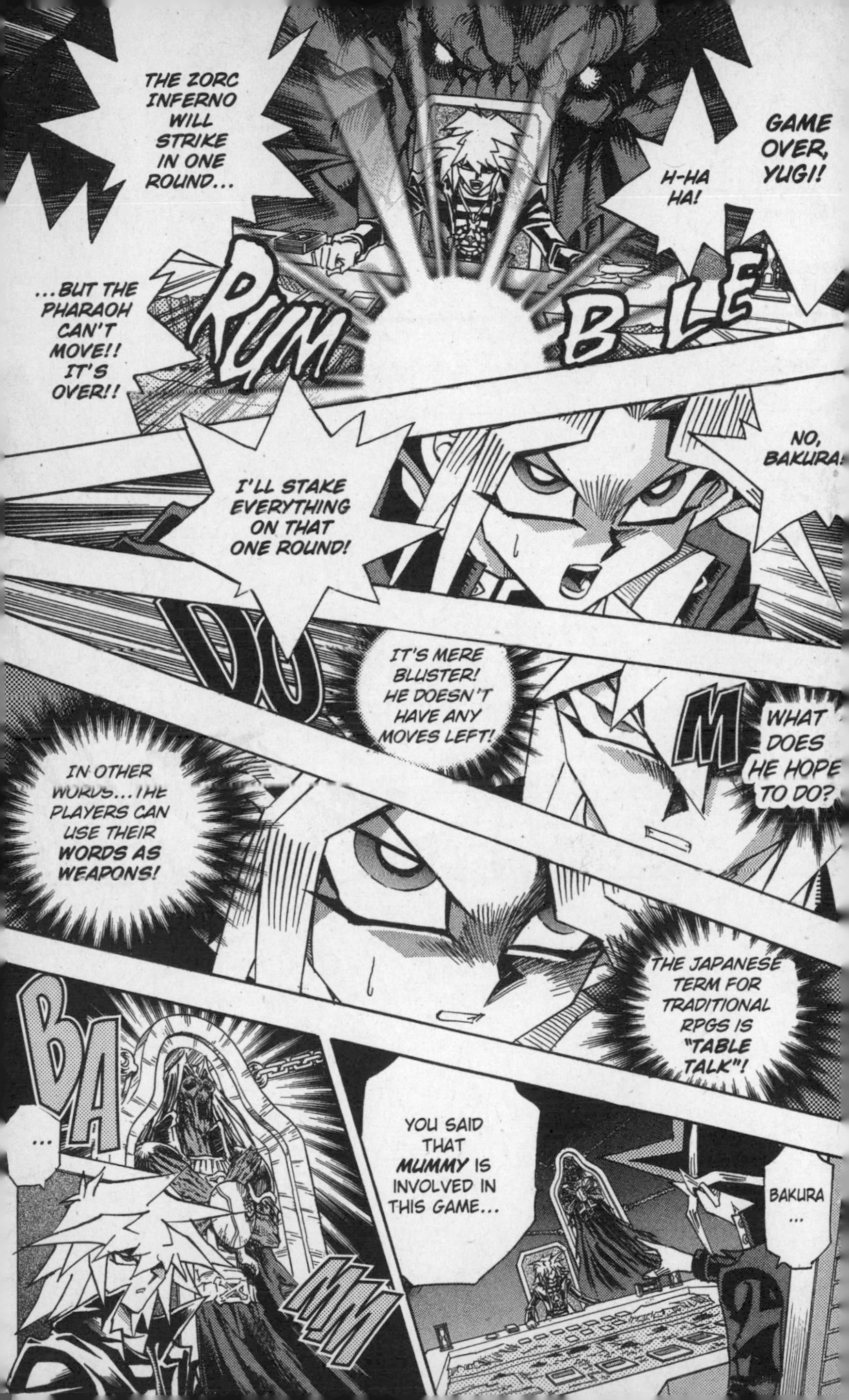
GAME OVER, YUGI!
H-HA HA!
THE ZORC INFERNO WILL STRIKE IN ONE ROUND...
...BUT THE PHARAOH CAN'T MOVE!! IT'S OVER!!
RUM
B LE
NO, BAKURA!
I'LL STAKE EVERYTHING ON THAT ONE ROUND!
DO
M
WHAT DOES HE HOPE TO DO?
IT'S MERE BLUSTER! HE DOESN'T HAVE ANY MOVES LEFT!
THE JAPANESE TERM FOR TRADITIONAL RPGS IS "TABLE TALK"!
IN OTHER WORDS...THE PLAYERS CAN USE THEIR WORDS AS WEAPONS!
BAKURA...
YOU SAID THAT MUMMY IS INVOLVED IN THIS GAME...
...
BA
MM

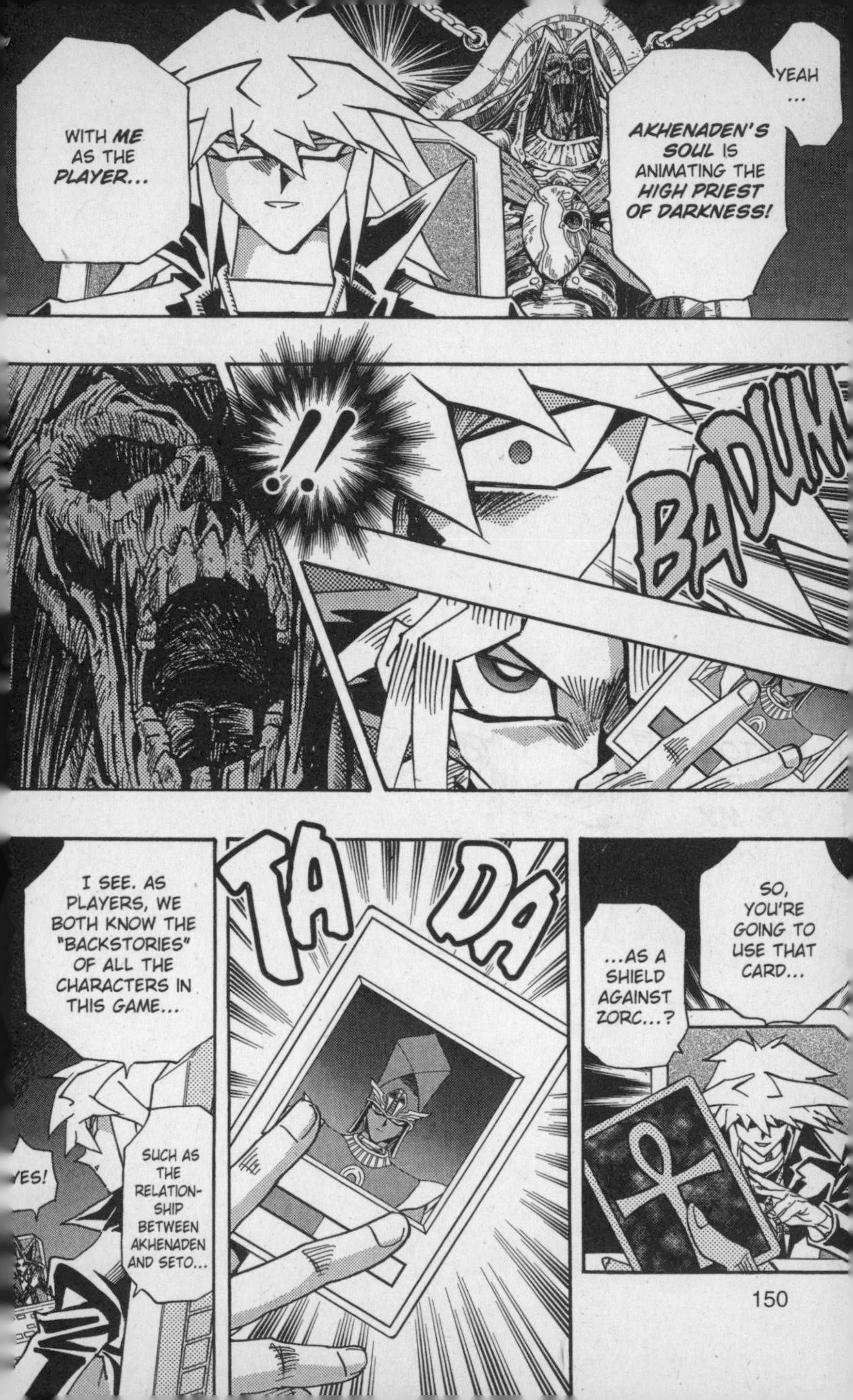
YEAH ... AKHENADEN'S SOUL IS ANIMATING THE HIGH PRIEST OF DARKNESS!
WITH ME AS THE PLAYER...
BADUM
!!
SO, YOU'RE GOING TO USE THAT CARD...
...AS A SHIELD AGAINST ZORC...?
TA DA
I SEE. AS PLAYERS, WE BOTH KNOW THE "BACKSTORIES" OF ALL THE CHARACTERS IN THIS GAME...
SUCH AS THE RELATIONSHIP BETWEEN AKHENADEN AND SETO...
ES!

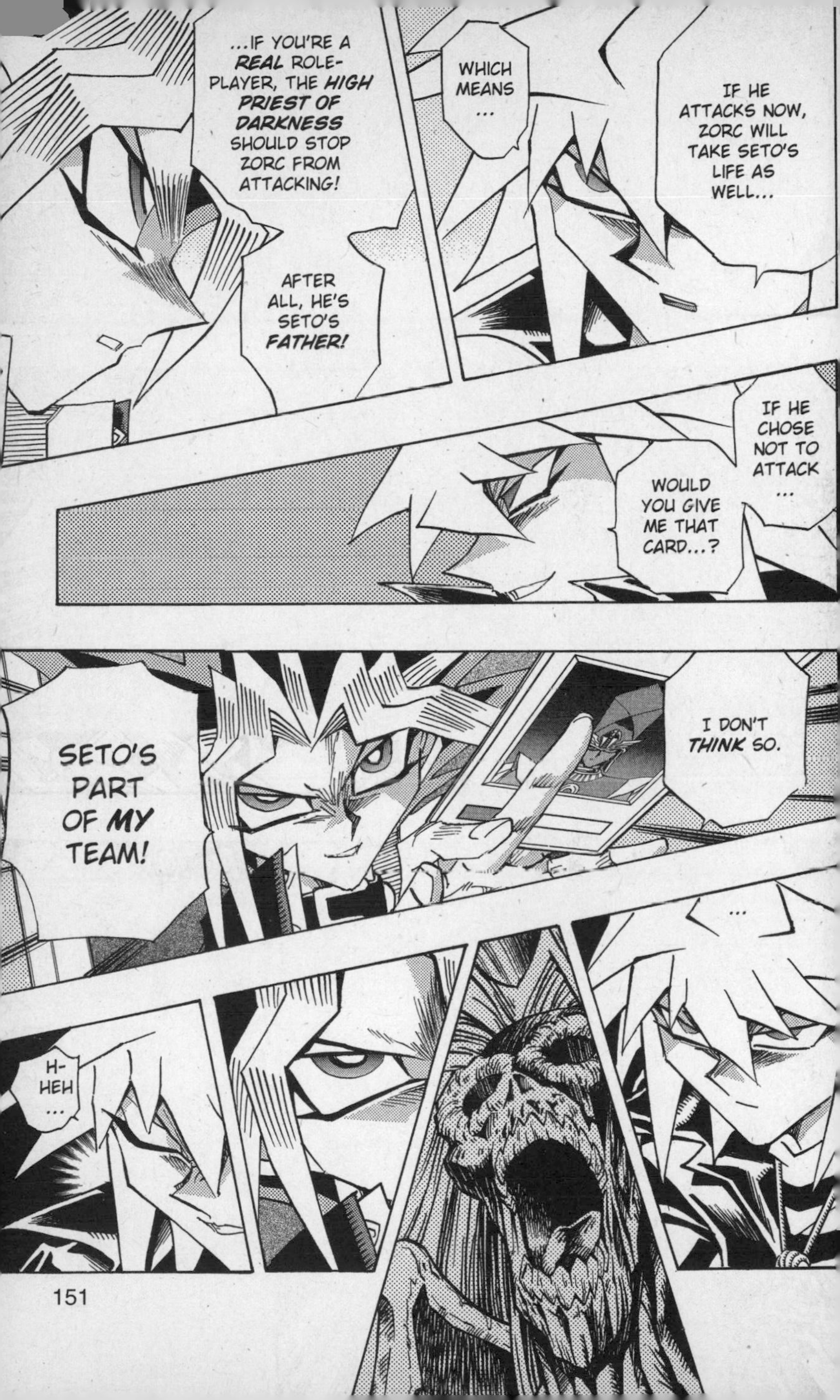
WHICH MEANS ...
IF HE ATTACKS NOW, ZORC WILL TAKE SETO'S LIFE AS WELL...
...IF YOU'RE A REAL ROLE-PLAYER, THE HIGH PRIEST OF DARKNESS SHOULD STOP ZORC FROM ATTACKING!
AFTER ALL, HE'S SETO'S FATHER!
IF HE CHOSE NOT TO ATTACK ...
WOULD YOU GIVE ME THAT CARD...?
I DON'T THINK SO.
SETO'S PART OF MY TEAM!
...
H-HEH ...

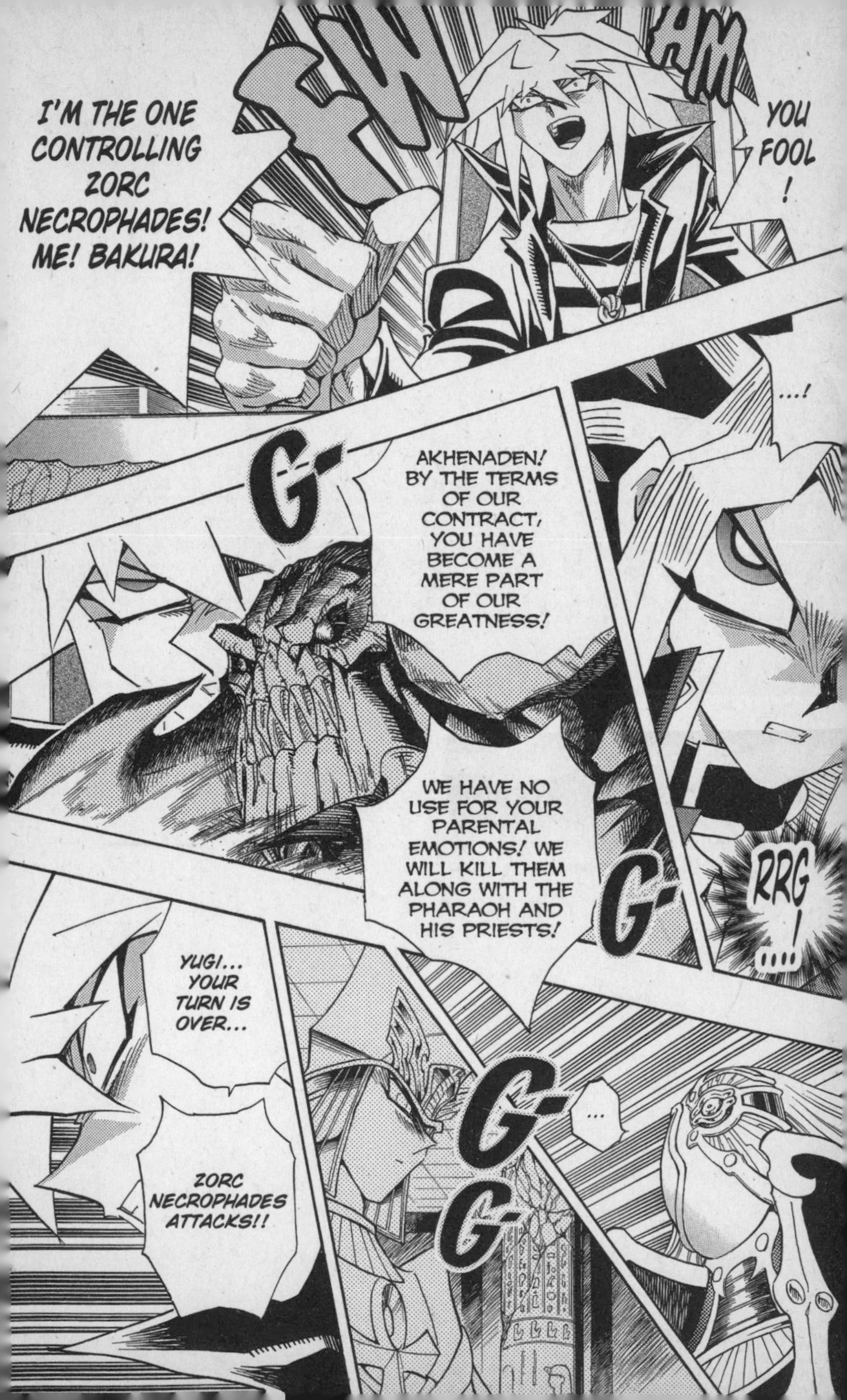
YOU FOOL!
I'M THE ONE CONTROLLING ZORC NECROPHADES! ME! BAKURA!
...!
RRG!
....!
G-
AKHENADEN! BY THE TERMS OF OUR CONTRACT, YOU HAVE BECOME A MERE PART OF OUR GREATNESS!
WE HAVE NO USE FOR YOUR PARENTAL EMOTIONS! WE WILL KILL THEM ALONG WITH THE PHARAOH AND HIS PRIESTS!
G-
...
G-
G-
YUGI... YOUR TURN IS OVER...
ZORC NECROPHADES ATTACKS!!

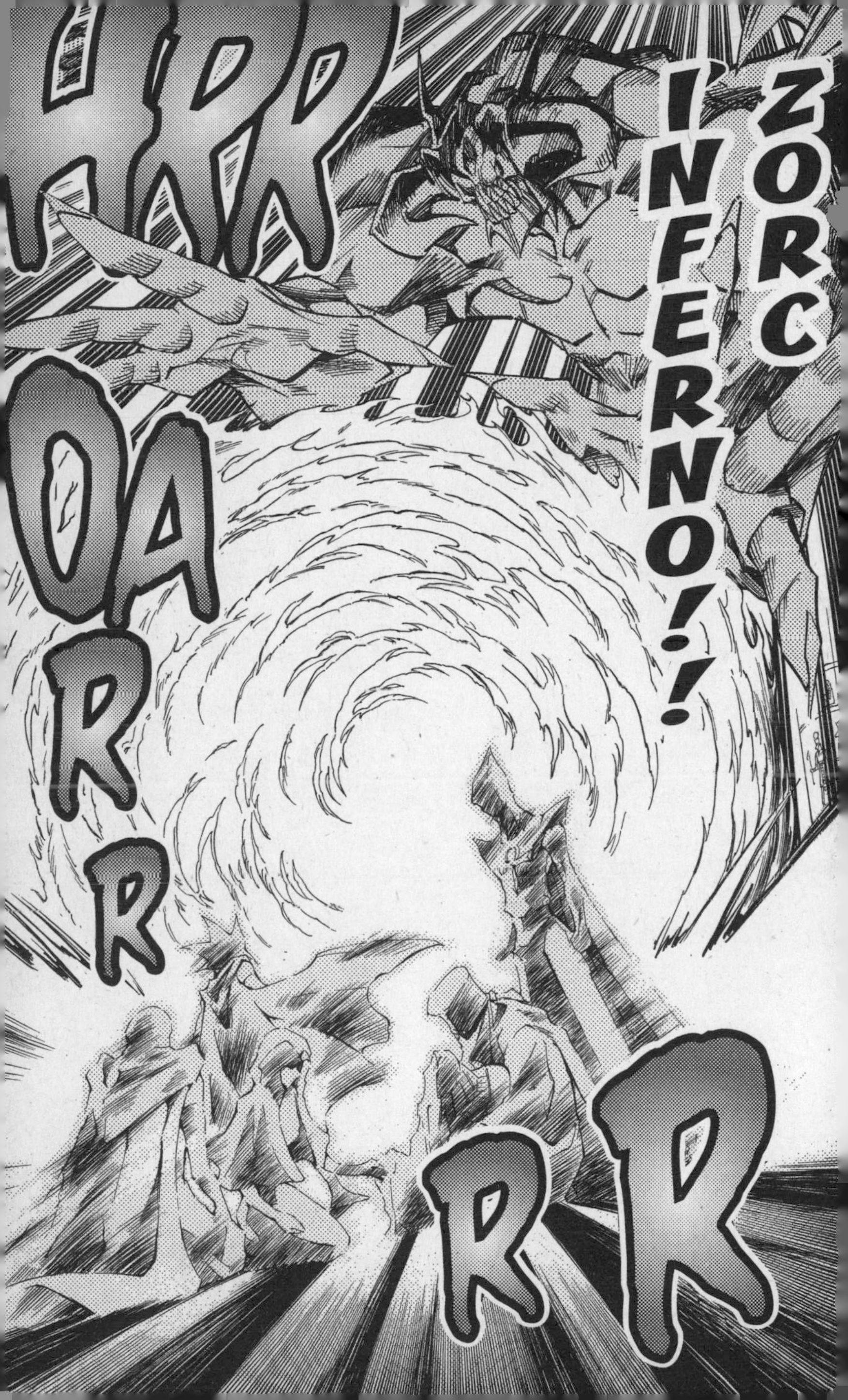
ZORC INFERNO!!
OARRRR

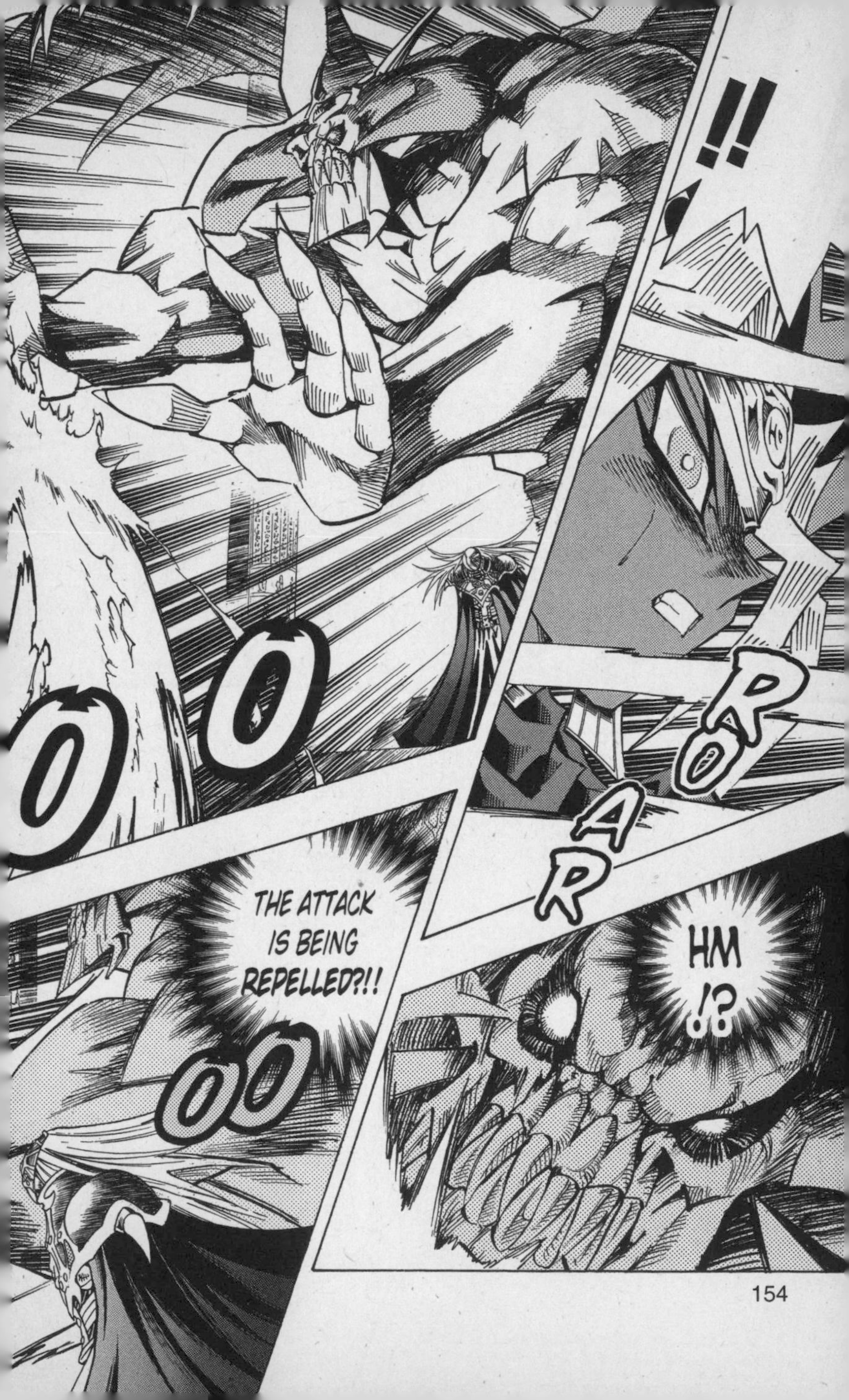
!!
ROAR
OO
HM !?
THE ATTACK IS BEING REPELLED?!!
OO

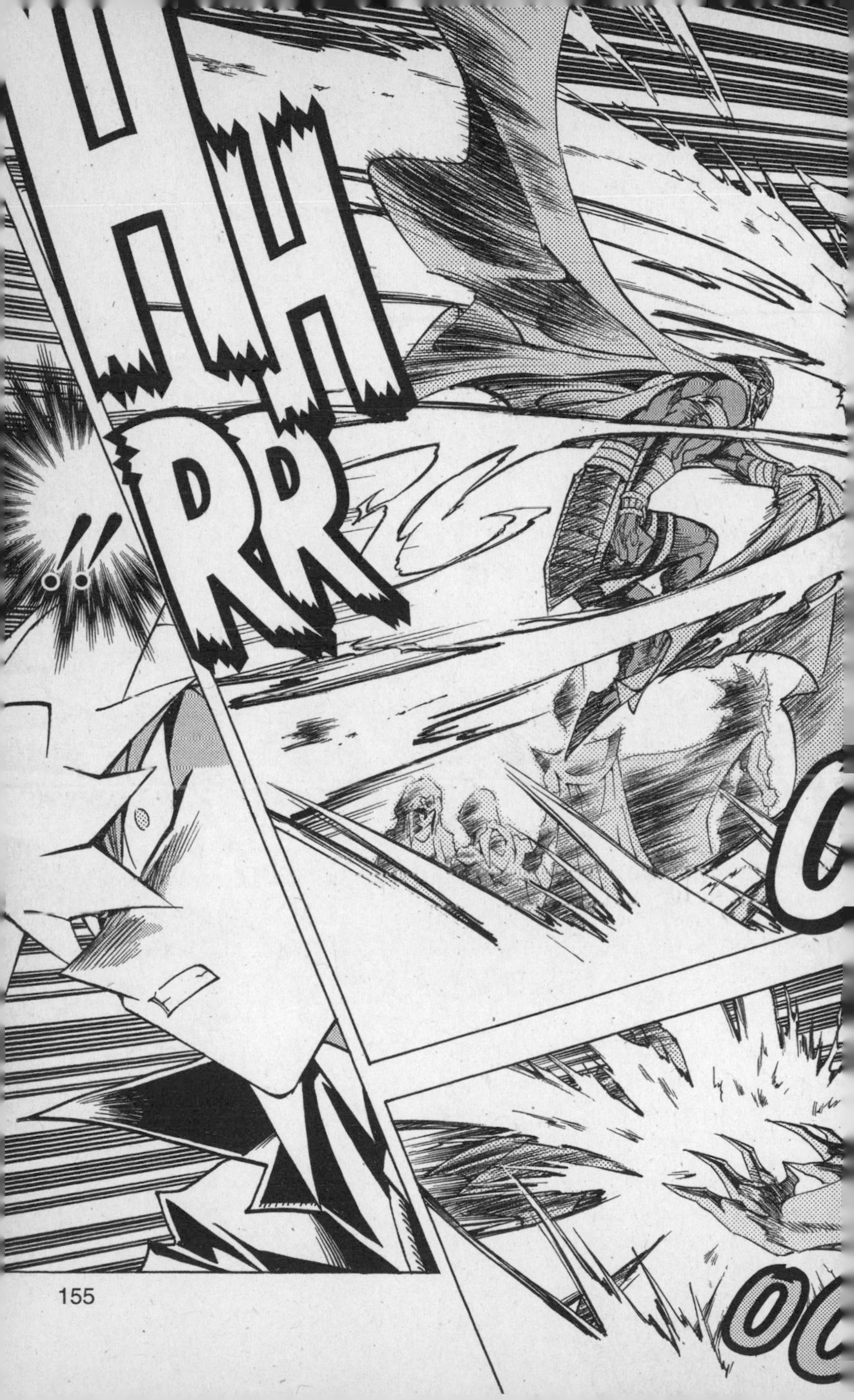

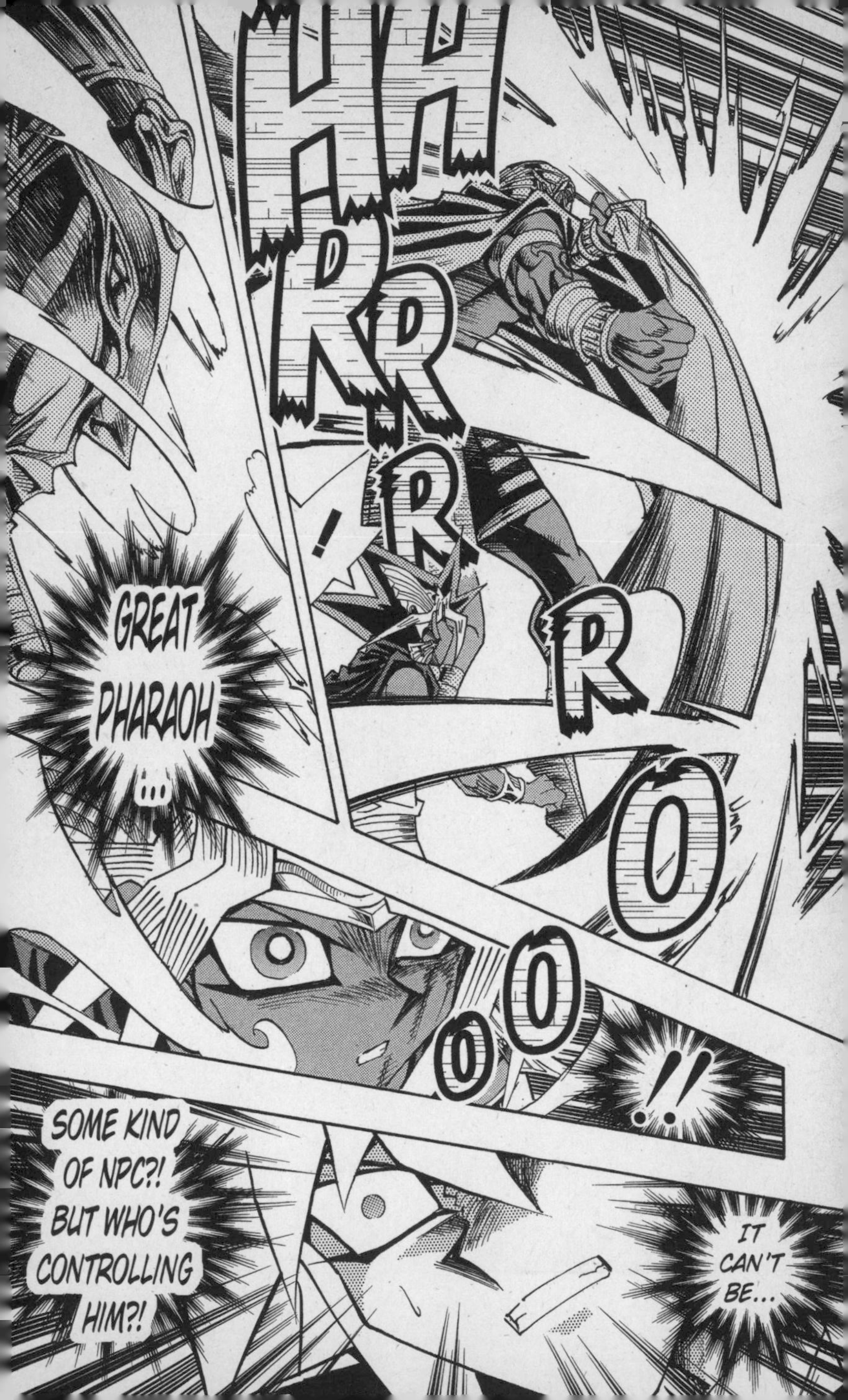
HHRRRROOOO!!
GREAT PHARAOH...
!
SOME KIND OF NPC?! BUT WHO'S CONTROLLING HIM?!
IT CAN'T BE...

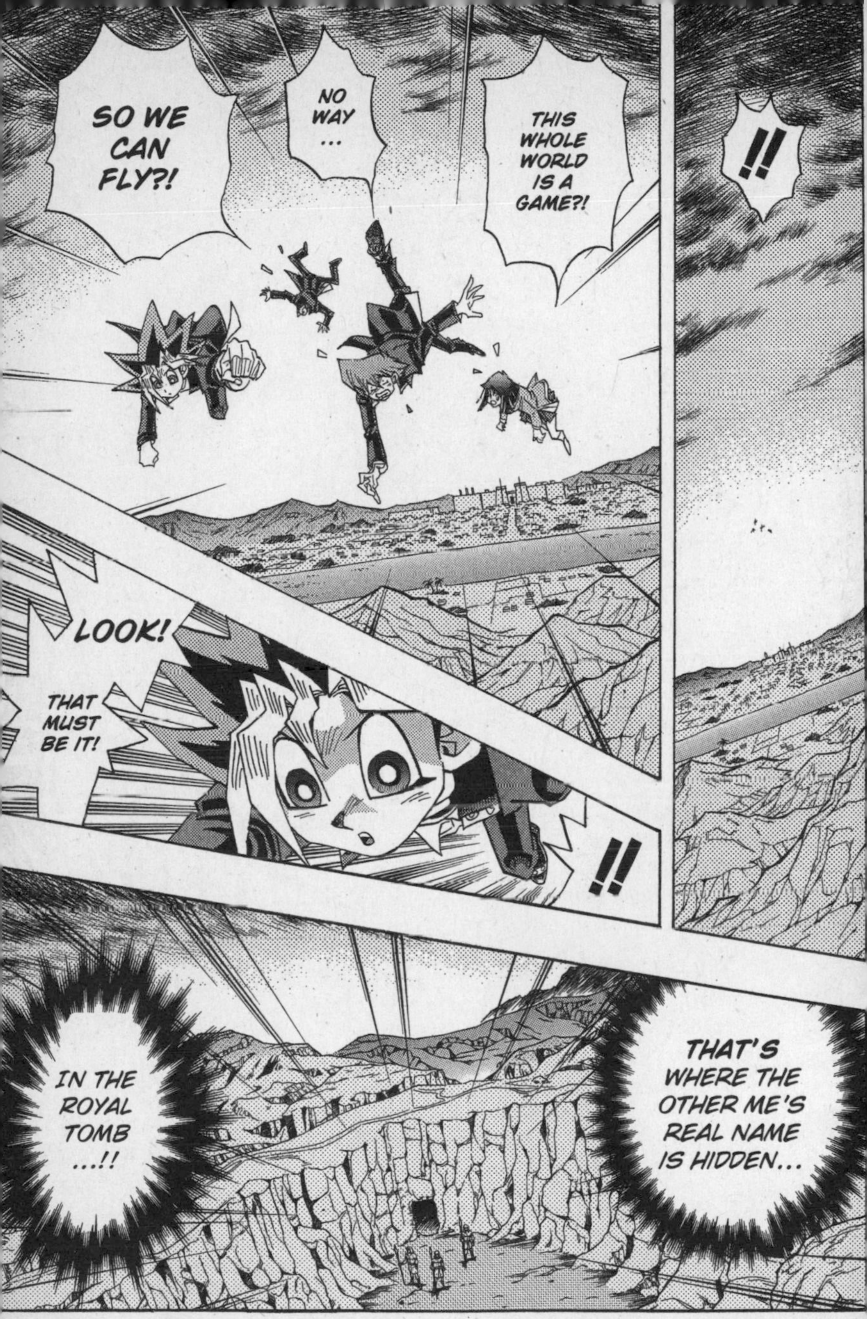
!!
THIS WHOLE WORLD IS A GAME?!
NO WAY ...
SO WE CAN FLY?!
!!
LOOK!
THAT MUST BE IT!
THAT'S WHERE THE OTHER ME'S REAL NAME IS HIDDEN...
IN THE ROYAL TOMB ...!!

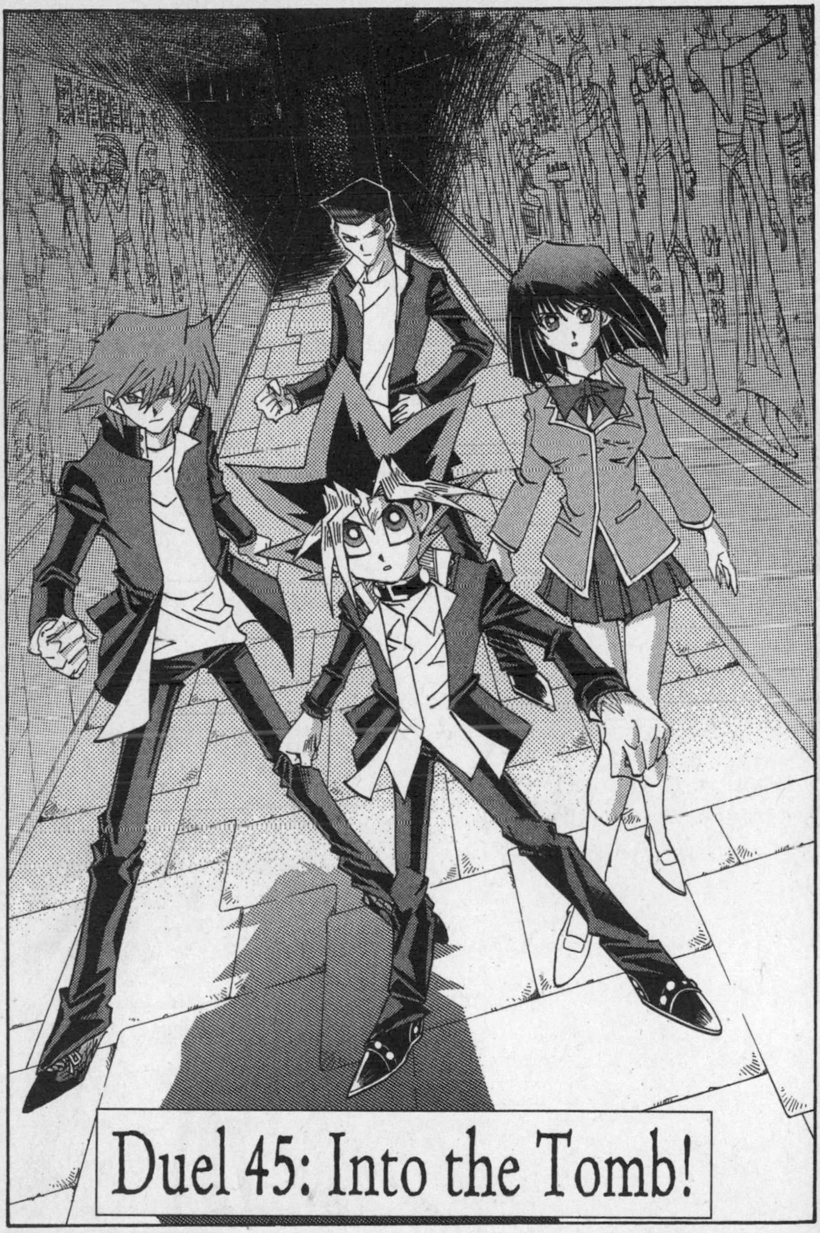
Duel 45: Into the Tomb!

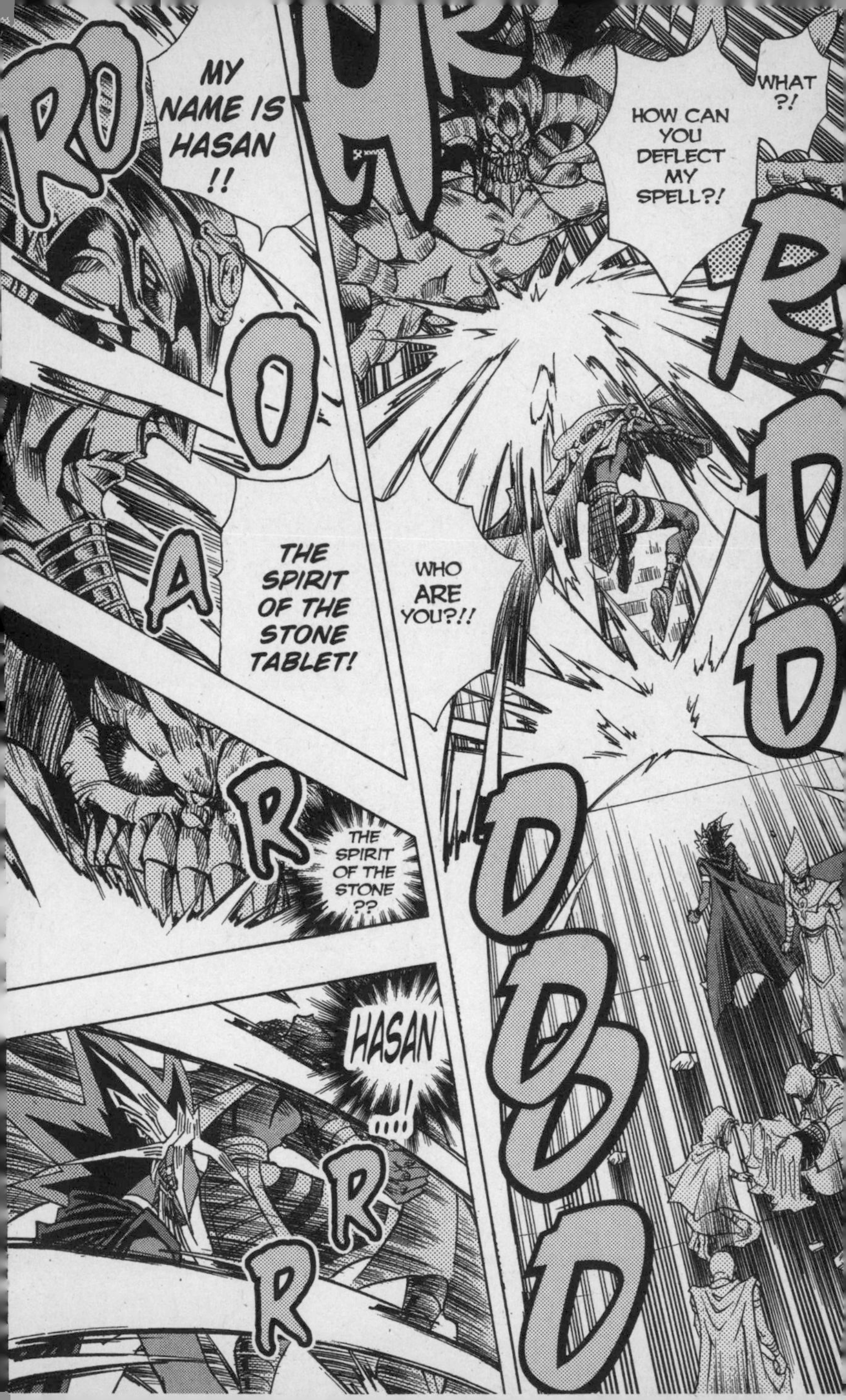
WHAT?!
HOW CAN YOU DEFLECT MY SPELL?!
WHO ARE YOU?!!
MY NAME IS HASAN!!
THE SPIRIT OF THE STONE TABLET!
THE SPIRIT OF THE STONE??
HASAN...!

READ THIS WAY

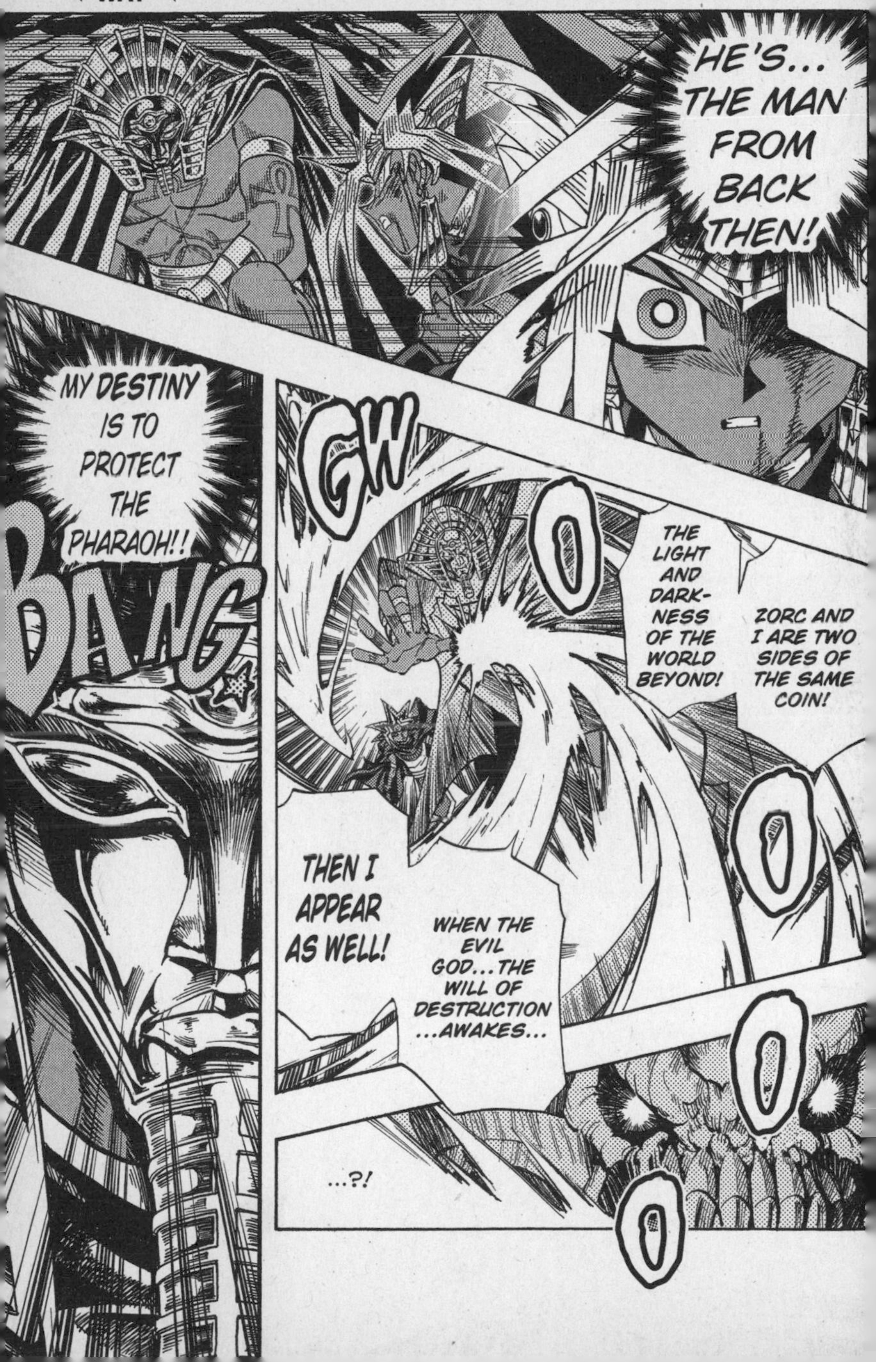
HE'S... THE MAN FROM BACK THEN!
ZORC AND I ARE TWO SIDES OF THE SAME COIN!
THE LIGHT AND DARK-NESS OF THE WORLD BEYOND!
GW
WHEN THE EVIL GOD... THE WILL OF DESTRUCTION ...AWAKES...
THEN I APPEAR AS WELL!
...?!
MY DESTINY IS TO PROTECT THE PHARAOH!!
BANG

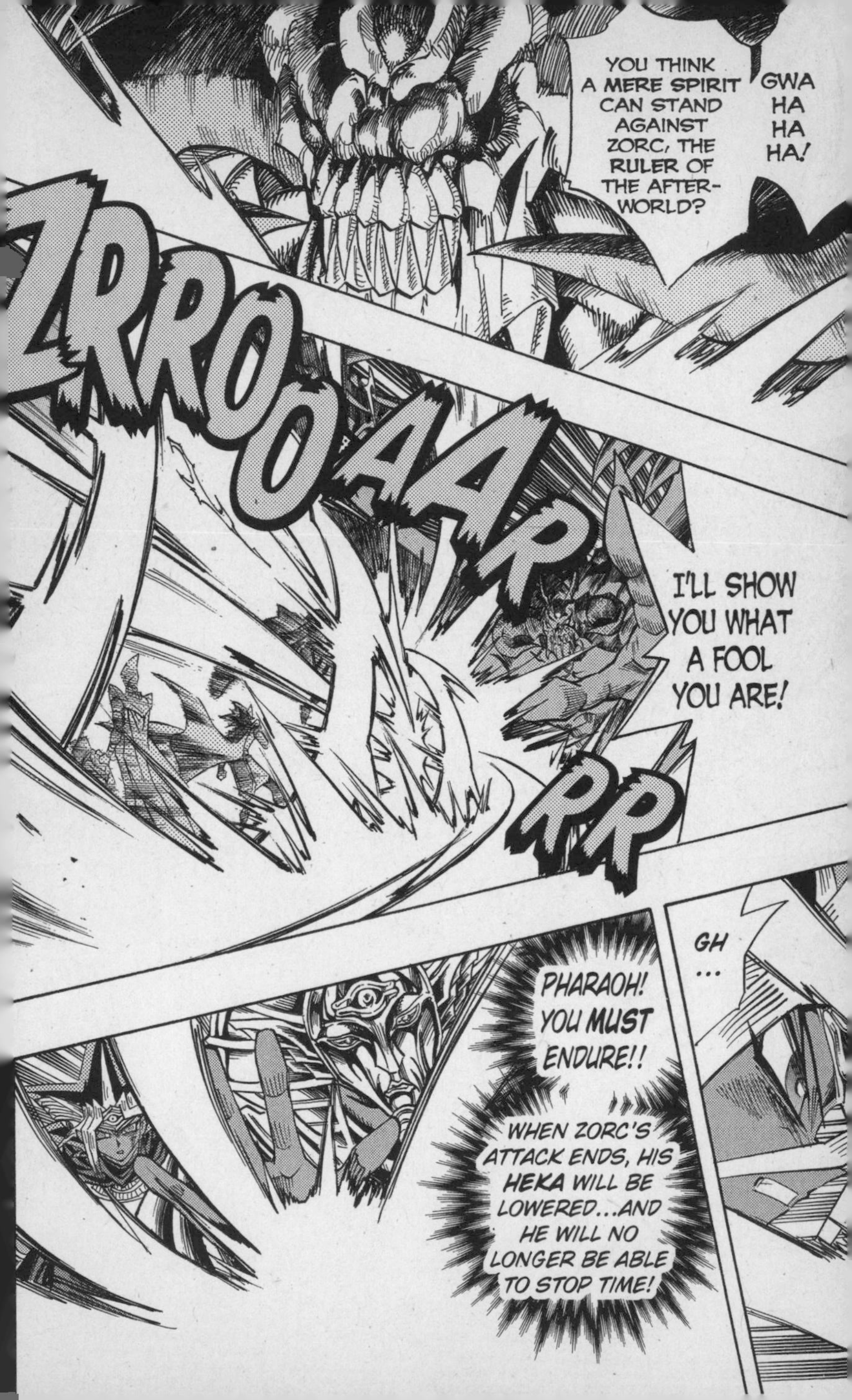
GWA HA HA HA!
YOU THINK A MERE SPIRIT CAN STAND AGAINST ZORC, THE RULER OF THE AFTER-WORLD?
ZRROOAAARRR
I'LL SHOW YOU WHAT A FOOL YOU ARE!
GH ...
PHARAOH! YOU MUST ENDURE!!
WHEN ZORC'S ATTACK ENDS, HIS HEKA WILL BE LOWERED...AND HE WILL NO LONGER BE ABLE TO STOP TIME!

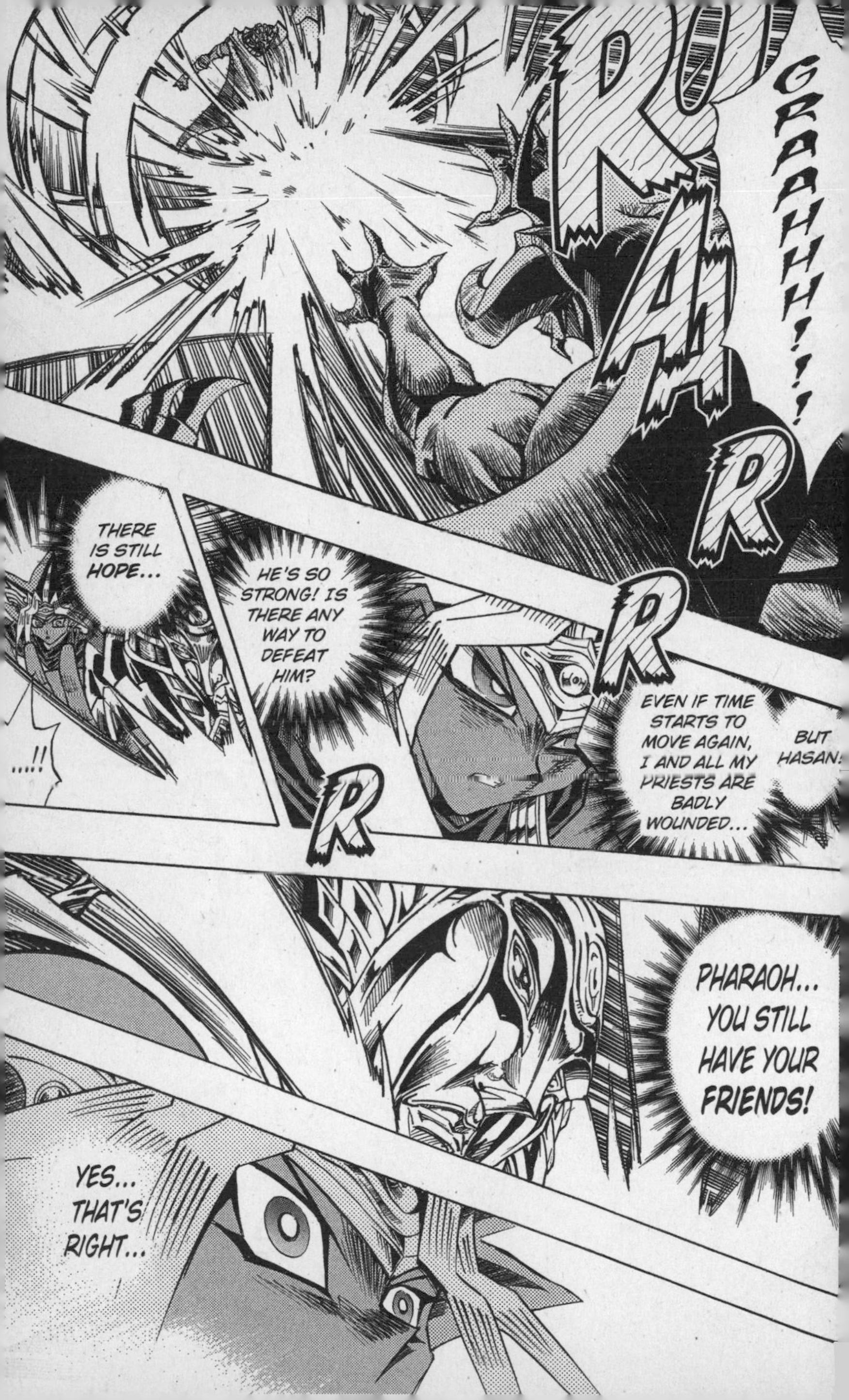
GRAAHHH!!!
BUT HASAN!
EVEN IF TIME STARTS TO MOVE AGAIN, I AND ALL MY PRIESTS ARE BADLY WOUNDED...
HE'S SO STRONG! IS THERE ANY WAY TO DEFEAT HIM?
THERE IS STILL HOPE...
...!!
PHARAOH... YOU STILL HAVE YOUR FRIENDS!
YES... THAT'S RIGHT...

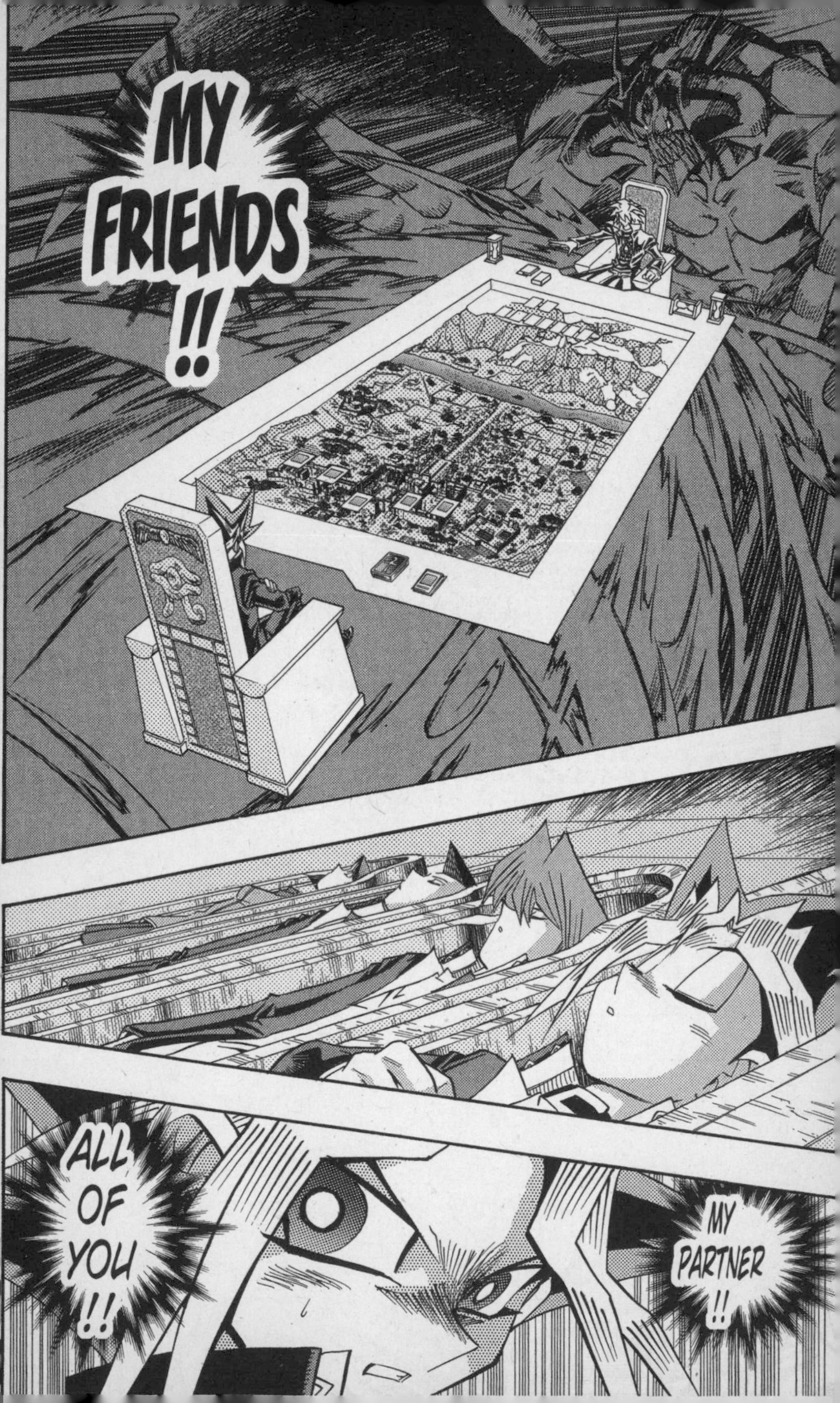
MY FRIENDS !!
MY PARTNER !!
ALL OF YOU !!

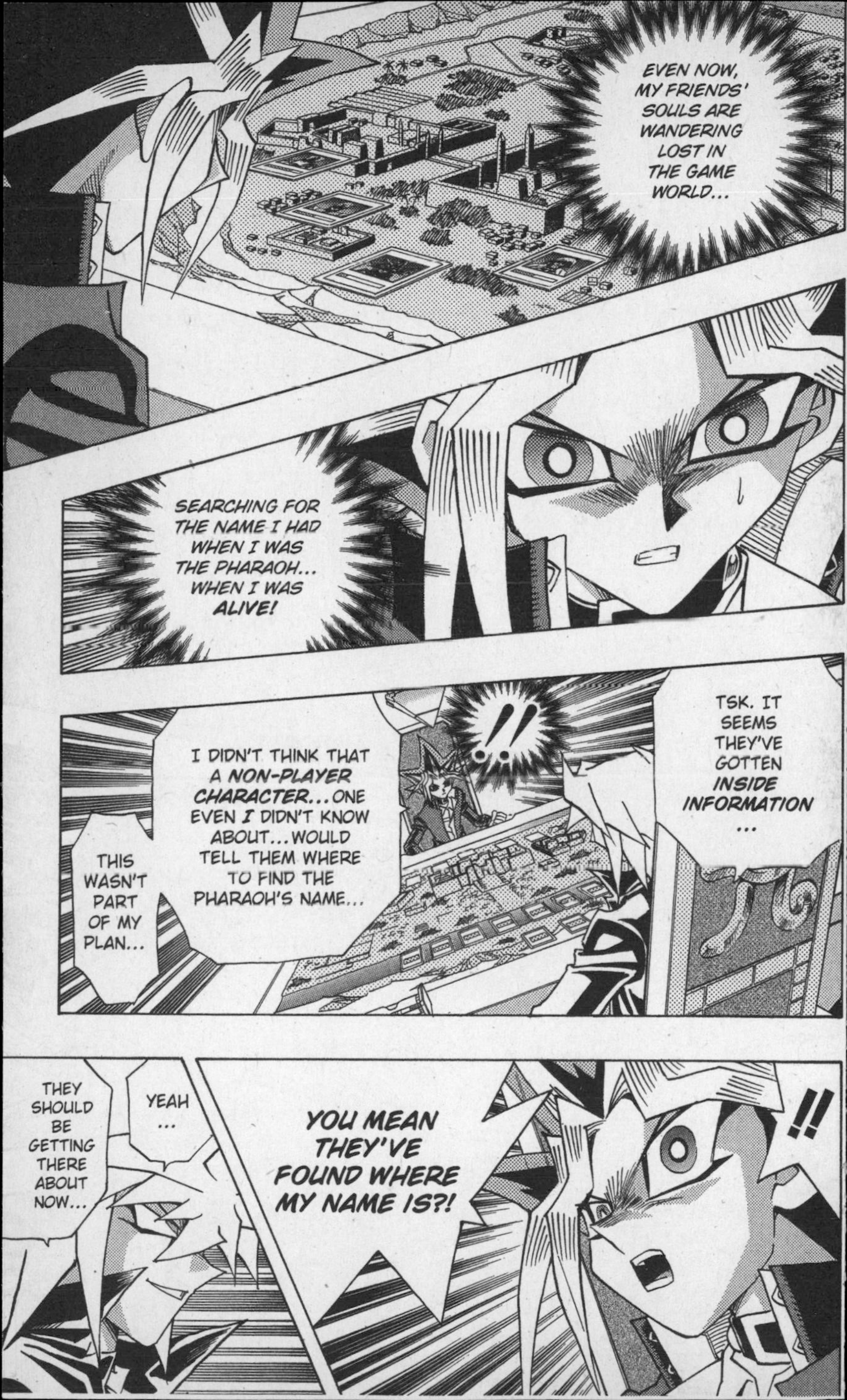
EVEN NOW, MY FRIENDS' SOULS ARE WANDERING LOST IN THE GAME WORLD...
SEARCHING FOR THE NAME I HAD WHEN I WAS THE PHARAOH... WHEN I WAS ALIVE!
TSK. IT SEEMS THEY'VE GOTTEN INSIDE INFORMATION...
!!
I DIDN'T THINK THAT A NON-PLAYER CHARACTER... ONE EVEN I DIDN'T KNOW ABOUT... WOULD TELL THEM WHERE TO FIND THE PHARAOH'S NAME...
THIS WASN'T PART OF MY PLAN...
!!
YOU MEAN THEY'VE FOUND WHERE MY NAME IS?!
YEAH...
THEY SHOULD BE GETTING THERE ABOUT NOW...

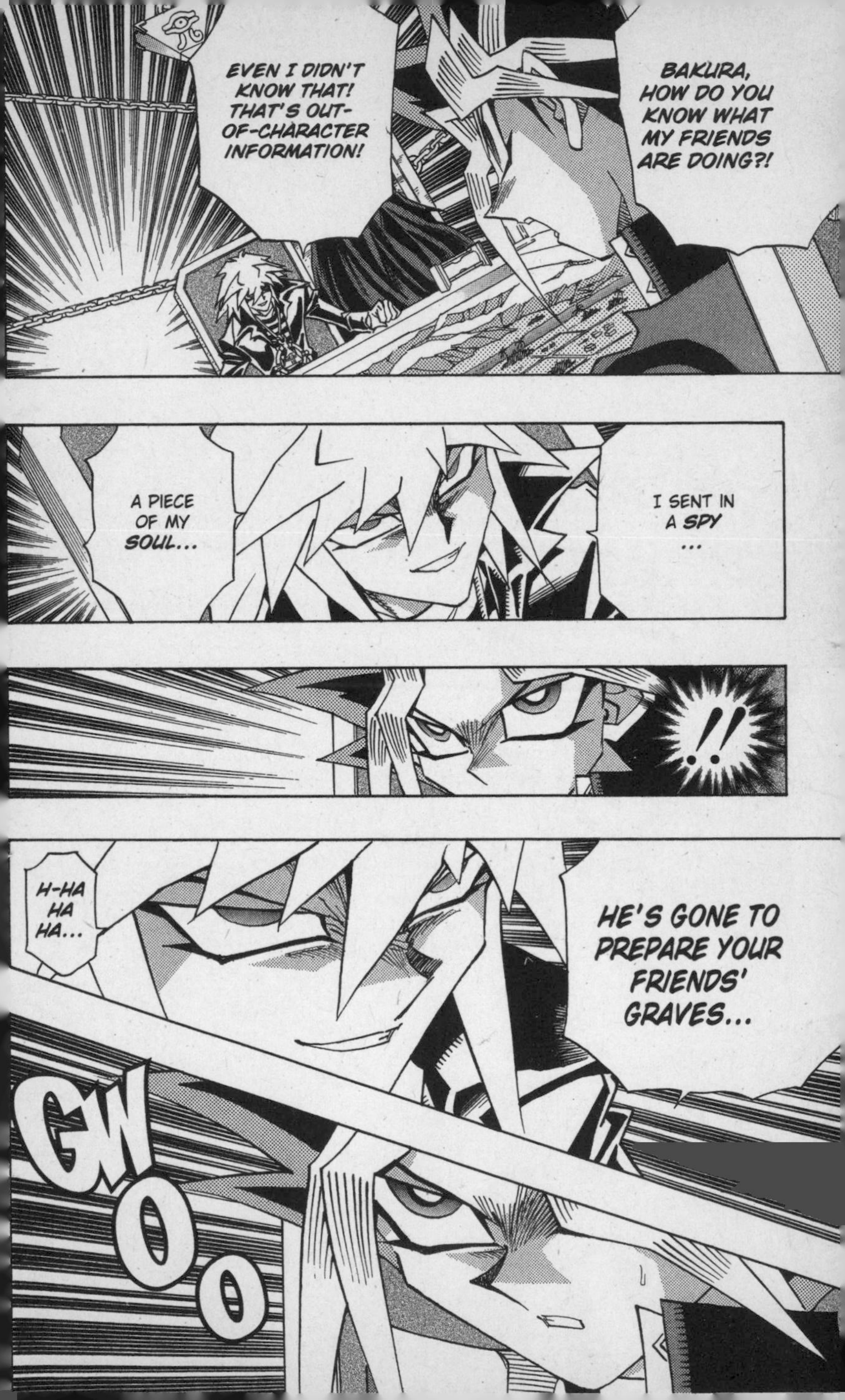
BAKURA, HOW DO YOU KNOW WHAT MY FRIENDS ARE DOING?!
EVEN I DIDN'T KNOW THAT! THAT'S OUT-OF-CHARACTER INFORMATION!
I SENT IN A *SPY* ...
A PIECE OF MY *SOUL*...
!!
HE'S GONE TO PREPARE YOUR FRIENDS' GRAVES...
H-HA HA HA...
GWOOO

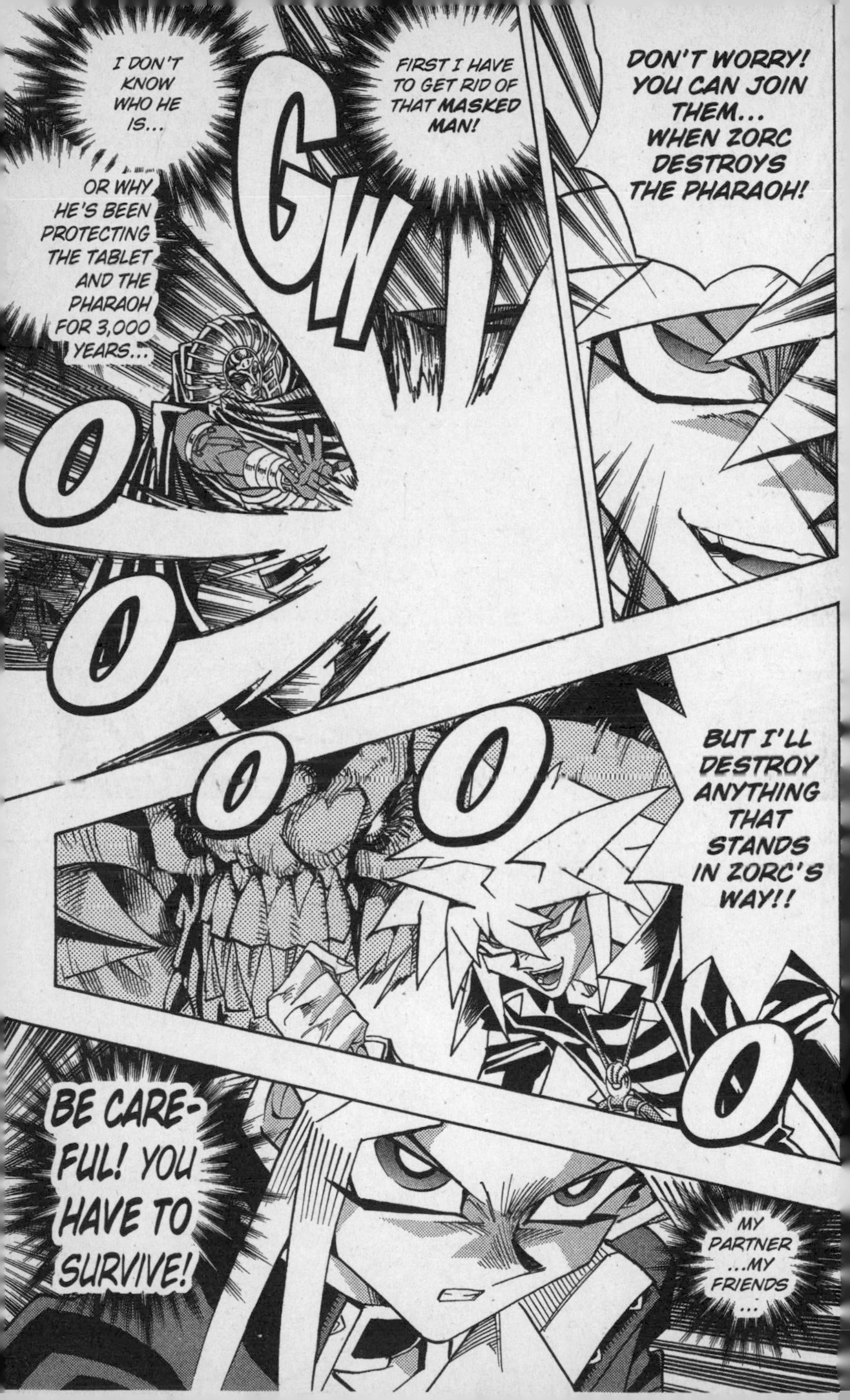
DON'T WORRY! YOU CAN JOIN THEM... WHEN ZORC DESTROYS THE PHARAOH!
I DON'T KNOW WHO HE IS...
OR WHY HE'S BEEN PROTECTING THE TABLET AND THE PHARAOH FOR 3,000 YEARS...
FIRST I HAVE TO GET RID OF THAT MASKED MAN!
GWOOOOOO
BUT I'LL DESTROY ANYTHING THAT STANDS IN ZORC'S WAY!!
MY PARTNER ...MY FRIENDS ...
BE CARE-FUL! YOU HAVE TO SURVIVE!

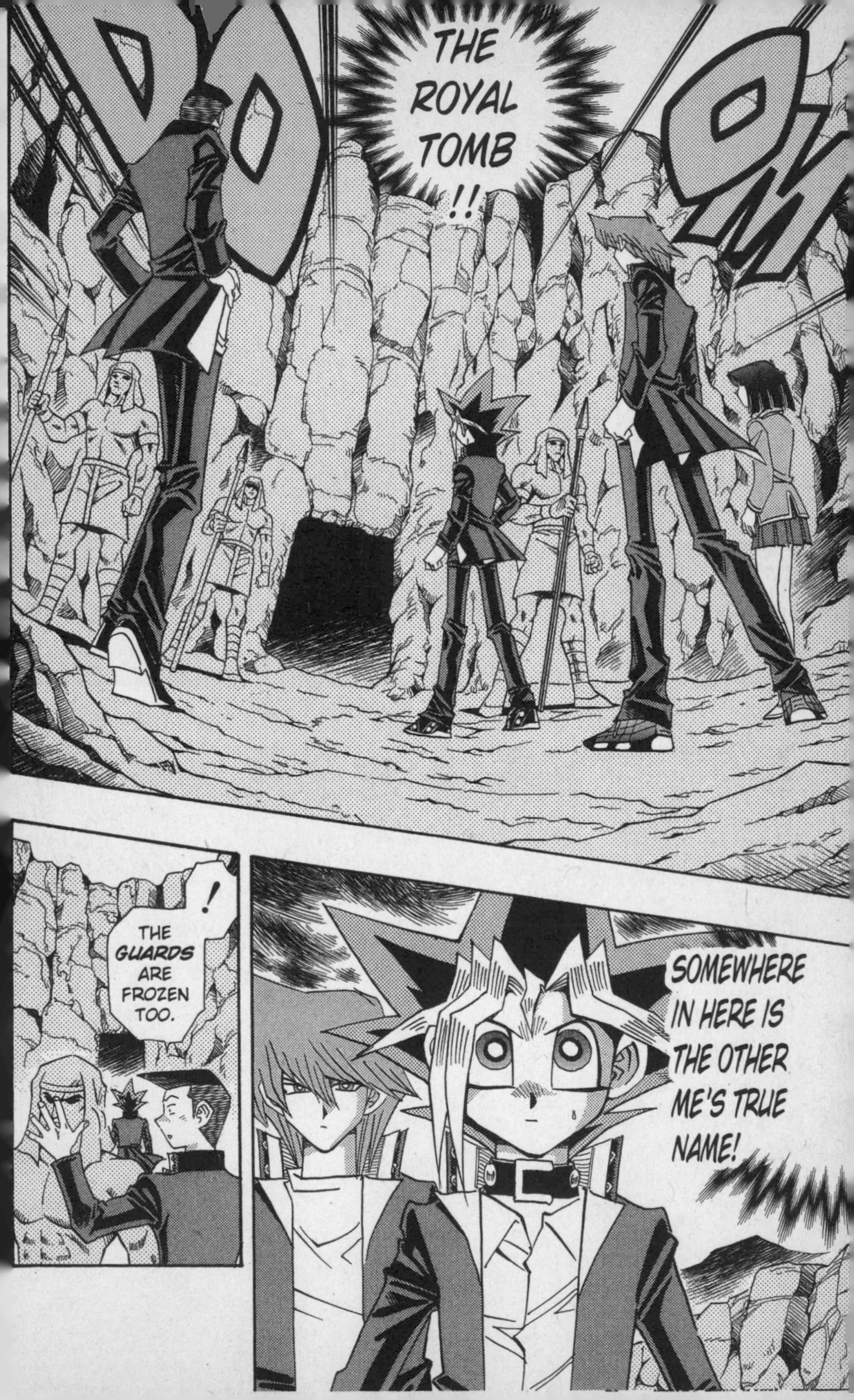
THE ROYAL TOMB!!
SOMEWHERE IN HERE IS THE OTHER ME'S TRUE NAME!
!
THE GUARDS ARE FROZEN TOO.

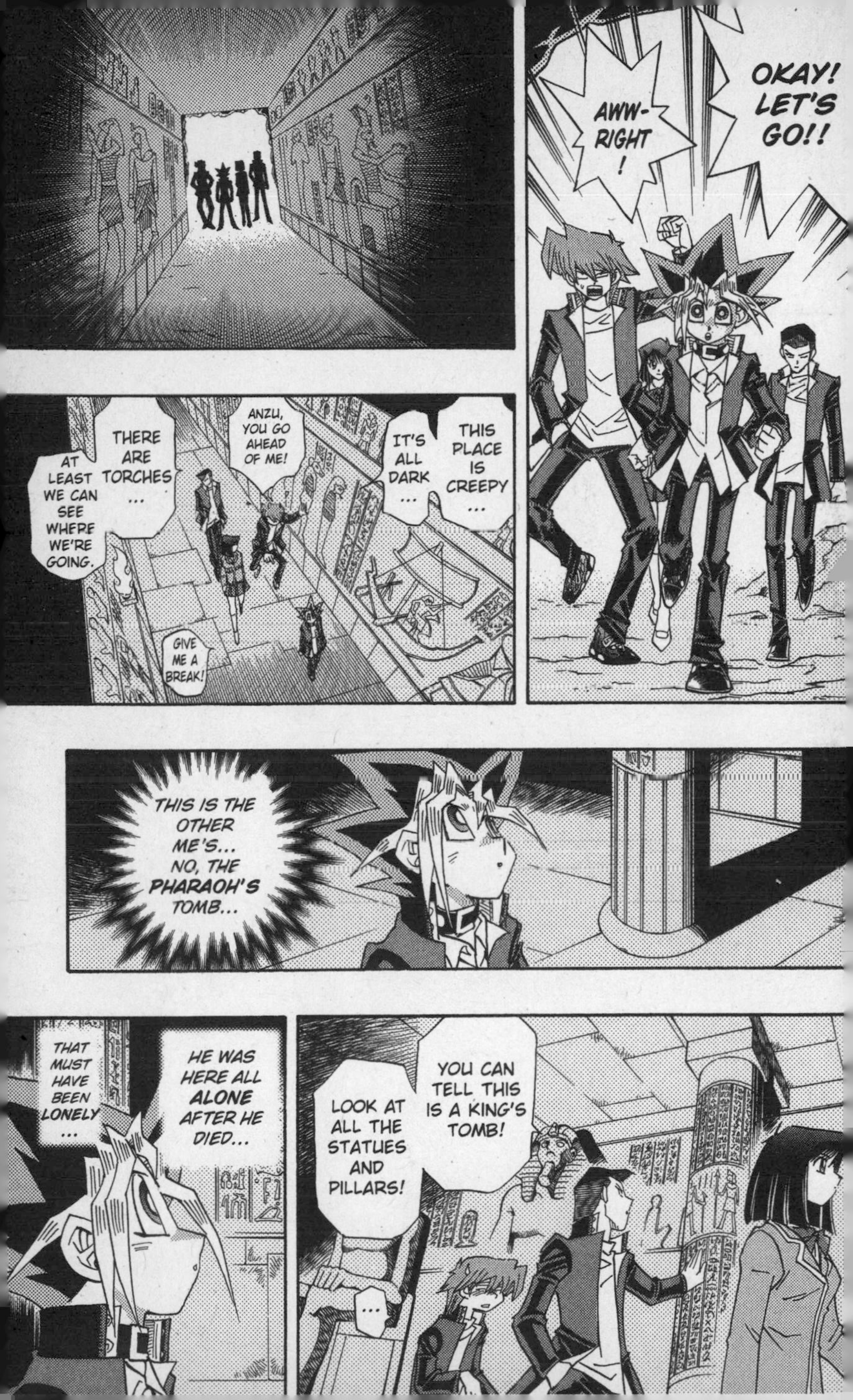

OKAY! LET'S GO!!
AWW-RIGHT!
THIS PLACE IS CREEPY...
IT'S ALL DARK...
ANZU, YOU GO AHEAD OF ME!
THERE ARE TORCHES...
AT LEAST WE CAN SEE WHERE WE'RE GOING.
GIVE ME A BREAK!
THIS IS THE OTHER ME'S... NO, THE **PHARAOH'S** TOMB...
YOU CAN TELL THIS IS A KING'S TOMB!
LOOK AT ALL THE STATUES AND PILLARS!
...
HE WAS HERE ALL **ALONE** AFTER HE DIED...
THAT MUST HAVE BEEN LONELY...

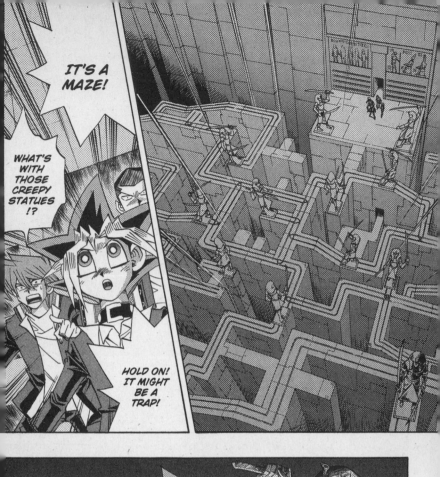

IT'S A MAZE!

WHAT'S WITH THOSE CREEPY STATUES !?

HOLD ON! IT MIGHT BE A TRAP!

...

IT LOOKS LIKE THAT SWORD COULD DROP AT ANY MOMENT...

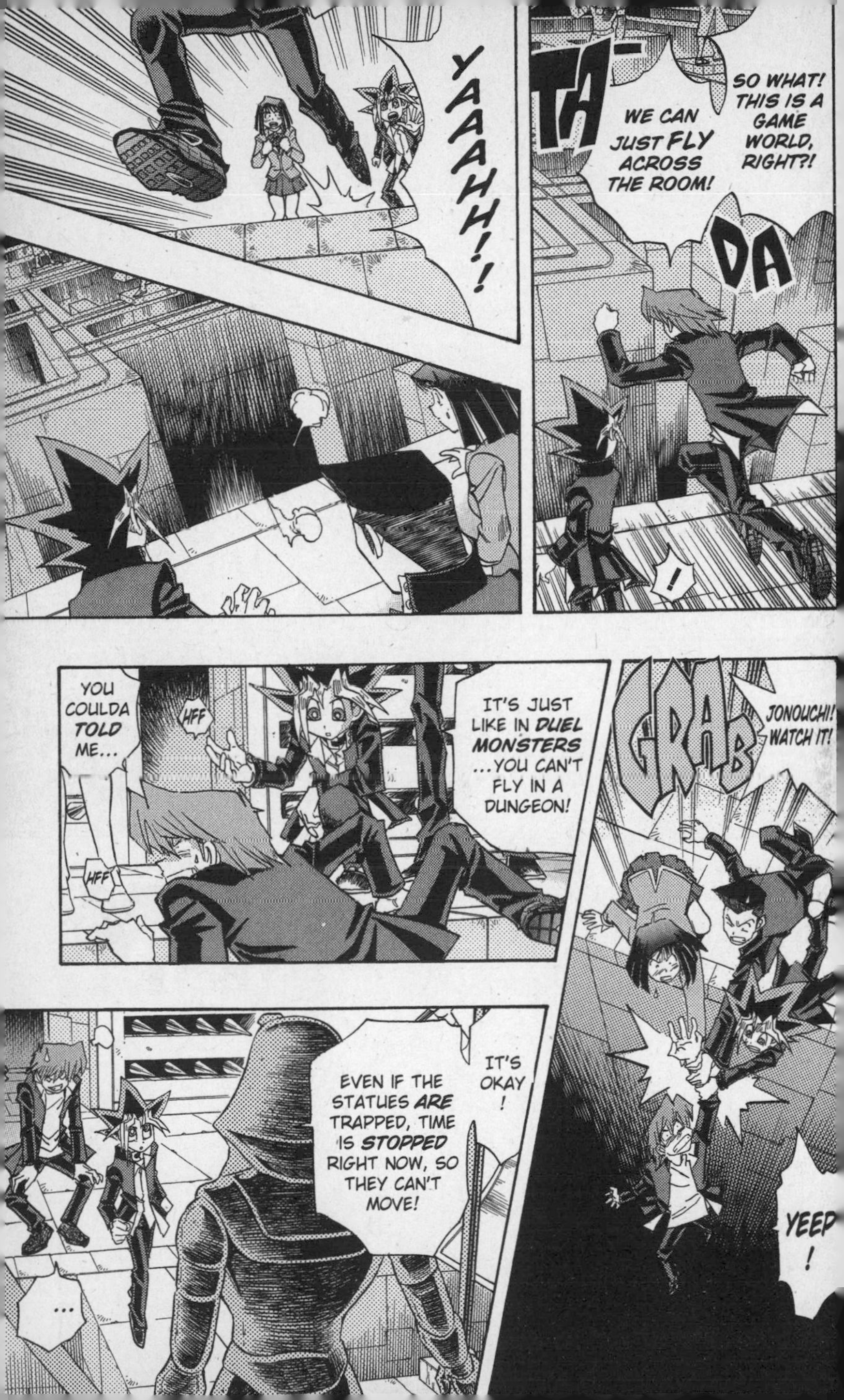
TA-
SO WHAT! THIS IS A GAME WORLD, RIGHT?!
WE CAN JUST FLY ACROSS THE ROOM!
DA
!
YAAAHH!!
GRAB
JONOUCHI! WATCH IT!
YEEP!
IT'S JUST LIKE IN DUEL MONSTERS ...YOU CAN'T FLY IN A DUNGEON!
HFF
YOU COULDA TOLD ME...
HFF
IT'S OKAY!
EVEN IF THE STATUES ARE TRAPPED, TIME IS STOPPED RIGHT NOW, SO THEY CAN'T MOVE!
...

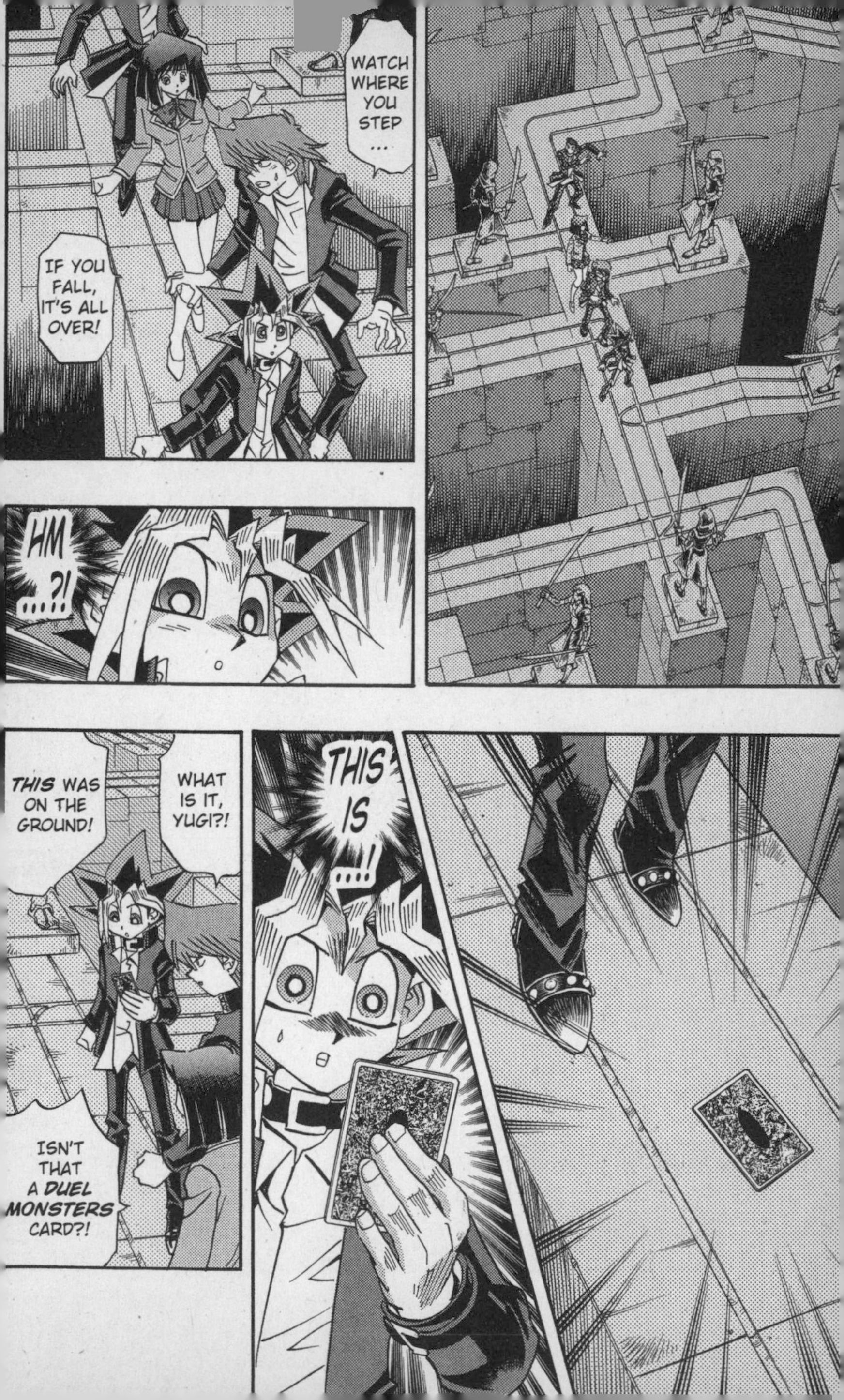
WATCH WHERE YOU STEP ...
IF YOU FALL, IT'S ALL OVER!
HM ...?!
THIS IS ...!!
WHAT IS IT, YUGI?!
THIS WAS ON THE GROUND!
ISN'T THAT A *DUEL MONSTERS* CARD?!

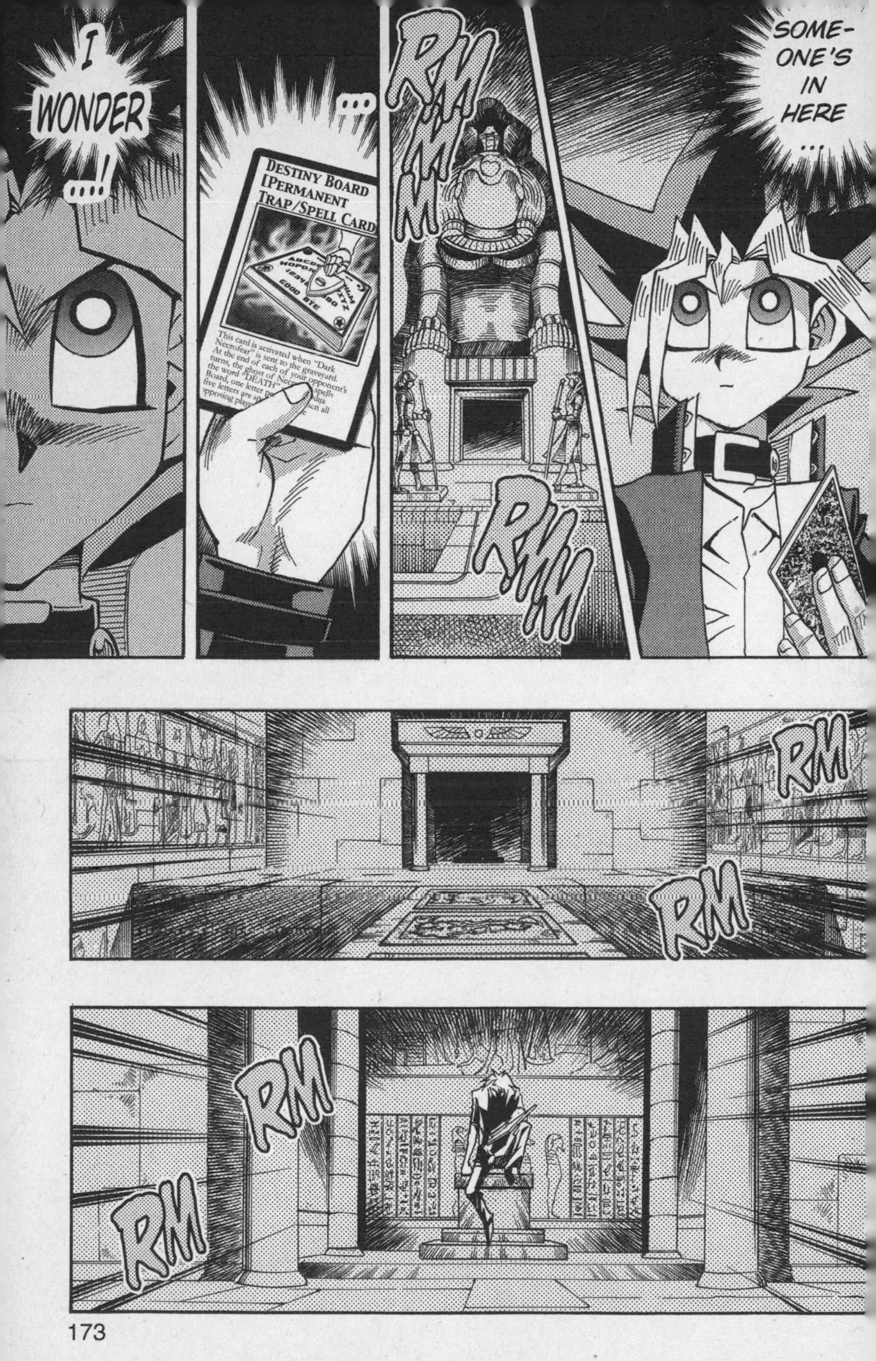
SOME-ONE'S IN HERE ...
RMMM
RMM
...
DESTINY BOARD [PERMANENT TRAP/SPELL CARD]
I WONDER ...!
RM
RM
RM
RM

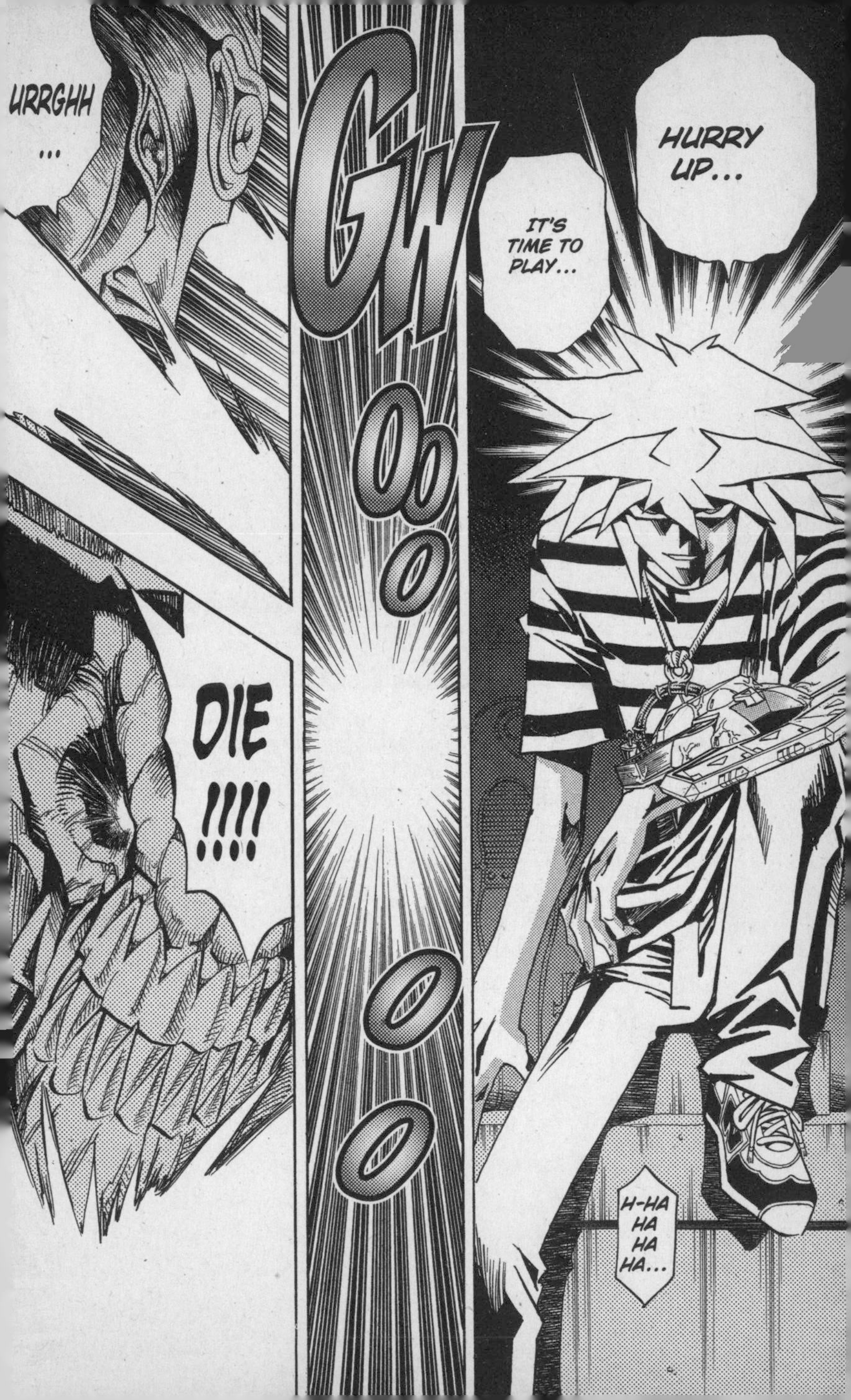
HURRY UP...
IT'S TIME TO PLAY...
H-HA HA HA HA...
GWOOOOO
URRGHH ...
DIE !!!!

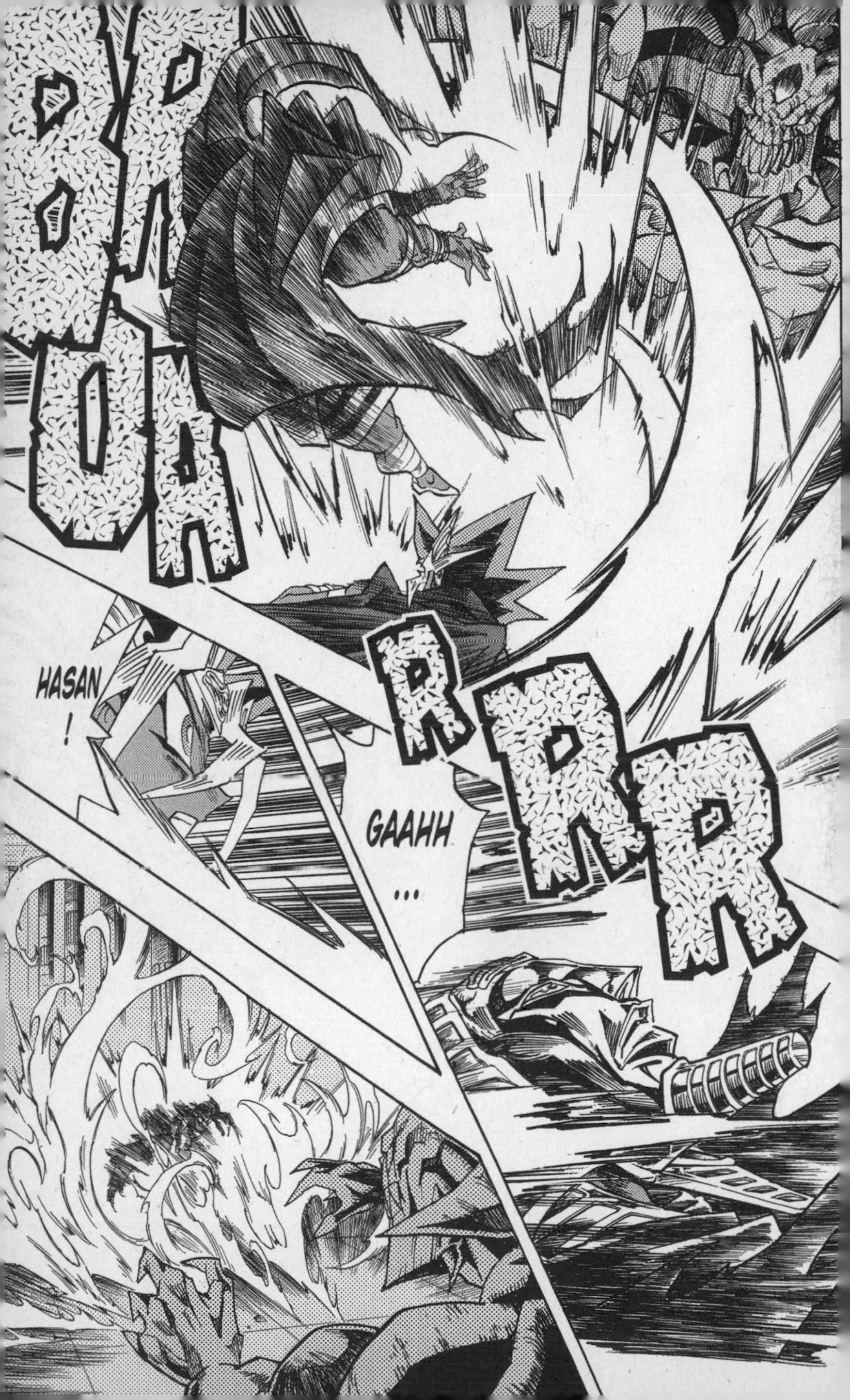
GAAHH...
HASAN!

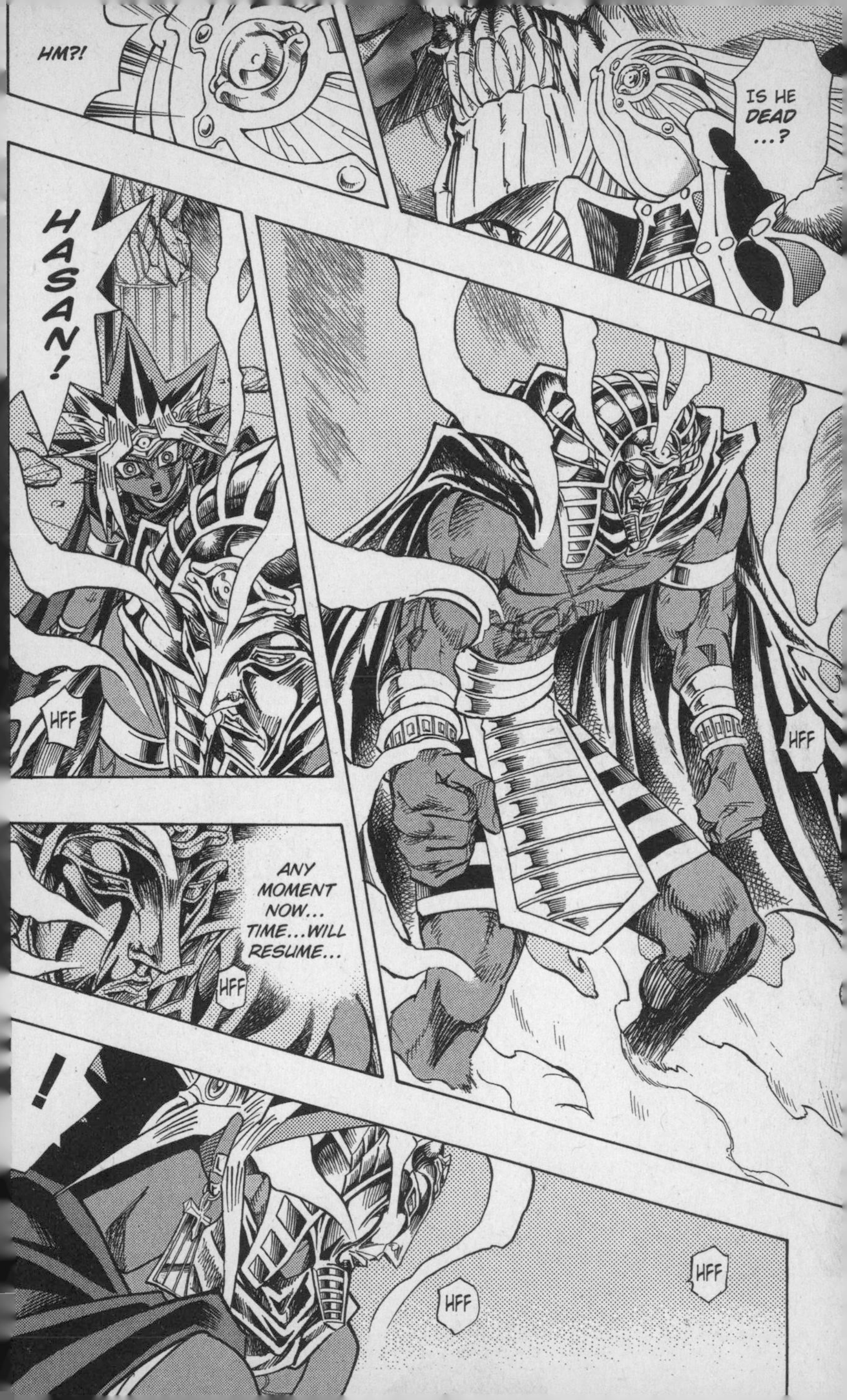
IS HE DEAD ...?
HM?!
HFF
HASAN!
HFF
ANY MOMENT NOW... TIME...WILL RESUME...
HFF
HFF
HFF
!

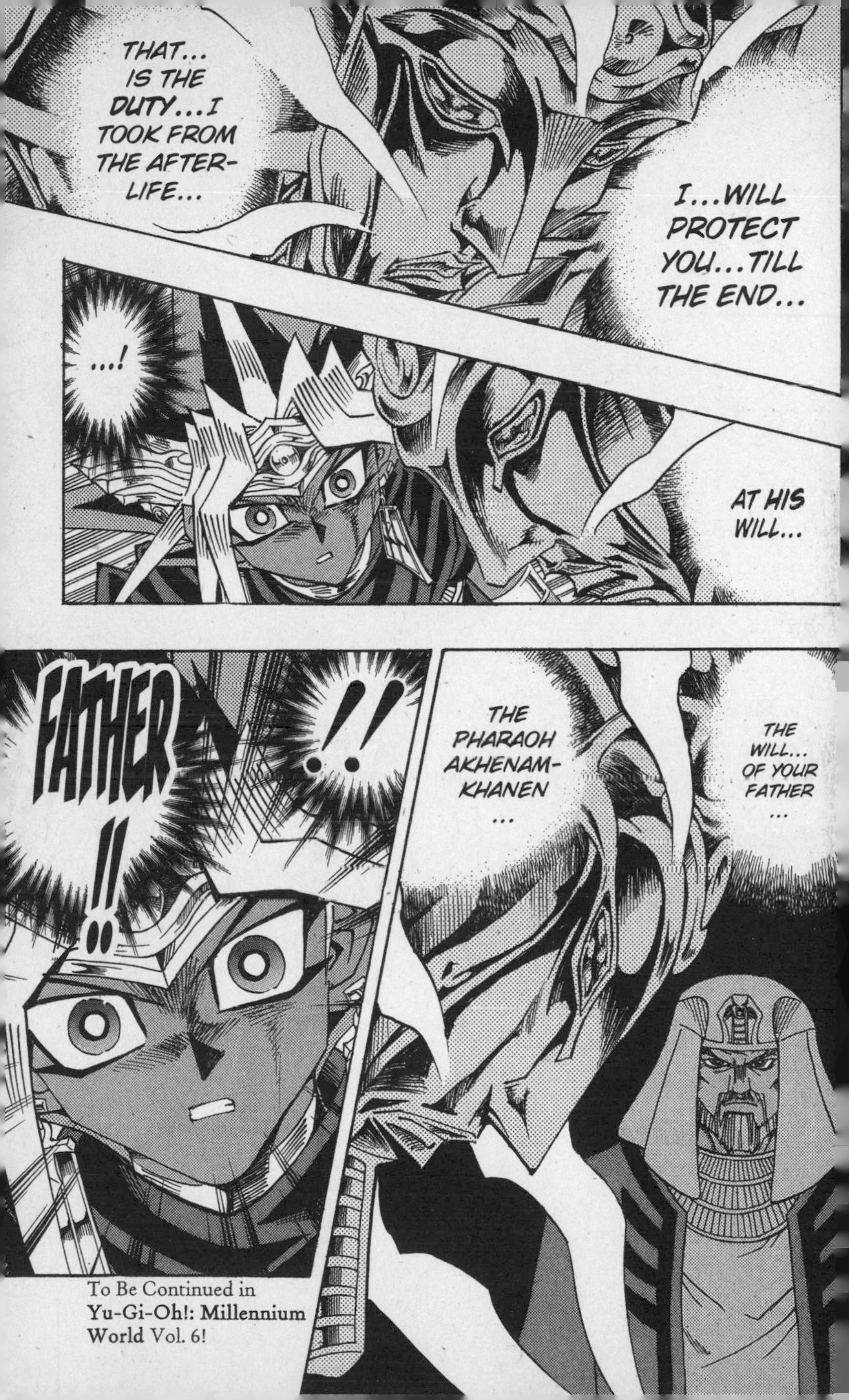
THAT... IS THE DUTY...I TOOK FROM THE AFTER-LIFE...
I...WILL PROTECT YOU...TILL THE END...
AT HIS WILL...
...!
THE WILL... OF YOUR FATHER...
THE PHARAOH AKHENAM-KHANEN...
!!
FATHER!!

To Be Continued in **Yu-Gi-Oh!: Millennium World** Vol. 6!

IN THE NEXT VOLUME...

In the World of Memories, it's the Battle of Armageddon, as the pharaoh and his allies fight the forces of Zorc Necrophades! While an army of corpses attacks Egypt, Siamun unleashes his secret monster, the forbidden one, who might be a match for the dark god! Meanwhile, Yugi, Jonouchi, Honda and Anzu enter the tomb, where they face Zorc's sinister servant, Bakura! Now Yugi must fight Bakura without the help of Yu-Gi-Oh. And the ultimate battle will be fought with the ultimate weapon...Duel Monsters cards!

COMING OCTOBER 2007!

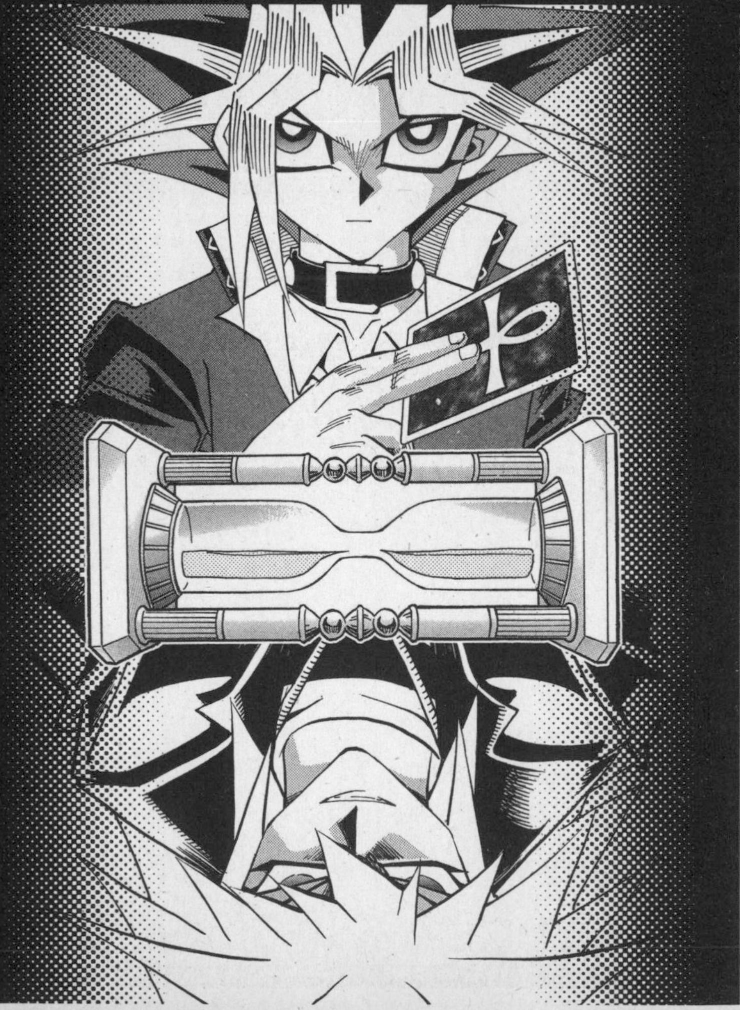

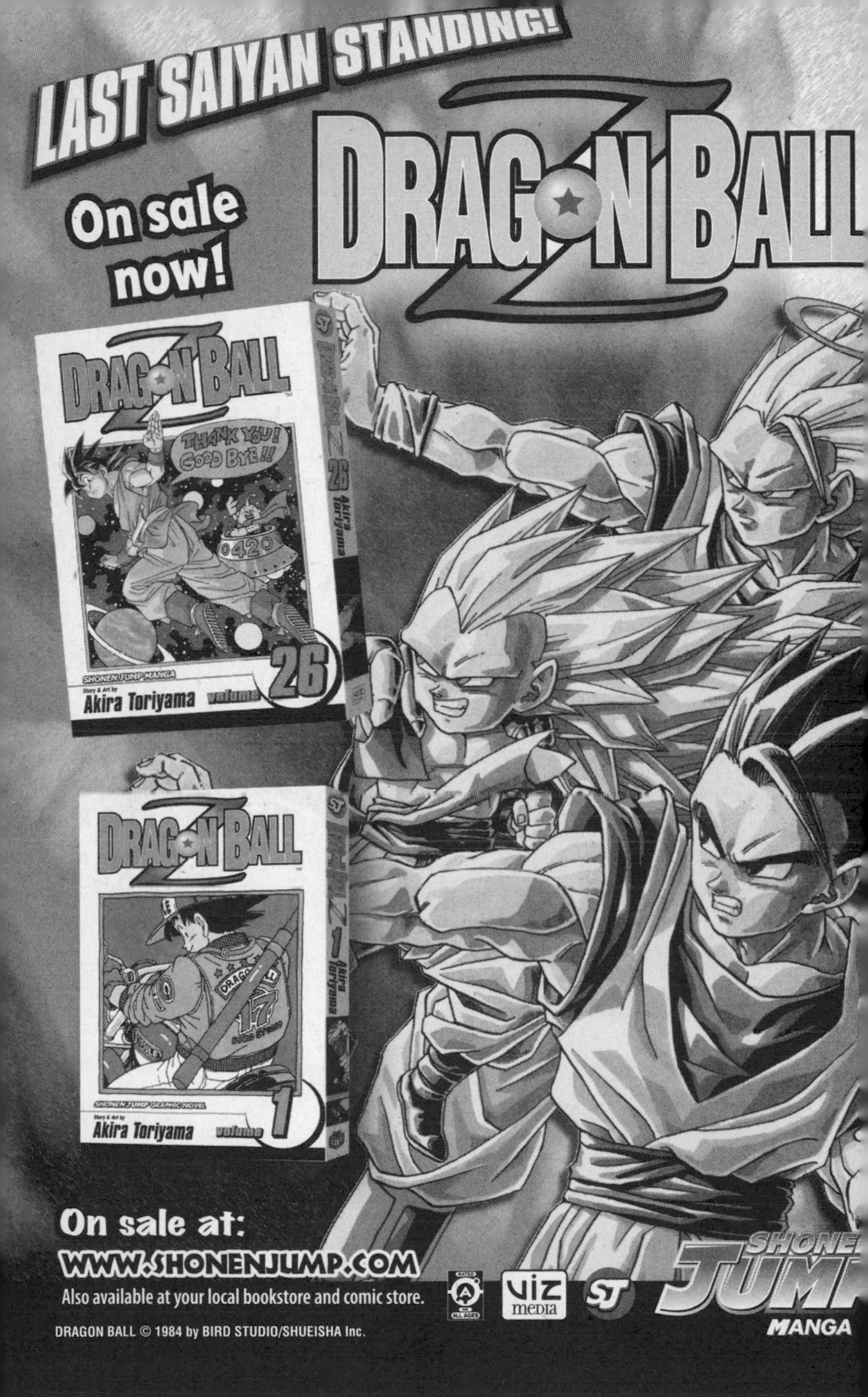
LAST SAIYAN STANDING!
DRAGON BALL Z
On sale now!
DRAGON BALL Z
THANK YOU! GOOD BYE!!
0420
SHONEN JUMP MANGA
26
Story & Art by
Akira Toriyama
volume 26
DRAGON BALL Z
SHONEN JUMP GRAPHIC NOVEL
Story & Art by
Akira Toriyama
volume 1
On sale at:
WWW.SHONENJUMP.COM
Also available at your local bookstore and comic store.
DRAGON BALL © 1984 by BIRD STUDIO/SHUEISHA Inc.
viz media
SHONEN JUMP MANGA

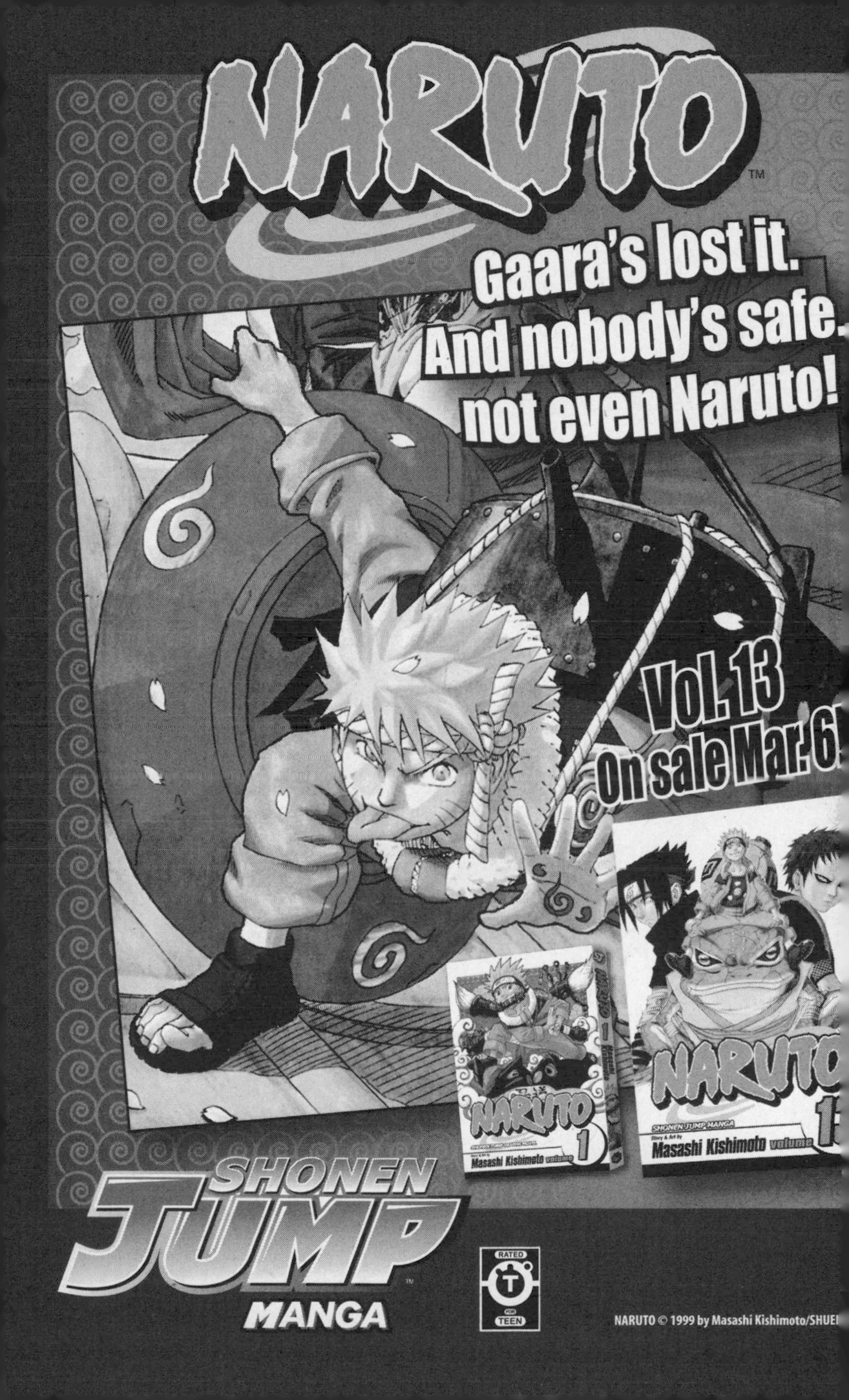
NARUTO™
Gaara's lost it.
And nobody's safe.
not even Naruto!
Vol. 13
On sale Mar. 6!
NARUTO
1
Masashi Kishimoto volume
NARUTO
SHONEN JUMP MANGA
Story & Art by
Masashi Kishimoto volume
SHONEN
JUMP™
MANGA
RATED
T
TEEN
NARUTO © 1999 by Masashi Kishimoto/SHUEI

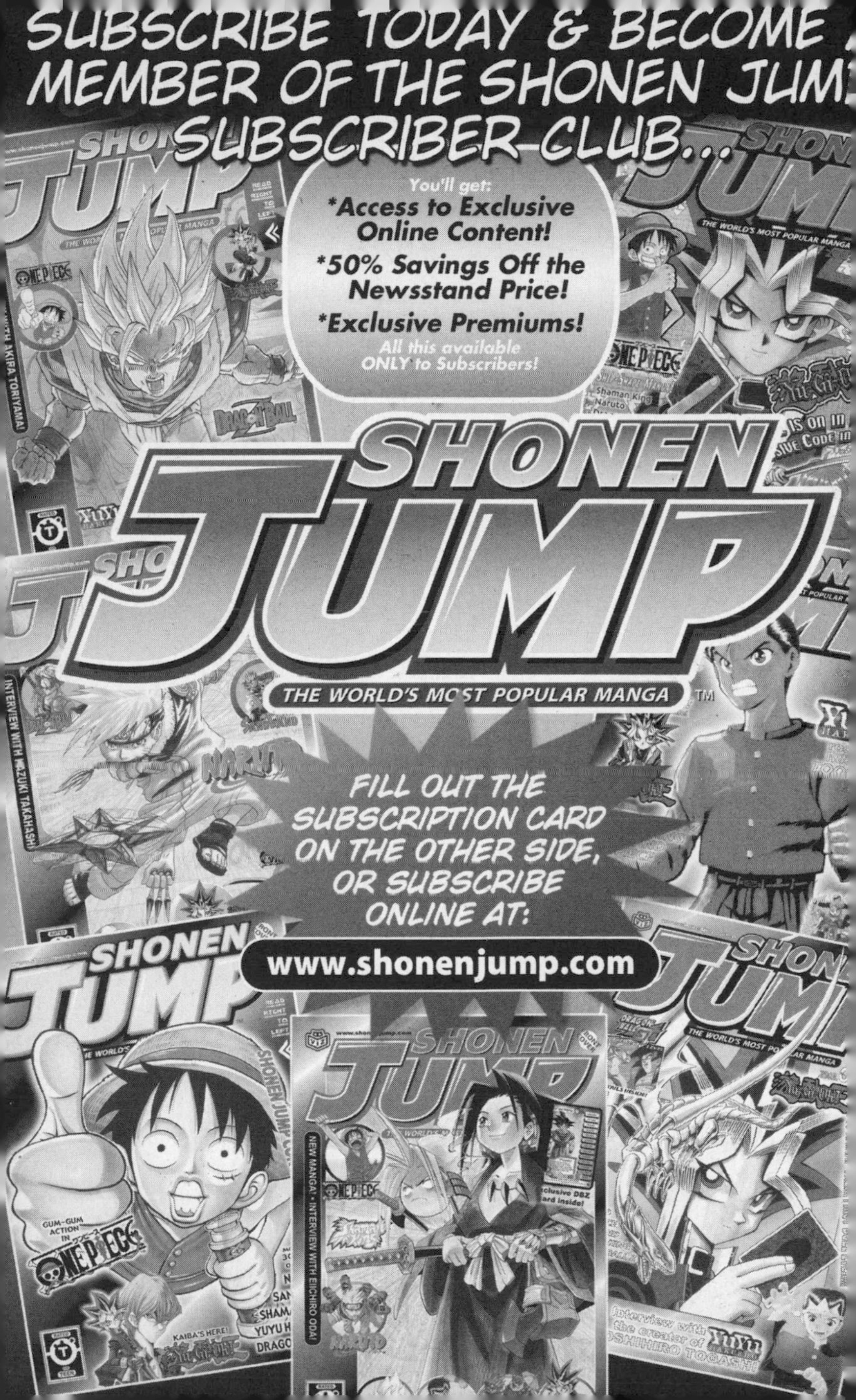
SUBSCRIBE TODAY & BECOME A MEMBER OF THE SHONEN JUMP SUBSCRIBER CLUB...
You'll get:
*Access to Exclusive Online Content!
*50% Savings Off the Newsstand Price!
*Exclusive Premiums!
All this available ONLY to Subscribers!
SHONEN JUMP
THE WORLD'S MOST POPULAR MANGA ™
FILL OUT THE SUBSCRIPTION CARD ON THE OTHER SIDE, OR SUBSCRIBE ONLINE AT:
www.shonenjump.com